VOICE   AUDIENCE   CONTENT

A Writer's Reader

Longman English and Humanities Series
Advisory Editor: Lee A. Jacobus
University of Connecticut, Storrs

VOICE
AUDIENCE
CONTENT

A Writer's Reader

SUSAN GIBSON

Northern Virginia Community College

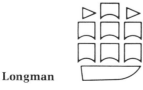

Longman *New York and London*

VOICE   AUDIENCE   CONTENT   *A Writer's Reader*

Longman Inc., New York
Associated companies, branches, and representatives throughout the world.

Developmental Editor: Gordon T. R. Anderson
Manufacturing and Production Supervisor: Louis Gaber
Composition: Book Composition Services
Printing and Binding: Maple Press

Library of Congress Cataloging in Publication Data

Main entry under title:

Voice, audience, content.

  (Longman English and humanities series)
  1. English language—Rhetoric.   2. College readers.
I. Gibson, Susan, 1946–   II. Series.
PE1417.V6   808'.04275   79–04275   79–10129
ISBN 0–582–28108–3

Manufactured in the United States of America

Acknowledgments

Northern Virginia Community College, Evergreen State College, The American College in Lucerne, Switzerland, the United States Coast Guard, Albany Business College, and Goddard College for permission to reprint text or photographs from their catalogues.

"Cleone Knox." From *The Diary of a Young Lady of Fashion in the Year 1764–1765* by Cleone Knox, edited by Alexander Blacker Kerr. Copyright 1926 by D. Appleton & Company. Reprinted by permission of Hawthorn Books, Inc.

"I'm Nobody! Who are you?" and "Apparently with no surprise" from *The Complete Poems of Emily Dickinson*, edited by Thomas H. Johnson. Reprinted by permission of Little, Brown and Company.

"Nick Carraway." Reprinted from *The Great Gatsby* by F. Scott Fitzgerald with the permission of Charles Scribner's Sons. Copyright 1925 by Charles Scribner's Sons.

"Charlie Chaplin." From *My Autobiography* by Charles Chaplin. Copyright © 1964 by Charles Chaplin. Reprinted by permission of Simon & Schuster, a Division of Gulf & Western Corporation.

"Liv Ullmann." From *Changing* by Liv Ullmann. Copyright © 1976, 1977 by Liv Ullmann. Reprinted by permission of Alfred A. Knopf, Inc.

"Robert Francis." From *The Trouble with Francis* by Robert Francis. Reprinted by permission of Robert Francis and the University of Massachusetts Press, copyright © 1971 by Robert Francis.

"Edna St. Vincent Millay, to her mother." From *Letters of Edna St. Vincent Millay.* Copyright 1952 by Norma Millay Ellis.

"George Bernard Shaw, to Alice Lockett." From *Bernard Shaw Collected Letters 1874–1897*, edited by Dan H. Laurence. Copyright 1965 by The Public Trustee as Trustee of the Estate of George Bernard Shaw. Published by Dodd, Mead & Company. Reprinted by permission of The Society of Authors on behalf of The Bernard Shaw Estate.

"Katherine Mansfield, to John Middleton Murry." From *Katherine Mansfield's Letters to John Middleton Murry, 1913–1922.* Copyright 1951 by Alfred A. Knopf. Reprinted by permission of Alfred A. Knopf, Inc.

"Mark Twain, to the Reverend Twichell." "Letter to Rev. Twichell, August 29, 1880" (pp. 383–85) from *Mark Twain's Letters,* Volume I edited by Albert Bigelow Paine. Copyright 1917 by Mark Twain Company. Reprinted by permission of Harper & Row, Publishers, Inc.

"Birhtwold: Speech from *The Battle of Maldon.*" "Beorhtweald's Great Exhortation," from *The Anglo-Saxon Poems in Bright's Anglo-Saxon Reader Done in a Normalized Orthography* by Francis P. Magoun, Jr. Published by Harvard University Press and reprinted by their permission.

"Diners Club." Letter reprinted by permission of Diners Club, a subsidiary of The Continental Corporation.

"National Foundation for Cancer Research." Letter reprinted by permission of the National Foundation for Cancer Research.

"Cabin Point." Letter reprinted by permission of Cabin Point, Inc.

"*The New Republic.*" Letter reprinted by permission of *The New Republic.*

"League of Women Voters." Letter reprinted by permission of the League of Women Voters of the United States.

"Dole Bananas." Advertisement reprinted by permission of Castle & Cooke, Inc. Copyright 1977.

"Exxon Corporation." Advertisement reprinted by permission of the Exxon Corporation.

"Crayola Crayons." Advertisement reprinted by permission of Binney & Smith, Makers of CRAYOLA ® Crayons.

"Conoco." Advertisement reprinted by permission of the Continental Oil Company.

"American Forest Institute." Advertisement reprinted by permission of the American Forest Institute.

"Volkswagen Dasher." Advertisement reprinted courtesy of Volkswagen of America.

"Oscar Mayer Bologna." Reprinted by permission of J. Walter Thompson Company.

"Primordial Chicken." From *The Impoverished Students' Book of Cookery, Drinkery, and House Keepery* by Jay F. Rosenberg. Copyright © 1965 by Jay F. Rosenberg. Reprinted by permission of Reed College Alumni Association.

"Chicken Cutlets." From *The Book of Household Management* by Mrs. Isabella Beeton. Published in the United States by Farrar, Straus & Giroux, Inc., and reprinted by their permission.

"George's Three-Alarm Chili." Courtesy George Mason Vaught.

"A Nice Cup of Tea." From *The Collected Essays, Journalism and Letters of George Orwell,* Volume 3, copyright © 1968 by Sonia Brownwell Orwell. Reprinted by permission of Harcourt Brace Jovanovich, Inc., and A. M. Heath and Company, Ltd.

"Treating Burns in the Mountains." From *Medicine for Mountaineering*, second edition, edited by James A. Wilkerson. Copyright © 1975 by The Mountaineers. Reprinted by permission of The Mountaineers.

"VISA/BankAmericard: In Case of Errors or Inquiries About Your Bill." Reprinted by permission of The Chase Manhattan Bank, N.A.

"The Word 'Slang.' " "The Word 'Jive.' " "The Word 'High.' " From *The American Heritage Dictionary of the English Language* edited by William Morris. Copyright © 1969, 1970, 1973, 1975, 1976, 1978 by Houghton Mifflin Company. Reprinted by permission of Houghton Mifflin Company.

"The Word 'Slang.' " "The Word 'Jive.' " "The Word 'High.' " From *The Random House College Dictionary*, Revised Edition. Copyright © 1975, 1979 by Random House, Inc. Reprinted by permission of Random House, Inc.

"The Word 'Slang.' " "The Word 'Jive.' " By permission. From *Webster's Third International Dictionary* © 1976 by G. & C. Merriam Co., Publishers of the Merriam-Webster Dictionaries.

"The Word 'Slang.' " From *The Oxford English Dictionary* by Sir James Augustus Henry Murray. Copyright 1933, © 1971 by Oxford University Press. Reprinted by permission of Oxford University Press.

"The Word 'Jive.' " "The Word 'High.' " From *Dictionary of American Slang*, 2nd Supplemented Edition by Harold Wentworth and Stuart Berg Flexner: definition of "jive" (p. 293), definition of "high" (p. 255). Copyright © 1975, 1967, 1960 by Harper & Row, Publishers, Inc. By permission of Thomas Y. Crowell.

"Meat Color Additives Linked to Cancer." From *The Washington Post*, 17 March 1971. Reprinted by permission of *The Washington Post*.

"Nitrates, Nitrites, and Nitrosamines" by I. A. Wolff and A. E. Wasserman. From *Science*, Vol. 177 (July 1972), pp. 15–19. Copyright 1972 by the American Association for the Advancement of Science and reprinted by their permission.

"Botulism and Nitrites" by I. A. Wolff and A. E. Wasserman. From *Science*, Vol. 180 (June 1973), p. 1322. Copyright 1973 by the American Association for the Advancement of Science and reprinted by their permission.

"Nitrites in Food" by W. Lijinsky. From *Science*, Vol. 182 (December 1973), pp. 1194–1196. Copyright 1973 by the American Association for the Advancement of Science and reprinted by their permission.

"Nitrites vs. Scientists or, Is That Coloring Really Necessary?" by Marian Burros. From *The Washington Post*, 25 July 1974. Reprinted by permission of *The Washington Post*.

"Bologna, Nitrite, and Your Health." Copyright 1976 by Consumers Union of United States, Inc., Mount Vernon, N.Y. 10550. Reprinted by permission from *Consumer Reports*, May 1976.

"Booker T. Washington: Atlanta Exposition Address." From *Up From Slavery* by Booker T. Washington published by Doubleday.

"Hubert Humphrey: *Beyond Civil Rights* (selection)." From *Beyond Civil Rights: A New Day of Equality* by Hubert H. Humphrey. Copyright © 1968 by Hubert H. Humphrey. Reprinted by permission of Random House, Inc.

"The Wife of Bath's Prologue (selection)." From *Chaucer's Poetry: An Anthology for the Modern Reader*, second edition, selected and edited by E. T. Donaldson. Copyright © 1958 by Ronald Press. Reprinted by permission of John Wiley & Sons, Inc.

"Mass Media's Conflicts of Interest" by Robert Cirino. From *We're Being More Than Entertained* by Robert Cirino. Copyright © 1977 by Robert Cirino. Reprinted by permission of the Lighthouse Press.

"Broadcasting—The Half-Opened Media" by Jerome A. Barron. From *Freedom of the Press for Whom?* by Jerome A. Barron. Copyright © 1973 by Indiana University Press and reprinted with their permission.

"Thank You, Walter Cronkite." Advertisement, Copyright © 1977 by Mobil Corporation and reprinted with their permission.

"Broadcast Advertising." From *Media and the First Amendment in a Free Society*. Copyright © 1972 by The Georgetown Law Journal Association; Copyright © 1973 by the University of Massachusetts Press and reprinted with their permission.

"A Modest Proposal to Pay for Excellence" by Martin Mayer. Reprinted with permission. This article appeared in the June 1978 issue of *American Film*.

"Robert Frost: The Way to the Poem" by John Ciardi. From *The Saturday Review*, 12 April 1958. "Letters to the Editor of *Saturday Review*." From *The Saturday Review*, 10 May 1958. "Letter to Letter-Writers" by John Ciardi. From *The Saturday Review*, 17 May 1958. © Saturday Review, 1958. All rights reserved.

"Stopping by Woods on a Snowy Evening." From *The Poetry of Robert Frost* edited by Edward Connery Lathem. Copyright 1923, © 1969 by Holt, Rinehart and Winston. Copyright 1951 by Robert Frost. Reprinted by permission of Holt, Rinehart and Winston, Publishers.

"The 'Death-Wish' in 'Stopping by Woods' " by James Armstrong. From *College English*, March 1964. Copyright © 1964 by the National Council of Teachers of English. Reprinted by permission of the publisher and the author.

"Toward Notes for 'Stopping by Woods': Some Classical Analogs" by Edward H. Rosenberry. From *College English*, April 1963. Copyright © 1963 by the National Council of Teachers of English. Reprinted by permission of the publisher and author.

"The Ghost of Christmas Past: 'Stopping by Woods on a Snowy Evening' " by Herbert R. Coursen, Jr. From *College English*, December 1962. Copyright © 1962 by the National Council of Teachers of English. Reprinted by permission of the publisher and author.

"Grammar don't matter?" by George C. Kohn. From *The Christian Science Monitor*, 15 July 1974. Reprinted by permission from The Christian Science Monitor. Copyright © 1974 The Christian Science Publishing Society. All rights reserved.

"Letters to the Education Editor of *The Christian Science Monitor*." From *The Christian Science Monitor*, 12 August 1974. Copyright © 1974 The Christian Science Monitor Publishing Society. All rights reserved.

"Miss Manners" by Judith Martin. From *The Washington Post*, 12 March 1978. Copyright © 1978 by The Washington Post and reprinted by permission.

"Why Can't Lawyers Talk Like Us?" by Stuart Auerbach. From *The Washington Post*, 15 January 1978. Copyright © The Washington Post and reprinted by permission.

To my first teachers Nancy and Bill

Preface to the Teacher

This is a supplementary text of readings to be used in conjunction with a rhetoric text and possibly a handbook. Chapters 1, 2, and 3 of part I of this book correspond to major subjects undertaken in most rhetorics: voice, audience, and the content of an argument. The prefaces to these sections are not intended to be complete introductions to these concepts, but should help the student to integrate his rhetoric text with his reader. Both the prefaces and the questions that follow each subsection will refer the student to rhetorical and grammatical terms that will need fuller explanation elsewhere in the composition course.

Part II of this book (Chapters 4–9) offers an alternative approach by grouping the writing selections thematically. These chapters will be most useful after some basic rhetorical principles have been mastered. They offer practice in distinguishing between styles and purposes in relation to the same general subject. In some cases they force the student to make choices between more and less trustworthy styles. The sections on the First Amendment, on marriage, and on cigarettes could be used in connection with the research paper. A few of the selections are models of professional research, some demonstrating the use of footnotes, while others can be used to help students identify less believable or irrelevant sources.

My chief aim in this book has been variety. I have tried to include short, usable examples of a spectrum of styles; the selections will be seen to vary in their success at accomplishing their purposes. When students can detect an inappropriate style or an unconvincing proof in the writing of others, they are better prepared to recognize a need for alterations in their own writing.

Contents

2 *Audience: Who's He Talking To?*

3   *Content: What's He Saying?*   79

7 *The Control of Television*   192

8 *Writing About Literature: "Stopping by Woods on a Snowy Evening"*   225

9 *Standards for Language* 251

Alternate Contents

This alternate listing may help you to find the example or style of writing that you are looking for. The categories are not mutually exclusive.

PART I

Introduction

What are the characteristics of good writing? Every writer must keep answering that question, for the answer changes from essay to essay and from situation to situation. And every writer must answer the question for himself. What am I aiming at? How will I know when it is finished?

Sometimes it is difficult to read one's own writing as others read it. It takes almost as much practice to be a good reader as it does to be a good writer, and the two skills are closely connected. Thoughtful reading of the work of other writers can teach you how to make the revisions you want in your own writing. The readings in this book have been selected and arranged to help you consider the range of possibilities available to you as a writer.

You undoubtedly have some ideas already about the characteristics of good writing. When you are revising something that you have written yourself, the problems uppermost in your mind may be things like spelling, grammar, organization, and clarity. These are certainly important. But when you recognize something as really *good* writing, you realize that it has other qualities as well. Students often tell me that good writing "gets the message across." While this is probably true, it is not especially helpful advice when you are trying to revise something. Good writers—and good readers—need more specific concepts to think about. The purpose of this book is to suggest some concepts that can help you become a better writer and reader and to give you practice in using these concepts.

Scholars who study language often identify three components of every communication: *somebody* wants to say *something* to *someone else.* Writers and readers who think consciously about each of these three components usually communicate well. I will discuss each of them briefly here.

First, *somebody* wants to say something. A writer, of course, is not actually present in front of his audience; he may be separated by thousands of miles or thousands of years. Nevertheless, as he puts words down on paper he creates an imaginary "voice," and the reader who "hears" this voice gets a more or less distinct impression of someone speaking to him. Sometimes this voice is called the *speaker* of a piece of writing, and sometimes it is called the *persona*. It is the "I" that does the talking to us.

You know from long experience that it is possible to pretend to be someone else when you are writing. Even when you are not pretending, you write with a different voice at different times. The "I" in your letter to your parents or children sounds like a different person from the one who speaks in that English paper you wrote last week. Because one person can write with many different voices, we have to be careful to distinguish between the voice and the writer, the real person, even though there is usually a similarity between the two. In the writing that I am composing right now, for instance, the voice is that of a teacher, although it's possible that I am not a teacher, and it's certainly true that I write with other voices at other times. When I sound warm and affectionate, or when I strive to use all the biggest words I know, or when I jot down information as quickly as possible, I am using different voices.

Second, a writer wants to say something to *someone else.* We will call this someone the "assumed audience" of the piece of writing. It may be a particular person, it may be someone unknown to the writer, it may be a large group of people. In any case, the things that the writer knows, or thinks he knows, about his audience help him decide what to say. We write differently for children and for adults. We write differently for our best friends and for our congressman. To use this piece of writing as an example again, we would say that the assumed or intended audience is students of composition.

Just as we had to distinguish between the writer and the voice, we sometimes have to remember the difference between the assumed audience and the actual audience. Someone who is not a composition student may read this introduction: a teacher, perhaps, or someone who is browsing at a used book sale. Nevertheless, we would still say that the assumed audience is students. And we could go on to analyze various assumptions that I am making about composition students. I have guessed that you already look out for spelling and grammar when you proofread, but that "voice" is a new concept for you. I have guessed that you sometimes write letters as well as papers. I have guessed that you are not interested in knowing who the scholars are who have suggested this model of communication. But if I am wrong in any of these guesses, I will communicate with you less effectively.

Third, the writer usually wants to communicate *something*. There are many words for this aspect of writing: *concepts, ideas, information, facts, claims, assertions, messages,* and so forth. I am going to call it simply *content*. In some ways, this is the most obvious component of communication. It is what we normally think we pay attention to. When you read for content, you will be judging writing by standards familiar to you: Is it clear? Is it accurate? Is it objective or biased? Is it reasonable?

The study of all aspects of content would take us far afield, into research methods, statistics, documentation, logic, and all the separate disciplines and studies that people write about. In this book, we will only be concerned with trying to separate content from other things and with noticing when specific claims are supported and when they are not.

Different types of claims require different types of support. Some claims are documented by reference to reports, tests, polls, or observations, from more or less reliable sources. Others depend on arguments put forward with more or less sound reasoning, and still others depend on values held by the writer, for which he may have no arguments or proofs at all. For instance, it is possible to find out from police records approximately how many people were killed by handguns in your city last year. This is a fact which can be determined with relative accuracy, but it does not in itself constitute an argument. If you want to argue that the licensing of handguns either will or will not reduce this number, you need to present reasons for this conclusion. Perhaps potential killers with licensed handguns will feel certain to be caught, and therefore will not shoot. Perhaps people will purchase fewer handguns if licenses are required. These reasons are of course much less certain than the fact of the number of deaths by gunshot wounds last year. Moreover, a writer's conclusions about an issue sometimes depend on certain overriding values for which the writer may not feel it necessary to supply reasons. For instance, one writer may feel that personal liberty is the greatest of all values; another may feel that the saving of even one life is more important than liberty. Each of these types of content —facts, reasons, and cherished beliefs—plays an important role in argument. Good writers and good readers need to be aware of which is which.

Here is a simple model of the three components of writing that I have been discussing:

VOICE

CONTENT   AUDIENCE

If you look at the table of contents for part I of this book, you will see that the three chapter headings correspond to the three points of the triangle. You will have an opportunity to study each of these three aspects of writing separately, in part I, before you study them all together in part II. However, it is important to remember that the separation in part I is artificial. Every piece of writing involves each of the three components to some degree, and many of the choices a writer makes can affect all three at once. For instance, if you change a word to suit your audience, you probably get a slight change in content or meaning as well. On a larger scale, a writer's assumptions about his audience nearly always affect his selection of a voice and his choices of information to include; or conversely, a writer may decide to aim for a particular audience because of the nature of his message: "Save Alaska!" "Buy a Cadillac!" The chapter divisions in part I are for learning purposes only. After all, you can't think about everything at once until you've had some practice thinking about everything separately.

In each of the chapters of part I, I have tried to pick out examples that will help you to concentrate on one aspect of the writing. For chapter 1, "Voice," I selected first some short passages about colleges. These selections are aimed at similar audiences—students thinking about where to go to college—and they are all introductory paragraphs which do not contain a great deal of specific information. The chief way in which these selections differ from one another is in the voices that they use to try to communicate the kind of places they are. The writers of autobiographies, in the next section of chapter 1, are not concerned with a specific audience, and the contents that they communicate are closely related to the voices that they have chosen to express themselves. So here, too, the writers' voices provide the main points of comparison between them. The personal letters have little information of importance to communicate, but each of these writers "keeps in touch" by using a voice that sounds like him- or herself.

In the examples in chapter 2, the writers' primary considerations are their audiences. Their voices and their selections of content are made with the audience clearly in mind. Political and military leaders need the support of followers above all. Everything they say is based on estimates of the best way to gain that support. So also the writers of direct mail and print advertisements want to persuade the audience, and you will be able to tell from the writing itself what guesses the writers have made about their audiences. But not all concern with audience necessarily implies persuasion. The writers of directions for doing things have to think clearly about what their audiences already know and do not know, but they don't have to persuade us to perform these operations.

In chapter 3, "Content," the differences among voices and audiences will be at a minimum, so that differences in content will become the focus of your comparison. Dictionaries have huge audiences whose only obvious characteristic is a desire for information about words. And dictionaries tend to adopt very similar voices. But they do differ in the content that they give us, perhaps more than you think. Similarly, all the examples in the section on nitrates are addressed to intelligent people who are worried about food additives, and all of them adopt a voice that sounds responsible and mature. But they disagree in their con-clusions, leaving you to ponder whether some are inaccurate, whose ar-guments are stronger, and how the basic values of the writers may differ. And finally, the writers who discuss equality have similar audiences and voices, but differ in their ideas about the subject.

Every writer should "get his message across." The problem is that all too often, writers get across messages that they never intended— messages about themselves, about what they think of their audience, or about how carefully they have researched their subject. You might think of the writer's job as *knowing* what his *whole* message is after he sees it written down and being able to change those aspects of the message that need changing to suit his purpose. To accomplish this step in the writing process, good reading is essential.

To sum up, this book suggests that there are three important ques-tions that you can ask about a piece of writing, either your own rough draft or someone else's finished piece. In shortened form, here are the questions:

* Who seems to be speaking?
* To whom does he or she seem to be speaking?
* What does it say?

When writing is really good, each of these components will be ad-justed to one another. Sometimes one aspect or another will receive primary emphasis, but if any one aspect is out of tune, the writing will seem lame. Overemphasis of any one component can be dangerous. You can get so interested in expressing a voice that you neglect to convey any content, and the writing may seem shallow; or an overemphasis on audience can make the writer seem to lack integrity, as if he'd be willing to lie or appear foolish just to please us; or an overemphasis on content can lead to a boring list of facts that no one needs to know. But the best writing contains a balance: a voice that expresses the writer's appropriate role, respectful assumptions about the audience and its desires, and content that is accurate and fair.

1

Voice: Who's Talking?

Writing is like walking onto a television stage set before a live camera. There you are, with all the floodlights shining on you, every expression and mannerism exposed. You can't tell how the audience is reacting, or what the reviews are going to be like. Think about how you feel when you have written down some words and handed in a paper—and off it goes, that little fragment of yourself, to be read by someone when you're not there, and probably judged and graded, too. What will your reader take you for? Do you sound like the heavy cop or the lady who sells paper towels? Will you "come across" the way you intended?

Writing is like acting because the writer takes on a role. For example, you would probably present yourself quite differently in a letter to your sister and in a complaint to the editor of a paper. For your sister, you might try to be amusing and warm, while for the newspaper you would be more likely to stress qualities like intelligence, orderliness, and social concern. The "roles" of being a brother and being a concerned citizen are different. We will call these roles and characteristics the *voice* of a piece of writing.

How is a voice expressed in writing? The answer to that question is almost as complicated as trying to say how personal characteristics are expressed in real people. Almost every choice a writer makes affects his or her voice. Vocabulary may be abstract or concrete, emotional or dry, full of strange words or full of ordinary ones. Sentences may be long or short, carefully structured or merely connected by *and*s and *but*s. Paragraphs may be long or short, and the whole piece of writing may be carefully organized or may wander off every which way. The writer may use expressions that we associate with a geographical area, or a movie star, or a certain line of work. You know more about what all these choices mean than you think you do. You have been using and listening to the language for a long time, and some of your decisions every day are based on "sizing up" people on the basis of the way they talk.

In the reading selections that follow, the writers face quite different kinds of problems: in the first section, they must speak as the voice of an educational institution; in the second section, their task is to present themselves as the heroes of their own autobiographies; and in the third section, they are writing friendly personal letters to keep a relationship going.

How do you talk like an institution? As you will see, the writers here came up with different solutions to that problem. They certainly do not write as *themselves;* we cannot tell whether they are young or old, men or women, drivers of Volkswagens or Cadillacs. But we can tell something about the impression they are trying to give us of their schools. Is it a competitive place, or a relaxed place? Do they seem to care about each student, or do they sound pretty mechanical? What sort of goals do they express—preparing you for a job, making you a useful citizen, enhancing your personal growth, or getting your money? As you read, think about the kinds of words and sentences they use, and how their choices about language create the "voice" of the college.

In the second section, the writer's task is both easier and harder—easier because the writer can speak more naturally, but harder, too, because expressing your "natural" self is almost impossible. (You can find out that this is true by trying it.) Get an overall impression of these voices first. Then look more closely at the writing itself, to discover how the effect is achieved. Look at vocabulary, organization, length of sentences and paragraphs, punctuation, and anything else that seems to stand out in the writer's style.

In the third section, the writers express a more informal side of themselves. The voices here reflect the different personalities and moods of parents and children, lovers and friends. These writers are not so careful to make their spelling and punctuation correct, and some even make "mistakes" on purpose. The job of a letter writer is to keep a relationship going, to use as nearly as possible the same voice that he or she would use if talking.

This chapter is designed to help you analyze the way other writers sound, that is, to help you describe their voices. While you learn to listen more carefully to other writers, you should practice writing yourself. As you become better at listening to others, you will also become better at hearing yourself. Actors sometimes look at their own facial expressions in mirrors and listen to their own voices on tape recorders. You, too, can "listen" to your own performance as a writer. Who do *you* sound like?

In summary, here are some important questions to ask when you want to analyze a writer's voice:

* What sort of vocabulary does the writer use?
* How long are the sentences?
* Are the sentences carefully constructed with complex grammatical units, or are they simple main clauses strung together with *ands* and *buts*?
* What marks of punctuation does the writer use?
* How long are the paragraphs? Are they carefully organized, with a thesis and development?

Colleges

Northern Virginia Community College

Purpose

Northern Virginia Community College is dedicated to the belief that each individual should be given a continuing opportunity for the development and extension of his skills and knowledge along with an opportunity to increase in awareness of his role in and responsibility toward society. The college, operating under an open admissions policy, accepts any person who has a high school diploma or the equivalent, or is at least 18 years of age, and in any case, is able to benefit from a program of instruction. The College is devoted to serving the educational needs of its community and assumes a responsibility for helping meet the requirements for trained manpower in its region through a cooperative effort with local industry, business professions, and government.

Educational opportunities are provided for post high school age youth and adults. These opportunities include high-quality instructional programs at the associate degree level, in occupational and technical programs designed to develop technicians, semi-professional workers and skilled craftsmen, as well as programs at the developmental level. A strong counseling program, including a number of other comprehensive student services are also provided to help each student make sound decisions regarding his occupational, educational, and personal goals and objectives. These services include: pre-college and freshman orientation, counseling, job placement, financial aid, student health service, psychological service, veterans affairs, and student activities.

Evergreen State College

Our Philosophy and Goals

Society needs trained minds; it needs new information, fresh ideas, and constructive, reliable responses to new problems from citizens capable of dealing creatively and positively with the complexities brought by rapid and massive change. Citizens of this society have their own needs: Flexibility, personal growth, and confidence, as well as a highly cultivated ability to learn new ideas and skills and to master quickly new bodies of information.

These demands shape the nature of undergraduate study at Evergreen which is designed to assist students to continue learning, to continue schooling their intelligences, to continue thinking things out, applying that new learning to the problems of contemporary life. Evergreen integrates formal education with the social, physical, and emotional development of students of diverse ages, cultural and economic backgrounds, interests, and outlooks.

Although Evergreen's academic programs are designed to enable students to sharpen basic intellectual skills, learn techniques for solving problems and develop an awareness of the implications of central human issues, the college places strong emphasis on the interrelationship of fields of knowledge rather than treating academic disciplines as entirely separate.

Evergreen encourages students to assume increasingly greater responsibility for their own work as they progress toward the Bachelor of Arts degree, with their studies matching their interests and career goals. Academic study achieves its best, Evergreen believes, when students can sample a reasonably wide range of actual jobs, working under conditions of genuine responsibility to themselves or as members of teams, subjecting this relevant experience to reflection about themselves and their futures.

Evergreen, in short, intends to develop a learning community that reflects the nature of the real world, where none of the problems humanity faces is simple and where none of the parts becomes, in its own conception, more important than the whole.

The American College

In the Coast Guard you'll learn the mechanics of saving lives.

When there's a family marooned by a flood, a sail boat in trouble on San Diego Bay, a boating accident on the Intracoastal Waterway, the Coast Guard goes.

It could be by helicopter, a motor lifeboat, or a sleek Coast Guard cutter. Whatever the way, we can't afford any mechanical failures.

We're in the business of saving lives, and we're proud of the job we do. Last year, we answered over 67,000 distress calls, and saved or otherwise prevented the loss of over $280,000,000 worth of property.

We need people with mechanical aptitudes in the Coast Guard. Young people who want to help others while they help themselves.

There are dozens of skills you can acquire: become an expert on gas and diesel engines, helicopter repairs, small boats, hydraulics.

Or, you can learn navigation, electronics, communications, or any number of useful, career-oriented vocations. Most importantly, you can learn at our expense.

The pay is good, too. Over $360 a month to start, with your first raise right after boot camp. And that's money you won't have to budget to room and board because we furnish those free. Plus free dental and medical care, and 30 days of paid vacation every year.

If you want to further your education and get college credits, we'll help. We'll also provide GI benefits when you get out. Or, if you decide to stay in, you'll get a bonus for re-enlisting plus excellent retirement benefits at an age when you can do something with them.

If you've got a way with things mechanical, give the Coast Guard serious thought. We want bright, young, eager people who want to do something with their lives. While you're helping others, you help yourself.

So, if you're a young person thinking hard about a good future, or between the ages of 17 and 26 and wanting that good future right now, call us toll free.

HELP OTHERS HELP YOURSELF.
800-424-8883
THE COAST GUARD.

Albany Business College

Behind the Scenes

ABC deals in realities—the realities of getting a good job and taking a meaningful place in your local community. The programs of study are based on the employment needs of the business world today—and in the foreseeable future. Emphasis is placed on the practical knowledge you'll need to get the position you want and advance rapidly.

ABC offers a wide variety of majors, both in Business Administration and Secretarial Science, for both men and women. Women may want to specialize in a Legal or Medical Secretarial major. Business Administration programs emphasize Accounting, Computer Programming or Retail Management.

In addition to the basics, there are many courses geared toward career advancement—like Psychology, Personnel Management, and Economics. And to improve your understanding of business in the society we live in, ABC has courses like Legal Principles, Insurance & Real Estate, and Income Tax.

All courses are taught by skilled professional educators, qualified both academically and in business experience. To them, you are not a number, but an individual entitled to all the help you need to successfully complete your course.

In addition, to insure your success and enjoyment in the program you choose, you receive frequent counseling both before and after entrance. Our business is people—helping them one at a time.

Goddard College

Any written statement about so complex an organism as a college can never be wholly adequate. The college changes as words are written about it; the words are generalizations, however much they strive to be concrete and specific; the writing is subjective, a reflection of what the writer can or will see at the time he writes.

So for others at Goddard, the college may be something different from what is here published, and these pages should be read with that caution in mind. On the other hand, the catalogue does indicate with some accuracy Goddard's aims and goals, and the procedures developed in the Resident Undergraduate Program to help students follow those aims and move toward those goals. It is to be hoped that it also communicates the college's particular atmosphere: that it is an exciting and challenging, sometimes puzzling and frustrating, but deeply rewarding place to be part of.

Goddard has been coeducational all its life. The text of the catalogue attempts to do justice to this happy fact by referring to individual students as "she" in one section or paragraph, and "he" in the next, each of course implying both.

QUESTIONS

1. Which of the selections appeals to you most? Why? Which school would you go to, if you had a free choice?

2. Think of adjectives to describe each institution, like *intellectual, friendly, personal, formal, silly*. Then try to explain why you get this impression.

3. Which of these institutions speaks directly to the student as "you"? Does this seem to be characteristic of formal voices, or of friendly ones?

4. Describe the kinds of attitudes that these voices express toward women students. Which school would be likely to have a women's center? Which schools seem to have no awareness of differences in sex? How can you tell?

5. Which of the colleges uses the most abstract vocabulary? the most concrete? In general, what happens to your voice if nearly all your vocabulary is abstract?

6. Which college uses the shortest sentences? the longest? What difference does this make?

7. Northern Virginia Community College uses a high proportion of passive verbs. Can you find them? How does the voice change when you make these verbs active?

8. A couple of these selections are actually advertisements. Do ads usually sound different from other types of writing? Which of the college catalogues sounds most like an ad? Why?

9. Each of the colleges would like to gain your trust; after all, you might be putting your education in their hands. Goddard tries to deserve your trust by being very careful about what they claim. Albany Business College does it by sounding confident. Which voice is more persuasive to you?

10. Look at the values implied in each of these passages. What are the things that each school expresses a concern about? For instance, which schools talk most about the student, and which seem to talk more about society? Do any of them make promises that you doubt they can keep?

11. In general, what are the advantages of using a formal voice? Are there any disadvantages? What can you gain or lose by adopting a friendly voice?

Autobiography

Cleone Knox

March 3rd.

    This morning had a vastly unpleasant interview with my Father. Last night, Mr. Ancaster, who is the indiscreetest young man alive, was seized suddenly while riding home along the shore with the desire to say good night to me. He climbed the wall, the postern gate being locked at that late hour, and had the Boldness to attempt to climb the ivy below my window; while but half way up the Poor Impudent young man fell. (If he hadn't Lord knows what would have happened for I am terribly catched by the Handsome Wretch.) As ill luck would have it Papa and Ned, who were conversing in the library, looked out at that moment and saw him lying Prostrate on the ground!

    No need to describe the scene that followed. My father it seems thinks me guilty of Indiscretion and Immodesty, though why I don't know, for I was sound asleep the whole time and never heard so much as an Oath (and I dare swear there were plenty flying round!). My father said some mighty unkind things to me this morning and I wept loudly for more than Half an Hour.

    Poor Mr. A. from all accounts is a Scoundrel, a Libertine and a Blackguard, and I have been forbidden ever to see, speak or indeed think of him again. Well, we shall see.

    I own I cannot imagine how it will all end. Pray Heaven there will not be a Recontre * between either of my Indignant male relatives and my unlucky admirer. 'Twould make a Scandal in the county we should never hear the end of.

    Men are such Damnable Fools there is no saying what they will do in a fury.

March 4th.

    Keep to my room to avoid the sour glances that are cast at me if I venture below. My father as grim as death will not say a word to me. Ned puts on monstrously Virtuous Prudish Airs. In short I am made to feel I am in disgrace. Declare I cannot see how I am to blame if a Foolish Headstrong young man attaches himself a trifle too warmly to me. Tried on my new striped silk gown which becomes me excessively well. Poor Mr. A. I doubt will never see me in it.

From Cleone Knox, *The Diary of a Young Lady of Fashion in the Year 1764–65*, ed. Alexander Blacker Kerr (New York: D. Appleton & Co., 1926).
* Old-fashioned word for duel.—ED.

March 5th.

Rain outside and gloom inside the house. Am vexed with all and everything, the weather, my father, Ned, Mr. A.'s Imprudence and the striped silk which has split under the arms to my vast annoyance. My father and Ned out shooting Seals on the rocks. I hope Ned may come home Better humoured.

March 6th.

This morning Betsy, looking very sly, brought me a Note from Mr. A., vowing Eternal Devotion and breathing horrible Vengeance against my hard hearted parent and Ned.

It seems that Mr. A. has entirely spoilt his Crimson Plush Suit, which is all Muddied and Filthy from his lying on the damp ground. Why he was riding in his best suit he alone can explain. Did he expect I should be so foolish as to admit him at that hour of the night?

At all events he holds my poor Charms responsible for this damage, and vows that nothing but a kiss will compensate him!

My father came in while I was reading it, which made me very confused. Dropped it on the fire but he gave me a suspicious glance.

March 8th.

Am to leave to-morrow for Ballywiticock House, to stay with my Cousin Charlotte, so my father announced to me yesterday. See plainly enough that this is nothing but a plot to keep me from Mr. A. Urged the rain, and bad roads in vain. Swore I could not abide Coz Charlotte's company for a day, far less a week. My father like all his Sex prides himself on his determination. I see Ned's doing in this. I could box his ears!

Emily Dickinson

I'm Nobody! Who are you?
Are you—Nobody—Too?
Then there's a pair of us?
Don't tell! they'd advertise—you know!

How dreary—to be—Somebody!
How public—like a Frog—
To tell one's name—the livelong June—
To an admiring Bog!

From *The Complete Poems of Emily Dickinson,* edited by Thomas H. Johnson (Boston: Little Brown & Co., 1960).

Jane Eyre

During these eight years my life was uniform: but not unhappy, because it was not inactive. I had the means of an excellent education placed within my reach; a fondness for some of my studies, and a desire to excel in all, together with a great delight in pleasing my teachers, especially such as I loved, urged me on: I availed myself fully of the advantages offered me. In time I rose to be the first girl of the first class; then I was invested with the office of teacher; which I discharged with zeal for two years: but at the end of that time I altered.

Miss Temple, through all changes, had thus far continued superintendent of the seminary: to her instruction I owed the best part of my acquirements; her friendship and society had been my continual solace: she had stood me in the stead of mother, governess, and latterly, companion. At this period she married, removed with her husband (a clergyman, an excellent man, almost worthy of such a wife) to a distant county, and consequently was lost to me.

From the day she left I was no longer the same: with her was gone every settled feeling, every association that had made Lowood in some degree a home to me. I had imbibed from her something of her nature and much of her habits: more harmonious thoughts: what seemed better regulated feelings had become the inmates of my mind. I had given in allegiance to duty and order; I was quiet; I believed I was content: to the eyes of others, usually even to my own, I appeared a disciplined and subdued character.

But destiny, in the shape of the Rev. Mr. Nasmyth, came between me and Miss Temple: I saw her in her traveling-dress step into a post-chaise, shortly after the marriage ceremony; I watched the chaise mount the hill and disappear beyond its brow; and then retired to my own room, and there spent in solitude the greatest part of the half-holiday granted in honor of the occasion.

I walked about the chamber most of the time. I imagined myself only to be regretting my loss, and thinking how to repair it; but when my reflections were concluded, and I looked up and found that the afternoon was gone and evening far advanced, another discovery dawned on me, namely, that in the interval I had undergone a transforming process; that my mind had put off all it had borrowed of Miss Temple—or rather that she had taken with her the serene atmosphere I had been breathing in her vicinity—and that now I was left in my natural element, and beginning to feel the stirring of old emotions. It did not seem as if a prop were withdrawn, but rather as if a motive were gone: it was not the power to be tranquil which had failed me, but the reason for tranquillity was no more. My world had for some years been in Lowood: my experience had been of its rules and systems; now I remembered that the real world was wide,

From Charlotte Brontë, *Jane Eyre* (New York: Harper, 1875).

and that a varied field of hopes and fears, of sensations and excitements, awaited those who had courage to go forth into its expanse, to seek real knowledge of life amidst its perils.

I went to my window, opened it, and looked out. There were the two wings of the building; there was the garden; there were the skirts of Lowood; there was the hilly horizon. My eye passed all other objects to rest on those most remote, the blue peaks: it was those I longed to surmount; all within their boundary of rock and heath seemed prison-ground, exile limits. I traced the white road winding round the base of one mountain, and vanishing in a gorge between two: how I longed to follow it farther! I recalled the time when I had traveled that very road in a coach; I remembered descending that hill at twilight: an age seemed to have elapsed since the day which brought me first to Lowood, and I had never quitted it since. My vacations had all been spent at school: Mrs. Reed had never sent for me to Gateshead; neither she nor any of her family had ever been to visit me. I had had no communication by letter or message with the outer world: school rules, school duties, school habits, and notions, and voices, and faces, and phrases, and costumes, and preferences, and antipathies: such was what I knew of existence. And now I felt that it was not enough: I tired of the routine of eight years in one afternoon. I desired liberty; for liberty I gasped; for liberty I uttered a prayer; it seemed scattered on the wind then faintly blowing. I abandoned it and framed a humbler supplication—for change, stimulus: that petition, too, seemed swept off into vague space: "Then," I cried, half desperate, "grant me at least a new servitude!"

Here a bell, ringing the hour of supper, called me down stairs.

Nick Carraway

My family have been prominent, well-to-do people in this Middle Western city for three generations. The Carraways are something of a clan, and we have a tradition that we're descended from the Dukes of Buccleuch, but the actual founder of my line was my grandfather's brother, who came here in fifty-one, sent a substitute to the Civil War, and started the wholesale hardware business that my father carries on to-day.

I never saw this great-uncle, but I'm supposed to look like him—with special reference to the rather hard-boiled painting that hangs in father's office. I graduated from New Haven in 1915, just a quarter of a century after my father, and a little later I participated in that delayed Teutonic migration known as the Great War. I enjoyed the counter-raid so thoroughly that I came back restless. Instead of being the warm center of

From F. Scott Fitzgerald, *The Great Gatsby* (New York: Charles Scribner's Sons, 1925).

the world, the Middle West now seemed like the ragged edge of the universe—so I decided to go East and learn the bond business. Everybody I knew was in the bond business, so I supposed it could support one more single man. All my aunts and uncles talked it over as if they were choosing a prep school for me, and finally said, "Why—ye-es," with very grave, hesitant faces. Father agreed to finance me for a year, and after various delays I came East, permanently, I thought, in the spring of twenty-two.

The practical thing was to find rooms in the city, but it was a warm season, and I had just left a country of wide lawns and friendly trees, so when a young man at the office suggested that we take a house together in a commuting town, it sounded like a great idea. He found the house, a weatherbeaten cardboard bungalow at eighty a month, but at the last minute the firm ordered him to Washington, and I went out to the country alone. I had a dog—at least I had him for a few days until he ran away—and an old Dodge and a Finnish woman, who made my bed and cooked breakfast and muttered Finnish wisdom to herself over the electric stove.

It was lonely for a day or so until one morning some man, more recently arrived than I, stopped me on the road.

"How do you get to West Egg village?" he asked helplessly.

I told him. And as I walked on I was lonely no longer. I was a guide, a pathfinder, an original settler. He had casually conferred on me the freedom of the neighborhood.

And so with the sunshine and the great bursts of leaves growing on the trees, just as things grow in fast movies, I had that familiar conviction that life was beginning over again with the summer.

Charlie Chaplin

At last the moment came. Sennett was away on location with Mabel Normand as well as the Ford Sterling Company, so there was hardly anyone left in the studio. Mr. Henry Lehrman, Keystone's top director after Sennett, was to start a new picture and wanted me to play a newspaper reporter. Lehrman was a vain man and very conscious of the fact that he had made some successful comedies of a mechanical nature; he used to say that he didn't need personalities, that he got all his laughs from mechanical effects and film cutting.

We had no story. It was to be a documentary about the printing press done with a few comedy touches. I wore a light frock coat, a top hat and a handlebar mustache. When we started I could see that Lehrman was groping for ideas. And of course, being a newcomer at Keystone, I was anxious to make suggestions. This was where I created antagonism with Lehrman.

From Charles Chaplin, *My Autobiography* (New York: Simon & Schuster, 1964).

In a scene in which I had an interview with an editor of a newspaper I crammed in every conceivable gag I could think of, even to suggesting business for others in the cast. Although the picture was completed in three days, I thought we contrived some very funny gags. But when I saw the finished film it broke my heart, for the cutter had butchered it beyond recognition, cutting into the middle of all my funny business. I was bewildered, and wondered why they had done this. Henry Lehrman confessed years later that he had deliberately done it, because, as he put it, he thought I knew too much.

The day after I finished with Lehrman, Sennett returned from location. Ford Sterling was on one set, Arbuckle on another; the whole stage was crowded with three companies at work. I was in my street clothes and had nothing to do, so I stood where Sennett could see me. He was standing with Mabel, looking into a hotel lobby set, biting the end of a cigar. "We need some gags here," he said, then turned to me. "Put on a comedy make-up. Anything will do."

I had no idea what make-up to put on. I did not like my getup as the press reporter. However, on the way to the wardrobe I thought I would dress in baggy pants, big shoes, a cane and a derby hat. I wanted everything a contradiction: the pants baggy, the coat tight, the hat small and the shoes large. I was undecided whether to look old or young, but remembering Sennett had expected me to be a much older man, I added a small mustache, which, I reasoned, would add age without hiding my expression.

I had no idea of the character. But the moment I was dressed, the clothes and the make-up made me feel the person he was. I began to know him, and by the time I walked onto the stage he was fully born. When I confronted Sennett I assumed the character and strutted about, swinging my cane and parading before him. Gags and comedy ideas went racing through my mind.

The secret of Mack Sennett's success was his enthusiasm. He was a great audience and laughed genuinely at what he thought funny. He stood and giggled until his body began to shake. This encouraged me and I began to explain the character: "You know this fellow is many-sided, a tramp, a gentleman, a poet, a dreamer, a lonely fellow, always hopeful of romance and adventure. He would have you believe he is a scientist, a musician, a duke, a polo player. However, he is not above picking up cigarette butts or robbing a baby of its candy. And, of course, if the occasion warrants it, he will kick a lady in the rear—but only in extreme anger!"

I carried on this way for ten minutes or more, keeping Sennett in continuous chuckles. "All right," said he, "get on the set and see what you can do there." As with the Lehrman film, I knew little of what the story was about, other than that Mabel Normand gets involved with her husband and a lover.

In all comedy business an attitude is most important, but it is not always easy to find an attitude. However, in the hotel lobby I felt I was an impostor posing as one of the guests, but in reality I was a tramp just wanting a little shelter. I entered and stumbled over the foot of a lady. I turned and raised my hat apologetically, then turned and stumbled over a cuspidor, then turned and raised my hat to the cuspidor. Behind the camera they began to laugh.

Quite a crowd had gathered there, not only the players of the other companies who left their sets to watch us, but also the stagehands, the carpenters and the wardrobe department. That indeed was a compliment. And by the time we had finished rehearsing we had quite a large audience laughing. Very soon I saw Ford Sterling peering over the shoulders of others. When it was over I knew I had made good.

At the end of the day when I went to the dressing room, Ford Sterling and Roscoe Arbuckle were taking off their make-up. Very little was said, but the atmosphere was charged with crosscurrents. Both Ford and Roscoe liked me, but I frankly felt they were undergoing some inner conflict.

It was a long scene that ran seventy-five feet. Later Mr. Sennett and Mr. Lehrman debated whether to let it run its full length, as the average comedy scene rarely ran over ten. "If it's funny," I said, "does length really matter?" They decided to let the scene run its full seventy-five feet. As the clothes had imbued me with the character, I then and there decided I would keep to this costume, whatever happened.

Liv Ullmann

I am sitting here, my thoughts carrying me around the world and within myself, trying to record the voyage on paper.

I want to write about love—about being a human being—about loneliness—about being a woman.

I want to write about an encounter on an island. A man who changed my life.

I want to write about a change that was accidental and a change that was deliberate.

I want to write about moments I regard as gifts, good moments and bad moments.

I don't believe that the knowledge or experience that is part of me is any greater than what others have.

I have attained one dream—and acquired ten new ones in its place. I have seen the reverse side of something that glitters.

It is not the Liv Ullmann people meet in magazines and newspapers that I shall be writing about. Some may think I have left out important

From Liv Ullmann, *Changing* (New York: Alfred A. Knopf, 1976).

facts about my life, but it has never been my intention to write an autobiography.

Ironically, my profession requires daily exhibition of body and face and emotions. Now I feel that I am afraid of revealing myself. Afraid that what I write will leave me vulnerable and no longer able to defend myself.

I am tempted to embroider, to make myself and my surroundings appear nice to win the reader's sympathy. Or to blacken things, to make them more exciting.

It is as if I am not convinced that reality itself is of interest.

"There's a young girl in me who refuses to die," wrote the Danish woman author Tove Ditlevsen.

I live, rejoice, grieve, and I am always struggling to become grown up. Yet every day, because something I do affects her, I hear that young girl within me. She who many years ago was I. Or who I thought was.

It is an eager and almost always protesting voice, although at times faint and full of yearning or sorrow. I don't want to heed it, because I know it has nothing to do with my adult life. But it makes me uncertain.

Some mornings I decide to live her life, be something other than what ordinarily is my daily role. I snuggle close to my daughter before she is awake, feel her warm, peaceful breathing, and hope that through her I may become what I wished to be.

Looking back on what I remember of my childhood's dreams, I see that they resemble many I still have, but I no longer live as if they were part of reality.

She who is in me and "refuses to die" is still hoping for something different. No success satisfies her, no happiness hushes her.

All the time I am trying to change myself. For I do know that there is much more than the things I have been near. I would like to be on the way toward this. To find peace, so that I can sit and listen to what is inside me without influence.

Robert Francis

When Nasrettin Hoca, celebrated medieval Turkish jester or stupid-shrewd man, was asked why he sat on his donkey backward, he said he wanted to see where he had been. Most donkey riders prefer to see where they are going, though it would seem that a little flexibility of the neck might permit anyone to look in both directions more or less at the same time. Certainly in that universal travel we call life all of us manage to keep

From Robert Francis, The Trouble with Francis (Amherst: University of Massachusetts Press, 1971).

an eye pretty constantly on both where we have been and where we are going, the chief difference between the two views being that the backward is considerably clearer than the forward. Yet most of this day-to-day looking back is fragmentary and evanescent. When our donkey is resting after the day's journey, perhaps on a little hill, we can take a more leisurely and lasting survey.

To write the story of one's life is to have the opportunity of combining two quite different experiences. The more obvious one is the living over of one's past. This is generally a pleasant experience since all that was good and happy in the past is good and happy to remember, however tinged it may be with nostalgia; whereas what was not good and happy is softened by time, takes its place in the context of the whole life, and can be remembered with humor and also with thankfulness that it is no more.

But at the same time that a man is living his life over in retrospect, he can stand aside from himself almost as if he were another person. He can be both observer and observed, both author and subject of his book. He can discover patterns in his past and make generalizations about it scarcely possible to one wholly engrossed in the flow of living or reliving. And this too is a good experience, for the nearer one comes to grasping his life as an integrated whole the nearer he is to saving himself from mere flux and fragmentation.

Of course there is a danger in finding order in one's past. Consciously or unconsciously one may represent that past as more orderly than in fact it was, or orderly in ways in which it was not. Yet if a man is determined to come as close as possible to the truth about himself, he must take the risk of distorting that truth. To give the details of one's life, however accurately, without trying to fit them together, is surely only a partial truth.

Let me start with one such generalization, one that seems to me both true and comprehensive enough to serve as a theme to which everything in this book might be related. If it is a paradox, it is a paradox in the sense of only an apparent contradiction. Indeed it did not use to seem strange to me that anyone should have a fortunate and for the most part happy life and at the same time be a pessimist. But evidently it has seemed strange to some people. I recall one friend's saying to me, when I had been trying to explain my *Weltanschauung*, "But why should *you* feel this way? Your life is good and happy." And another friend in writing about my poetry asked why Robert Francis should speak of evil. What evil had *he* ever known?

It seems generally agreed that a man's outlook on life, his optimism or his pessimism, parallels his personal situation. If he himself is healthy and happy, he is impressed with all the other healthy and happy people around him. He is an optimist. But if he is unhealthy and unhappy, he tends to see the whole universe suffering from the same ills. He is a pessimist.

This is where I make an exception. I have been growing healthier and happier over the years; yet when I look around me I am more impressed with the ills of life, the injustices, frustrations, and agonies, than with anything else. I am, therefore, what might be called a happy pessimist. And this is not because I enjoy my pessimism, as some pessimists seem to do, but in spite of, very much in spite of, my somber view of the human situation.

Perhaps it could be called a tragic view I take, but "tragic" is not tragic enough to describe it. For in true tragedy there is a redeeming element, and there is no redeeming element in my ultimate view of life.

In speaking of pessimists and optimists I know I am using very clumsy and unsatisfactory terms. By derivation a pessimist ought to be someone who believes that all is for the worst in this the worst of all possible worlds. Most pessimists are not so pessimistic. For precise thinking and expression we ought to have other words, a whole spectrum of words. But we don't.

Not only are the degrees of pessimism or of optimism infinite, but so are the possibilities of combining the two in the same life. A Frenchman, for instance, might be quite pessimistic about the political situation of France, and yet be an optimist in regard to French cuisine. If the political situation changes for the better, he ceases to be a pessimist or becomes at least less pessimistic. But if he should suffer a *crise de foie* he becomes a pessimist again but for a different reason.

I leave it to the reader to decide in what respects and to what extent I am a pessimist, though he will probably have to wait till the last chapter to find out. As for the other part of my theme—the gradual increase of my good health and good fortune—the reader may expect to find substantiation all along the way.

QUESTIONS

1. Think up one adjective to describe the impression that you get of each of these writers. See if your classmates agree with you.

2. Which of the writers use the longest sentences? the most complex grammar? What effect does their grammar have on their voice? For instance, which writers seem to have planned carefully what they are going to say, and which seem to be jotting down whatever comes into their heads?

3. Writers use punctuation in different ways. For instance, Cleone Knox uses a lot of Initial Capital Letters. How does this habit affect her voice? If you use a lot of parentheses (who does that?), you break a thought in the middle (like this) and risk sounding scatterbrained. And exclamation points!!! What about question marks? Some writers make use of the semicolon; this formal mark usually creates a sense of balance and control. Can punctuation help to define a voice?

4. Charlie Chaplin sometimes uses the jargon of the film industry—words that are characteristically used by people in that profession. Find some examples. Then look at the vocabularies of the other writers. What characteristics stand out? Who uses emotional words? old-fashioned words? clichés? abstract words?

5. Which of the writers use the longest paragraphs? the shortest? Does this have any effect on the voice?

6. Look at the organization of each sample. Is the writer consciously trying to make a single point about him- or herself? Is there a thesis statement? Or is the writer saying several unconnected things?

7. Robert Francis says that he has an opportunity to "discover patterns" and "make generalizations" about his past. What is the danger involved in doing this, according to him? Why is it worth doing anyway? Do the other writers see patterns in their lives?

8. Most of these voices make direct statements about themselves. Jane Eyre says that she was "beginning to feel the stirring of old emotions." Liv Ullmann says, "All the time I am trying to change myself." Are these statements believable? What is there in the writing that helps us to believe them?

9. Several of these writers mention clothes. To Charlie Chaplin, clothes are all-important for creating the character that appeared in the movies. Find other references to clothing. Is what people wear usually important to their sense of identity?

   Do clothes help us form an understanding of other people? How can a writer make up for the fact that his voice has no clothes, no appearance? Can things like punctuation, organization, and type of vocabulary provide clues for the reader, the way clothing does?

10. Go back to one of the writers you have talked about and summarize everything that was said about him or her. Does it all add up to a pretty consistent picture? When you put together your observations about sentence length, kinds of vocabulary, use of punctuation, and so on, are they all consistent with the adjective you first picked out to describe the writer?

Personal Letters

Edna St. Vincent Millay, to her mother

Vassar College
Poughkeepsie, N. Y.
[May 7, 1914]
Wednesday.

Dear Mother,—
    I love you. In a few minutes I'm going to be home. We've drawn lots
for next year's rooms, & I have a perfectly wonderful single in North, a
corner room with two windows & lots of room for everything. North was
the most popular hall. Catherine Filene & Harry are right down
stairs from me, & Margaret & Kim down below them. (Catherine & Harry
are in here & they both send you their love.)
    I shall have the cutest room. I'm going to get me a little alcohol
tea-kettle so I can have tea, & bring back my lovely tea-set for show, &
use my cute one. I'm going to subscribe for a couple of good magazines
& a newspaper, so the room'll look alive, so to speak. And I'm going to try
most always to have a flower. I'll have to buy a little furniture—we
get it here second-hand from the seniors. Desk & extra cot, etc.
    O, I'm so crazy to get home!—Seems to me I can't wait, tho I'm crazy
about the college & everything.—My history teacher who is perfectly
dear but very dignified & has never unbent the least little bit before today,
said this morning, àpropos of my absentminded disregard of a certain
hard & fast rule, "Well, why didn't you think, you naughty little
thing?"
    Was that a scolding,—or not?
    Four weeks from tomorrow I take my last exam. Martha Bull
wants me to stay over for Commencement,—the 10th, but I can't. Couldn't
stand it.
    It's lovely weather here now. That helps. But I tell you I'm all ready
to be home.—What a wonderful summer we'll have, 'spite of Latin Prose,
& all the rest!—Please make 'em plant some pansies, if nuffin' else.

Yo' lovin' chile,
Vincent.

John, to his mother

Hiya Ma!
   Very good to hear from you, am glad to hear things at home are going
well. Things here are relatively excellent. Lots of work, history,
economics and psychology are my main courses, the others are art
history and a little English. The English is pretty poor, which is to bad.
Maybe I can pick this up later. Foods fine (don't worry!) roomate
wears P.J.'s and doesn't drink beer. All of them are incredibly smart,
however, I think I can hold my own. Its interesting what you said about
competition, for this is obviously a very competitive situation. It's
healthy though, it makes me work.
   People are generally very nice, the freshmen far less freaky than
I had expected. The upper classmen get a little "different" however I
say this only on the basis of their outward appearance, for I have no
classroom contact with them at all, which is too bad. The city gets me
down once an a while, its a rather depressing place, no where to go to be
really alone, not even parks (!) Ah well. Have to decide on a major.

> Take care
> Love
> John

Pop, to Deborah

19 Sep 64

Debby darling:
   Even David conceded tother day that things didnt seem quite the
same around here with old Debs gone. I had a dream about it, myself.
Seems you were about three years old, and lost somehow, lagged
behind or something, and I had to go back and retrieve you. Aw. Touchin,
like. Actually the night we got back from dropping you nightmares
were in order: whadda trip. I lost us again a couple of times. Finally we
stopped at a Howy J's and had a big feed, sirloins, and managed to
stagger back home. But then, I must say, life on the ranch has seemed to
go along about as always, even in your lamented absence. Bob was here
for two nights. David may have an apartment with his friends, & on
the other hand he may not. Nancy has been painting still lifes (lives?)
featuring kitchen edibles. A very nice one with lettuce, lemons, eggs, and
an eggplant tumbling out of a paper bag, cornucopia-style. When one
needs an egg, as I did last night while constructing a meat loaf, and it isn't
to be found in the fridge, one repairs to the studio and cops a prop.
   Do I take it your roommate did turn up? She turns out to be, I

conjecture, six feet six with a harelip, and she belches all night? She does? We were all glad to receive your picture of the college president. Intellectual people always look so intellectual, I always say.

One of the benefits of sending Debby to college that I hadn't anticipated is the pleasure of writing her letters, but now I see that I have neither news nor entertainment to offer. At least you can be thankful it's not advice. We did have the feeling, leaving you Wednesday, that we were leaving you in good hands, and I don't mean your dorm mother's hands. I guess I really mean Debby's hands.

well, send us some NEWS, whyntcha???

yr Pop

Mother, to Deborah

Jan. 6

Dear Deb—

It is 10° below zero this morning and my car didn't start—your father's did, however, so I think we are still mobile.

We had a marvelous time last weekend in Boston—we stayed at a Posh Hotel and went to Larry's wedding—Whew! Speak of Style—Rich, old Boston family! We were (all 300 of us) given a daisy as we entered the church—Singers, bridesmaids, flower girl, printed up service and Gloria in the midst of it all being very charming.

Well back to Monday & I've got a cold & the kids in school are all sulks. Thats the way it goes!

Sam is catting around. Says he has to go to the library every other night. The excuses don't change much over the years.

love Mother

George Bernard Shaw, to Alice Lockett

[36 Osnaburgh Street NW]
5th November 1883

Here is your letter—not that I have anything to say, but because you expect it. At least you said so. I walked home from Liverpool St. [Station], and got frightfully wet (I believe I am in for an attack of rheumatic fever at least) all because you would not wait half a minute whilst I went back for an umbrella. Wretch that you were to catch that train, and fool that I am to put myself in the way of caring whether you caught it or not! I will be your slave no longer: you used me vilely when we met before, and you disappointed me horribly tonight. I recant every word I have ever said to you, and plead temporary insanity as my excuse for having uttered them. I am exceedingly glad that I had not to wait another half hour at that waiting room. I detest the entire universe. I did nothing all the time but tell you monstrous lies—I wonder you can be so credulous as to believe my transparent flatteries. I say the same things to everybody. I believe in my soul that you never meant to catch that train—that you were as much disappointed as I when you found it had not gone. As much disappointed, that is, as I pretended to have been. In reality, I was overjoyed. You told me I was in an unamiable humor. Behold the fruits of it. Must I eternally flatter flatter flatter flatter flatter? When you sit bolt upright opposite me in a railway carriage, you look like a Chinese idol. What! I feel like the Chinaman, do I? Not in the least, I assure you. I felt a thrill of delight when you said you were going to Glostershire. Heaven knows when I shall recover this wetting. If ever woman was undeservedly beloved (supposing any man could be found mad enough to love you a little at odd moments when your complexion is unusually beautiful) you are she.

> yours
> with the most profound
> Indifference
> and in the most entire
> Freedom
> from any attraction on the
> part of
> Any Woman Living

> GBS

Katherine Mansfield, to John Middleton Murry

> Mylor,
> Very late Friday night,
> (August, 1916)

My own,

I shall not be able to post this letter until I have heard from you where you are going to sleep after tonight. Nevertheless I must write and tell you. . . .

That it only dawned on me this evening that perhaps you will not be here again for a long time . . . that you won't see the dahlias of this year again reflected in your mirror and that the lemon verbena in a jar on my table will all be withered and dry.

As I thought that, sitting, smoking in the dusky room, Peter Wilkins
[a black kitten] came in with a fallen-all-too-fallen leaf in his mouth,
and I remembered that the Michaelmas daisies were out and, lo! it
was autumn.

Is it just my fancy—the beauty of this house tonight? This round
lamp on the round table, the rich flowers, the tick of the clock dropping into the quiet—and the dark outside and the apples swelling and a
swimming sense of deep water. May brought me this evening some of this
year's apples. . . . 'Good to eat.' They are small and coloured like pale
strawberries. I wish that you were with me, my love. It is not because
you are absent that I feel so free of distraction, so poised and so still. I feel
that I am free even of sun and wind, like a tree whose every leaf has
'turned'.

I love you tonight beyond measure. Have I ever told you how I love
your shoulders. When I hold you by your shoulders . . . put my arm
round you and feel your fine delicious skin warm and yet cool, like milk,
and your slender bones—the bones of your shoulders. . . .

Goodnight, my heart.

I am your own girl.

Mark Twain, to the Reverend Twichell

Quarry Farm, Aug. 29 ['80].

Dear old Joe,—Concerning Jean Clemens, if anybody said he "didn't
see no p'ints about that frog that's any better'n any other frog," I should
think he was convicting himself of being a pretty poor sort of observer. . . . I will not go into details; it is not necessary; you will soon be in
Hartford, where I have already hired a hall; the admission fee will be
but a trifle.

It is curious to note the change in the stock-quotation of the Affection Board brought about by throwing this new security on the market.
Four weeks ago the children still put Mamma at the head of the list right
along, where she had always been. But now:

Jean
Mamma
Motley ⎱
Fraulein ⎰ cats.
Papa

That is the way it stands, now. Mamma is become No. 2; I have
dropped from No. 4, and am become No. 5. Some time ago it used to be
nip and tuck between me and the cats, but after the cats "developed"
I didn't stand any more show.

I've got a swollen ear; so I take advantage of it to lie abed most of the day, and read and smoke and scribble and have a good time. Last evening Livy said with deep concern, "O dear, I believe an abscess is forming in your ear."

I responded as the poet would have done if he had had a cold in the head—

> "Tis said that abscess conquers love,
> But O believe it not."

This made a coolness.

Been reading Daniel Webster's Private Correspondence. Have read a hundred of his diffuse, conceited, "eloquent," bathotic (or bathostic) letters written in that dim (no, vanished) Past when he was a student; and Lord, to think that this boy who is so real to me now, and so booming with fresh young blood and bountiful life, and sappy cynicisms about girls, has since climbed the Alps of fame and stood against the sun one brief tremendous moment with the world's eyes upon him, and then—f-z-t-! where is he? Why the only long thing, the only real thing about the whole shadowy business is the sense of the lagging dull and hoary lapse of time that has drifted by since then; a vast empty level, it seems, with a formless spectre glimpsed fitfully through the smoke and mist that lie along its remote verge.

Well, we are all getting along here first-rate; Livy gains strength daily, and sits up a deal; the baby is five weeks old and—but no more of this; somebody may be reading this letter 80 years hence. And so, my friend (you pitying snob, I mean, who are holding this yellow paper in your hand in 1960,) save yourself the trouble of looking further; I know how pathetically trivial our small concerns will seem to you, and I will not let your eye profane them. No, I keep my news; you keep your compassion. Suffice it you to know, scoffer and ribald, that the little child is old and blind, now, and once more toothless; and the rest of us are shadows, these many, many years. Yes, and your time cometh!

Mark.

QUESTIONS

1. Describe briefly the personality that each writer expresses in his letter. What words or phrases are especially important in defining this personality?

2. Which writers seem to be having a good time writing the letter? How can you tell?

3. What other feelings do the letters communicate?

4. Compare the openings or salutations of the letters. Describe the differences in voice that these openings suggest. Is the rest of the letter always consistent with the opening?

5. One of the letters uses a great number of dashes. How does this affect the sound of the voice?

6. Some of the writers misspell words or make grammatical mistakes. What do these errors communicate? Is the message that errors give us always inappropriate in a personal letter? Do any of the writers make "errors" on purpose?

7. Some of these letters were written by professional writers, and some were not. Do you find the letters of the professionals better? Are they more interesting? Do they contain more specific detail? Do they do a better job of making the writer seem to be almost present?

8. Which of these letters would you like to receive? Which would you like to have written?

2

Audience: Who's He Talking To?

Just as every piece of writing has its own voice, so every piece of writing also has an assumed audience. Sometimes a writer knows specifically who will read his writing, as for instance when a student writes a paper for a teacher or sends a letter to a friend. I think nearly everyone finds it more difficult to write to a stranger, to ask for information, say, or to request a job interview. When you know your audience, you can make some good guesses about how they will "take" your style. You know which teachers will be annoyed by slang and which ones will complain if they think you are showing off your abstract vocabulary. But when, as sometimes happens, you have to write a paper the first day in class, your task is more difficult. And this audience problem becomes much more difficult when you expect your writing to be read, not by one person, but by many people. In these situations, the writer has to define the character of the audience. We say that the writer makes *assumptions* about the eudience. He or she guesses that they have certain values, certain likes and dislikes. An overwhelming concern with audience is a particular characteristic of persuasive writing, but every writer needs to consider the audience to some extent.

The first group of passages in this chapter are examples of leaders exhorting their people to support them. In the older pieces, two generals urge their soldiers on to battle. In the modern pieces, leaders of government ask all the citizens for their support of a goal which the leader is defining. You will note, of course, that the leader defines his objectives in ways that should seem attractive to the audience. He also tries to get them to identify with him—as warriors, Americans, Englishmen, defenders of liberty, or whatever. At all times, the speaker is carefully considering who his listeners are.

The second group of passages comes from the world of advertising and public relations. Some are samples from the letters you call "junk mail" and usually throw away. They ask you to join an organization or to buy something, perhaps even an idea or a set of values. Some are ads that ask you to buy a particular brand of product; other ads are "selling" an image of a company or a public policy that will benefit the company. Why is it that, although persuasion is a respectable and even a noble aim in some cases, we tend to look down our noses at advertising? Are there reasonable and unreasonable methods to use in persuasion? Part of that answer lies in the assumptions that the letters and ads make about us, the audience. A few ads talk to us as responsible citizens and consumers, but many assume that we are vain and foolish.

As you read these two sections, you may still want to consider the voice that the writer creates. But this time, ask yourself what assumptions about the audience are revealed by this selection of a voice. Does the voice assume that we are intelligent and well informed? Does the writer ask us to consider our own interests, and if so, what does he think we're interested in? Our money? Our comfort? Our ambition? And finally, of course, do you feel comfortable being the audience that this writer expects you to be?

In persuasive writing, as in self-expression, the writer may choose some words that are heavily connotative or emotional. But these words will not necessarily reflect the writer's values. The writer will choose value-words and emotion-words which he assumes that the audience cares about. If Americans are supposed to believe in freedom, and you are trying to persuade them to support you, you might just throw in the word *freedom* from time to time, without ever being specific about what you mean. If the politician uses such *buzz-words* a great deal, we know that he assumes that his audience is not very sophisticated.

Aristotle wrote that there are three different ways to persuade an audience: through your own character, through the listeners' emotions, and through reasoning. The character approach means using your voice to do the persuading. The writer tries to show that he is sensible, sympathetic to the concerns of the audience, and a person of high morals or ideals. The emotional approach may try to make the audience either feel good about the writer's cause or feel fearful or hateful toward the issues or people on the other side. Arguing by using good reasons shows the greatest respect for your audience, but often it is not as successful as an appeal to the feelings. Most persuasive writers use a combination of all three approaches.

The last section of this chapter, "Directions," illustrates how writers who are not interested in persuasion also have to think about their audience. These writers have to imagine the situation their reader is in, what materials are available to him, and what he already knows or doesn't know.

I have suggested several different kinds of questions to ask about the writer's audience. Here they are in summary:

* Who is/are the assumed audience?
* What guesses has the writer made about the nature of the audience?
* Does the writer try to get the audience to identify with him?
* Does the writer use one of Aristotle's three methods of persuasion?

Leaders

Birhtwold

Speech *from* The Battle of Maldon

The speech below is from a long poem in a language called "Old English," which was spoken in England from about the seventh century until about the eleventh. In spite of the poem's age, some of the forebears of our own English words are recognizable. The poem, *The Battle of Maldon,* describes a time in the year 991 when Vikings from Scandinavia attacked the English near Maldon in Essex. Birthnoth, the leader of the Saxon militia, is killed, and many of the Saxon soldiers flee. But Birhtwold (or Beorhtweald) urges them in this speech to fight on to their deaths, as he intends to do himself.

> Beorht-weald maðelode,   bord hafenode—
> se wæs eald ʒenéat—   æsc acweahte;
> hé full bealdlíce   beornas lǽrde:
> "Hyʒe sceal þý heardra,   heorte þý cœnre,
> mód sceal þý máre   þý úre mæʒen lýtlaþ.
> Hér liʒeþ úre ealdor   eall forhéawen,
> gód on gréote.   Á mæʒ gnornian
> se-þe nú fram þis wíʒ-plegan   wendan þenćeþ.
> Ić eom fród féores;   fram ić ne wille,
> ac ić mé be healfe   mínum hláforde,
> be swá léofum menn   licgan þenće."

Birhtwold spoke, raised his shield—he was an old retainer—shook his ash-spear; full boldly he exhorted the men: "Purpose shall be the firmer, heart the keener, courage shall be the more, as our might lessens. Here lies our lord all hewn down, good man on ground. Ever may he lament who now thinks to turn from war-play. I am old of life; from here I will not turn, but by my lord's side, by the man I loved, I intend to lie."

Henry V

Speech from Shakespeare's Henry V

In this next speech, another English leader and warrior, King Henry V, urges his soldiers on to an attack. They are engaged in an invasion of France, and this time the English soldiers will be successful.

SCENE I.—*France. Before Harfleur.*

Alarums. Enter KING HENRY, EXETER, BEDFORD, GLOUCESTER, *and* Soldiers,
    with scaling ladders.
    K. Hen. Once more unto the breach, dear friends, once more;
Or close the wall up with our English dead!
In peace there's nothing so becomes a man
As modest stillness and humility:
But when the blast of war blows in our ears,
Then imitate the action of the tiger;
Stiffen the sinews, summon up the blood,
Disguise fair nature with hard-favour'd rage;
Then lend the eye a terrible aspect;
Let it pry through the portage of the head
Like the brass cannon; let the brow o'erwhelm it
As fearfully as doth a galled rock
O'erhang and jutty his confounded base,
Swill'd with the wild and wasteful ocean.
Now set the teeth and stretch the nostril wide,
Hold hard the breath, and bend up every spirit
To his full height! On, on, you noblest English!
Whose blood is fet from fathers of war-proof;
Fathers that, like so many Alexanders,
Have in these parts from morn till even fought,
And sheath'd their swords for lack of argument.
Dishonour not your mothers; now attest
That those whom you call'd fathers did beget you.
Be copy now to men of grosser blood,
And teach them how to war. And you, good yeomen,

Whose limbs were made in England, show us here
The metle of your pasture; let us swear
That you are worth your breeding; which I doubt not;
For there is none of you so mean and base
That hath not noble lustre in your eyes.
I see you stand like greyhounds in the slips,
Straining upon the start. The game's afoot:
Follow your spirit; and, upon this charge
Cry 'God for Harry! England and Saint George!'

[*Exeunt. Alarum, and chambers go off.*]

President Kennedy

Inaugural Address (20 January 1961)

Mr. Chief Justice, President Eisenhower, Vice President Nixon, President Truman, reverend clergy, fellow citizens, we observe today not a victory of party, but a celebration of freedom—symbolizing an end, as well as a beginning—signifying renewal, as well as change. For I have sworn before you and Almighty God the same solemn oath our forebears prescribed nearly a century and three quarters ago.

The world is very different now. For man holds in his mortal hands the power to abolish all forms of human poverty and all forms of human life. And yet the same revolutionary beliefs for which our forebears fought are still at issue around the globe—the belief that the rights of man come not from the generosity of the state, but from the hand of God.

We dare not forget today that we are the heirs of that first revolution. Let the word go forth from this time and place, to friend and foe alike, that the torch has been passed to a new generation of Americans—born in this century, tempered by war, disciplined by a hard and bitter peace, proud of our ancient heritage—and unwilling to witness or permit the slow undoing of those human rights to which this Nation has always been committed, and to which we are committed today at home and around the world.

Let every nation know, whether it wishes us well or ill, that we shall pay any price, bear any burden, meet any hardship, support any friend, oppose any foe, in order to assure the survival and the success of liberty.

This much we pledge—and more.

To those old allies whose cultural and spiritual origins we share, we pledge the loyalty of faithful friends. United, there is little we cannot do in a host of cooperative ventures. Divided, there is little we can do—for we dare not meet a powerful challenge at odds and split asunder.

To those new States whom we welcome to the ranks of the free, we pledge our words that one form of colonial control shall not have passed away merely to be replaced by a far greater iron tyranny. We shall not always expect to find them supporting our view. But we shall always hope to find them strongly supporting their own freedom—and to remember that, in the past, those who foolishly sought power by riding the back of the tiger ended up inside.

To those peoples in the huts and villages across the globe struggling to break the bonds of mass misery, we pledge our best efforts to help them help themselves, for whatever period is required—not because the Communists may be doing it, not because we seek their votes, but because it is right. If a free society cannot help the many who are poor, it cannot save the few who are rich.

To our sister republics south of our border, we offer a special pledge—to convert our good words into good deeds, in a new alliance for progress, to assist free men and free governments in casting off the chains of poverty. But this peaceful revolution of hope cannot become the prey of hostile powers. Let all our neighbors know that we shall join with them to oppose aggression or subversion anywhere in the Americas. And let every other power know that this hemisphere intends to remain the master of its own house.

To that world assembly of sovereign states, the United Nations, our last best hope in an age where the instruments of war have far outpaced the instruments of peace, we renew our pledge of support—to prevent it from becoming merely a forum for invective—to strengthen its shield of the new and the weak—and to enlarge the area in which its writ may run.

Finally, to those nations who would make themselves our adversary, we offer not a pledge but a request: that both sides begin anew the quest for peace, before the dark powers of destruction unleashed by science engulf all humanity in planned or accidental self-destruction.

We dare not tempt them with weakness. For only when our arms are sufficient beyond doubt can we be certain beyond doubt that they will never be employed.

But neither can two great and powerful groups of nations take comfort from our present course—both sides overburdened by the cost of modern weapons, both rightly alarmed by the steady spread of the deadly atom, yet both racing to alter that uncertain balance of terror that stays the hand of mankind's final war.

So let us begin anew—remembering on both sides that civility is not a sign of weakness, and sincerity is always subject to proof. *Let us never negotiate out of fear. But let us never fear to negotiate.*

Let both sides explore what problems unite us instead of laboring those problems which divide us.

Let both sides, for the first time, formulate serious and precise proposals for the inspection and control of arms—and bring the absolute power to destroy other nations under the absolute control of all nations.

Let both sides seek to invoke the wonders of science instead of its terrors. Together let us explore the stars, conquer the deserts, eradicate disease, tap the ocean depths, and encourage the arts and commerce.

Let both sides unite to heed in all corners of the earth the command of Isaiah—to "undo the heavy burdens and to let the oppressed go free."

And if a beachhead of cooperation may push back the jungle of suspicion, let both sides join in creating a new endeavor, not a new balance of power, but a new world of law, where the strong are just and the weak secure and the peace preserved.

All this will not be finished in the first 100 days. Nor will it be finished in the first 1,000 days, nor in the life of this administration, nor even perhaps in our lifetime on this planet. But let us begin.

In your hands, my fellow citizens, more than in mind, will rest the final success or failure of our course. Since this country was founded, each generation of Americans has been summoned to give testimony to its national loyalty. The graves of young Americans who answered the call to service surround the globe.

Now the trumpet summons us again—not as a call to bear arms, though arms we need; not as a call to battle, though embattled we are; but a call to bear the burden of a long twilight struggle, year in, and year out, "rejoicing in hope, patient in tribulation"—a struggle against the common enemies of man: tyranny, poverty, disease, and war itself.

Can we forge against these enemies a grand and global alliance, North and South, East and West, that can assure a more fruitful life for all mankind? Will you join in that historic effort?

In the long history of the world, only a few generations have been granted the role of defending freedom in its hour of maximum danger. I do not shrink from this responsibility—I welcome it. I do not believe that any of us would exchange places with any other people or any other generation. The energy, the faith, the devotion which we bring to this endeavor will light our country and all who serve it—and the glow from that fire can truly light the world.

And so, my fellow Americans, ask not what your country can do for you: Ask what you can do for your country.

My fellow citizens of the world: Ask not what America will do for you, but what together we can do for the freedom of man.

Finally, whether you are citizens of America or citizens of the world, ask of us the same high standards of strength and sacrifice which we ask of you. With a good conscience our only sure reward, with history the final judge of our deeds, let us go forth to lead the land we love, asking His blessing and His help, but knowing that here on earth God's work must truly be our own.

President Johnson

Address on U.S. Policies in Vietnam (Delivered at Johns Hopkins University, 7 April 1965)

Last week 17 nations sent their views to some two dozen countries having an interest in Southeast Asia. We are joining those 17 countries and stating our American policy tonight, which we believe will contribute toward peace in this area of the world.

I have come here to review once again with my own people the views of the American Government.

Tonight Americans and Asians are dying for a world where each people may choose its own path to change. This is the principle for which our ancestors fought in the valleys of Pennsylvania. It is the principle for which our sons fight tonight in the jungles of Vietnam.

Vietnam is far away from this quiet campus. We have no territory there, nor do we seek any. The war is dirty and brutal and difficult. And some 400 young men—born into an America that's bursting with opportunity and promise—have ended their lives on Vietnam's steaming soil.

Why must we take this painful road?

Why must this nation hazard its ease and its interests and its power for the sake of a people so far away?

We fight because we must fight if we are to live in a world where every country can shape its own destiny. And only in such a world will our own freedom be finally secure.

This kind of a world will never be built by bombs or bullets. Yet the infirmities of man are such that force must often precede reason—and the waste of war the works of peace.

We wish that this were not so. But we must deal with the world as it is, if it is ever to be as we wish.

The world as it is in Asia is not a serene or peaceful place. The first reality is that North Vietnam has attacked the independent nation of South Vietnam: its object is total conquest.

Of course, some of the people of South Vietnam are participating in attack on their own government, but trained men and supplies, orders and arms flow in a constant stream from north to south. This support is the heartbeat of the war and it is a war of unparalleled brutality.

Simple farmers are the targets of assassination and kidnapping; women and children are strangled in the night because their men are loyal to their government. And helpless villages are ravaged by sneak attacks. Large-scale raids are conducted on towns, and terror strikes in the heart of cities.

The confused nature of this conflict cannot mask the fact that is: it is the new face of an old enemy.

Over this war and all Asia is another reality: the deepening shadow of Communist China. The rulers in Hanoi are urged on by Peking. This is a regime which has destroyed freedom in Tibet, which has attacked India and has been condemned by the United Nations for aggression in Korea.

It is a nation which is helping the forces of violence in almost every continent. The contest in Vietnam is part of a wider pattern of aggressive purposes.

Why are these realities our concern?

Why are we in South Vietnam?

We are there because we have a promise to keep.

Since 1954 every American President has offered support to the people of South Vietnam. We have helped to build, and we have helped to defend. Thus, over many years we have made a national pledge to help South Vietnam defend its independence. And I intend to keep that promise.

To dishonor that pledge, to abandon this small and brave nation to its enemies, and to the terror that must follow, would be an unforgivable wrong. ·

We are also there to strengthen world order. Around the globe, from Berlin to Thailand, are people whose well-being rests in part on the belief that they can count on us if they are attacked. To leave Vietnam to its fate would shake the confidence of all these people in the value of an American commitment; and in the value of America's word.

The result would be increased unrest and instability—and even wider war.

We are also there because there are great stakes in the balance. Let no one think for a moment that retreat from Vietnam would bring an end to conflict. The battle would be renewed in one country and then another. The central lesson of our time is that the appetite of aggression is never satisfied.

To withdraw from one battlefield means only to prepare for the next. We must say in Southeast Asia, as we did in Europe, in the words of the Bible, "Hitherto shalt thou come; but no further."

There are those who say that all our efforts there will be futile; that China's power is such that it is bound to dominate all Southeast Asia. But there is no end to that argument until all of the nations of Asia are swallowed up.

There are those who wonder why we have a responsibility there. Well, we have it there for the same reason that we have a responsibility for the defense of Europe. World War II was fought in both Europe and Asia and when it ended we found ourselves with continued responsibility for the defense of freedom.

Our objective is the independence of South Vietnam, and its freedom from attack. We want nothing for ourselves—only that the people of South Vietnam be allowed to guide their own country in their own way.

We will do everything necessary to reach that objective. And we will do only what is absolutely necessary.

In recent months attacks on South Vietnam were stepped up. Thus it became necessary for us to increase our response and to make attacks by air. This is not a change of purpose. It is a change in what we believe that purpose requires.

We do this in order to slow down aggression.

We do this to increase the confidence of the brave people of South Vietnam who have bravely borne this brutal battle for so many years with so many casualties.

And we do this to convince the leaders of North Vietnam, and all who seek to share their conquest, of a very simple fact:

We will not be defeated.

We will not grow tired.

We will not withdraw, either openly or under the cloak of a meaningless agreement.

We know that air attacks alone will not accomplish all of these purposes. But it is our best and prayerful judgment that they are a necessary part of the surest road to peace.

We hope that peace will come swiftly. But that is in the hands of others besides ourselves. And we must be prepared for a long-continued conflict. It will require patience as well as bravery, the will to endure as well as the will to resist.

I wish it were possible to convince others with words of what we now find it necessary to say with guns and planes. Armed hostility is futile. Our resources are equal to any challenge because we fight for values and we fight for principles rather than territory or colonies. Our patience and our determination are unending.

Once this is clear, then it should also be clear that the only path for reasonable men is the path of peaceful settlement.

Such peace demands an independent South Vietnam—securely guaranteed and able to shape its own relationships to all others, free from outside interference, tied to no alliance, a military base for no country.

These are the essentials of any final settlement.

We will never be second in the search for such a peaceful settlement in Vietnam.

There may be many ways to this kind of peace: in discussion or negotiation with the governments concerned, in large groups or in small ones, in the reaffirmation of old agreements or their strengthening with new ones.

We have stated this position over and over again 50 times and more to friend and foe alike. And we remain ready, with this purpose, for unconditional discussions.

And until that bright and necessary day of peace we will try to keep conflict from spreading. We have no desire to see thousands die in battle—Asians or Americans. We have no desire to devastate that which the people of North Vietnam have built with toil and sacrifice. We will use our power with restraint and with all the wisdom that we can command.

But we will use it.

This war, like most wars, is filled with terrible irony. For what do the people of North Vietnam want? They want what their neighbors also desire—food for their hunger, health for their bodies, a chance to learn, progress for their country, and an end to the bondage of material misery. And they would find all of these things are more readily in peaceful association with others than in the endless course of battle.

These countries of Southeast Asia are homes for millions of impoverished people. Each day these people rise at dawn and struggle through until the night to wrestle existence from the soil. They are often wracked by disease, plagued by hunger, and death comes at the early age of 40.

Stability and peace do not come easily in such a land. Neither independence nor human dignity will ever be won, though, by arms alone.

It also requires the work of peace.

The American people have helped generously in times past in these works, and now there must be a much more massive effort to improve the life of man in that conflict-torn corner of our world.

The first step is for the countries of Southeast Asia to associate themselves in a greatly expanded cooperative effort for development.

We would hope that North Vietnam would take its place in the common effort just as soon as peaceful cooperation is possible.

The United Nations is already actively engaged in development in this area, and as far back in 1961 I conferred with our authorities in Vietnam in connection with their work there. And I would hope tonight that the Secretary General of the United Nations could use the prestige of his great office and his deep knowledge of Asia to initiate as soon as possible with the countries of that area a plan for cooperation in increased development.

For our part I will ask the Congress to join in a billion-dollar American investment in this effort as soon as it is under way.

And I would hope that all other industrialized countries, including the Soviet Union, will join in this effort to replace despair with hope and terror with progress. The task is nothing less than to enrich the hopes and the existence of more than 100 million people, and there is much to be done.

The vast Mekong River can provide food and water and power on a scale to dwarf even our own TVA.

The wonder of modern medicine can be spread through villages where thousands die every year from lack of care.

Schools can be established to train people in the skills that are needed to manage the process of development.

And these objectives, and more, are within the reach of a cooperative and determined effort. I also intend to expand and speed up a program to make available our farm surplus to assist in feeding and clothing the needy in Asia.

We should not allow people to go hungry and wear rags, while our own warehouses overflow with an abundance of wheat and corn and rice and cotton.

So I will very shortly name a special team of outstanding patriotic distinguished Americans to inaugurate our participation in these programs. This team will be headed by Mr. Eugene Black, the very able former president of the World Bank.

In areas that are still ripped by conflict, of course, development will not be easy. Peace will be necessary for final success. But we cannot and must not wait for peace to begin this job.

This will be a disorderly planet for a long time. In Asia, as elsewhere, the forces of the modern world are shaking old ways and uprooting ancient civilizations. There will be turbulence and struggle and even violence. Great social change, that we see in our own country now, does not always come without conflict.

We must also expect that nations will on occasion be in dispute with us. It may be because we are rich or powerful, or because we have made some mistakes, or because they honestly fear our intentions.

However, no nation need ever fear that we desire their land or to impose our will or to dictate their institutions.

But we will always oppose the effort of one nation to conquer another nation. We will do this because our own security is at stake. But there is more to it than that. For our generation has a dream. It is a very old dream. But we have the power and now we have the opportunity to make that dream come true.

For centuries, nations have struggled among each other. But we dream of a world where disputes are settled by law and reason. And we will try to make it so.

For most of history, men have hated and killed one another in battle. But we dream of an end to war. We will try to make it so.

For all existence, most men have lived in poverty, threatened by hunger. But we dream of a world where all are fed and charged with hope. And we will help to make it so.

The ordinary men and women of North Vietnam and South Vietnam, of China and India, of Russia and America, are brave people. They are filled with the same proportions of hate and fear, of love and hope. Most of them want the same things for themselves and their families. Most of them do not want their sons to ever die in battle; or to see their homes, or the homes of others, destroyed.

Well, this can be their world yet. Man now has the knowledge— always before denied—to make this planet serve the real needs of the people who live on it.

I know this will not be easy. I know how difficult it is for reason to guide passion, and love to master hate. The complexities of this world do not bow easily to pure and consistent answers.

But the simple truths are there just the same. We must all try to follow them as best we can.

We often say how impressive power is. But I do not find it impressive at all. The guns and the bombs, the rockets and the warships, are all symbols of human failure. They are necessary symbols. They protect what we cherish. But they are witness to human folly.

A dam built across a great river is impressive.

In the countryside where I was born, and where I live, I have seen the night illuminated and the kitchens warmed and the homes heated where once the cheerless night and the ceaseless cold held way. And all this happened because electricity came to our area along the humming wires of the R.E.A.

Electrification of the countryside—yes, that too is impressive. A rich harvest in a hungry land is impressive.

The sight of healthy children in a classroom is impressive. These, not mighty arms, are the achievements which the American nation believes to be impressive.

And if we are steadfast, the time may come when all other nations will also find it so.

Every night before I turn out the lights to sleep I ask myself this question: "Have I done everything that I can do to unite this country? Have I done everything I can to help unite the world, to try to bring peace and hope to all the peoples of the world? Have I done enough?"

Ask yourselves that question in your homes and in this hall tonight. Have we, each of us, all done all we could? Have we done enough? We may well be living in the time foretold many years ago when it was said:

"I call heaven and earth to record this day against you; that I have set before you life and death, blessing and cursing. Therefore choose life that both thou and thy seed may live."

This generation of the world must choose: destroy or build, kill or aid, hate or understand.

We can do all these things on a scale that's never been dreamed of before. Well, we will choose life. And so doing we will prevail over the enemies within man and over the natural enemies of all mankind.

To Dr. Eisenhower and Mr. Garland, and this great institution—Johns Hopkins—I thank you for this opportunity to convey my thoughts to you and to the American people.

Good night.

President Nixon

Address on the Situation in Southeast Asia (Televised Speech, 8 May 1972)

Good evening:

Five weeks ago, on Easter weekend, the Communist armies of North Vietnam launched a massive invasion of South Vietnam, an invasion that was made possible by tanks, artillery, and other advanced offensive weapons supplied to Hanoi by the Soviet Union and other Communist nations.

The South Vietnamese have fought bravely to repel this brutal assault. Casualties on both sides have been very high. Most tragically, there have been over 20,000 civilian casualties, including women and children, in the cities which the North Vietnamese have shelled in wanton disregard of human life.

As I announced in my report to the Nation 12 days ago, the role of the United States in resisting this invasion has been limited to air and naval strikes on military targets in North and South Vietnam. As I also pointed out in that report, we have responded to North Vietnam's massive military offensive by undertaking wide-ranging new peace efforts aimed at ending the war through negotiation.

On April 20, I sent Dr. Kissinger to Moscow for 4 days of meetings with General Secretary Brezhnev and other Soviet leaders. I instructed him to emphasize our desire for a rapid solution to the war and our willingness to look at all possible approaches. At that time, the Soviet leaders showed an interest in bringing the war to an end on a basis just to both sides. They urged resumption of negotiations in Paris, and they indicated they would use their constructive influence.

I authorized Dr. Kissinger to meet privately with the top North Vietnamese negotiator, Le Duc Tho, on Tuesday, May 2, in Paris. Ambassador Porter, as you know, resumed the public peace negotiations in Paris on April 27 and again on May 4. At those meetings, both public and private, all we heard from the enemy was bombastic rhetoric and a replaying of their demands for surrender. For example, at the May 2 secret meeting, I authorized Dr. Kissinger to talk about every conceivable avenue toward peace. The North Vietnamese flatly refused to consider any of these approaches. They refused to offer any new approach of their own. Instead, they simply read verbatim their previous public demands.

Here is what over 3 years of public and private negotiations with Hanoi has come down to: The United States, with the full concurrence of our South Vietnamese allies, has offered the maximum of what any President of the United States could offer.

We have offered a deescalation of the fighting. We have offered a cease-fire with a deadline for withdrawal of all American forces. We have offered new elections which would be internationally supervised with the

Communists participating both in the supervisory body and in the elections themselves.

President Thieu has offered to resign one month before the elections. We have offered an exchange of prisoners of war in a ratio of 10 North Vietnamese prisoners for every one American prisoner that they release. And North Vietnam has met each of these offers with insolence and insult. They have flatly and arrogantly refused to negotiate an end to the war and bring peace. Their answer to every peace offer we have made has been to escalate the war.

In the 2 weeks alone since I offered to resume negotiations, Hanoi has launched three new military offensives in South Vietnam. In those 2 weeks the risk that a Communist government may be imposed on the 17 million people of South Vietnam has increased, and the Communist offensive has now reached the point that it gravely threatens the lives of 60,000 American troops who are still in Vietnam.

There are only two issues left for us in this war. First, in the face of a massive invasion do we stand by, jeopardize the lives of 60,000 Americans, and leave the South Vietnamese to a long night of terror? This will not happen. We shall do whatever is required to safeguard American lives and American honor.

Second, in the face of complete intransigence at the conference table do we join with our enemy to install a Communist government in South Vietnam? This, too, will not happen. We will not cross the line from generosity to treachery.

We now have a clear, hard choice among three courses of action: Immediate withdrawal of all American forces, continued attempts at negotiation, or decisive military action to end the war.

I know that many Americans favor the first course of action, immediate withdrawal. They believe the way to end the war is for the United States to get out, and to remove the threat to our remaining forces by simply withdrawing them.

From a political standpoint, this would be a very easy choice for me to accept. After all, I did not send over one-half million Americans to Vietnam. I have brought 500,000 men home from Vietnam since I took office. But, abandoning our commitment in Vietnam here and now would mean turning 17 million South Vietnamese over to Communist tyranny and terror. It would mean leaving hundreds of American prisoners in Communist hands with no bargaining leverage to get them released.

An American defeat in Vietnam would encourage this kind of aggression all over the world, aggression in which smaller nations armed by their major allies, could be tempted to attack neighboring nations at will in the Mideast, in Europe, and other areas. World peace would be in grave jeopardy.

The second course of action is to keep on trying to negotiate a settlement. Now this is the course we have preferred from the beginning and we shall continue to pursue it. We want to negotiate, but we have made every reasonable offer and tried every possible path for ending this war at the conference table.

The problem is, as you all know, it takes two to negotiate and now, as throughout the past 4 years, the North Vietnamese arrogantly refuse to negotiate anything but an imposition, an ultimatum that the United States impose a Communist regime on 17 million people in South Vietnam who do not want a Communist government.

It is plain then that what appears to be a choice among three courses of action for the United States is really no choice at all. The killing in this tragic war must stop. By simply getting out, we would only worsen the bloodshed. By relying solely on negotiations, we would give an intransigent enemy the time he needs to press his aggression on the battlefield.

There is only one way to stop the killing. That is to keep the weapons of war out of the hands of the international outlaws of North Vietnam.

Throughout the war in Vietnam, the United States has exercised a degree of restraint unprecedented in the annals of war. That was our responsibility as a great Nation, a Nation which is interested—and we can be proud of this as Americans—as America has always been, in peace not conquest.

However, when the enemy abandons all restraint, throws its whole army into battle in the territory of its neighbor, refuses to negotiate, we simply face a new situation.

In these circumstances, with 60,000 Americans threatened, any President who failed to act decisively would have betrayed the trust of his country and betrayed the cause of world peace.

I therefore concluded that Hanoi must be denied the weapons and supplies it needs to continue the aggression. In full coordination with the Republic of Vietnam, I have ordered the following measures which are being inplemented as I am speaking to you.

All entrances to North Vietnamese ports will be mined to prevent access to these ports and North Vietnamese naval operations from these ports. United States forces have been directed to take appropriate measures within the internal and claimed territorial waters of North Vietnam to interdict the delivery of any supplies. Rail and all other communications will be cut off to the maximum extent possible. Air and naval strikes against military targets in North Vietnam will continue.

These actions are not directed against any other nation. Countries with ships presently in North Vietnamese ports have already been notified that their ships will have three daylight periods to leave in safety. After that time, the mines will become active and any ships attempting to leave or enter these ports will do so at their own risk.

These actions I have ordered will cease when the following conditions are met:

First, all American prisoners of war must be returned.

Second, there must be an internationally supervised cease-fire throughout Indochina.

Once prisoners of war are released, once the internationally supervised cease-fire has begun, we will stop all acts of force throughout Indochina, and at that time we will proceed with a complete withdrawal of all American forces from Vietnam within 4 months.

Now, these terms are generous terms. They are terms which would not require surrender and humiliation on the part of anybody. They would permit the United States to withdraw with honor. They would end the killing. They would bring our POW's home. They would allow negotiations on a political settlement between the Vietnamese themselves. They would permit all the nations which have suffered in this long war—Cambodia, Laos, North Vietnam, South Vietnam—to turn at last to the urgent works of healing and of peace. They deserve immediate acceptance by North Vietnam.

It is appropriate to conclude my remarks tonight with some comments directed individually to each of the major parties involved in the continuing tragedy of the Vietnam war.

First, to the leaders of Hanoi, your people have already suffered too much in your pursuit of conquest. Do not compound their agony with continued arrogance; choose instead the path of a peace that redeems your sacrifices, guarantees true independence for your country, and ushers in an era of reconciliation.

To the people of South Vietnam, you shall continue to have our firm support in your resistance against aggression. It is your spirit that will determine the outcome of the battle. It is your will that will shape the future of your country.

To other nations, especially those which are allied with North Vietnam, the actions I have announced tonight are not directed against you. Their sole purpose is to protect the lives of 60,000 Americans, who would be gravely endangered in the event that the Communist offensive continues to roll forward, and to prevent the imposition of a Communist government by brutal aggression upon 17 million people.

I particularly direct my comments tonight to the Soviet Union. We respect the Soviet Union as a great power. We recognize the right of the Soviet Union to defend its interests when they are threatened. The Soviet Union in turn must recognize our right to defend our interests.

No Soviet soldiers are threatened in Vietnam. Sixty thousand Americans are threatened. We expect you to help your allies, and you cannot expect us to do other than to continue to help our allies, but let us, and let all great powers, help our allies only for the purpose of their defense, not for the purpose of launching invasions against their neighbors.

Otherwise the cause of peace, the cause in which we both have so great a stake, will be seriously jeopardized.

Our two nations have made significant progress in our negotiations in recent months. We are near major agreements on nuclear arms limitation, on trade, on a host of other issues.

Let us not slide back toward the dark shadows of a previous age. We do not ask you to sacrifice your principles, or your friends, but neither should you permit Hanoi's intransigence to blot out the prospects we together have so patiently prepared.

We, the United States and the Soviet Union, are on the threshold of a new relationship that can serve not only the interests of our two countries, but the cause of world peace. We are prepared to continue to build this relationship. The responsibility is yours if we fail to do so.

And finally, may I say to the American people, I ask you for the same strong support you have always given your President in difficult moments. It is you most of all that the world will be watching.

I know how much you want to end this war. I know how much you want to bring our men home. And I think you know from all that I have said and done these past 3½ years how much I, too, want to end the war to bring our men home.

You want peace. I want peace. But, you also want honor and not defeat. You want a genuine peace, not a peace that is merely a prelude to another war.

At this moment, we must stand together in purpose and resolve. As so often in the past, we Americans did not choose to resort to war. It has been forced upon us by an enemy that has shown utter contempt toward every overture we have made for peace. And that is why, my fellow Americans, tonight I ask for your support of this decision, a decision which has only one purpose, not to expand the war, not to escalate the war, but to end this war and to win the kind of peace that will last.

With God's help, with your support, we will accomplish that great goal.

Thank you and good night.

QUESTIONS

1. Define the audience for each of these speeches. Who are they? Does the writer expect them to share any characteristics, any goals, or any values?

2. Decide which of the speeches rely most on reason, which rely on emotion, and which emphasize the good qualities of the speaker himself. Are there any speeches that will not fit into these categories? Are there any that fit more than one?

3. A good way to get an audience's attention is to surprise it, and one way to surprise it is to show that two opposite or unlikely things are true at once, or that the normal state of affairs has been reversed. We remember the phrase "The last shall be first" because of the pair of opposites it contains. Explain how Birhtwold uses this device. Can you find other examples in other selections?

4. "Images"—pictures created by words that you can almost see in your mind—can be a powerful tool of persuasion. Find several images in Henry V's speech. What emotions might be associated with these images? Do any of the other writers in this section use images to persuade?

5. Circle all the places where Johnson uses the pronoun *we*. How would the speech be different if he had said *I* or *you*? Does he really mean *all* American citizens? Why isn't he more careful to specify who he means? Compare Kennedy's use of *we*.

6. Identify "buzz-words" in Kennedy's speech, words that are sure to get a positive response from almost any American audience. Do you think he uses too many of them?

7. Kennedy organizes many of his paragraphs through the use of "parallel structure." Do either of the other presidents use it?

8. Why does Johnson quote from the Bible, rather than some other book?

9. Do the presidents believe that Americans care about their history? What national values in this history do they expect us to identify with?

Direct Mail and Print Advertising

Diners Club

Dear Mr. Doe,

A person of your position certainly knows distinction. That's precisely why I'm sending you this special invitation to apply for membership in Diners Club.

In fact, Mr. Doe, Diners' exceptional combination of worldwide coverage, added financial and travel services, and personal prestige cannot be matched by any other card! If you qualify for our card, you will soon see for yourself that Diners offers more advantages to its members.

Why in Virginia alone, you'd have immediate acceptance in 664 hotels, motels, resorts, night spots and restaurants. Rent-a-cars? Every chain serving your state—Avis, Hertz, National, all of them, plus 28 independents too. Airlines? Every single one without exception. And top stores, and specialty shops too. Then there are over 2,139 different gasoline, tire and repair stations.

And your home state is just the beginning. Waiting for you is immediate acceptance at over 350,000 of the finest establishments in more than 150 countries. You see, Diners invented the whole idea of the executive card back in 1950. We were first in the U.S., then first in Europe, Latin America, Africa and Asia too. Currently, there are very few leading hotels, motels, resorts and, of course, restaurants in the U.S. and abroad that do not honor Diners.

What's more, many of our establishments actually refuse one or more of the other major cards!

Yes, Diners is the card to carry, Mr. Doe. Our coverage is truly extensive. And so are our other services.

There's a toll-free reservation service for thousands upon thousands of participating hotels and motels in every state of the Union. Emergency cash advances are available at 82 Diners Club international offices in 43 countries. And registered members also have the right to cash a personal check for up to $250 at participating hotels in the U.S. and Canada. If you become a member, you may also obtain travel, accident, even hospital-medical insurance at low-cost group rates. There's even a personal loan service that allows Diners members to apply, privately by mail, for loans of up to $25,000.00—indicating the high personal prestige associated with our cardholders.

This prestige is genuine too, because we have purposely set our standards for membership exceptionally high. In fact, we often turn down prospective members other cards would accept!

But I've made it relatively easy for you to apply for your Diners Club card at this time. The Top-Priority form attached is designed with a person of your position in mind, straightforward and efficient.

Your form is already registered in your name and takes but a few minutes to complete and mail. You can be sure it will receive immediate attention when received at this office. And, if your application is approved, you'll have the extra convenience—and "clout"—of a Diners Club card in your wallet!

In fact, I'm so sure that a Diners Club card belongs in your wallet, that I'm issuing this special invitation.

So, to apply for your Diners Club card, the first card in America and around the world, complete the Top-Priority form at—

tached. Then place it in the postage—paid "wallet" envelope, and
mail quickly——no later than ten days from now.

> Very truly yours,
> Arthur Grimes
> Membership Chairman

AG/agg

P.S. When my friends used to ask me how many establishments ac—
cept a Diners Club card, I'd say 350,000 and let it go at that.
But most didn't seem to realize just how huge that is. So
now I tell them this: If, starting right now, you went to a
different Diners Club establishment every single hour,
24 hours a day, every single day, 365 days a year, you
wouldn't be back here until the year 2016!

National Foundation for Cancer Research

7315 Wisconsin Avenue • Bethesda, Maryland 20014
(301) 654-1250

<u>May I List Your Name on the Honor Roll</u>

<u>Of Those Who Are Helping Us Find a Cure for Cancer?</u>

Dear Concerned Fellow Citizen:

I'm writing you today for an important purpose. It's to in—
vite you to join with many other far—sighted, intelligent men and
women who are contributing to National Foundation for Cancer Re—
search's far—reaching cancer research programs.

We are actively developing a cure for cancer. If you will con—
tribute towards this goal, I promise that your name will be in—
scribed in perpetuity upon the HONOR ROLL of those who gave so
cancer might join smallpox, polio, diptheria, typhus, and other
almost—forgotten disease plagues of the past.

Our Scientific Director, Dr. Albert Szent—Gyorgyi, M.D.,
Ph.D., is recognized as an authentic genius. He single—handedly
discovered Vitamin C and won the Nobel Prize for Science. His work
has saved the lives of countless human beings. His imaginative
mind is well on the way towards unlocking the riddle of a cancer
cure.

Today, the outlook is highly promising. Certain types of
cancer are being controlled. The results we are striving for, pay—

ing for, and praying for, are nearly at hand. We're at the threshold. That's why your assistance now is so vitally important.

Yes, your immediate help is vital. Every day a cancer cure is postponed means another 9,500 Americans are doomed to die. During the two minutes you've been reading this letter of mine, 132 men, women and children have died of cancer!

Frightening isn't it? Yet, if you and others come forward now to help, we can end the threat that now hangs over all of us, our friends, and our loved ones. My mother was recently operated on for cancer, so I have experienced as you may have, the fear and helplessness that accompanies this disease.

National Foundation for Cancer Research is in the front lines in the fight against cancer. Dr. Szent-Gyorgyi has phoned this morning to inform me that the moment of truth is approaching. I couldn't tell him we may not have enough money to support his research much longer. Honestly, how can we stop now when another few months could make the difference?

Yet, medical and scientific research is horribly expensive. And unless I can raise $175,000 to support this cancer research program during the coming fiscal year, all the work and money already spent may have been in vain. It's a very serious situation.

Of course, we could beg Washington for help. But, all we would get is government red tape and bureaucracy . . . we need help now to meet the laboratory salaries and rent.

This is why, even though I'm not accustomed to writing people I've never met and asking them for money, I beg you to help us bring a quick end to cancer's continuing toll.

Any amount you send the Foundation, whether $100, $50, $10, $5, or any other sum you can spare will enable us to continue doing battle against one of mankind's most remorseless plagues.

Please let me hear from you soon. I'll be awaiting your reply.

Sincerely,
Franklin C. Salisbury
Executive Director

P.S. When a cure is found it will take a great deal of time to distribute this knowledge to everyone. I promise that you and your loved ones will be among the first to be informed. Please help us speed that day. Let me add your name to our HONOR ROLL now.

A Non-Profit Donor Supported Association Dedicated to Stopping Cancer . . . "In Our Lifetime"

Cabin Point

1676   In The Heart of Historyland   1978

June 5, 1978

Dear Friend:

This is your personal invitation to take advantage of our 1978 Sales Program which is an offering of lots at Cabin Point.

You may purchase a $5,489 lot for only $4,989. This offer is well within your budget as it requires a down payment of only $89, and the balance with 6% simple interest is payable in easy monthly payments of $58.84 for 108 months. This price of $4,989 also includes all costs, such as drawing of deeds, street improvements, surveying, and closing cost . . . there are no hidden charges. Do not confuse this offer with other developments. Warranty Deed and Title Insurance are available.

This historic Virginia estate known as Cabin Point is being offered for sale on an individual lot basis to a select few. There are over five miles of wooded waterfront along the Potomac River and Cabin Point lakes. These lakes form wonderful well-protected harbors for the boating enthusiasts. There will be ten miles of all-weather roads carving their way through majestic Virginia woodlands. For the exclusive use of club members and their guests, there is an olympic-sized pool, tennis, club house, parks with playground attractions, boat launching ramps, boating, water skiing, beaches and above all, the quiet and tranquility only a secluded Virginia estate can offer. This is a sensibly restricted subdivision including beautiful waterfront lots, with lots to fit most everyone's budget and taste.

This special advertising offer is made in good faith as part of our overall Sales Program. To qualify for this beautiful lot, it will be necessary for you to drive to Cabin Point.

This offer is limited and is subject to cancellation at any time. To serve you better and to avoid confusion, this offer must either be accepted or rejected at the time you inspect the property. If married, both husband and wife must be present at the time of inspection. The reason this opportunity is offered to you is for the word-of-mouth advertising which you, as a satisfied customer, may give your friends, neighbors, and relatives—thereby saving us thousands of dollars in advertising costs.

You will not be required to purchase additional property or to build. All of our lots are at least 1/3 of an acre and exceed the minimum-size required in Virginia. Choice waterfront and waterview lots are available. DON'T DELAY. THIS OFFER IS AVAILABLE FOR ONLY A LIMITED TIME, AS SPECIFIED BELOW.

You may inspect this lot anytime between 9 A.M. and sundown. This offer will be held open to you only until SUNDAY, JUNE 11, 1978, at 8:30 P.M.

Bring this letter with you to qualify for this special offer.

Very sincerely yours,
L. H. Wilson

The New Republic

Dear Reader:

How long has it been since you've read something ornery? That's right, ornery. Cussed. Contrary. It's a great old tradition in American journalism but today it's more often honored in the breach.

Today most weekly newsmagazines are the products of corporate and group journalism—slickly packaged food for thought. And, like most packaged food, they're bland.

But not The New Republic. For more than 60 years, we've answered to no one but ourselves. We're a magazine of serious, informed, opinionated, un-bland individuals.

Of course, the only way you'll really know what we mean is to read us. And at the end of this letter is an offer that makes it easy for you to do just that.

But meanwhile, consider some of our people . . .

A tradition of lively writing.

The New Republic has always been a home for iconoclasts. From Walter Lippmann and H. L. Mencken (the original curmudgeon) to Lillian Hellman and Lewis Mumford.

Today we continue that untraditional tradition. With John Osborne ("the best political reporter in Washington," said Henry Kissinger, who was often on the receiving end of Osborne's barbs).

And Stanley Kauffmann ("America's hardest critic to please"). And Richard Strout, who for 34 years has written the magazine's most famous column—TRB.

And contributors such as John Hersey, Robert Coles, Joyce Carol Oates, Richard Rovere and Alfred Kazin.

And new writers.

We've also added a host of new contributors—including Tad Szulc (who has a knack for being where wars and revolutions are), Henry Fairlie (an expert of devastating British wit) and "Suetonius" (the pseudonym for a Washington insider with strong views).

And new editors—managing editor Michael Kinsley, executive editor Morton Kondracke and literary editor Roger Rosenblatt.

Altogether, they're a collection of individuals who see things differently—and write about them differently.

We give our writers room.

Because the other three weekly newsmagazines divide them- selves into regular departments, they feel they have to report what happened each week in each department—whether it was important or not.

At The New Republic, we figure you read at least one of these newsweeklies and at least one daily newspaper. You already know what the news is.

So our editors and contributors are free to tell you what they think the news means.

In depth. And, if need be, at length. So The New Republic has something of the feel of a monthly magazine. But because we are a weekly, we give you immediate facts and insights about the news—to help you make sense of it while it's still happening.

That's what's really important.

A lively new look.

The New Republic has learned that lively writing and lively graphics go hand in hand.

So we now run covers by Andy Warhol, Ben Shahn, Red Grooms and Rembrandt and drawings by Jamie Wyeth. We regularly print political cartoons, drawings of literary figures, photographs and photomontages. And we use color type and whole pages of color to make sure your eye doesn't miss a single interesting item.

Now we have some of the slick look of the other newsweeklies—but beneath our surface sophistication there's also a real sophistication.

Expose your mind?

As we said, we're not out to compete with the other weekly newsmagazines. There just aren't enough readers who want "small insurrections" fomented in their minds every week (fomented by people such as J. K. Galbraith, Michael Harrington, Irving Howe and Oriana Fallaci).

But if you'd like to be exposed to some sometimes ornery, cussed and downright contrary ideas, we'll make it easy.

Simply send in the enclosed reply card and we'll send you an issue of The New Republic—with our compliments. And the next 47 issues for only $12.00.

That's half the normal subscription price of $24—a great opportunity. Now don't you be contrary and pass it up.

Sincerely yours,
Robert J. Myers
Publisher

League of Women Voters of the United States
1730 M St., NW, Washington, D.C. 20036   (202) 296-1770

June 1977

Dear Friends:

Few things are harder to change by peaceful means than the living habits of an entire nation. Yet every thoughtful assessment of the present energy crisis concludes that just such changes will have to take place in the United States, starting now.

Three years ago, the League of Women Voters Education Fund saw that any realistic national energy policy will be doomed without the wholehearted cooperation of the American public. Changes in living habits, after all, call for changes in public attitudes. To set such a process in motion, the Education Fund decided to mobilize a national education program to bring energy issues and choices to grassroots America. Such an ambitious undertaking has a chance of success (where others may fail) partly because the LWVEF works in cooperation with the 137,000 members of the League of Women Voters of the United States in 1,401 Leagues and in every state—dedicated to public service and skilled in communicating complex issues in everyday language in their home communities—and partly because of the credibility the LWVEF has built over the years as an impartial organization with "no axe to grind." Ever since 1974, the LWVEF energy education program has been expanding—an energy task force which has now been succeeded by an energy department . . . energy information written in non-technical language and distributed to the League network and through it to the public . . . regional energy workshops . . . a major fund raising campaign for community energy education.

In early June 1977 the LWVEF brought together a team of League and community leaders from every state to meet with some of the top energy spokesmen from government, industry, academic circles and environmental groups. Participants received thorough background in energy issues and intensive training in techniques for communicating the problems and alternatives to citizens. Each team is pledged to conduct a program of citizen education in its home state.

Besides energy, the LWVEF is concerned with environmental quality, land use, women's rights, problems of poverty and discrimination, international relations, good government practices and unbiased voter information before elections. Leagues across the country take advantage of the LWVEF publications, workshops, conferences, etc., by conducting educational programs on these national issues, tailored to the uniqueness of each state or region or town. League members have demonstrated their ability to reach citizens from all walks of life, including the local power structure. The well-organized framework of the Leagues and active participation of members assures broad dissemination of the work of the LWVEF.

Since its founding in 1957, the Education Fund has been eligible to receive tax-deductible contributions under section 501(c)(3) of the Internal Revenue Code. Because the LWVEF is not a membership organization, its educational and research work is supported almost entirely by grants and contributions from individuals, corporations, foundations, unions and government agencies, either for specific projects or for general support. We were particularly gratified by the generous contributions to offset the costs of the Presidential Debates for which the LWVEF recently received the George Foster Peabody Broadcasting Award for 1976.

The kind of money we need most is that which is unrestricted—
money which is not earmarked for any one project. That is what
keeps the show on the road and it is to that end that we are asking
for your support. Your contribution, of course, would be tax-
deductible. Incidentally, I happen to think that if the American
people understand their energy choices now, our living habits may
be less severely affected in the future. Please join our efforts by
sending your donation.

Sincerely,
Ruth C. Clusen
President

The Education Fund is one of two organizations at the national
level of the League, the other being the League of Women Voters of
the United States. The League of Women Voters of the United
States, a membership organization, is also nonpartisan but it
takes stands on issues following consensus by the state and local
Leagues across the country. Since it lobbies for these positions,
contributions are not tax-deductible unless they qualify as a
business expense.

HE SHORT STOP SNACK.

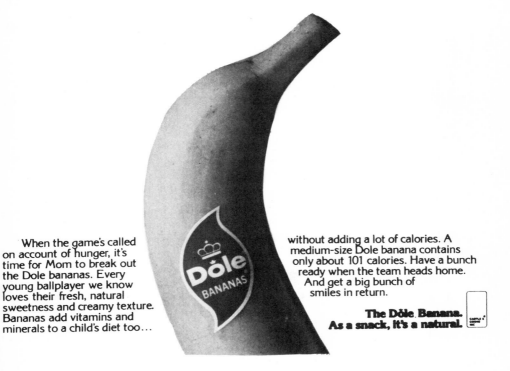

When the game's called on account of hunger, it's time for Mom to break out the Dole bananas. Every young ballplayer we know loves their fresh, natural sweetness and creamy texture. Bananas add vitamins and minerals to a child's diet too... without adding a lot of calories. A medium-size Dole banana contains only about 101 calories. Have a bunch ready when the team heads home. And get a big bunch of smiles in return.

**The Dole Banana.
As a snack, it's a natural.**

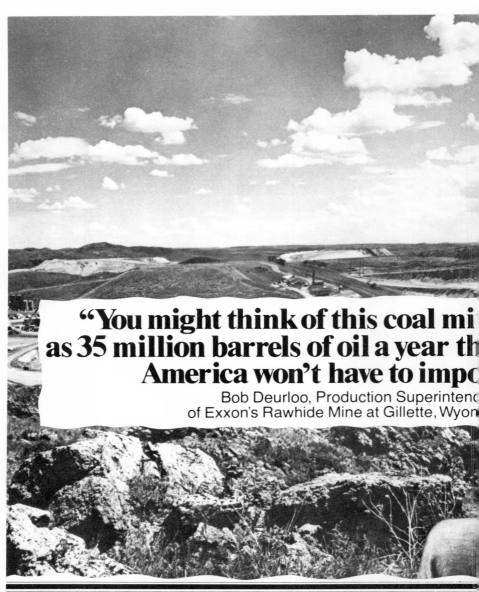

"You might think of this coal mi[ne]
as 35 million barrels of oil a year th[at]
America won't have to imp[ort]"

Bob Deurloo, Production Superinten[dent]
of Exxon's Rawhide Mine at Gillette, Wyo[ming]

Energy for a s[

America's coal – resource that is being developed to help meet our country's growing energy needs.

Coal is America's most plentiful energy resource. By developing more of it to fuel electric power plants and industries, America can reduce its dependence on foreign oil.

Exxon's new mine at Gillette, Wyoming will be able to produce 12 million tons of coal a year, enough energy to replace 35 million barrels of imported oil. And we're reclaiming the land we mine to return it to use as range land.

We have also been operating a 3-million-ton-a-year underground mine in Carlinville, Illinois since 1970, and have just opened a new underground mine at Albers, Illinois. Soon, we will be opening a third underground mine near Huntington, West Virginia and a second surface mine in Wyoming.

The capacity of all these mines will be the energy equivalent of about 3 days' supply of oil for America.

Exxon is working on ways to make better use of coal reserves—research into better ways to mine coal, better ways to burn it, and new ways to convert it into clean-burning synthetic gas and liquid fuels.

Our coal development is part of Exxon's activities to find and to supply more energy for America, from America.

EXXON

ong America

Mankind doesn't need any one form of energy.
Mankind needs energy.

For the foreseeable future, no one form of energy can meet all our needs.

We don't have enough domestic petroleum. Coal can't power cars today. Nuclear energy, at least in this century, can't generate all our electricity.

So the energy we need must come from a combination of sources.

At Conoco, we produce the key fuels—oil, natural gas, coal and uranium. And what we learn in the process helps us develop new sources as well.

We're working on ways to produce oil from tar sands and ways to change coal into synthetic gas and oil. We're also working on methanol, derived from coal or natural gas, as an alternative to present-day liquid fuels.

Because mankind needs more than one form of energy, we need to make more than one kind of effort.

Doing more with energy.

OPERATION DOUBLE TREE IS WORKING IN THE SOUTH.

Once written off as nearly extinct, the forests of the South have staged an amazing comeback.

As a result, economists who only a few years ago predicted a world shortage of wood and wood fiber, now see hope of supply keeping pace with demand within a generation—thanks to the almost legendary resilience of the Southern pine and an idea called Operation Double Tree.

Double Tree is the forest industry's name for intensive forest management that can double the amount of wood from the nation's productive forestland. And do it in such a way that everyone can share in the multiple benefits.

An Ideal Climate.

Double Tree is more than a slogan. It's already working in forests all across the country. And the South has truly helped pioneer the way.

This is because the South has some of the most productive forestland on the North American continent. The climate is moist and warm, ideal for growing trees ten months out of the year.

Scientists and forest products companies are finding new ways to make the South's forests even more productive: using more of every tree they harvest. And replanting as soon as possible with fast-growing seedlings that resist disease.

An ideal climate has made the South the nation's proving ground for modern forest research.

A Long Way To Go.

These new techniques are being used on privately owned lands, as well as those owned by industry and government. This is especially important in the South, where almost 73% of the commercial forest* is owned by individuals.

So Operation Double Tree *is* working. But we still have a long way to go.

Overall, the American forest is still only half as productive as it could be. And this is a waste of one of our most valuable natural resources.

It's the kind of waste we can't af-

ford. In the U.S. alone, the demand for wood and paper products is expected to double in the next 50 years.

But working together, all timber growers—private owners, industry and government—can learn to make the most productive use of our remaining commercial forests.

For more information, write for our free booklet, "Managing the Great American Forest," Southern Forest Institute, 3395 Northeast Expressway, Atlanta, Georgia 30341.

SOUTHERN FOREST INSTITUTE
A Division of
AMERICAN FOREST INSTITUTE

Commercial forest is forest capable of, and available for, growing trees for harvest.

The two loblolly pines below are shown 51 percent of actual size. The smaller one is 18 years old. It grew in a natural stand of trees. The larger one is only 16. But it grew on a plantation where it thrived on the benefits of good forest management.

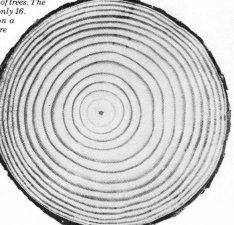

DASHER OUTCLASSES MERCEDES 280E AND ROLLS-ROYCE IN SURPRISING WAYS.

Imagine a Volkswagen limousine. Got it? Good!

You have now grasped the concept of the VW Dasher.

The Dasher Sedans are our most sumptuous cars; they outclass some very classy machines in some very surprising ways.

If you own a Mercedes-Benz 280E, you will be depressed to discover that the Dasher 2-door Sedan with standard transmission not only goes from 0 to 50 miles per hour quicker than the Mercedes,* but carries more in its trunk.

If you're about to spring for a Rolls-Royce, hold the phone. The Dasher holds more in its trunk than the Rolls, too.

Fine as they may be, neither the Mercedes nor the Rolls has front-wheel drive. The Dasher does, and it makes all the difference in poor driving conditions.

The Mercedes, the Rolls and the Dasher do have their similarities.

All 3 have dignified interiors, with handsome, thoughtful appointments like reclining bucket seats, remote control outside mirrors and quartz electric clocks.

But finally, there are two particularly impressive dissimilarities. For one, Dasher costs about $10,000 less than the Mercedes, and about $39,000 less than the Rolls. Then of course, only the Dasher has a ⓦ right there up front. *with automatic transmission

VOLKSWAGEN DOES IT AGAIN

©VOLKSWAGEN OF AMERICA, INC.

This is why we make bologna the way we do.

Oscar Mayer

1. One of the characteristic devices of direct mail advertising is flattery of the consumer. Find examples of this.

2. Why do most of these letters use double spaces between paragraphs? What is the purpose of including a "P.S."?

3. Which of these letters include statistics? Do the figures appeal to our minds or to our emotions?

4. What techniques have the writers used to make themselves sound like ordinary people? Why might they do this?

5. How does the National Foundation for Cancer Research define the group that it is inviting us to join? Try writing a definition of this group that makes the members sound ridiculous.

6. Which letter does the best job of clearly describing the association or product it is selling?

7. Describe the assumed audience of each advertisement and letter. Can you tell anything about their age, sex, income level, or opinions?

8. What groups or stereotypes do the advertisers expect their audiences to identify with?

9. Ads often use puns, alliteration, or other examples of wordplay to get our attention. Can you find any examples here?

10. Most ads, of course, appeal to our emotions rather than our minds. But some of these seem to be making a rational argument. Why would an advertiser choose this approach? Are you convinced by the arguments?

11. Which of the audiences addressed in these letters and ads would you rather be? Why?

Directions

Primordial Chicken

CHICKENS

The chicken is a noble little beastie. It is cheap, nourishing, easy to prepare, and tastes exceedingly good. The average Impoverished Student can eat ½ of the average fatted chicken at a sitting. (N.B., if your girlfriend is an Impoverished Student and says that she "eats like a bird," don't take her literally—birds eat several *times* their own weight daily. But take the hint.) By cooking chickens, you will discover that you can cook other things besides casseroles. So will your compatriots. This will prove an enlightening experience for both sets. You will increase the range of your culinary experience; your compatriots will be impressed. This is as enlightening an experience as you can expect from *any* cookbook.

I include no recipe for fried chicken, southern or otherwise, because of the following premiss:

PREMISS: You already have a recipe for fried chicken. If you don't, ask your mother for one. All fried chicken tastes pretty much alike. (So shoot me!)

Primordial Chicken₁

This recipe is so named because it is the minimum sort of thing one can do to chicken and still have it taste exceedingly good. Based upon the statistics quoted above, you will need

1 cut-up frying chicken per each two persons

Procedure: Rub each piece of chicken lightly with oil. Rub each piece of oiled chicken heavily with salt, pepper, garlic salt, and *tarragon*. Broil for about 10–12 minutes on each side, after sneakily coating your broiler with aluminum foil to nullify washing problems.

Everyone *must* eat Primordial Chicken with his fingers. That's an order!

Primordial Chicken₂

To make Primordial Chicken₂, all you have to do is follow the recipe for Primordial Chicken₁, substituting *rosemary* for *tarragon* throughout. The result tastes different, but just as good. With the fingers, please!

Chicken Cutlets (an Entrée)

926. INGREDIENTS.—2 chickens; seasoning to taste of salt, white pepper, and cayenne; 2 blades of pounded mace, egg and bread crumbs, clarified butter, 1 strip of lemon rind, 2 carrots, 1 onion, 2 tablespoonfuls of mushroom ketchup, thickening of butter and flour, 1 egg.

Mode.—Remove the breast and leg bones of the chickens; cut the meat into neat pieces after having skinned it, and season the cutlets with pepper, salt, pounded mace, and cayenne. Put the bones, trimmings, &c., into a stewpan with 1 pint of water, adding carrots, onions, and lemon-peel in the above proportion; stew gently for 1½ hours, and strain the gravy. Thicken it with butter and flour, add the ketchup and 1 egg well beaten; stir it over the fire, and bring it to the simmering-point, but do not allow it to boil. In the meantime, egg and bread-crumb the cutlets, and give them a few drops of clarified butter; fry them a delicate brown, occasionally turning them; arrange them pyramidically on the dish, and pour over them the sauce.

Time.—10 minutes to fry the cutlets. *Average cost*, 2s, each,
Sufficient for an entrée.
Seasonable from April to July.

FOWLS AS FOOD.—Brillat Savarin, pre-eminent in gastronomic taste, says that he believes the whole gallinaceous family was made to enrich our larders and furnish our tables; for, from the quail to the turkey, he avers their flesh is a light aliment, full of flavour, and fitted equally well for the invalid as for the man of robust health. The fine flavour, however, which Nature has given to all birds coming under the definition of poultry, man has not been satisfied with, and has used many means—such as keeping them in solitude and darkness, and forcing them to eat—to give them an unnatural state of fatness or fat. This fat, thus artificially produced, is doubtless delicious, and the taste and succulence of the boiled and roasted bird draw forth the praise of the guests around the table. Well-fattened and tender, a fowl is to the cook what the canvas is to the painter; for do we not see it served boiled, roasted, fried, fricasseed, hashed, hot, cold, whole, dismembered, boned, broiled, stuffed, on dishes, and in pies,—always handy and ever acceptable?

George's Three-Alarm Chili

2 cups dry pinto beans
T vegetable oil
1 large onion, coarsely chopped
1 green pepper, sliced
1 lb. ground beef
1 16-oz. can tomatoes
1 6-oz. can tomato paste
1 oz. (5–6 T) hot chili powder
3 jalapeno peppers, minced fine
salt and pepper

1. Soak beans overnight in lightly salted water. Simmer 2–3 hours or until tender but not mushy.
2. Sauté onion and green pepper in the oil in a heavy pot or large skillet, until onion becomes transparent. Add ground beef and cook until browned, stirring frequently.
3. Add remaining ingredients. Simmer one hour. Season to taste; more chili powder or jalapeno may be added at this time. Serve over rice.

(Courtesy George Mason Vaught)

A Nice Cup of Tea

If you look up "tea" in the first cookery book that comes to hand you will probably find that it is unmentioned; or at most you will find a few lines of sketchy instructions which give no ruling on several of the most important points.

This is curious, not only because tea is one of the mainstays of civilisation in this country, as well as in Eire, Australia and New Zealand, but because the best manner of making it is the subject of violent disputes.

When I look through my own recipe for the perfect cup of tea, I find no fewer than eleven outstanding points. On perhaps two of them there would be pretty general agreement, but at least four others are acutely controversial. Here are my own eleven rules, every one of which I regard as golden:

First of all, one should use Indian or Ceylonese tea. China tea has virtues which are not to be despised nowadays—it is economical, and one can drink it without milk—but there is not much stimulation in it. One does not feel wiser, braver or more optimistic after drinking it. Anyone who uses that comforting phrase "a nice cup of tea" invariably means Indian tea. Secondly, tea should be made in small quantities—that is, in a teapot. Tea out of an urn is always tasteless, while army tea, made in a cauldron, tastes of grease and whitewash. The teapot should be made of china or earthenware. Silver or Britannia-ware pots produce inferior tea and enamel pots are worse: though curiously enough a pewter teapot (a rarity nowadays) is not so bad. Thirdly, the pot should be warmed beforehand. This is better done by placing it on the hob than by the usual method of swilling it out with hot water. Fourthly, the tea should be strong. For a pot holding a quart, if you are going to fill it nearly to the brim, six heaped teaspoons would be about right. In a time of rationing this is not an idea that can be realised on every day of the week, but I maintain that one strong cup of tea is better than 20 weak ones. All true tea-lovers not only like their tea strong, but like it a little stronger with each year that passes—a fact which is recognised in the extra ration issued to old-age pensioners. Fifthly, the tea should be put straight into the pot. No strainers, muslin bags or other devices to imprison the tea. In some countries teapots are fitted with little dangling baskets under the spout to catch the stray leaves, which are supposed to be harmful. Actually one can swallow tea-leaves in considerable quantities without ill effect, and if the tea is not loose in the pot it never infuses properly. Sixthly, one should take the teapot to the kettle and not the other way about. The water should be actually boiling at the moment of impact, which means that one should keep it on the flame while one pours. Some people add that one should only use water that has been freshly brought to the boil, but I have never noticed that this makes any difference. Seventhly, after making the tea, one should stir it, or better, give the pot a good shake, afterwards allowing the leaves to settle. Eighthly, one should drink out of a breakfast cup—that is the cylindrical type of cup, not the flat, shallow type. The breakfast cup holds more, and with the other kind one's tea is always half cold before one has well started on it. Ninthly, one should pour the cream off the milk before using it for tea. Milk that is too creamy always gives tea a sickly taste. Tenthly, one should pour tea into the cup first. This is one of the most controversial points of all; indeed in every family in Britain there are probably two schools of thought on the subject. The milk-first school can bring forward some fairly strong arguments, but I maintain that my own argument is unanswerable. This is that, by putting the tea in first and then stirring as one pours, one can exactly regulate the amount of milk whereas one is liable to put in too much milk if one does it the other way round.

Lastly, tea—unless one is drinking it in the Russian style—should be drunk *without sugar*. I know very well that I am in a minority here. But still, how can you call yourself a true tea-lover if you destroy the flavour of your tea by putting sugar in it? It would be equally reasonable to put pepper or salt. Tea is meant to be bitter, just as beer is meant to be bitter. If you sweeten it, you are no longer tasting the tea, you are merely tasting the sugar; you could make a very similar drink by dissolving sugar in plain hot water.

Some people would answer that they don't like tea in itself, that they only drink it in order to be warmed and stimulated, and they need sugar to take the taste away. To those misguided people I would say: Try drinking tea without sugar for, say, a fortnight and it is very unlikely that you will ever want to ruin your tea by sweetening it again.

These are not the only controversial points that arise in connection with tea-drinking, but they are sufficient to show how subtilised the whole business has become. There is also the mysterious social etiquette surrounding the teapot (why is it considered vulgar to drink out of your saucer, for instance?) and much might be written about the subsidiary uses of tea-leaves, such as telling fortunes, predicting the arrival of visitors, feeding rabbits, healing burns and sweeping the carpet. It is worth paying attention to such details as warming the pot and using water that is really boiling, so as to make quite sure of wringing out of one's ration the twenty good, strong cups that two ounces, properly handled, ought to represent.

Treating Burns in the Mountains

The severity of a burn depends upon the size of the area it covers, the depth to which it extends, and its location on the body. Few individuals survive burns which involve more than fifty percent of the body surface.

From James A. Wilkerson (ed.), *Medicine for Mountaineering*, 2nd ed. (Seattle: The Mountaineers, 1975).

In contrast, few burns covering less than twenty percent of the body prove fatal if given proper care. Burns of the face and neck, hands, arm pits, and crotch are frequently more incapacitating because specialized organs and complex anatomical structures are involved or the areas are difficult to keep clean.

Burns are classified as first, second, or third degree according to the depth to which damage extends. First degree burns are superficial, do not kill any of the tissue, and only produce redness of the skin. Second degree burns cause death of the upper portion of the skin, resulting in blisters. Third degree burns produce death of the full thickness of the skin and may extend deeply into the underlying tissues. Third degree burns, if more than one inch in diameter, do not heal unless covered by skin grafts, and can produce extensive, deforming scars.

An extensive, deep burn incurred in a remote mountainous area can be a catastrophe, particularly if the fluids needed to replace those lost into the burned tissues are not available. Evacuation must be carried out at once by the fastest means available.

First degree burns may require no treatment. Therapy for more severe burns consists of both care for the local injury and treatment of the effects of the burn on the entire body.

Local Therapy

Immediately after the burn is incurred all clothing and jewelry covering the injury should be removed. If the burn is small and not very deep, immersion in cold water helps reduce the pain. Cold injury must be avoided. The burned area should be carefully washed with sterile cotton soaked with warm, previously boiled water and liquid soap. All debris, dirt, and fragments of loose skin must be removed. (These measures are surprisingly painless if carried out gently.) The burn should be covered with a layer of a sterile dressing made of material (such as gauze impregnated with petroleum jelly) which does not stick to the wound. A thick, bulky dressing should be placed on top of this layer. This dressing should be held in place by a snug bandage which applies a moderate amount of pressure to the damaged area. Ointments or creams should never be placed on a second or third degree burn. These materials have no benefit whatsoever, greatly increase the danger of infection, and make the wound difficult to clean. (Gauze impregnated with petroleum jelly is a prepackaged, sterile dressing obtainable from the manufacturers of dressings and bandages, not ordinary gauze on which some petroleum jelly has been smeared.)

If the burn occupies less than fifteen percent of the body surface area and does not involve the face, neck, hands, or genital area, the patient may not need to be evacuated. The bandage must be left in place without being disturbed for at least six to eight days. Changing the bandage prior to this time introduces the danger of infection without benefiting the patient. Only after about a week has elapsed can an accurate distinction between first, second, and third degree burns be made. If a third degree burn is present, the patient usually should be evacuated, although a small third degree burn would not always require interruption of an outing scheduled to end within a week or ten days.

If the burn is found to be only first degree or superficial second degree with no blisters present when the bandage is removed, no further treatment is required. Even bandaging is not necessary unless the area requires protection from trauma.

If blisters, either intact or ruptured, are present, the wound should be redressed with a similar bandage to protect any intact blisters and prevent infection. This dressing can be changed every three or four days until healing is complete.

Third degree burns at six to eight days are covered by a thick, leathery layer of parched, dead skin which may range in color from white to dark brown or black. This area is completely insensitive to touch. In cases in which there is some doubt about the depth of the injury, gentle testing for anesthesia with a sterile object is a good way of determining whether the burn has extended through the full thickness of the skin.

If a third degree burn is found, the injury should be covered with an identical bandage and plans begun to evacuate the patient. If the burn is small and does not particularly incapacitate the victim there is no urgency about evacuation. However, these burns do not heal without skin grafts. Some eight to ten days after injury the layer of dead skin begins to crack and loosen around the edges. Infection inevitably follows, even under optimal circumstances, and can have dire consequences.

If the burn is incapacitating from the onset, either from its extent or location, the victim should be evacuated at once without waiting to determine the depth of the wound.

VISA/BankAmericard

In Case of Errors or Inquiries About Your Bill

The Federal Truth in Lending Act requires prompt correction of billing mistakes.

1. If you want to preserve your rights under the Act, here's what to do if you think your bill is wrong or if you need more information about an item on your bill:

    a. Do not write on the bill. On a separate sheet of paper write (you may telephone your inquiry but doing so will not preserve your rights under this law) the following:

        i. Your name and account number (if any).

ii. A description of the error and an explanation (to the extent you can explain) why you believe it is an error.

If you only need more information, explain the item you are not sure about and, if you wish, ask for evidence of the charge such as a copy of the charge slip. Do not send in your copy of a sales slip or other document unless you have a duplicate copy for your records.

iii. The dollar amount of the suspected error.

iv. Any other information (such as your address) which you think will help the Bank to identify you or the reason for your complaint or inquiry. It will be helpful to include the Reference Number for the disputed items as shown on the bill.

b. Send your billing error notice to the address on your bill which is listed after the words: "Inquiries may be made to," or similar wording.

Mail it as soon as you can, but in any case, early enough to reach the Bank within 60 days after the bill was mailed to you. If you have authorized your bank to automatically pay from your checking or savings account any credit card bills from that bank, you can stop or reverse payment on any amount you think is wrong by mailing your notice so the Bank receives it within 16 days after the bill was sent to you. However, you do not have to meet this 16-day deadline to get the Bank to investigate your billing error claim.

2. The Bank must acknowledge all letters pointing out possible errors within 30 days of receipt, unless the Bank is able to correct your bill during that 30 days. Within 90 days after receiving your letter, the Bank must either correct the error or explain why the Bank believes the bill was correct. Once the Bank has explained the bill, the Bank has no further obligation to you even though you still believe that there is an error, except as provided in paragraph 5 below.

3. After the Bank has been notified, neither the Bank nor an attorney nor a collection agency may send you collection letters or take other collection action with respect to the amount in dispute; but periodic statements may be sent to you, and the disputed amount can be applied against your credit limit. You cannot be threatened with damage to your credit rating or sued for the amount in question, nor can the disputed amount be reported to a credit bureau or to other creditors as delinquent until the Bank has answered your inquiry. *However, you remain obligated to pay the parts of your bill not in dispute.*

4. If it is determined that the Bank has made a mistake on your bill, you will not have to pay any finance charges on any disputed amount. If it turns out that the Bank has not made an error, you may have to pay finance charges on the amount in dispute, and you will have to make up any missed minimum or required payments on the disputed amount.

Unless you have agreed that your bill was correct, the Bank must send you a written notification of what you owe; and if it is determined that the Bank did make a mistake in billing the disputed amount, you must be given the time to pay which you normally are given to pay undisputed amounts before any more finance charges or late payment charges on the disputed amount can be charged to you.

5. If the Bank's explanation does not satisfy you and you notify the Bank *in writing* within 10 days after you receive its explanation that you still refuse to pay the disputed amount, the Bank may report you to credit bureaus and other creditors and may pursue regular collection procedures. But the Bank must also report that you think you do not owe the money, and the Bank must let you know to whom such reports were made. Once the matter has been settled between you and the Bank, the Bank must notify those to whom the Bank reported you as delinquent of the subsequent resolution.

6. If the Bank does not follow these rules, the Bank is not allowed to collect the first $50 of the disputed amount and finance charges, even if the bill turns out to be correct.

7. If you have a problem with property or services purchased with a credit card, you may have the right not to pay the remaining amount due on them, if you first try in good faith to return them or give the merchant a chance to correct the problem. There are two limitations on this right:

a. You must have bought them in your home state, or if not within your home state, within 100 miles of your current mailing address; and

b. The purchase price must have been more than $50.

However, these limitations do not apply if the merchant is owned or operated by the Bank, or if the Bank mailed you the advertisement for the property or services.

QUESTIONS

1. Which writers try to persuade us that the process described is worth undertaking?

2. If you don't believe you could complete some of these activities, why not? Is it that you lack tools, materials, or practice, or is there something wrong with the writing?

3. Search these directions for words or processes that the writer assumes the reader already understands. For instance, to make "George's Three-Alarm Chili" you have to know how to "sauté." What do you have to know in order to follow the directions for treating a burn, or correcting your BankAmericard bill?

4. Which of the three recipes assumes that the readers have lots of cooking experience? Which assumes that they have almost none?

5. Orwell's directions for making tea appeared in a newspaper in England in 1946. In what ways are his directions adapted to people in that time and place?

6. Suggest some visual aids for these directions.

7. Some of the writers have unusual voices. Describe the characters who seem to be speaking in "Primordial Chicken" and "A Nice Cup of Tea." Do these voices steer the directions toward particular audiences?

8. Are there any writers who may not *want* the audience to understand perfectly?

3

Content: What's He Saying?

We have seen that a piece of writing "says" different kinds of things: it speaks with a certain voice, and it "says" that the writer has certain expectations about the audience. But, of course, the *content* of writing is equally important: the information it conveys, the arguments it puts forward, the claims that it makes. These claims should be, as far as possible, true; they should be supported by reasonable evidence; and they should be clear.

Perhaps the most important thing to remember about content is that no piece of writing can give *all* the facts on any topic. Every time a writer presents information, he goes through a process of selection, guided by his purpose and by his sense of what the audience needs to know. It is boring to read what is already commonly known, and it can be equally boring to read unusual facts that are not related to any purpose. Remember the poor third-grader who said, "This book told me more than I wanted to know about penguins." We all have a tendency to think we have said everything when we have given a lot of facts. Usually, however, facts are only a background used to support a point of view, to which the particular purposes, goals, and values of the writer also contribute.

Most formal essays take the form of a *thesis*—a claim that is put forward—followed by evidence and arguments that support the thesis. Evidence might take the form of facts, or examples, or statements from authorities. There are several formal systems that can be used to describe the relationship between the thesis and the supporting arguments. You will probably encounter a study of both induction and deduction during your years in college. But even without formal study, some standards for the presentation of evidence can be arrived at through common sense.

One important standard is that the evidence presented should be balanced. That is, the writer should not intentionally "slant" his case; if he knows of important arguments or statistics on the other side, he has a responsibility to mention them and to explain why he is not convinced by them. A second important standard is relevance. If you are trying to argue that lower speed limits reduce highway fatalities, it does no good to present information on the number of victims who can be saved through improved ambulance service. Third, a writer should indicate the source of any controversial facts and figures that he uses. If you claim, for instance, that four out of five doctors recommend Brand X, you need to explain how you arrived at this information. How were the doctors selected, and what exactly were they asked? In formal reports, the sources of information are indicated by footnotes.

The content of writing should be accurate, fair, and interesting to the audience; nearly everyone agrees that it should also be clear. But what is clarity, and how is it to be achieved? Sometimes when we say that something is "clear" we mean that it is easy for us to understand. We are familiar with all the words; the sentence structure contains nothing unusual; we can follow the writer's line of thought from one point to the next, because the ideas are well organized. All of these things have something to do with clarity, but they also indicate that clarity is not absolute. It depends on the audience. What is clear between one physicist and another may be gobbledygook to me, and what is clear in a letter between friends might have no meaning to anyone else. Thus one important test of clarity is that the writing can be easily understood by the audience for whom it is intended.

There is another aspect of clarity, however, that does not change from audience to audience. Some words have a limited, specific application; others are ambiguous. The meaning of *elephant*, for instance, is quite clear to anyone who is familiar with the word. You will probably never be confused about whether something is or is not an elephant. But other common words—*boy* is an example—are less clear. Exactly when does a person stop being a boy and become a man? Many people are borderline. As you can see by this example, most language is at least somewhat ambiguous, and this is not always a bad thing. But clear language should strive for the most precise meaning possible.

It often happens that abstract words are less clear than concrete or specific ones, so a good rule of thumb for clarity is to be as concrete as possible. "Pay your bills on time" is both clearer and more concrete than "Accept financial responsibility." Someone might imagine that the second statement means to take out a lot of loans, but the first is not likely to be interpreted in a variety of ways. Sometimes writers make use of technical words, or jargon, because these are the only words that have the specific meaning needed. Doctors and lawyers are famous for being difficult for the public to understand, because of their special vocabulary. Doctors need words for parts of the body and processes that most of us have never heard of. When doctors write for other doctors, jargon may be a good choice, though it would not be clear to a patient.

Sometimes writers are intentionally unclear. This usually happens when the writer's purpose is to sell us something or get us to do something. These writers might not be benefited if the audience fully understood their purposes or products. For instance, oil companies often speak of "our" national resources when they mean resources that are owned by the companies themselves. They blur the distinction between public and private ownership, between "us" as the oil company and "us" as all Americans. Sometimes products use chemical names, like *hexachlorophene*, which they know are unclear to most people, but which sound impressive. Or you have probably seen a politician wiggle out of a tricky question by giving an ambiguous answer. Even a few legal documents are intentionally unclear, to prevent clients, tenants, or employees from fully understanding their rights. Such uses of language are dishonest, but quite common.

This chapter should help to build your respect for orderly, clear and well-documented information, but it should also warn you that there are certain dangers in reading to get just the "facts." We Americans have a great deal of respect for science and technology and the well-being that they have brought to most of us, and we extend that sense of importance to language that seems to be scientific, factual, or objective. As you will see in the examples that follow, however, no writing can be strictly factual, and perhaps even objectivity is not often a reasonable goal. Writing is not really done by computers, though some writing appears that way. We must always remember that a particular writer has chosen to include some facts and leave out others, and to express these facts with some words rather than others. Reading for content means reading with an awareness of these choices.

The selections that follow are divided into three groups. The first group comes from dictionaries, which are among the most widely used and most trusted sources of information. But as you will see, different dictionaries provide different emphases and wording that make for differences in the content itself.

The second section contains reports of various types on a common topic. Many of these are the kinds of sources that you might use in doing a research paper. Some illustrate the use of footnotes to document sources of information. You will be trying to compare the reports for usefulness and fairness. They all share the problems of trying to be clear and accurate, and they all hope that their readers will find them to be trustworthy sources of information.

The last section illustrates how an abstract word—in this case, *equality*—can mean different things in different contexts. Nearly everyone believes in equality, but the word is so unclear that we may *not* agree on any specific policies. Your job in this section will be to figure out just what definition of *equality* the writer has in mind.

In brief, here are some important questions to ask about content:

* What is the thesis? What are the supporting arguments?
* Which parts of the argument are factual and rational, and which are the opinions of the writer?
* Are the facts balanced, relevant, and well documented?
* Is the language clear or ambiguous?

Dictionaries: Information and Attitude

The Word *Slang*

American Heritage Dictionary

slang (släng) *n.* **1.** The nonstandard vocabulary of a given culture or subculture, consisting typically of arbitrary and often ephemeral coinages and figures of speech characterized by spontaneity and raciness. **2.** Language peculiar to a group; argot or jargon. [Origin obscure.] —**slang′i·ly** *adv.* —**slang′i·ness** *n.* —**slang′y** *adj.*

Random House College Dictionary

slang[1] (slang), *n.* **1.** very informal usage in vocabulary and idiom that is characteristically more metaphorical, playful, elliptical, vivid, and ephemeral than ordinary language. **2.** (in English and some other languages) speech and writing characterized by the use of vulgar and socially taboo vocabulary and idiomatic expressions. **3.** jargon. **4.** argot; cant. —*v.i.* **5.** to use slang or abusive language. —*v.t.* **6.** to assail with abusive language. [?]

Webster's Third New International Dictionary

³slăng \"\ *n* -s [origin unknown] **1** : language peculiar to a particular group: as **a** : the special and often secret vocabulary used by a class (as thieves, beggars) and usu. felt to be vulgar or inferior : ARGOT **b** : the jargon used by or associated with a particular trade, profession, or field of activity **2** : a nonstandard vocabulary composed of words and senses characterized primarily by connotations of extreme informality and usu. a currency not limited to a particular region and composed ·typically of coinages or arbitrarily changed words, clipped or shortened forms, extravagant, forced, or facetious figures of speech, or verbal novelties usu. experiencing quick popularity and relatively rapid decline into disuse **syn** see DIALECT
⁴slang \"\ *adj* **1** : of, constituting, or expressed in slang **2** : SLANGY, VULGAR, RAKISH
⁵slang \"\ *vb* -ED/-ING/-S *vt* **1** *slang, Brit* : CHEAT, SWINDLE, DUPE **2** *chiefly Brit* : to abuse with words : censure abusively or with harsh or coarse language ~ *vi* : to use slang or vulgar abuse : talk in a slangy manner

Oxford English Dictionary

Slang (slæŋ), *sb.*³ [A word of cant origin, the ultimate source of which is not apparent. It is possible that some of the senses may represent independent words. In all senses except 1 only in slang or canting use.

The date and early associations of the word make it unlikely that there is any connexion with certain Norw. forms in *sleng*- which exhibit some approximation in sense.]

1. The special vocabulary used by any set of persons of a low or disreputable character; language of a low and vulgar type. (Now merged in c.)

In the first quot. the reference may be to customs or habits rather than language : cf. the use of SLANG *a.* 2 b.

1756 TOLDERVY *Hist. 2 Orphans* I. 68 Thomas Throw had been upon the town, knew the slang well. **1774** KELLY *School for Wives* III. ix, There is a language we [bailiffs] sometimes talk in, called slang. **1809** E. S. BARRETT *Setting Sun* I. 106 Such grossness of speech, and horrid oaths, as shewed them not to be unskilled in the slang or vulgar tongue of the lowest blackguards in the nation. **1824** SCOTT *Redgauntlet* ch. xiii, What did actually reach his ears was disguised..completely by the use of cant words, and the thieves-Latin called slang. *a* **1839** PRAED *Poems* (1864) II. 117 And broaches at his mother's table The slang of kennel and of stable.

b. The special vocabulary or phraseology of a particular calling or profession; the cant or jargon of a certain class or period.

1802-12 BENTHAM *Ration. Judic. Evid.* (1827) IV. 306 Giving, in return for those fees, scraps of written lawyer's slang. **1834** H. J. ROSE *Apol. Study of Divinity* (ed. 2) 15 However tempting the scientific *slang*, if I may so term it, of the day may be. **1857** KINGSLEY *Lett.* (1878) II. 43, I have drawn, modelled in clay and picture fancied, so much in past years, that I have got unconsciously into the slang. **1872** GEO. ELIOT *Middlem.* xi, Correct English is the slang of prigs who write history and essays. And the strongest slang of all is the slang of poets.

c. Language of a highly colloquial type, considered as below the level of standard educated speech, and consisting either of new words or of current words employed in some special sense.

1818 KEBLE in Sir J. T. Coleridge *Mem.* (1869) 75 Two of the best [students] come to me as a peculiar grinder (I must have a little slang). **1848** THACKERAY *Van. Fair* xliii, He was too old to listen to the banter of the assistant-surgeon and the slang of the youngsters. **1868** DORAN *Saints &*

Sinners I. 107 He [Latimer] occasionally employed some of the slang of the day to give force to his words. **1887** R. N. CAREY *Uncle Max* xv, If I had ever talked slang, I might have said that we chummed together famously.

attrib. and *Comb.* **1846** MRS. GORE *Engl. Char.* (1852) 139 Like a door from which some slang-loving roué has wrenched the knocker. **1850** *N. & Q.* Ser. I. 369/2 That great slang-manufactory for the army, the Royal Military College, Sandhurst.

d. Abuse, impertinence. (Cf. SLANG *v.* 3, 4.)

1835 LOCKHART in *Scott's Fam. Lett.* (1894) II. 297 This Mr. H. gave grand slang to the Porters, etc., who crowded the vessel on our anchoring : 'Your fingers are all thumbs, I see ', etc.

† **2.** Humbug, nonsense. *Obs.*⁻¹

1762 FOOTE *Orator* I. Wks. 1799 I. 192 Have you seen the bills?..What, about the lectures? ay, but that's all slang I suppose; no, no. No tricks upon travellers.

† **3.** A line of work; a 'lay'. *Obs.*⁻¹

c **1789** G. PARKER *Life's Painter* 120 How do you work now?..O, upon the old slang, and sometimes a little lully-prigging.

4. A licence, *esp.* that of a hawker.

1812 J. H. VAUX *Flash Dict., Slang,*..a warrant, license to travel, or other official instrument. **1865** *Slang Dict.* 234 'Out on the slang,' i. e. to travel with a hawker's licence. **1896** *Westm. Gaz.* 9 Dec. 2/1 You don't want for much to start with ;.. ½ sovereign..for a (slang) licence is plenty.

5. A travelling show.

1859 *Slang Dict.* 94 *Slang*, a travelling show. **1873** LELAND *Egypt. Sketch Bk.* 63 There is a great deal of the Rommany or Gipsy element .. wherever the 'slangs' or exhibition affairs show themselves.

b. A performance.

1861 MAYHEW *Lond. Lab.* III. 101, I am talking of a big pitch, when we go through all our 'slang', as we say.

c. *attrib.*, as **slang cove, cull,** a showman.

c **1789** G. PARKER *Life's Painter* 130 To exhibit any thing in a fair or market,.. that's called slanging, and the exhibiter is called the slang cull. **1851** MAYHEW *Lond. Lab.* I. 353 We did intend petitioning.., but I don't suppose it would be any go, seeing as how the slang coves (the showmen) have done so, and been refused.

6. A short weight or measure. (Cf. SLANG *a.* 3.)

1851 MAYHEW *Lond. Lab.* I. 32/2 There's plenty of costers wouldn't use slangs at all, if people would give a fair price. *Ibid.* II. 90/1 Some of the street weights, a good many of them, are slangs.

The Word *Jive*

American Heritage Dictionary

jive (jīv) *n. Slang.* **1.** Jazz or swing music. **2.** The jargon of jazz musicians and enthusiasts. **3.** Deceptive, nonsensical, or glib talk. [Origin unknown.]

Random House College Dictionary

jive (jīv), *n., v.*, **jived, jiv·ing.** —*n.* **1.** swing music. **2.** *Slang.* the jargon of jazz and swing musicians and jazz, swing, and jitterbug devotees, esp. of the 1940's. **3.** *Slang.* unintelligible or deceptive talk. —*v.i.* **4.** to play jive. [?]

Webster's Third New International Dictionary

¹**jive** \'jīv\ *n* -s [origin unknown] **1 a** *slang* : glib, deceptive, or foolish talk **b** : the jargon of narcotics addicts or of jazz music and nightclub life **c** : a special jargon of difficult or slang terms ⟨a sort of academic ~ interlarded with lengthy and undigested quotations —Dwight MacDonald⟩ **2** : hot jazz or the jitterbugging sometimes performed to it
²**jive** \"\ *vb* -ED/-ING/-S *vi* **1** *slang* : to talk jive : fool around : KID **2 a** : to dance to hot jazz; *esp* : JITTERBUG **b** : to play hot jazz ~ *vt* **1** *slang* : TEASE, KID **2** : to play (music) hot ⟨small bands *jiving* in cellar clubs⟩

Dictionary of American Slang

jive   *n.*   **1** Ordinary, tiresome, or misleading talk or actions; exaggerations, flattery; distraction; insincere, uncouth talk or conduct; anything that should be ignored; boloney; bull. 1954 [c1920]: ". . . There was lots of just plain common shooting and cutting. But . . . that jive didn't faze me at all. I was so happy to have some place to blow my horn." Louis Armstrong, *Satchmo, My Life in New Orleans*, 150. 1941: "Don't hand me any more of that jive." *Life*, Jan. 27, 78. *Orig. Negro use, and orig. perhaps alternate sp. of "gieve."* **2** Gaudy articles, merchandise, or clothing. 1954 [c1920]: "When we collected our pay I did not know what to buy so I bought a lot of cheap jive at the five and ten cent store to give to the kids. . . ." Louis Armstrong, *Satchmo, My Life in New Orleans*, 193. **3** [taboo] Sex; sexual intercourse. **4** Fast popular music with a strongly accented two- or four-beat rhythm, as played by the pop. big swing bands c1938–c1945: fast swing music; jazz as it developed in the 1930's; swing. 1943: "G.M. [Glenn Miller]! Man, what solid jive." Max Shulman, *Barefoot Boy With Cheek*, 90. *By far the most common use.* **5** Marijuana. *Never common.* See **gyve.**   *v.t.* To mislead with words; to deceive; to kid.   *v.i.* **1** To play or dance to jive music; to jam. *Note that all the above meanings are equated with meanings of "jazz." Thus, "jive" replaced "jazz" to some extent, c1938–c1945, linguistically as well as musically.* **2** To make sense; to equate or match two items; to match with the known facts. *Very common since c1940. Prob. from "jibe."* **3** To talk idly or confusedly, in a jazzy rhythm and up-to-date slang.   *adj.* Any person, place, group, object, or idea associated with teenagers or swing music. *c1938–c1945. One could see a jive movie with Benny Goodman, then go to a jive joint for some beer and to hear some jive records on the juke box.*   **jiving**   *adj.* **1** Playing jive adroitly or in an exciting manner. *Jive use c1935.* → **2** Playing swing adroitly or in an exciting manner. *Some swing use.* **3** Attracting attention or showing off while playing cool or far-out music, as by blowing very high notes, playing very fast, or accenting close-harmony bass notes, while demonstrating little musicianship or comprehension of the piece, chord relationships, or arrangement. *This derisive cool and far-out use shows what these groups think of jive.*

The Word *High*

American Heritage Dictionary

high (hī) *adj.* **higher, highest. 1.** Extending or projecting far upward; tall; elevated. **2.** Having a specified elevation: *ten feet high.* **3.** Being at or near its peak or culmination: *high noon.* **4.** Beginning to decompose, as meat; excessively gamy. **5.** Far removed in time; remote: *high antiquity.* **6.** Piercing in tone or sound: *a high note.* **7.** Situated far from the equator: *a high latitude.* **8.** Of great moment or importance. **a.** Pre-eminent in rank or standing: *the high priest.* **b.** Serious; weighty; grave: *high treason.* **9.** Lofty or exalted in quality, character, or style: *"the glorious language and high metaphors of St. Paul"* (Walton). **10. a.** Of great quantity, magnitude, or degree: *a high temperature.* **b.** Of great force or violence: *high winds.* **11.** Costly or expensive; dear: *high prices.* **12.** Showing pride, arrogance, or disdain. **13.** In a state of excitement or euphoria; elated: *high spirits.* **14.** *Slang.* Intoxicated by alcohol or a narcotic. **15.** At an advanced stage of development or complexity. **16.** *Phonetics.* Pronounced with part of the tongue close to the palate: *a high vowel.* —*n.* **1.** A high place or region. **2.** *Abbr.* **h., H.** The transmission gear of an automotive vehicle producing maximum speed. **3.** A center of high atmospheric pressure; anticyclone. **4.** *Slang.* Intoxication or euphoria induced by a stimulant or narcotic. —**high and dry. 1.** Helpless; destitute. **2.** Out of water. Said of ships. —**high and low.** Here and there; all around; everywhere. —**high and mighty.** Arrogant; domineering; disdainful. [Middle English *hei, high,* Old English *hēah.* See **keu-²** in Appendix.*] —**high′ly** *adv.*

Synonyms: *high, tall, lofty, towering, elevated.* These adjectives mean standing out or otherwise distinguished because of height. *High* and *tall,* the most general terms, are sometimes interchangeable. In general *high* refers to what rises a considerable distance from a base or is situated at a level well above another level considered as a base: *a high mountain; a high ceiling; a high shelf. Tall* describes what rises to a considerable extent; it often refers to living things and to what has great height in relation to breadth or in comparison with like things: *a tall man; tall trees; a tall building. Lofty* describes what is imposingly or inspiringly high. *Towering* suggests height that causes awe or makes something stand out conspicuously. *Elevated* stresses height in relation to immediate surroundings; it refers principally to being raised or situated above a normal level or above the average level of an area.

Dictionary of American Slang

high   *adj.* **1** Drunk. *Usu. pleasantly or happily drunk; not drunk to the point of unconsciousness.* 1944: "... After seeing him 'a bit high.'" Fowler, *Good Night,* 262. "High, slightly alcoholic, above the earth!" A. Miller, *Death of a Salesman,* 106. *Very common.* See Appendix, Drunk. **2** Under the influence of a narcotic drug, esp. marijuana, and esp. when the feeling is pleasant and makes one carefree and lighthearted. 1956: "The coarse [marijuana] seeds are made into cigarettes and the user smokes them in big puffs getting high—a state in which time seems to stand still, where the top of the head is filled with all heaven, and everything seems easy to do, better, stronger, and longer." S. Longstreet, *The Real Jazz Old and New,* 144. 1957: "On that occasion, Gee assertedly supplied the drugs, spoon and needle, and then they planned to meet again at 4 P.M. He was there till about 3:30 A.M. When he wandered out, he was high, but not drunk." E. Kirkman & H. Less, N.Y. *Daily News,* Sept. 14, 4/2. *Orig. addict use, c1930; now widely known.*

high (hī), *adj.* **1.** having a considerable reach or extent upward; lofty; tall. **2.** having a specified extent upward. **3.** situated above the ground or some base; elevated. **4.** intensified; greater than usual; exceeding the common degree or measure; strong or intense: *high speed; high color.* **5.** expensive, costly, or dear: *high prices; high rents.* **6.** exalted in rank, station, etc.; of exalted character or quality. **7.** *Music.* **a.** acute in pitch. **b.** a little sharp, or above the desired pitch. **8.** produced by relatively rapid vibrations; shrill. **9.** extending to or from an elevation: *a high dive.* **10.** great in quantity, as number, degree, or force. **11.** chief; principal; main. **12.** of great consequence; important; grave; serious. **13.** lofty; haughty; arrogant. **14.** advanced to the utmost extent or to the culmination: *high tide.* **15.** elated; merry or hilarious. **16.** rich, extravagant, or luxurious: *high living.* **17.** *Informal.* intoxicated with alcohol or drugs. **18.** remote: *high latitude.* **19.** extreme in opinion or doctrine, esp. religious or political. **20.** designating or pertaining to highland or inland regions. **21.** having considerable energy or potential power. **22.** *Auto.* of, pertaining to, or operating at the gear transmission ratio at which the speed of the engine crankshaft and of the drive shaft most closely correspond. **23.** *Phonet.* (of a vowel) articulated with the upper surface of the tongue relatively close to some portion of the palate, as the vowels of *eat* and *boot.* Cf. **close** (def. 50), **low**¹ (def. 31). **24.** (of meat, esp. game) tending toward a desirable or undesirable amount of decomposition; slightly tainted. **25.** *Baseball.* (of a pitched ball) crossing the plate at a level above the batter's shoulders. **26.** *Cards.* **a.** having greater value than other denominations or suits. **b.** able to take a trick; being a winning card. —*adv.* **27.** at or to a high point, place, or level. **28.** in or to a high rank or estimate: *He aims high in his political ambitions.* **29.** at or to a high amount or price. **30.** in or to a high degree. **31.** luxuriously; richly; extravagantly. **32.** *Naut.* as close to the wind as is possible while making headway with sails full. **33. fly high,** to be full of hope or elation. **34. high and dry, a.** (of a ship) grounded so as to be entirely above water at low tide. **b.** deserted; stranded. **35. high and low,** in every possible place; everywhere. —*n.* **36.** *Auto.* high gear. **37.** *Informal.* See **high school. 38.** *Meteorol.* a pressure system characterized by relatively high pressure at its center. Cf. **anticyclone, low**¹ (def. 45). **39. on high, a.** at or to a height; above. **b.** in heaven. [ME *heigh,* var. of *hegh, hey, heh,* OE *hēah, hēh;* c. D *hoog,* Icel *hār,* Sw *hög,* G *hoch* (OHG *hoh*), Goth *hauhs,* Lith *kaūkas* swelling, *kaukarà* hill]

—**Syn. 1.** HIGH, LOFTY, TALL refer to something that has considerable height. HIGH is a general term, and denotes either extension upward or position at a considerable height: *six feet high; a high shelf.* LOFTY denotes imposing or even inspiring height: *lofty crags.* TALL is applied either to something that is high in proportion to its breadth, or to anything higher than the average of its kind: *a tall tree, building.* **6.** elevated, eminent, distinguished. —**Ant. 1.** low.

QUESTIONS

1. What kinds of information do dictionaries give, in addition to definitions? Find examples of such information in the entries reproduced here.

2. How would you rate these dictionaries on clarity? Are the definitions easy to understand? Are they precise?

3. Do the dictionaries convey an attitude toward slang? toward jive? Do all the dictionaries convey the same attitude? Do you think that most users of the words *slang* and *jive* share these attitudes?

4. Dictionary makers discover what words mean by paying attention to how people use them. Sometimes they include quotations from people who used the word in writing. Judging by the quotations selected, what groups of people are the dictionaries listening to? Who is Dwight MacDonald? Who is Louis Armstrong? Why do you suppose *jive* does not appear at all in the *Oxford English Dictionary?*

5. Have the dictionaries accurately defined your own use of these words? For instance, when you say, "slang," do *you* mean the special vocabulary of thieves, vagabonds, etc.? Which definition, or part of a definition, comes closest to your own meaning?

6. Each of the dictionaries labels *jive* as slang. Do you think they are right, according to their own definitions of *slang?* What about the definitions of *high* that are labeled slang?

7. Think of words that you would not normally use in an English paper, but that you do use regularly at home. Look them up in several dictionaries in the library. Do the dictionaries state or imply any attitudes toward these words? Is your own dictionary a reliable guide to who accepts or uses a word and who does not?

   (It might interest you to know that *Webster's Third New International Dictionary* is famous for what it says about *ain't.*)

Reporting and Arguing: Nitrates and Nitrites

Meat Color Additives Linked to Cancer

Washington Post (*17 March 1971*)

A medical researcher said on Capitol Hill yesterday that a needlessly large cancer toll is the possible price Americans pay for the chemical treatment of hams, other cured meat products, and smoked fish to keep them pink, red or otherwise appetizingly colored.

The scientist, Dr. William Lijinsky of the University of Nebraska Medical Center, also said that the suspect chemical, nitrite, may contribute significantly to the incidence of lung cancer in cigarette smokers, and may create a cancer potential from the use of beer, wine, cereals and certain widely used medicines.

Lijinsky suggested the Food and Drug Administration forbid "cosmetic" uses of nitrite and allow only enough of it in meat and fish products to preserve them in a wholesome condition. This would reduce present permitted levels by 90 to 95 per cent.

"We are greatly concerned" by research reports such as Lijinsky's, Dr. Clayton Yeutter, administrator of the Agriculture Department's Consumer and Marketing Service told the House Intergovernmental Relations Subcommittee.

But FDA commissioner Charles C. Edwards indicated that the fears of the Omaha scientist may be over-drawn.

"So far it is only a possibility," Dr. Edwards told subcommittee Chairman L. H. Fountain (D.—N.C.). "No one has yet established that this possibility is real. . . . Additional data must be developed. We are trying to develop this evidence."

The three witnesses gave the opening testimony in a round of hearings on the effectiveness of FDA and Agriculture Department programs to protect the public from potentially unsafe food additives and medicated animal feeds.

Lijinsky, who has a National Cancer Institute grant for his studies at Nebraska's Eppley Institute, was concerned with nitrite primarily as one of the two ingredients that combine to form potent carcinogens (cancer-causing substances) called nitrosamines.

Nitrosamines are created in the stomach under the stimulus of acids continually secreted by granular cells, but can travel through the body to cause cancer in the lungs or other organs of laboratory animals.

"No species examined, nor any tissue or organ seems to be resistant to the induction of tumors by one nitrosamine or another," he said. "It is most unlikely that man would be the only resistant species."

The second ingredient of nitrosamines, amines, has been found in tobacco smoke, in addition to the foods and beverages listed earlier, Lijinsky said.

Turning to medicines, he said that several hundred are amines, including Ritalin, which is often used to control overly active children; other tranquilizers; Preludin, among other appetite suppressants, and antihistamines.

The obvious way to reduce the possible cancer threat from nitrosamines is to decrease the intake of nitrite, Lijinsky said.

He recommended that the FDA reduce the maximum permissible concentration of nitrite in cured meat products and smoked fish to 10 to 20 parts per million. Already, he said, the FDA has established a tolerance of only 10 parts per million for preserving and fixing the color of smoked tuna.

For decades, the Agriculture Department and FDA have allowed 200 parts per million. According to a report made by the department 45 years ago, and cited yesterday by the subcommittee staff, the 200-part figure is simply the highest concentration found in hams after curing in a type of wine solution still used today.

He said that meat products commonly contain lower concentrations of 50 to 150 parts. But, he added, there have been occasional reports "of very much higher concentrations" of nitrite in smoked fish and bacon, possibly because of "careless manufacturing procedure."

Nitrates, Nitrites, and Nitrosamines

Science (7 July 1972)

Extensive research is needed to establish how great a food hazard these nitrogenous substances present.

I. A. Wolff and A. E. Wasserman

The potential hazards of nitrosamines as toxicants formed in, or as a result of eating, certain foodstuffs have been described in newspapers (1), in testimony before congressional committees (2), in technical articles (3), and in consumer publications (4). We believe it appropriate therefore to review the status of knowledge of these substances to gain perspective and to distinguish between actual and potential occurrence of these compounds or their formation in vivo (or both). Some authors have carried out test tube reactions between nitrite and secondary amines and have indicated that these precursor substances are components of a number of foods we eat or drugs we take (5). However, it does not necessarily follow that by either in vitro or in vivo mechanisms we are being exposed to nitrosamines from a variety of sources. Evidence for the presence or formation of nitrosamines in foods is limited and some of the earlier reports of nitrosamines in human nutrients may have been based on inadequate analytical procedures (6). Furthermore, because pharmacological data on the action of various nitrosamines are incomplete at this time, we believe that it is not yet possible scientifically to ascertain the true danger from nitrosamines in our environment. The demonstrated carcinogenicity of many of these compounds, however, indicates that well-planned, long-range research is mandatory to obtain the needed answers.

Not only may nitrites conceivably serve as reactants with amines or amides to form toxic nitroso compounds, but the nitrites—and their precursor nitrates—have themselves been implicated in causing toxicity in animals and humans, and particularly in children. Ecologists have expressed concern regarding nitrate concentrations in the environment and the effect on the food and water supply.

Nitrates

Our major intake of nitrates in foodstuffs comes primarily from vegetables or water supplies that are high in nitrate content, or from nitrates used as additives in the meat-curing process.

Nitrates are natural constituents of plants. They are present in large quantities in many vegetables, but they occur in only minor amounts in

Dr. Wolff is director of the Eastern Regional Research Laboratory, and Dr. Wasserman is Investigations Head in the Meat, Hides and Leather Laboratory of the Eastern Regional Research Laboratory, Eastern Marketing and Nutrition Research Division, Agricultural Research Service, U.S. Department of Agriculture, Philadelphia, Pennsylvania 19118.

fruit (7). Spinach, beets, radishes, eggplant, celery, lettuce, collards, and turnip greens are among the vegetables that generally contain very high concentrations of nitrates (7). The nitrate content of some samples may be more than 3000 parts per million. However, the absolute values reported vary extremely because of genetic, environmental, sampling, and maturity factors.

The most important factors that favor large accumulation of nitrate in vegetables include (i) a nitrate-rich environment such as may be caused by high levels of fertilization, especially during the ripening period (8); (ii) species that are prone to accumulate nitrate (9); (iii) plant nutrient deficiencies (such as that caused by a lack of molybdenum) (10); (iv) conditions of reduced light intensity during maturation (11); (v) lack of water (12); and (vi) plant damage from chemical treatments (13). Interactions among these factors complicate the picture and account for the wide ranges of values reported for nitrate of the same vegetables.

A person is likely to consume as much or more nitrates from his vegetable intake as from the cured meat products he eats (14). Sodium or potassium nitrate is permitted as an additive to meat products in the United States at levels of 2¾ ounces to 3½ ounces per 100 pounds of meat (15). In some countries, not including the United States, addition of small amounts of nitrate is permitted in the manufacture of some varieties of cheese (7).

Concern has frequently been expressed about the high nitrate content of some water supplies, particularly those from wells. This nitrate comes from many sources, including precipitation, soil and rock, agricultural use of fertilizers, nitrogen fixation by microorganisms and plants, and especially decomposition of plant and sewage wastes followed by the leaching of nitrates into groundwater. Health agencies have issued reports that, for water to be safe for domestic use, the concentration of nitrate should not exceed 10 parts per million expressed as nitrate-nitrogen (16). Numerous examples may be found in which the nitrate content of well water is in excess of this amount (17). This situation presents some hazard of potential toxicity. However, the usual nitrate intake of an adult may be less from the water supply than from either the vegetables or meat products ordinarily consumed (7).

In the quantities normally occurring in food or feed, nitrates become toxic only under conditions in which they are, or may be, reduced to nitrites. Otherwise, at reasonable concentrations, nitrate ions are rapidly excreted in the urine. The nitrites, then, constitute the principal toxic agent, and high intake of nitrates constitutes a hazard primarily under conditions that are favorable for their reduction to nitrite. Four such situations in which this may occur are well documented.

(1) The microbial environment in the rumen of cattle causes reduction of nitrate to nitrite. Subsequent absorption of the nitrite ion may result in toxicity to cattle. Hence a danger is present when feeds or water of high nitrate content are consumed (18). In the host, the enlarged cecum

and colon also provide a location for microbial reduction of nitrate, and subsequent toxic effects (19).

(2) The lesser stomach acidity of infants under about 4 months of age may permit the growth of microorganisms that can reduce nitrate to nitrite. As a result, providing water of high nitrate content to infants is a real hazard. Numerous deaths from this cause have been recorded (20).

(3) When spinach, whether processed or unprocessed, is stored under conditions that permit the growth of microorganisms, nitrate may be reduced to nitrite. A number of cases of toxicity in infants have been reported from spinach left at room temperature for some time after cooking or after a jar of baby food was opened. Conceivably, such nitrite toxicity may also develop in other vegetables or in prepared foods of high nitrate content, but most of the cases reported deal particularly with spinach (21).

(4) Reduction of nitrate to nitrite has occurred in damp forage materials that were high in nitrate content. Ingestion by livestock proved toxic (22). Also, release of oxides of nitrogen from ensiled forages may be hazardous to man and animals (23).

In the curing of meat, some of the added nitrate is usually reduced to nitrite but authentic cases of toxic effects from added nitrate only were not found.

Thus, nitrates are not toxic per se, but may under some circumstances be the starting point for a chain of reactions that result in the conversion to toxic substances. Hence, prudence dictates that we monitor the nitrate content of our foods, feeds, and water supplies, divert any samples of particularly high content into channels where they will do no harm, and be aware of actions that can lead to decreasing the use and amount of nitrate in foods when such decrease becomes warranted.

Nitrites

The proved toxicity of nitrites is due primarily to their interaction with blood pigment to produce methemoglobinemia, and their presumptive toxicity relates to their possible reaction, under normally encountered situations, with amines or amides to form toxic nitroso compounds.

Hemoglobin (Hb), the respiratory pigment containing Fe(II), normally transports oxygen to the tissues as a loose complex—oxyhemoglobin (Hb · O_2). After the iron is oxidized to the ferric state, the pigment loses its ability to transport oxygen and forms a brown compound, methemoglobin (MetHb). The presence of nitrite in the blood results in MetHb formation. When the methemoglobin concentration exceeds 70 percent, asphyxia occurs, although at lower levels the reaction is reversible (24). The nitrite is very strongly bound to the heme of methemoglobin (25).

Although there are a number of instances in cattle of nitrite poisoning from water or forage, or in infants from nitrite-containing spinach, the incidence of toxicity is really quite low and the intakes required for serious toxic effects are usually large. As was mentioned in the previous section, the nitrites are in these instances derived from reduction of nitrates. Poisoning of adult humans by nitrite apparently has not been a problem. However, accidental addition of excessive amounts of nitrite to foods has led to instances of poisoning of both adults (26) and children (27).

Nitrites are more toxic than nitrates, and restriction of the daily intake for man to 0.4 milligram per kilogram of body weight is recommended (28). However, nitrites have been used therapeutically as medication for vasodilation and as an antidote for cyanide poisoning in doses of 30 to 300 milligrams without severe toxic effects (29). Consumption levels that may cause long-term hazards in man have not been established.

Nitrates and Nitrites in Cured Meat and Fish

The principal source of nitrite in our diets is processed (cured) meat or fish, and nitrites are considered a potential reactant precursor for nitrosamines.

Originally meat was cured in brine containing potassium nitrate as one of the ingredients. However, the actual curing agent was found to be the nitrite produced by the bacterial reduction of the nitrate salt. When it was shown that nitrite could be substituted for nitrate in the cure solution with the production of a more uniform and completely satisfactory product in a shorter period of time, a legal limit of no more than 200 milligrams of residual nitrite (calculated as $NaNO_2$) per kilogram of meat was established (30). The action of nitrite in the cure process is threefold: (i) formation of characteristic color, (ii) production of cured flavor, and (iii) antibacterial activity.

The role of nitrite in color formation is to furnish nitric oxide which reacts with myoglobin (Mb) to give nitrosylmyoglobin (MbNO) the red-pink pigment of cured meat. Although the fate of nitrite after addition to meat is not fully known, the following reactions have been postulated to occur in the presence of added reductants (AH_2) (31).

$$NaNO_2 + H^+ \rightarrow HNO_2 + Na^+$$
$$2HNO_2 \rightarrow N_2O_3 + H_2O$$
$$N_2O_3 + AH_2 \rightarrow AHNO + HNO_2$$
$$AHNO \rightarrow AH \cdot + NO$$
$$NO + MetMb \rightarrow MetMbNO$$
$$MetMbNO + AH_2 \rightarrow MbNO$$

In the presence of ascorbic acid, cysteine, quinones, or other reductants, nitrous acid, formed from the nitrite ion, is reduced to nitric oxide, which forms a complex with metmyoglobin (MetMb). The nitrosylmetmyoglobin (MetMbNO) is reduced by ascorbic acid to nitrosylmyoglobin. Nitrosylhemochrome, the cure pigment, results when the product is heated.

Another mechanism for the production of nitric oxide (NO) proposes (32) the reduction of nitrite mediated by reduced cytochrome c [Fe(II)Cyto c] and reduced nicotinamide adenine dinucleotide (NADH):

$$\text{No}_2 + \text{Fe(II)Cyto c} \rightarrow \text{NOFe(III)Cyto c}$$
$$\text{NOFe(III)Cyto c} + \text{NADH} \rightarrow \text{NO} + \text{Fe(II)Cyto c}$$

Cured meat flavor is a function of the activity of nitrite on meat components. While emphasis has been placed on the reaction of nitrite with meat pigments, the so-called "cosmetic effect," and on the antibacterial action of the compound, little attention has been paid to the development of the characteristic cured flavor. However, there have been several reports on the effect of nitrite on the flavor of bacon, ham, and frankfurters (33). Initial studies indicate that flavor can be obtained at concentrations of nitrite lower than the legal limits. There is no information available at this time, however, about the reactions or the meat components involved.

The antibacterial effects of nitrite appear to be necessary to maintain the stability of cured canned meat products exposed to less-than-sterilizing heat treatment. The growth of *Clostridium botulinum* and toxin production are inhibited. While the mode of action of nitrite is still unknown, it has been reported that division of vegetative cells does not occur in the presence of this ion (34). Growth of surviving organisms is also inhibited by the action of residual nitrite.

Inhibition of the growth of *C. botulinum* in these meat products is a complex phenomenon involving interaction of the number of spores present, the amount of heat applied, and the concentrations of sodium chloride and sodium nitrite used (35). The interdependence of these factors is so great that minor changes in the conditions of one may require balancing modifications in all the others. The pH of the product may also play an important role in the bactericidal effect of nitrite, although it is difficult to adjust the pH of meat. It has been shown in model systems that there is approximately a tenfold increase in antibacterial effect with a decline of one pH unit in the range of pH 7.5 to 6.0 (36). Under the more acid conditions, larger concentrations of undissociated nitrous acid are available and, according to Shank *et al.* (37), this is the molecular species responsible for inhibition of the growth of clostridia. The dynamics of nitrous acid formation may be shown as a cyclic reaction:

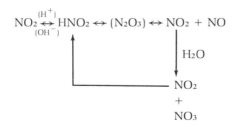

Concomitant oxidation-reduction reactions lead to the formation of nitric oxide and nitrogen dioxide. The latter reacts with water forming nitrate ion and nitrite ions, which reenters the cycle. At the pH of greatest antibacterial activity (pH 4.5 to 5.5) the amount of nitrous acid present is at a maximum.

A number of episodes of botulism in recent years were caused by consumption of improperly handled or improperly processed fish or fish products (38). Control of *C. botulinum* in these products is attained by the use of sodium nitrite cure preparations. The preservation of fresh fish fillets or lightly smoked saltwater fish—such as salmon, tuna, halibut, and cod (39)—as well as freshwater fish—chub, for example (38)—has been described. Federal regulations limiting the residual nitrite in smoked, cured tuna to 10 mg/kg and in sable, salmon, and shad to no more than 200 mg/kg have been established. The nitrite content of smoked chub must be not less than 100 mg/kg (30).

The use of nitrite in the preservation of fish may result in the formation of nitrosamines. Certain species of fish, particularly of saltwater fish (40), contain large quantities of trimethylamine, trimethylamine oxide, and dimethylamine which may react with nitrite to form N-nitrosodimethylamine.

N-Nitroso Compounds

The reaction of nitrite with some classes of amines is a matter of public health interest at this time. Nitrosamines have been used as intermediates in a number of industrial processes (41); hence exposure to these compounds may be more widespread than assumed. Animal studies have shown that N-nitrosamines and the related N-nitrosamides are carcinogenic (42), and they may be mutagenic and teratogenic (43) as well. Nitrosamines having a wide variety of molecular structures are carcinogenic; of the approximately 100 compounds tested, about 75 percent produced lesions in test animals. Various tissues respond to the action of these compounds, some of them specifically to a certain nitrosamine or to groups of nitrosamines. The effects of nitrosamines can be elicited by several routes of administration—oral, intravenous, inhalation, subcutaneous, intraperitoneal, and topical. Local sarcomas have been observed rarely at the site of injection; the carcinogenic activity usually occurs elsewhere. It would seem, therefore, that the nitrosamines themselves are not carcinogens but may behave as carcinogen precursors (44). Studies with radioactive tracers suggest metabolic degradation of the nitroso compound to form an alkylating radical or ion that attacks the 7-position of guanine in nucleic acids. Although no cancer in man has yet been traced to nitrosamines as causative agents, the experimental results in animals suggest that these compounds also would be carcinogenic to man.

The acute toxicity or eventual carcinogenicity of the nitrosamines may, depending on the compound and the circumstances, show itself at very low dosages (43). Results of feeding studies are not yet decisive as to precise dose-response relationships. In a study with rats given a single dose, concentrations of N-nitrosodimethylamine greater than 5 ppm induced tumors in more than 70 percent of the animals, whereas continuous feeding of 1 ppm in the diet has been suggested as a threshold dose (45).

N-Nitrosamines, principally N-nitrosodimethylamine, have been reported in a number of foods. However, improved analytical procedures and recognition of artifacts in the preparations have now led to questions concerning the validity of these reports.

Nitrosation has in the past been considered to occur with secondary amines only. Recent studies have indicated that nitrosamines are also formed from tertiary amines and quaternary ammonium compounds that occur naturally in foods (46) and drugs (47).

The nitrosation reaction may proceed chemically or it may occur as a result of the metabolic activity of microorganisms. Ease of nitrosation, chemically, may be influenced by many factors, including the basicity of the amine (48), pH (49), substrate concentration (49), and the presence of some inorganic ions (50). The thiocyanate ion is of particular interest. This ion is normally present in human saliva in amounts ranging from 12 to 33 mg/100 ml (higher amounts are found in the saliva of smokers) and is capable of increasing the rate of nitrosation of morpholine (51).

In addition to the potential of formation of nitrosamine in processed foods, there may be nitrosamine formation in the gastrointestinal tract from ingested nitrite and secondary amines or their precursors (52). In several in vitro studies nitrosamine was formed from amines and nitrite in media in which intestinal microorganisms were growing (53, 54). In other tests, with human patients exhibiting conditions in which there was no, or only low, stomach acidity, nitrosation of diphenylamine, a nontoxic easily nitrosated amine, occurred (55). The appearance of tumors in various organs or the methylation of the 7-position in the nucleic acid guanine in rats that had ingested amines or amides and nitrite was considered presumptive evidence for the formation of nitroso compounds (56). The role of the intestinal bacteria in nitrosation under these conditions, however, is still not clear. Under healthy conditions the human stomach and upper gastrointestinal tract contain very few organisms (57), but when the acidity decreases, conditions may be favorable for the presence of nitrate-reducing, nitrosating bacteria. Nitrates and nitrites ingested with food or water are normally absorbed very rapidly from the stomach and upper gastrointestinal tract, appearing eventually in the urine. Thus, though the residence time of the nitrates and nitrites may be too short for gastric involvement, the potential exists for bladder involvement. It has been shown that rats with experimentally induced bladder infections of Escherichia coli excreted nitrosated piperidine after they had ingested the amine and a water solution of nitrate (53).

Correlation between many preformed nitrosamines and tumor induction in animals has been demonstrated. However, the relation between nitrite (nitrate) and amines (or their precursors), the end formation of nitrosamines in foods or in vivo, and their carcinogenic effect is still tenuous. While nitrosamine formation occurs more or less readily in vitro, in the normal, healthy human gastric conditions do not seem to be favorable for nitrosamine formation. At this time there is not enough information concerning the naturally occurring amines and their precursors, the pH changes in the stomach during digestion, the rate of absorption of the reactants, or the role of the intestinal flora.

The number of reports of nitrosamines in foods confirmed by mass spectrometry, the only procedure currently recognized as definitive, is very limited. Important gaps in our information exist. In addition to lack of information about all the compositional factors of the foods, we are also ignorant of the processing factors that could lead to nitrosamine formation.

Other environmental factors have been mentioned as potential sources of nitrosamines. Tobacco smoke has been implicated in the development of lung cancer. The tobacco plant is rich in amines, and an even larger number of these compounds has been identified in tobacco smoke as a result of the pyrolysis of the nitrogenous constituents of the plant (58). Nitrate is also present either as a plant constituent or it may have been added during processing. Under these conditions the presence of nitrosamines has been reported in tobacco (59) and in tobacco smoke (58, 60). However, reports of nitrosamines in tobacco smoke should be evaluated for reliability of analytical methods used, and the possibility that they may be formed (artifacts) in the collecting traps should be considered (58).

A number of commonly used drugs that are taken either in large doses or for long periods of time contain secondary amine groups or structures that may be amine precursors. There is some interest in the potential internal nitrosation of such drugs if ingested with nitrite or water containing high levels of nitrate. Model studies (47) reacting nitrite with oxytetracycline and antipyrine yielded N-nitrosodimethylamine, and N-nitrosodiethylamine was obtained when the drug disulfiram was used. Although no nitrosamine could be isolated from the system containing nitrite and tolbutamide, nitrosohexamethyleneimine was formed from tolazamide. Extended studies with more drugs and investigation of the applicability of model systems to the human experience are needed.

Summary

We are faced with evaluating the potential hazard of nitrate, nitrite, and nitrosamines in our environment. The extent of real danger is not yet known, but deliberate consideration of the available information would suggest that the hazard is not sufficiently great to cause alarm. There may be some who advocate immediate elimination of or drastic reduction in amounts of nitrite or nitrate in cured meat and fish. Before actions such as these would be taken, we should be very sure that we are not forgoing the needed preservative effects of nitrite, which protects us against serious outbreaks of food poisoning. We could be replacing one hazard by another, more serious one.

There is under way in the scientific community a commendable amount of research on many aspects of this important problem. This effort is necessary because so little is known of the possible in vivo synthesis of nitrosamines.

Thus we should continue to regard nitrites and nitrosamines as possible important toxicants but should be cautious about taking any action relative to modification of our food supply until we are sure the action is needed, justified, and proper.

References and Notes

1. Baltimore Sun, 14 December 1970; Washington Post, 17 March 1971; Wall Street Journal, 17 March 1971.
2. Wall Street Journal, 17 March 1971; Philadelphia Inquirer, 7 April 1971.
3. Food Process. **32** (5), 21 (1971).
4. Consumer Bulletin, March 1971, p. 25.
5. W. Lijinsky and S. S. Epstein, Nature **225**, 21 (1970); W. Lijinsky, in Proceedings of the Conference on Nitrosamines, Heidelberg, 1971, in preparation.
6. K. Heyns and H. Koch, Z. Lebensmittel-Unters. Forsch. **145**, 76 (1971); E. Kröller, Deut. Lebensmittel-Rundsch. **63**, 303 (1967); R. Preussmann, G. Neurath, G. Wulf-Lorestzen, D. Dajber, H. Hengy, Z. Anal. Chem. **202**, 187 (1964); N. P. Sen, D. C. Smith, L. Schwinghamer, J. J. Marleau. J. Ass. Offic. Anal. Chem. **52**, 47 (1969).
7. M. R. Ashton, British Food Manufacturing Industries Research Association Literature Survey No. 7 (April 1970).
8. W. Schuphan and H. Schottmann, Z. Lebensmittel-Unters. Forsch. **128**, 71 (1965); G. ap Griffith, J. Sci. Food Agr. **11**, 626 (1960); A. Ulrich, D. Ririe, F. J. Hills, A. G. George, M. D. Morse, C. M. Johnson, Calif. Agr. Exp. Sta. Bull. No. 766 (1959).
9. A. Gul and B. J. Kolp, Agron. J. **52**, 504 (1960); J. F. Zieserl, Jr., W. L. Rivenbark, R. H. Hageman, Crop Sci. **3** (1), 27 (1963).
10. E. J. Rubins, Soil. Sci. **81**, 191 (1956); K. H. Schütte, The Biology of Trace Elements, (Lippincott, Philadelphia, 1964).
11. C. S. Gilbert. H. F. Eppson, W. B. Bradley, O. A. Beath, Wyo. Agr. Exp. Sta. Bull. No. 277 (1946); N. O. Bathurst and K. J. Mitchell, N. Z. J. Agr. Res. **1**, 540 (1958).
12. J. J. Hanway and A. J. Englehorn, Agron. J. **50**, 331 (1958); W. B. Davidson, J. L. Doughty, J. L. Bolton, Can. J. Comp. Med. Vet. Sci. **5**, 303 (1941).
13. L. M. Stahler and E. I. Whitehead, Science **112**, 749 (1950); C. J. Willard, North Central Weed Control Conf. Proc. Annu. Meet. **7**, 110 (1950).
14. W. D. Richardson, J. Amer. Chem. Soc. **29**, 1757 (1907).
15. Code of Federal Regulations, Title 9 (revised as of 1 January 1971).
16. World Health Organization, Expert Committee on Maternal and Child Health, Official Records of the World Health Organization **13**, 19 (1949); U.S. Public Health Serv. Publ. 956 (1962).
17. C. Simon, H. Manzke, H. Kay, G. Mrowetz, Z. Kinderheilk. **91**, 124 (1964).
18. W. B. Bradley, A. O. Beath, H. F. Eppson, Science **89**, 365 (1939); M. L. Sapiro, S. Hoflund, R. Clark, J. I. Quin, Onderstepoort J. Vet. Sci. Anim. Ind. **22**, 357 (1949).
19. W. B. Bradley, H. F. Eppson, O. A. Beath, Wyo. Agr. Exp. Sta. Bull. No. 241 (1940); W. B. Davidson, J. L. Doughty, J. L. Bolton, Can. J. Comp. Med. Vet. Sci. **5**, 303 (1941).
20. Z. Knotek and P. Schmidt, Pediatrics **34**, 78 (1964); U. Werner, W. Thal, W. D. Wuttke, Deut. Med. Wochenschr. **90**, 124 (1965); C. Simon, H. Manzke, H. Kay, G. Mrowetz, Z. Kinderheilk. **91**, 124 (1964).
21. W. Schuphan, Z. Ernaehrungswiss. **5**, 207 (1965); C. Simon, Lancet **1966-I**, 872 (1966);

————, H. Kay, G. Mrowetz, *Deut. Lebensmittel-Rundsch.* **61,** 75 (1965); A. Sinios and W. Wodsak, *Deut. Med. Wochenschr.* **90,** 1856 (1965).

22. O. E. Olson and A. L. Moxon, *J. Amer. Vet. Med. Ass.* **100,** 403 (1942).

23. W. H. Peterson, R. H. Burris, R. Sant, H. N. Little, *J. Agr. Food Chem.* **6,** 121 (1958); J. V. Scaletti, C. E. Gates, R. A. Briggs, L. M. Schuman, *Agron. J.* **52,** 369 (1960).

24. W. E. J. Phillips, *Food Cosmet. Toxicol.* **9,** 219 (1971).

25. B. S. Walker, W. C. Boyd, I. Asimov, *Biochemistry and Human Metabolism* (Williams & Wilkins, Baltimore, 1957).

26. B. Roueché, *Eleven Blue Men and Other Narratives of Medical Detection* (Little, Brown, Boston, 1954).

27. Sixth Report of the Joint FAO/WHO Expert Committee on Food Additives, *FAO Nutr. Meet. Rep. Ser. No. 31* (1962).

28. J. D. Orgeron, J. D. Martin, C. T. Caraway, R. M. Martine, G. H. Hauser, *Public Health Rep.* **72,** 189 (1957).

29. *Merck Index* (Merck, Rahway, N.J., ed. 8, 1968).

30. Code of Federal Regulations, Title 21, Sec. 121. 1064 and Sec. 121.1230 (revised as of 1 January 1971).

31. J. B. Fox, Jr. and J. S. Thomson, *Biochemistry* **2,** 465 (1963).

32. C. L. Walters, A. McM. Taylor, R. J. Casselden, N. Ray, *British Food Manufacturing Industries Research Association, Research Report No. 139* (1968).

33. J. Brooks, R. B. Haines, T. Moran, J. Pace (Great Britain Department of Science and Industrial Research;, *Food Invest. Spec. Rep.* **49,** 1 (1940); H. W. Barnett, H. R. Nordin, H. D. Bird, L. J. Rubin, paper presented at the 11th European Meeting of Meat Research Workers (1965); I. C. Cho and L. J. Bratzler, *J. Food Sci.* **35,** 668 (1970); A. E. Wasserman and F. Talley, *ibid.,* in press.

34. C. L. Duncan and E. M. Foster, *Appl. Microbiol.* **16,** 406 (1968); H. Pivnick, M. A. Johnston, C. Thacker, R. Loynes, *Can. Inst. Food Technol. J.* **3,** 103 (1970).

35. H. Pivnick, H. W. Barnett, H. R. Nordin, L. J. Rubin, *Can. Inst. Food Technol. J.* **2,** 141 (1969); H. Reimann, *Food Technol. London* **17,** 39 (1963); T. A. Roberts and M. Ingram, *J. Food Technol.* **1,** 147 (1966); J. H. Silliker, R. A. Greenberg, W. R. Schack, *Food Technol. London* **12,** 551 (1958).

36. C. L. Duncan and E. M. Foster, *Appl. Microbiol.* **16,** 401 (1968); T. A. Roberts and M. Ingram, *J. Food Technol.* **1,** 147 (1966).

37. J. L. Shank, J. H. Silliker, R. H. Harper, *Appl. Microbiol.* **10,** 185 (1962).

38. K. G. Weckel and S. Chien, *University of Wisconsin College of Agriculture and Life Sciences, Research Report No. 51* (1969).

39. H. L. A. Tarr and P. A. Sunderland, *Fish. Res. Board Can. Progr. Rep. Pac. Coast Sta. No. 40* (1939), p. 14.

40. G. A. Reay and J. M. Shewan, *Advan. Food Res.* **2,** 343 (1949); N. P. Sen, D. C. Smith, L. Schwinghamer, B. Howsam, *Can. Inst. Food Technol. J.* **3,** 66 (1970).

41. E. G. Maitlen, U.S. Pat. 2,970,939 (1961); M. R. Lytton, E. A. Wielicki, E. Lewis, U.S. Pat. 2,776,946 (1957); K. Klager, U.S. Pat. 3,192,707 (1965).

42. P. N. Magee and J. M. Barnes, *Brit. J. Cancer* **10,** 114 (1956); H. Druckrey, R. Preussmann, S. Ivankovic, D. Schmähl, *Z. Krebsforsch.* **69,** 103 (1967).

43. P. N. Magee and J. M. Barnes, *Advan. Cancer Res.* **10,** 163 (1967).

44. H. Druckrey, R. Preussmann, S. Ivankovic, *Ann. N.Y. Acad. Sci.* **163,** Art. 2, 676 (1969).

45. B. Terracini, P. N. Magee, J. M. Barnes, *Brit. J. Cancer* **21,** 559 (1967).

46. W. Fiddler and J. W. Pensabene, *Nature* **236,** 307 (1972).

47. W. Lijinsky, in *Proceedings of the Conference on Nitrosamines, Heidelberg, 1971,* in preparation.

48. J. Sander, F. Schweinsberg, H.-P. Menz, *Hoppe-Seyler's Z. Physiol. Chem.* **349,** 1691 (1968).

49. S. S. Mirvish, *J. Nat. Cancer Inst.* **44,** 633 (1970).

50. E. Boyland, in *Proceedings of the Conference on Nitrosamines, Heidelberg, 1971,* in preparation.

51. ————, E. Nice, K. Williams, *Food Cosmet. Toxicol.* **9,** 639 (1971).

52. W. Lijinsky and S. S. Epstein, *Nature* **225**, 2f (1970); N. P. Sen, D. C. Smith, L. Schwinghamer, *Food Cosmet. Toxicol.* **7**, 301 (1969).
53. G. Hawksworth and M. J. Hill, *Biochem. J.* **122**, 28P (1971).
54. J. Sander, *Hoppe-Seyler's Z. Physiol. Chem.* **349**, 429 (1968).
55. J. Sander and F. Seif, *Arzneimittel-Forsch.* **19**, 1091 (1969).
56. R. Montesano and P. N. Magee, *Int. J. Cancer* **7**, 249 (1971); J. Sander and G. Bürkle, *Z. Krebsforsch.* **73**, 54 (1969).
57. T. Bauchop, *Annu. Rev. Microbiol.* **25**, 429 (1971).
58. G. Neurath, *Experientia* **23**, 400 (1967).
59. W. J. Serfontein and J. H. Smit, *Nature* **214**, 169 (1967).
60. D. E. Johnson, J. D. Millar, J. W. Rhoades, *Nat. Cancer Inst. Monogr.* **28**, 181 (1968); E. L. Wynder and D. Hoffman, Eds. *Tobacco and Tobacco Smoke* (Academic Press, New York, 1967).

Botulism and Nitrites

Letters to Science

In their article of 7 July 1972 (p. 15), I. A. Wolff and A. F. Wasserman imply that the addition of nitrite is necessary to prevent the growth of *Clostridium botulinum* in cured meat and smoked fish products. In fact, the conjunction of many factors, of which nitrite is only one, produces the bactericidal effect. It is not known what other combinations of heat, salt, and pH might accomplish the same effect in the absence of nitrite.

What is known is that many products, such as bacon, to which nitrites are now added, involve no botulism hazard because they are fried. Others, such as frankfurters, can be processed without nitrite to remove any such hazard. The Berkeley Co-Op, for example, has marketed such a product for some time with great success. As the Fountain subcommittee hearings in March 1971 demonstrated, the use of nitrite in the processing of smoked fish products is a relatively recent practice, and the levels added are frequently far below what the Food and Drug Administration claims to be necessary to prevent botulism. In fact, some states prohibit the addition of nitrate or nitrite to smoked fish products and instead require processing at 180°C to obviate any botulism risk. Japan has totally banned the use of nitrites in fish products.

While it is true that some early reports of N-nitrosamines in foods are of questionable validity, some more recent positive findings have been confirmed. For instance, the presence of the carcinogen nitrosopyrrolidine in cooked bacon and sausage has been confirmed at between 30 and 106 parts per billion. The very limited number of samples for nitrosamines taken by the U.S. Department of Agriculture makes any positive findings in the food supply highly suggestive.

It is true that "there is not enough information" to determine the probability of nitrosamine formation in vivo in humans. Nevertheless, nitrosamine formation from the interaction of nitrates and secondary amines have been established in vivo in cats and rabbits, species whose gastric juices have a pH similar to that of man. And the presence of nitrosodiphenylamine was detected in the stomachs of 31 human subjects who were fed a combination of nitrate and secondary amines (1).

It is precisely the numerous uncertainties and gaps in knowledge about nitrites and nitrosamines which Wolff and Wasserman identify that compel one to disagree with their conclusion that "the hazard is not sufficiently great to cause alarm." Apparently, they would have an unsuspecting public bear the burden of these uncertainties, despite ample evidence that nitrites are not always necessary to prevent botulism and that alternative means of safe processing are available which do not involve risks such as these posed by nitrite. The law and common sense both require that these risks be resolved.

Peter H. Schuck

Consumers Union,
1714 Massachusetts Avenue, NW,
Washington, D.C. 20036

Harrison Wellford

Center for Study of Responsive Law,
P.O. Box 19367,
Washington, D.C. 20036

Reference

1. P. N. Magee, Food Cosmet. Toxicol. **3**, 207 (1971).

Schuck and Wellford are to be commended on their concern for the consumer. We, too, share this concern. We also are in accord with the last sentence of their letter. However, we repeat our contention that the resolution of the risks must be based on considered evaluation of all the information available. Furthermore, sufficient foresight must be applied to prevent undesirable effects induced by any changes imposed. Our article was a brief compilation and summary of information from several diverse fields to provide a background, as well as to stimulate thought, interest, and research on a sensitive problem of public health interest. Schuck and Wellford have used in part data published since our paper was prepared to question our conclusions. In the same interval, however, a number of encouraging reports have also appeared, as we indicated they might. Van Logten et al. (1) reported no tumors or cancerous lesions in rats fed for 2 years on a diet consisting of 40 percent cured meat processed with nitrate in such a manner that 60 micrograms per kilogram (parts per billion) of total nitrosamines were found in the meat. In our laboratory, sodium ascorbate was shown to inhibit or prevent formation of N-nitrosodimethylamine in frankfurters (2), and preliminary data indicate

N-nitrosopyrrolidine formation in bacon may be similarly affected. Modification of manufacturing practices may be required when these results, together with information from other laboratories, are evaluated.

One alternative proposed by Schuck and Wellford does not seem acceptable. According to them, many products, such as bacon, could contain botulin toxin, but there would be no hazard because they are fried prior to consumption. We question whether appropriate regulatory agencies would be willing to approve such products. Consumers and consumer organizations themselves might want to raise serious questions about such an approach.

The urgency stressed by Schuck and Wellford about elimination of nitrate should, in our opinion, be tempered with caution, in view of the many scientific unknowns and the long history of usage with apparent safety. There is still no correlation of the quantities of nitrosamines that might possibly be ingested under normal conditions with the development of harmful effects—either in humans or in animals. The nitrosamines pose a serious *potential* hazard, and intensive investigation of the many facets of the problem is definitely needed and under way. At this time a satisfactory solution to the problem looks promising. This may involve modifications of curing processes, utilization of nitrite substitutes, reduction of nitrite concentration, or in some cases elimination of nitrite. To us it seems somewhat premature to judge the preferred approach or approaches.

A. E. Wasserman
I. A. Wolff

Eastern Regional Research Laboratory,
Agricultural Research Service,
U.S. Department of Agriculture,
600 East Mermaid Lane,
Philadelphia, Pennsylvania 19118

References

1. M. J. Van Logten, E. M. den Tonkelaar, R. Kroes, J. M. Berkvens, G. J. van Esch, *Food Cosmet. Toxicol.* **10**, 475 (1972).
2. W. Fiddler, E. G. Piotrowski, J. W. Pensabene, A. E. Wasserman, *Proceedings of the 18th Meeting of the Meat Research Workers* (Meat Research Workers, Guelph, Ontario, 1972), p. 416.

Nitrites in Foods

Letter to Science *(21 December 1973)*

A. E. Wasserman and I. A. Wolff, who discuss the use of nitrate in their reply to P. H. Schuck and H. Wellford (Letters, 29 June, p. 1322), do not deal adequately with the question of the use of nitrite in cured meat and fish products, which Schuck and Wellford suggest is an unnecessary hazard to health. Wasserman and Wolff also ignore the problem of formation of carcinogenic nitrosamines in vivo (1), which Schuck and Wellford address in their letter. It is this amply demonstrated possibility which poses the greatest hazard to the public, and is the major reason for the proposal to eliminate nitrite from our food whenever possible.

A limit of 200 parts per million (ppm) of *residual* nitrite in food (meat) set in 1926 is arbitrary and has no scientific basis. The preservative effect depends on the amount of nitrite added to the food before processing (a minimum, so it is said, of 150 ppm). After processing, the residual nitrite can be, and often is, as little as 10 ppm in, for example, ham or canned luncheon meat. It is this residual nitrite which takes part in nitrosamine formation in vivo, and it would seem that an upper limit of 200 ppm is far higher than indicated by good manufacturing practice, and high enough to be a threat to health.

Wasserman and Wolff state that there is a long history of usage of nitrate (and, by implication, of nitrite) with apparent safety. This is an unwarranted conclusion, since cancer is a widespread and common affliction, the cause of which is unknown. Evidence is accumulating about the formation of nitrosamines from nitrite and secondary or tertiary amines (agrichemical residues, drugs, and so forth), both in food and in vivo, which suggests that nitrosamines formed in this way are a cause of cancer (2), perhaps the major one. If, as Wasserman and Wolff suggest, the avoidance of botulinus poisoning takes precedence over the possible carcinogenic hazard from nitrosamine formation, consistency would demand that food manufacturers add nitrite to all products in which a botulism hazard exists. One can assume that this is their recommendation for vichyssoise soup and processed mushrooms, large batches of which have been recalled in the past year or so because of the finding of *Clostridium botulinum* contamination in some samples. The feeding study of Van Logten et al. (3), cited by Wasserman and Wolff, is irrelevant, as the usually accepted practice in toxicology was not followed, namely the administration of greatly exaggerated doses (often 100 times or more the human exposure) to compensate for the small number of animals (180) in the experiment. The results of this 2-year feeding test (in which *nitrite* was added to the meat) cannot possibly be extrapolated to the experience of millions of humans who might consume proportionate doses of nitrite for 50 years or more. Moreover, this experiment did not test the possibility of formation of nitrosamines in the stomach.

Wasserman and Wolff state that there is no correlation of the amounts of nitrosamines that might be ingested under normal conditions with development of harmful effects, in man or animals. I draw their attention to the philosophy behind the Delaney Amendment—any amount of a known carcinogen is a hazard. To talk of the *potential* hazard of nitrosamines found in food is obfuscation, since these are carcinogens several orders of magnitude more potent than aminotriazole or cyclamates, which have been banned by the government. The benefit of the doubt should be given to the public rather than to the food processors. Surely it is time that nitrites (and nitrates) were removed from the GRAS (generally regarded as safe) list, as were cyclamates, until such time as they are proved safe for human consumption beyond a reasonable doubt.

W. Lijinsky

Biology Division,
Oak Ridge National Laboratory,
Oak Ridge, Tennessee 37830

References

1. W. Lijinsky and S. S. Epstein, *Nature (Lond.)* **225,** 21 (1970).
2. W. Lijinsky, H. W. Taylor, C. Snyder, P. Nettesheim, *ibid.* **224,** 176 (1973).
3. M. J. Van Logten, E. M. den Tonkelaar, P. Kroes, J. M. Berkvens, G. J. van Esch, *Food Cosmet. Toxicol.* **10,** 475 (1972).

Nitrites vs. Scientists or, Is That Coloring Really Necessary?
Washington Post (*25 July 1974*)

Marian Burros

About 99.9 per cent of the bacon, hot dogs, ham, bologna, salami and corned beef Americans consume by the ton, contains a chemical some scientists consider more hazardous than substances which have been banned from the food supply. Yet the U.S. Department of Agriculture Nitrate Panel has recommended only minimal reduction of the chemical, sodium nitrate, which is used in processed meats.

After working for three years on the problem, Dr. William Lijinsky, an eminent cancer researcher, is acutely disappointed by the panel's findings. He had expected a more meaningful reduction of nitrite, which he considers "more potent than cyclamates." Not all scientists agree with him, however.

Until 1971 there was very little concern, except among a few researchers, about the use of sodium nitrite and sodium nitrate to color, flavor and preserve virtually all processed meats.

By then, sufficient experiments had established that nitrites and nitrates (which are converted to nitrites by bacteria) combine with amines, found in other foods, drugs, tobacco and beverages, to form nitrosamines, powerful carcinogens (cancer-producing agents). Much of the supporting data on the hazards of nitrites has been gathered by Lijinsky.

In 1971, he appeared before the House Inter-Governmental Relations Subcommittee which was examining the Food and Drug Administration's contention that nitrites and nitrosamines present "no imminent hazard" to man, and that no reduction in the amount of nitrites used in food was necessary. Lijinsky, a researcher in chemical carcinogens at Oak Ridge (Tenn.) National Laboratory, testified to the contrary. And that was the beginning of his inadvertent involvement in the politics of nitrites.

To him the evidence pointed in one direction only: the reduction of nitrites in the food supply. He said, "Nitrosamines are among the most potent carcinogens we know and are certainly the most widely acting group of carcinogens. They seem to be most effective in eliciting tumors when they are applied as small doses over a long period, rather than as large single doses. These are precisely the conditions under which we would be exposed to nitrosamines if they are, indeed, formed by the interaction of amines with nitrites in our diet."

In his experiments with combinations of nitrites and amines in laboratory test animals, using both injection and feeding techniques, Lijinsky had found ". . . approximately 100 nitrosamines . . . the vast majority [being] carcinogenic. . . . No species examined, nor any tissue or organ seems to be resistant to the induction of tumors by one nitrosamine or another. It is most unlikely that man would be the only resistant species."

But to those whose business depends on sodium nitrite for coloring, flavoring and in some instances, preserving meat, the evidence was not convincing and they brought to bear the formidable pressure of their industry to prevent the USDA from taking any action.

The culmination of the uneven battle—several dedicated independent scientific researchers plus a few consumer groups against the highly organized meat industry—resulted in last week's recommendations which Lijinsky says are "hardly world-shaking."

The panel suggested a reduction of residual nitrite levels from the previous limit of 200 parts per million (ppm) to 100 or 125 ppm, for all but one category of processed meats. (A recommendation of 50 ppm was made for canned sterilized products whose safety is assured by sterilization.) Lijinsky had suggested 20 ppm. In some instances, he agrees, small amounts of nitrite may be necessary to prevent the formation of clostridium botulinum (which causes the often-fatal disease, botulism).

Even though he has lost his fight, for the moment, Lijinsky continues to believe that "you achieve more by not beating people over the head." This rational attitude, however, did not earn him a place on the USDA Nitrite Panel formed in September, 1973.

"I consider myself persona non grata on the USDA Nitrite Panel." Consumer activists, who asked for an independent scientist on the panel and were turned down, thought Lijinsky would have been the perfect choice. Why he was not included, Lijinsky says, "is something I cannot answer."

He admits to being prejudiced about the panel before he testified in front of it this past April. But "having been there and having had an excellent reception . . . I thought they would be more receptive to a lower count." Their recommendations came as a "surprise."

He believes that the panel was misled and that it did not "appreciate the other side of the picture," i.e., the hazards of nitrosamines. And he blames himself: "We probably didn't make a good enough case. I think we're up against some very stubborn forces like the meat industry and the ones who make decisions in the regulatory agencies, who don't like to change things."

Several years ago, however, Lijinsky was willing to give the meat industry the benefit of the doubt about the safety of nitrites: "I don't think the meat industry was spreading untruths. I think it's been ignorance. I would not accuse them of malice."

Still, he said in his testimony before the Nitrate Panel: "There is the suspicion that high nitrite levels sometimes are compensation for poor manufacturing quality. This suspicion is fortified by the remarks I heard at a meeting of the nitrosamine group sponsored by the FDA. These were in response to my question asking why bratwurst is not processed with nitrite. . . . The reply, which I could hardly believe, was that the shelf life and conditions of manufacture of bratwurst were such that nitrite was not necessary, implying that nitrite is used principally to overcome shortcomings in manufacture and distribution of some of the other products in which it is used."

Further, he questioned whether nitrite is really needed at all. "Some years ago, when concern about formation of nitro compounds from nitrite and amines was not widespread, a reporter called several meat processors and asked why nitrite was used in meat curing. The comments he received were that nitrite was used for color and taste, but there was no mention of preservation or preventing botulism. The latter seems to have been discovered as a reason for using nitrite only recently."

In a pamphlet, "Sidelights of Sausage," put out by the American Meat Institute, the industry states: "nitrite and nitrate help in developing appetizing meat color." There is no mention of nitrites as a preservative for safety. An AMI spokesman called the statement "incomplete."

For his part, Lijinsky, who has been working on cancer research for 12 years, doesn't really believe that a safe level of nitrites exists. So he has chosen not to eat foods which contain them.

Thus, it was something of a shock at a recent lunch with a reporter in Washington, to find several pieces of ham in what the waiter had assured him was a cheese omelette. He carefully pushed them aside.

While he does not "dictate" to his family on the subject of processed meats, none is served in his home.

None is served to the family cat, either, whose diet consists of "canned food without nitrite."

Bologna, Nitrite, and Your Health

Consumer Reports (*May 1976*)

Nitrate has served as a food preservative since ancient times. It was used in the deserts of Asia before Homer's day, and Romans added it to a brine to cure meat. Not until this century, however, did chemists discover that the active agent wasn't nitrate itself, but *nitrite*—a reaction product of nitrate converted by bacterial action. More recently, scientists also discovered that nitrite may pose a serious threat to health.

Nitrate and nitrite are currently added to more than 12 billion pounds of food annually in the United States, usually in the form of sodium nitrate or sodium nitrite. They are used in smoked fish and in most cured meats, including bologna, salami, pepperoni, bacon, frankfurters, corned beef, pastrami, canned ham, and a variety of sausages.

Whether converted from nitrate or added directly, nitrite helps to impart a characteristic cured flavor and color to the food. It also inhibits the growth of some harmful bacteria, notably the type responsible for the deadly toxin that causes botulism.

But a heavy dose of nitrite is poisonous. About five grams of sodium nitrite can kill an adult, and as little as half a gram can make an adult acutely ill. The U.S. Department of Agriculture (USDA) currently permits a limit of 200 parts per million of sodium nitrite in food. At that level, a person would have to eat about 5½ pounds of bologna or 50 frankfurters at a time to get half a gram of sodium nitrite. Accordingly, normal portions of bologna or other cured meats are immediately harmful only when large amounts of nitrite are added to food by mistake, although some individuals who are sensitive to nitrite may experience severe headaches from eating normally processed cured foods.

Potentially much more serious—and the subject of considerable debate—is a suspected link between nitrite and cancer. Nitrite itself is not carcinogenic. But under certain circumstances, nitrite can combine with substances called amines, which are found in food, in tobacco smoke, in some common drugs, and in the human body. The combination of nitrite and amines forms nitrosamines, a group of substances that have produced malignant tumors in a wide variety of test animals.

As yet, there is no direct evidence that nitrosamines cause cancer in humans. Nor is there any proof that ingesting nitrites will produce nitrosamines in the human body. And some scientists believe that the stomach of a healthy human may inhibit nitrosamine formation.

But wide gaps still exist in current knowledge of digestive processes, and what may apply to a healthy person may not hold true for a sick one. Further, nitrosamines can develop in food itself. Trace quantities have already been detected in bologna, frankfurters, bacon, and other cured products. Over the last year, for example, scientists in Canada's Health Protection Branch found nitrosamines in seven out of 24 bologna samples tested. The amounts detected ranged from 14 to 60 parts per billion. Fried bacon shows trace amounts of nitrosamines fairly consistently. According to the USDA, the amounts detected most recently tend to range from about 10 to 20 parts per billion.

The trace amounts of nitrosamines identified in food are far lower than the levels that have produced tumors in animals. Those levels range upward from a minimum of 2000 parts per billion. However, if it is true that nitrosamines *can* induce cancer in humans, even small amounts may be unsafe.

In short, the question of whether nitrite is a significant hazard to the public is still unresolved. And there are respected scientists arguing on either side of the issue. Sitting resolutely on the fence, meanwhile, is the USDA—the Federal agency that's supposed to protect consumers in this matter.

The USDA has recently proposed new limits on the amount of nitrite to be permitted in various cured meats. In some respects, the limits are significantly lower than existing ones, which have not changed since 1925. But the new proposed standards are essentially similar to what industry is already practicing in 1976. So any gain in safety is likely to be minimal.

According to the USDA, the use of nitrite must be retained to protect the public against botulism poisoning. But the use of nitrite isn't the only way to prevent botulism; it's merely the easiest way to do it without reducing the shelf life or altering the characteristic flavor or texture of cured foods somewhat. Bologna without nitrite can be made just as safe from botulism as bologna with nitrite. Some specialized food stores already have nitrite-free products on the shelves. Such products may be labeled with an expiration date and instructions for freezing or refrigerating.

In 1972 the National Research Council urged public agencies and industry to find substitutes for nitrate and nitrite in foods. Thus far, the main response of the USDA and industry has been to explore ways of retaining the additives in lower amounts. We believe the suspicions about nitrate and nitrite are sufficiently serious for the USDA to set a target date for banning both of those additives from the food supply.

QUESTIONS

1. Rate each of these reports on clarity. Which are easiest to understand, and which are the most difficult? Which make the most specific claims, and which stick to more abstract or ambiguous statements?

2. Some of these writers make use of the jargon of cancer research. Look up the meanings of these words:

in vivo	*carcinogen*	*mutagenic*
in vitro	*sarcoma*	*correlation*
metabolic	*ingest*	*lesion*
toxicity	*reactant*	

Now find places in the reports where these words are used. Are they necessary for their particular meaning, or could a simpler word have been substituted?

3. Although each of these reports seems to be primarily concerned with the subject matter, some are obviously written for different audiences than others. Identify as closely as possible the intended audience for each report. Explain how you can tell.

4. Identify the information that all the reports, or nearly all, agree upon. For instance, do they all agree that nitrites pose a "potential hazard"? Discuss the difference between a "hazard" and a "potential hazard."

5. Identify as specifically as possible the areas in which the writers disagree. Does the disagreement seem to stem mostly from facts, or does it stem from differing values that the writers hold?

6. What persons officially decide whether cured meat sold in the United States may contain nitrites, and in what amounts? Which writers provide this information?

7. Consider the two newspaper reports. One of them is "signed"—that is, the reporter's name is given. In general, what is the difference between a signed article and an unsigned one? Is the Burros story different in its approach and content from the other one?

8. Wolff and Wasserman use a great many verbs in the passive voice. Locate several of these and try to change the sentence so that the verb is active. What information do you need in order to do this?

9. Do any of the reports seem to be persuasive as well as informative? Do any of them approach the audience through their emotions as well as through their reason? Are any of them entirely without persuasion?

10. Consider each of the following topics for a research paper:

> Do Nitrites Cause Cancer?
> Should Nitrites Be Banned?
> A Case History in Consumer Politics
> How Our Government Protects Us
> A Biography of William Lijinsky
> Bias in Reporting
> The Role of the Department of Agriculture in Consumer Protection

Which of these subjects would you be qualified to write on after reading the sources here? Which of these titles suggest that the paper will be partly persuasive? Choose one of these topics, or a better one, and make a list of further sources that you would consult in order to write the paper.

Variations on a Single Word: Equality

The Declaration of Independence (1776)

When in the Course of human events, it becomes necessary for one people to dissolve the political bands which have connected them with another, and to assume among the Powers of the earth, the separate and equal station to which the Laws of Nature and of Nature's God entitle them, a decent respect to the opinions of mankind requires that they should declare the causes which impel them to the separation.

We hold these truths to be self-evident, that all men are created equal, that they are endowed by their Creator with certain unalienable Rights, that among these are Life, Liberty and the pursuit of Happiness.

The Fourteenth Amendment (1868)

SEC. 1. All persons born or naturalized in the United States, and subject to the jurisdiction thereof, are citizens of the United States and of the State wherein they reside. No State shall make or enforce any law which shall abridge the privileges or immunities of citizens of the United States; nor shall any State deprive any person of life, liberty, or property, without due process of law; nor deny to any person within its jurisdiction the equal protection of the laws.

The Seneca Falls Declaration of Sentiments and Resolutions (1848)

Most of the American women who joined abolitionist movements before the Civil War believed that they were working for the rights of women as well as blacks. One of the most powerful expressions of what these women wanted came from a convention of feminists, headed by Elizabeth Cady Stanton and Lucretia Mott, held in Seneca Falls, New York in 1848. When the Fourteenth Amendment finally passed, it did not extend its guarantee of "equal protection of the laws" to women, and yet these writers included so much more than law in their understanding of what it would mean to be an "equal" citizen.

1. Declaration of Sentiments

When, in the course of human events, it becomes necessary for one portion of the family of man to assume among the people of the earth a position different from that which they have hitherto occupied, but one to which the laws of nature and of nature's God entitle them, a decent respect to the opinions of mankind requires that they should declare the causes that impel them to such a course.

We hold these truths to be self-evident: that all men and women are created equal; that they are endowed by their Creator with certain inalienable rights; that among these are life, liberty, and the pursuit of happiness; that to secure these rights governments are instituted, deriving their just powers from the consent of the governed. Whenever any form of government becomes destructive of these ends, it is the right of those who suffer from it to refuse allegiance to it, and to insist upon the institution of a new government, laying its foundation on such principles, and organizing its powers in such form, as to them shall seem most likely to effect their safety and happiness. Prudence, indeed, will dictate that governments long established should not be changed for light and transient causes; and accordingly all experience hath shown that mankind are more disposed to suffer while evils are sufferable, than to right themselves by abolishing the forms to which they are accustomed. But when a long train of abuses and usurpations, pursuing invariably the same object, evinces a design to reduce them under absolute despotism, it is their duty to throw off such government, and to provide new guards for their future security. Such has been the patient sufferance of the women under this government, and such is now the necessity which constrains them to demand the equal station to which they are entitled.

The history of mankind is a history of repeated injuries and usurpations on the part of man toward woman, having in direct object the establishment of an absolute tyranny over her. To prove this, let facts be submitted to a candid world.

He has never permitted her to exercise her inalienable right to the elective franchise.

He has compelled her to submit to laws, in the formation of which she has no voice.

He has withheld from her rights which are given to the most ignorant and degraded men—both natives and foreigners.

Having deprived her of this first right of a citizen, the elective franchise, thereby leaving her without representation in the halls of legislation, he has oppressed her on all sides.

He has made her, if married, in the eye of the law, civilly dead.

He has taken from her all right in property, even to the wages she earns.

He has made her, morally, an irresponsible being, as she can commit many crimes with impunity, provided they be done in the presence of her husband. In the covenant of marriage, she is compelled to promise obedience to her husband, he becoming, to all intents and purposes, her master—the law giving him power to deprive her of her liberty, and to administer chastisement.

He has so framed the laws of divorce, as to what shall be the proper causes, and in case of separation, to whom the guardianship of the children shall be given, as to be wholly regardless of the happiness of women—the law, in all cases, going upon a false supposition of the supremacy of man, and giving all power into his hands.

After depriving her of all rights as a married woman, if single, and the owner of property, he has taxed her to support a government which recognizes her only when her property can be made profitable to it.

He has monopolized nearly all the profitable employments, and from those she is permitted to follow, she receives but a scanty remuneration. He closes against her all the avenues to wealth and distinction which he considers most honorable to himself. As a teacher of theology, medicine, or law, she is not known.

He has denied her the facilities for obtaining a thorough education, all colleges being closed against her.

He allows her in Church, as well as State, but a subordinate position, claiming Apostolic authority for her exclusion from the ministry, and, with some exceptions, from any public participation in the affairs of the Church.

He has created a false public sentiment by giving to the world a different code of morals for men and women, by which moral delinquencies which exclude women from society, are not only tolerated, but deemed of little account in man.

He has usurped the prerogative of Jehovah himself, claiming it as his right to assign for her a sphere of action, when that belongs to her conscience and to her God.

He has endeavored, in every way that he could, to destroy her confidence in her own powers, to lessen her self-respect and to make her willing to lead a dependent and abject life.

Now, in view of this entire disfranchisement of one-half the people of this country, their social and religious degradation—in view of the unjust laws above mentioned, and because women do feel themselves aggrieved, oppressed, and fraudulently deprived of their most sacred rights, we insist that they have immediate admission to all the rights and privileges which belong to them as citizens of the United States.

Booker T. Washington: Atlanta Exposition Address (1895)

Booker T. Washington was a conservative black leader who emphasized the need for self-improvement through vocational training in the decades after the Civil War. Most of his views are either treated with scorn by contemporary civil rights leaders or excused as being politically necessary for his time. Judging by the passage below, especially by his interpretation of "equal and exact justice," why do you suppose Washington is so harshly judged?

I do not believe that any state should make a law that permits an ignorant and poverty-stricken white man to vote, and prevents a black man in the same condition from voting. Such a law is not only unjust, but it will react, as all unjust laws do, in time; for the effect of such a law is to encourage the Negro to secure education and property, and at the same time it encourages the white man to remain in ignorance and poverty. I believe that in time, through the operation of intelligence and friendly race relations, all cheating at the ballot-box in the South will cease. It will become apparent that the white man who begins by cheating a Negro out of his ballot soon learns to cheat a white man out of his, and that the man who does this ends his career of dishonesty by the theft of property or by some equally serious crime. In my opinion, the time will come when the South will encourage all of its citizens to vote. It will see that it pays better, from every standpoint, to have healthy, vigorous life than to have that political stagnation which always results when one-half of the population has no share and no interest in the Government.

As a rule, I believe in universal, free suffrage, but I believe that in the South we are confronted with peculiar conditions that justify the protection of the ballot in many of the states, for a while at least, either by an educational test, a property test, or by both combined; but whatever tests are required, they should be made to apply with equal and exact justice to both races.

Supreme Court: Plessy v. Ferguson (1896)

Plessy v. Ferguson is the title of a famous Supreme Court case of 1896 in which the Court interpreted the meaning of the Fourteenth Amendment. The case dealt specifically with public transportation. The Court decided that state laws could establish separate railroad cars for blacks and whites, as long as the cars themselves were equal, or similar. This decision implied that segregation was legal in all public places.

We consider the underlying fallacy of the plaintiff's argument to consist in the assumption that the enforced separation of the two races stamps the colored race with a badge of inferiority. If this be so, it is not by reason of anything found in the act, but solely because the colored race chooses to put that construction upon it. The argument necessarily assumes that if, as has been more than once the case, and is not unlikely to be so again, the colored race should become the dominant power in the state legislature, and should enact a law in precisely similar terms, it would thereby relegate the white race to an inferior position. We imagine that the white race, at least, would not acquiesce in this assumption. The argument also assumes that social prejudice may be overcome by legislation, and that equal rights cannot be secured to the Negro except by an enforced commingling of the two races. We cannot accept this proposition. If the two races are to meet on terms of social equality, it must be the result of natural affinities, a mutual appreciation of each other's merits and a voluntary consent of individuals.

Supreme Court: Brown v. Board of Education (1954)

In Brown v. Board of Education of Topeka (1954), the Supreme Court disagreed with the Court's interpretation of "equal protection" in Plessy v. Ferguson and overturned that decision. A man named Oliver Brown, with other black parents, had tried to enroll his child in a neighborhood elementary school that accepted only white students. The Supreme Court considered several similar cases at once and decided that separate schools are "inherently unequal." The passage below comes from the decision written by Chief Justice Earl Warren.

In each of the cases, minors of the Negro race, through their legal representatives, seek the aid of the courts in obtaining admission to the public schools of their community on a nonsegregated basis. In each instance, they have been denied admission to schools attended by white children under laws requiring or permitting segregation according to race. This segregation was alleged to deprive the plaintiffs of the equal protection of the laws under the Fourteenth Amendment. In each of the cases other than the Delaware case, a three-judge federal district court denied relief to the plaintiffs on the so-called "separate but equal" doctrine announced by this Court in Plessy v. Ferguson, 163 U.S. 537. Under that doctrine, equality of treatment is accorded when the races are provided substantially equal facilities, even though these facilities be separate. In the Delaware case, the Supreme Court of Delaware adhered to that doctrine, but ordered that the plaintiffs be admitted to the white schools because of their superiority to the Negro schools.

The plaintiffs contend that segregated public schools are not "equal" and cannot be made "equal," and that hence they are deprived of the equal protection of the laws. Because of the obvious importance of the question presented, the Court took jurisdiction. . . .

Today, education is perhaps the most important function of state and local governments. Compulsory school attendance laws and the great expenditures for education both demonstrate our recognition of the importance of education to our democratic society. It is required in the performance of our most basic public responsibilities, even service in the armed forces. It is the very foundation of good citizenship. Today it is a principal instrument in awakening the child to cultural values, in preparing him for later professional training, and in helping him to adjust normally to his environment. In these days, it is doubtful that any child may reasonably be expected to succeed in life if he is denied the opportunity of an education. Such an opportunity, where the state has undertaken to provide it, is a right which must be made available to all on equal terms.

We come then to the question presented: Does segregation of children in public schools solely on the basis of race, even though the physical facilities and other "tangible" factors may be equal, deprive the children of the minority group of equal educational opportunities? We believe that it does.

In Sweatt v. Painter, supra [339 U.S. 629, 70 S.Ct. 850], in finding that a segregated law school for Negroes could not provide them equal educational opportunities, this Court relied in large part on "those qualities which are incapable of objective measurement but which make for greatness in a law school." In McLaurin v. Oklahoma State Regents, supr [339 U.S. 637, 70 S.Ct. 853], the Court, in requiring that a Negro admitted to a white graduate school be treated like all other students, again resorted to intangible considerations: ". . . his ability to study, to engage in discussions and exchange views with other students, and, in general, to learn his profession." Such considerations apply with added force to children in grade and high schools. To separate them from others of similar age and qualifications solely because of their race generates a feeling of inferiority as to their status in the community that may affect their hearts and minds in a way unlikely ever to be undone. . . .

We conclude that in the field of public education the doctrine of "separate but equal" has no place. Separate educational facilities are inherently unequal. Therefore, we hold that the plaintiffs and others similarly situated for whom the actions have been brought are, by reason of the segregation complained of, deprived of the equal protection of the laws guaranteed by the Fourteenth Amendment. This deposition makes unnecessary any discussion whether such segregation also violates the Due Process Clause of the Fourteenth Amendment.

Hubert Humphrey: *Beyond Civil Rights* (1968)

The passage below, which continues the debate over what it means to be "equal," comes from a book written by Democratic leader Hubert Humphrey during his presidential campaign in 1968.

There is still this separate country of poverty, a shrinking yet still large fraction of the American population (more numerous, in fact, than most of the nations on the globe), that is more or less shut out of the material benefits and opportunities of American democracy. One-third are Negro, barred from full participation both by a heritage of poverty and by racial discrimination.

The first priority, in this "next and more profound stage" of the equal rights movement, is to bring forward into American society these people who have been left behind for so long a time.

I can't give the details of policy proposals here; there isn't space, and this book isn't the place. But I can suggest a guideline or two.

A program for equality must now become a program for *participation*.

It must be a deliberate, sensitive, planned program to allow people to come in—to help them attain the ability to walk through those gates of opportunity.

It must be a program not of the federal government alone, but also of states and cities; not of government alone, but of the private sector and voluntary associations, too, working together—"creative federalism."

It must be a program not of handouts or of charity, but of opening new opportunities for self-help and dignity.

It must enable citizens to participate in politics, in a broad range of social institutions, and above all—in the American economy.

From Hubert H. Humphrey, *Beyond Civil Rights: A New Day of Equality* (New York: Random House, 1968).

QUESTIONS

1. Explain as specifically as you can what *equal* or *equality* means to each writer.

2. Which writers would probably agree on a wide variety of issues, and which ones would you expect to have strong disagreements?

3. Do you think that the income tax imposes an equal burden on all citizens? Explain how an answer to that question might depend on the meaning of *equal*.

4. The women who wrote the "Declaration of Sentiments" at Seneca Falls in 1848 were also concerned with the meaning of another word: *men*. Find examples of the use of this word in books, newspapers, and magazines and try to decide whether it usually includes women or usually does not. Can you find any examples which, like the Declaration of Independence, are ambiguous?

5. Make an argument showing that what Humphrey calls a "program for equality" could just as well be called a "program for special favors." Then try to make an answer to your own argument.

6. Explain how each of these writers might interpret the phrase *equal educational opportunity.*

7. Bring to class examples of other words that mean different things to different people or at different times.

PART II

Introduction

Part I of this book introduced three different aspects of written composition: the voice, the audience, and the content. Part II illustrates some of the variety of messages that result when writers start with the same general subject but create different voices, make different assumptions about their audiences, and select different information.

Each chapter of part II starts with a short introduction outlining a general subject that might be a writing assignment. Here are the "assignments":

1. Make a careful observation of some natural object or scene, and write a description of it.
2. Do some research on the subject of cigarette smoking, and make a report.
3. State your views on the institution of marriage.
4. Explore the conflict between TV broadcasting and the First Amendment. Try to arrive at a solution.
5. Write a paper on a poem by Robert Frost.
6. Write an essay on what you think are the most important criteria for making judgments about language.

The professional writers whose essays follow started with some such general idea or purpose. But as you will see, these subjects leave plenty of latitude. There is certainly no right answer or perfect paper. Writers choose different aspects of their subjects and use different tones of voice. Some of them want to persuade us, and others don't seem to care about us. Some of the writings are interesting, some are boring, some are logical, some are confused. You might want to try your hand at these assignments before you look at the examples offered in the book. Or you might study the selections first, to get ideas and to think about what makes a piece of writing a success.

The questions at the end of each chapter ask about the selections' voices, audiences, and contents. Your job is to get the whole message from each selection.

4

Looking at Nature

What do you see when you go outdoors? That depends not only on *where* you are but on *who* you are and *to whom* you're talking. We see what is important to us, and we describe our world in relation to our own purposes and interests and those of our audience.

"Narcissus" Taylor's Encyclopedia of Gardening

NARCISSUS (nar-sis' sus). Important, chiefly hardy, bulbous plants of the family Amaryllidaceae, comprising about 40 species, most of them European, very widely grown for ornament or fragrance, and including such well-known plants as the daffodil, jonquil, paper-white, the Chinese sacred lily, and the poet's narcissus. All bear bulbs. Leaves generally rush-like or more or less terete in cross-section in the jonquil and its relatives, but flat or nearly so in the common daffodil, basal in all sorts, and usually about the length of the flowering stalk. Flowers prevailingly white or yellow, often nodding. Calyx and corolla not separable as such, but modified in two ways: (1) The flower having a central crown (corona) which is long and tubular (in the trumpet narcissus or daffodil); or (2) the central crown (corona) reduced to a shallow, ring-like cup (as in the jonquil and poet's narcissus). Outside of this central corolla-like organ are the six segments which comprise the petals and sepals. In the group with a long tubular corona there is the typical hose-in-hose effect of one flower growing within another. Stamens 6, usually hidden in the crown. Fruit a 3-lobed, many-seeded capsule. The species have been much hybridized so that those below are somewhat uncertain as to exact botanical identity, although they represent the chief sorts in cult. (*Narcissus* is possibly named for the mythological youth so fond of his own reflection that after long gazing at it he was changed into the flower.) They are sometimes called Lent lilies.

To Daffodils

Robert Herrick

Fair Daffodils, we weep to see
    You haste away so soon:
As yet the early-rising Sun
    Has not attain'd his noon.
        Stay, stay,
    Until the hasting day
        Has run
    But to the even-song;
And, having pray'd together, we
    Will go with you along.

We have short time to stay, as you,
    We have as short a Spring;
As quick a growth to meet decay
    As you, or any thing.
        We die,
    As your hours do, and dry
        Away
    Like to the Summer's rain;
Or as the pearls of morning's dew
    Ne'er to be found again.

The Daffodils

William Wordsworth

I wander'd lonely as a cloud
That floats on high o'er vales and hills,
When all at once I saw a crowd,
A host of golden daffodils,
Beside the lake, beneath the trees,
Fluttering and dancing in the breeze.

Continuous as the stars that shine
And twinkle on the milky way,
They stretch'd in never-ending line
Along the margin of a bay:
Ten thousand saw I at a glance
Tossing their heads in sprightly dance.

The waves beside them danced, but they
Out-did the sparkling waves in glee:—
A Poet could not but be gay
In such a jocund company!
I gazed—and gazed—but little thought
What wealth the show to me had brought,

For oft, when on my couch I lie
In vacant or in pensive mood,
They flash upon that inward eye
Which is the bliss of solitude;
And then my heart with pleasure fills,
And dances with the daffodils.

"Apparently With No Surprise"   Emily Dickinson

Apparently with no surprise
To any happy Flower
The Frost beheads it at its play—
In accidental power—
The blonde Assassin passes on—
The Sun proceeds unmoved
To measure off another Day
For an Approving God.

Pied Beauty   Gerard Manley Hopkins

Glory be to God for dappled things—
  For skies of couple-colour as a brinded cow;
    For rose-moles all in stipple upon trout that swim;

Fresh-firecoal chestnut-falls; finches' wings;
  Landscape plotted and pieced—fold, fallow, and plough;
    And áll trádes, their gear and tackle and trim.

All things counter, original, spare, strange;
  Whatever is fickle, freckled (who knows how?)
    With swift, slow; sweet, sour; adazzle, dim;
He fathers-forth whose beauty is past change:
                    Praise him.

Looking Down on Improved Property

or *An Airplane View of Man and Land*

May Theilgaard Watts

The two men with briefcases, waiting beside me at Gate 5, were bragging to each other, in a refined way, about their evergreens.

The man with the hand-painted tie, who had left the hose running on his best specimens and hoped his wife would remember to move it, owned an even fifty of them—seventy-five, if you counted the two-year-old transplants he was raising in the nursery row.

The man with the long cigarette holder had only twenty-six, but they were big and dense, having been kept on a rigid pruning schedule; and they included two specimens of Carolina hemlock, and two gold-tipped, ball-shaped arborvitae. It sounded as if, on a quality basis, or a cubic-foot basis, or a tonsorial basis, he might be ahead.

Eventually, perhaps, Dun and Bradstreet may list a man's evergreen status. As a criterion of success, it seems to be finding popular acceptance, especially in landscapes from which Nature long ago eliminated the evergreen.

The conversation had started with an appraisal of the plantings around that Chicago airport, where the inevitable competition was evident, between man's choice of plant material and Nature's choice. About man's choice there was no question. It was evergreens and tailored lawn. But Nature had other ideas, raggedly informal—such ideas as the native pioneers, cottonwood and box-elder; or the foreign camp followers, ailanthus trees and dandelions.

How long would it be, I wondered, before that seedling cottonwood would be discovered by the authorities, trespassing there between the Pfitzer junipers and the arborvitaé; or that vigorous ailanthus sapling that had pre-empted the angle in the concrete wall as its universally established domain.

Then a woman with an orchid breasted up to the fence just beyond the two conifer-proprietors.

The orchid's dramatic lower petal was extended with a receptive gesture. Flowers certainly offer more decorative landing places than airlines do, I thought, as I looked at that extraordinary threshold that the orchid holds out to insects.

That particular orchid offered a landing place like sculptured purple marble inlaid with lines of gold that converged at the luminous portal to the business section of the flower. But the glamorous structure was not functioning, except as a badge of solvency, like the briefcasers' evergreens.

As I tore my eyes away from the orchid, I saw yet another landing place, a lowly one. There was a dandelion blooming in a crack at the edge of the cement runway. It appeared to be functioning; at least, a fly was on it, apparently drinking. Whether or not he was paying for his drink by delivering pollen, I could not see, and November was hardly the time for maturing seeds, anyhow.

That landing place was as different from the orchid's pastel colored one as the entrance to Coney Island is different from a vaulted portal with a purple wedding carpet laid before it—and as much more likely to lead to vigorous, abundant progeny.

The dandelion was holding its nectar in shallow goblets, not too deep for the tongues of numerous insects. Its presence was advertised by a color visible to the partially color-blind bee, a color conspicuous in the sunlight. Its form was as economical of expenditure for display as the orchid's form was spendthrift. The dandelion was composed of many flowers, a hundred or more, packed tightly into a head, and pooling their expenditure on stem and petal material.

And each of these yellow flowers makes only one seed, while the orchid (if its elaborately specialized pollination mechanism has an opportunity for functioning) makes thousands and thousands of seeds. Here the tables are turned—now the orchid, so spendthrift of advertising and allure, proves niggardly in its seed-packaging. Each little embryo plant starts out with such a meager endowment of food that its chances for survival are slight. But the dandelion's embryo is provisioned with a supply of food adequate to give it a bounding start in life.

The lasting qualities of these two landing places speak, too, of their individual problems. The orchid, poised on a branch in a steamy atmosphere, needs to last a long time while it awaits the languid, fluttering approach of the pollinating visitor that may not come for many days. But the dandelion, pioneering in earth's wounds, has many a bustling visitor hurtling in to drink. It requires no durable substance. No wonder the orchid rides the perfumed pearl-gray lapel and mink, while the dandelion gets the dust of the runway blown across its face.

Then the DC3 was ready. It lifted us, orchid, briefcases, and all, up over backyards and alleys that are the fouled nests of humans, and over the unyielding geometry of the industrial districts, where Nature's only opportunity for shaping curves is the smoke.

From Chicago to Dayton, we looked down on a battle, the battle between man's passion for square corners and Nature's penchant for curves.

Across one stretch of country the grid of lines was so accurate, the lines so straight, that I thought that the terrain down there must be as flat as a billiard table, until I noticed that the shadow of our plane was riding humps down there.

It was not only the roads that made squares. The rivets on the wing of the plane were a geometric pattern riding over that other geometric pattern down below—a pattern made of fields, and fences, corn rows, wood lots, orchard rows, cemetery plots, and lines of plowing and mowing and irrigation, and sidewalks and driveways of city subdivisions—so uniform that they looked like products of a punch press.

Under this net, Nature was squirming and resisting.

She was scrawling a meandering stream zigzag across the ritual of straight lines. And where a farmer had turned his back for a moment, she was rubbing a thumb across and blurring the precision of impeccable fence rows with a welter of hawthorns, wild plums, and wild roses. It was easy to identify the hawthorns from the DC3. There is no mistaking the gray foam of them. And the rest of the fraternity inevitably comes along when the hawthorn invades the fence row.

In one place the farmer's fence had been shifted slightly by an undermining gully.

It could be seen, from this height, that Nature was tampering even with the over-all pattern of man's wheat and rye fields, by overlaying the flat squares with a dappled marbling that was sheet erosion.

The pattern of the square is a rare one in living things. Flowers are most often five-parted, less often three-parted, and seldom four-parted. It is true, there are some four-parted ones: the mustards, poppies, and olives are in fours; and the mints have square stems, as do the blue ash and usually the euonymus. But even these squares are softened by flowing contours.

The spiral appears over and over again: in the center of a sunflower head; in the outward corkscrewing of a twig; in the downward thrust of a root tip; in the ascent of a vine. The circle and the five-pointed star are often repeated, the triangle, too. But not the square.

Just when it seemed as if man's geometry was everywhere an alien temporary mold that had nothing in common with Nature's lines, just then we noticed paths, footpaths that crossed fields near the edge of town, or made a short cut to a country school or a crossroads community.

These little paths ambled and sauntered. They swung out into curves for no apparent reason. But there must have been a rise of ground, or a depression at each curve, not visible from the air.

Cow paths, too, followed the contour.

Then we saw a country road, dark-colored, with edges that were blurred probably by elderberry, blackberry, bittersweet. It ambled and

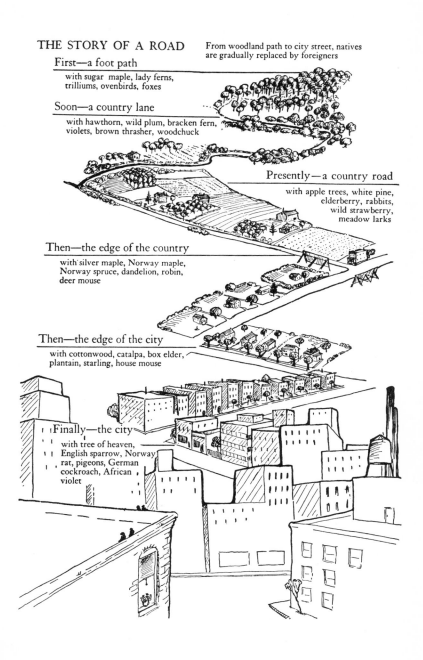

THE STORY OF A ROAD

From woodland path to city street, natives are gradually replaced by foreigners

First—a foot path

with sugar maple, lady ferns, trilliums, ovenbirds, foxes

Soon—a country lane

with hawthorn, wild plum, bracken fern, violets, brown thrasher, woodchuck

Presently—a country road

with apple trees, white pine, elderberry, rabbits, wild strawberry, meadow larks

Then—the edge of the country

with silver maple, Norway maple, Norway spruce, dandelion, robin, deer mouse

Then—the edge of the city

with cottonwood, catalpa, box elder, plantain, starling, house mouse

Finally—the city

with tree of heaven, English sparrow, Norway rat, pigeons, German cockroach, African violet curved like the little paths. It wandered through a small town, and then, abruptly, it straightened with a jerk, and cut like a gash across a large town. As it entered the outskirts of the large town, it passed close to an area marked by a snarl of exaggeratedly curveting roads and sidewalks, with dark masses of evergreens. That must have been Suburbia.

It occurred to me that there, in the life story of a road, just as in the story of a filling lake, or the story of a dune, or a bog, the vertical and the horizontal successions would be the same. A barefoot boy might follow a deer path through the woods, among lady ferns, trilliums, sugar maples; he might continue on as the path became wider, with a plank laid down here and there; he might find himself presently on a dirt road; and then he might be walking on a cement sidewalk beside a paved street; and finally he might find that the sidewalk ran close beside the pavement on the one side and beside the front of a building on the other, while fireplugs and newsstands grew where lady ferns had been. That would be the "horizontal succession." But, if he had the time, he could stand perfectly still on the deer path, and simply wait until the same changes came to the path. It might take a long time. It might all happen within a lifetime, but if the deer path lay near a growing town the changes would come eventually. That would be the "vertical succession."

There are aspects of the land that are revealed to the air traveler, though they are seldom seen otherwise.

The shame of many a farmer, for example, is laid bare. Gullies, far from the public road, and heretofore hidden from the passer-by, are all too apparent from the air. It will be interesting to see whether the spotlight of public scrutiny will have an effect on these indecent scrawls.

Another thing revealed from the air was bee-hives, long white rows of them. They looked like sugar cubes along the end of an orchard in one place, ambling beside a brook in another, and strung out along the edge of an open field in another.

Then we began to notice differences in the occasional stretches of woods beneath us. There were many woodlands that were transparent right down to the ground. Those were evidently the ones that had been grazed, or perhaps burned over each spring. Probably both, because the same kind of farmer that allows his woods to be grazed is likely to burn them over too.

There were woods that were not grazed. We could not look down through those—even though November had stripped all but the white oaks of their leaves. It was easy to understand that raindrops, dropping from our viewpoint and passing through that layered vegetation, would be broken and broken again, until they sank, captured, into the leaf mold. But on the grazed forest, where seedlings and shrubs and saplings had been eliminated, raindrops would hammer down with a gouging force; the few raspberries and thistles would not break their force enough to matter.

Those grazed forests would be gone, soon, unable to reproduce themselves in the face of the cows.

We looked down on many planted wood lots. Almost all of them were as accurately-squared lots as the rest of the scenery. I wondered how many of those farmers knew about the interesting piece of research on bird population that had been done by the Academy of Sciences in Chicago. If they knew about the evidence that bird population varies directly as the amount of edge on a forest, they would surely feel inclined to work some scallops, bays, peninsulas, onto the edges of those wood lots, and double their bird population.

We landed at South Bend. The evergreens were neat. So was the grass. The dandelions, cottonwood seedlings, and an ailanthus tree were doing their bit toward blurring the man-made straight edges.

At Fort Wayne, Indiana, we made another landing. The evergreens, grass, dandelions, and cottonwoods were there, too—and a few ungainly box-elders.

We left the plane at Dayton, and walked over to the bus, past dandelions, grass, clipped evergreens, and an invading ailanthus tree.

BIBLIOGRAPHICAL NOTES

Nesting Birds and the Vegetation Substrata by William J. Beecher. Chicago Ornithological Society, Chicago, 1942.
Hedgerows by Nicholas Drahos, *Cornell Rural School Leaflet* **40** (Fall, 1946), Number 2.
Pleasant Valley by Louis Bromfield. Harper, New York, 1945.
Bees: Their Vision, Chemical Senses, and Language by Karl von Frisch. Cornell University Press, Ithaca, New York, 1950.
"A Comparison of Reproductive Potential in Two Rat Populations" by David E. Davis. *Ecology* **32** (July, 1951), 469-475.
Airways of America by A. K. Lobeck. The Geographical Press, Columbia University, New York, 1933.

The Journals of Lewis and Clark

Tuesday July 16th 1805.

Drewyer killed a buffaloe this morning near the river and we halted and breakfasted on it. here for the first time I ate of the small guts of the buffaloe cooked over a blazing fire in the Indian stile without any preperation of washing or other clensing and found them very good. After breakfast I determined to leave Capt. C. and party, and go on to the point where

From Bernard DeVoto (ed.), *The Journals of Lewis and Clark* (Boston: Houghton Mifflin Company, 1953).

the river enters the Rocky Mountains and make the necessary observations against their arrival; accordingly I set out with the two invalleds Potts and LaPage and Drewyer.

July 16th Tuesday 1805 [Clark]

a fair morning after a verry cold night, heavy dew,   dispatched one man back for an ax left a fiew miles below, and Set out early   passed about 40 Small Camps, which appeared to be abandoend about 10 or 12 days,   Suppose they were Snake Indians,   a fiew miles above I Saw the poles Standing in their position of a verry large lodge of 60 feet Diameter, & the appearance of a number of Leather Lodges about,   this Sign was old & appeared to have been last fall   great number of buffalow   the river is not So wide as below from 100 to 150 yards wide & Deep Crouded with Islands & Crooked   Some scattering timber on its edge Such as Cotton wood Cotton willow, willow and box elder, the S[h]rubs are arrow wo[o]d red wood, Choke cherry, red berries, Goose beries, Sarvis buries, red & Yellow Currents a Sp[e]cie of Shomake &c.

I camped on the head of a Small Island near the Stard. Shore at the Rockey Mountains   this Range of mountains appears to run NW & SE and is about 800 feet higher than the Water in the river faced with a hard black rock   the current of the River from the Medison river to the Mountain is gentle, bottoms low and extensive, and its General Course is S. 10° W. about 30 miles on a direct line.

July 17th Wednesday 1805

Set out early this morning and crossed the rapid at the Island cald. pine rapid with Some dificuelty,   at this rapid I came up with Capt. Lewis & partey   took a Medn. altitude & we took Some Luner Observations &c. and proceeded on,   the emence high Precipces oblige all the party to pass & repass the river from one point to another   the river confined in maney places in a verry narrow chanel from 70 to 120 yards wide bottoms narrow without timber and maney places the Mountain[s] approach on both Sides,   The river crooked bottoms narrow, Clifts high and Steep,   I assended a Spur of the Mountain, which I found to be highe & dificuelt of axcess, Containing Pitch Pine & Covered with grass   Scercely any game to be seen. The yellow Current now ripe also the fussey [fuzzy] red Choke Cheries getting ripe. Purple Current[s] are also ripe. Saw Several Ibix or mountain rams to day

Walden

Now that the cars are gone by and all the restless world with them, and the fishes in the pond no longer feel their rumbling, I am more alone than ever. For the rest of the long afternoon, perhaps, my meditations are interrupted only by the faint rattle of a carriage or team along the distant highway.

Sometimes, on Sundays, I heard the bells, the Lincoln, Acton, Bedford, or Concord bell, when the wind was favorable, a faint, sweet, and, as it were, natural melody, worth importing into the wilderness. At a sufficient distance over the woods this sound acquires a certain vibratory hum, as if the pine needles in the horizon were the strings of a harp which it swept. All sound heard at the greatest possible distance produces one and the same effect, a vibration of the universal lyre, just as the intervening atmosphere makes a distant ridge of earth interesting to our eyes by the azure tint it imparts to it. There came to me in this case a melody which the air had strained, and which had conversed with every leaf and needle of the wood, that portion of the sound which the elements had taken up and modulated and echoed from vale to vale. The echo is, to some extent, an original sound, and therein is the magic and charm of it. It is not merely a repetition of what was worth repeating in the bell, but partly the voice of the wood; the same trivial words and notes sung by a wood-nymph.

At evening, the distant lowing of some cow in the horizon beyond the woods sounded sweet and melodious and at first I would mistake it for the voices of certain minstrels by whom I was sometimes serenaded, who might be straying over hill and dale; but soon I was not unpleasantly disappointed when it was prolonged into the cheap and natural music of the cow. I do not mean to be satirical, but to express my appreciation of those youths' singing, when I state that I perceived clearly that it was akin to the music of the cow, and they were at length one articulation of Nature.

Regularly at half-past seven, in one part of the summer, after the evening train had gone by, the whip-poor-wills chanted their vespers for half an hour, sitting on a stump by my door, or upon the ridge-pole of the house. They would begin to sing almost with as much precision as a clock, within five minutes of a particular time, referred to the setting of the sun, every evening. I had a rare opportunity to become acquainted with their habits. Sometimes I heard four or five at once in different parts of the wood, by accident one a bar behind another, and so near me that I distinguished not only the cluck after each note, but often that singular buzzing sound like a fly in a spider's web, only proportionally louder. Sometimes one would circle round and round me in the woods a few feet

From Henry David Thoreau, *Walden and Other Writings*, ed. with an introduction by Brooks Atkinson (New York; Random House, 1965).

distant as if tethered by a string, when probably I was near its eggs. They sang at intervals throughout the night, and were again as musical as ever just before and about dawn.

When other birds are still, the screech owls take up the strain, like mourning women their ancient u-lu-lu. Their dismal scream is truly Ben Jonsonian. Wise midnight hags! It is no honest and blunt tu-whit tu-who of the poets, but, without jesting, a most solemn graveyard ditty, the mutual consolations of suicide lovers remembering the pangs and the delights of supernal love in the infernal groves. Yet I love to hear their wailing, their doleful responses, trilled along the woodside; reminding me sometimes of music and singing birds; as if it were the dark and tearful side of music, the regrets and sighs that would fain be sung. They are the spirits, the low spirits and melancholy forebodings, of fallen souls that once in human shape night-walked the earth and did the deeds of darkness, now expiating their sins with their wailing hymns or threnodies in the scenery of their transgressions. They give me a new sense of the variety and capacity of that nature which is our common dwelling. *Oh-o-o-o-o that I never had been bor-r-r-r-n!* sighs one on this side of the pond, and circles with the restlessness of despair to some new perch on the gray oaks. Then—*that I never had been bor-r-r-r-n!* echoes another on the farther side with tremulous sincerity, and—*bor-r-r-r-n!* comes faintly from far in the Lincoln woods.

I was also serenaded by a hooting owl. Near at hand you could fancy it the most melancholy sound in Nature, as if she meant by this to stereotype and make permanent in her choir the dying moans of a human being,—some poor weak relic of mortality who has left hope behind, and howls like an animal, yet with human sobs, on entering the dark valley, made more awful by a certain gurgling melodiousness,—I find myself beginning with the letters *gl* when I try to imitate it,—expressive of a mind which has reached the gelatinous, mildewy stage in the mortification of all healthy and courageous thought. It reminded me of ghouls and idiots and insane howlings. But now one answers from far woods in a strain made really melodious by distance,—*Hoo hoo hoo, hoorer hoo*; and indeed for the most part is suggested only pleasing associations, whether heard by day or night, summer or winter.

I rejoice that there are owls. Let them do the idiotic and maniacal hooting for men. It is a sound admirably suited to swamps and twilight woods which no day illustrates, suggesting a vast and undeveloped nature which men have not recognized. They represent the stark twilight and unsatisfied thoughts which all have. All day the sun has shone on the surface of some savage swamp, where the single spruce stands hung with usnea lichens, and small hawks circulate above, and the chickadee lisps amid the evergreens, and the partridge and rabbit skulk beneath; but now a more dismal and fitting day dawns, and a different race of creatures awakes to express the meaning of Nature there.

Late in the evening I heard the distant rumbling of wagons over

bridges,—a sound heard farther than almost any other at night,—the bay-
ing of dogs, and sometimes again the lowing of some disconsolate cow in
a distant barn-yard. In the meanwhile all the shore rang with the trump of
bullfrogs, the sturdy spirits of ancient wine-bibbers and wassailers, still
unrepentant, trying to sing a catch in their Stygian lake,—if the Walden
nymphs will pardon the comparison, for though there are almost no
weeds, there are frogs there,—who would fain keep up the hilarious rules
of their old festal tables, though their voices have waxed hoarse and
solemnly grave, mocking at mirth, and the wine has lost its flavor, and
become only liquor to distend their paunches, and sweet intoxication
never comes to drown the memory of the past, but mere saturation and
waterloggedness and distention. The most aldermanic, with his chin
upon a heart-leaf, which serves for a napkin to his drooling chops, under
this northern shore quaffs a deep draught of the once scorned water, and
passes round the cup with the ejaculation tr-r-r-oonk, tr-r-r-oonk,
tr-r-r-oonk! and straightway comes over the water from some distant cove
the same password repeated, where the next in seniority and girth has
gulped down to his mark; and when this observance has made the circuit
of the shores, then ejaculates the master of ceremonies, with satisfaction,
tr-r-r-oonk! and each in his turn repeats the same down to the least dis-
tended, leakiest, and flabbiest paunched, that there be no mistake; and
then the bowl goes round again and again, until the sun disperses the
morning mist, and only the patriarch is not under the pond, but vainly
bellowing troonk from time to time, and pausing for a reply.

I am not sure that I ever heard the sound of cock-crowing from my
clearing, and I thought that it might be worth the while to keep a cockerel
for his music merely, as a singing bird. The note of this once wild Indian
pheasant is certainly the most remarkable of any bird's, and if they could
be naturalized without being domesticated, it would soon become the
most famous sound in our woods, surpassing the clangor of the goose and
the hooting of the owl; and then imagine the cackling of the hens to fill the
pauses when their lords' clarions rested! No wonder that man added this
bird to his tame stock,—to say nothing of the eggs and drumsticks. To
walk in a winter morning in a wood where these birds abounded, their
native woods, and hear the wild cockerels crow on the trees, clear and
shrill for miles over the resounding earth, drowning the feebler notes of
other birds,—think of it! It would put nations on the alert. Who would not
be early to rise, and rise earlier and earlier every successive day of his life,
till he became unspeakably healthy, wealthy, and wise? This foreign
bird's note is celebrated by the poets of all countries along with the notes
of their native songsters. All climates agree with brave Chanticleer. He is
more indigenous even than the natives. His health is ever good, his lungs
are sound, his spirits never flag. Even the sailor on the Atlantic and Pacific
is awakened by his voice; but its shrill sound never roused me from my
slumbers. I kept neither dog, cat, cow, pig, nor hens, so that you would
have said there was a deficiency of domestic sounds: neither the churn nor

the spinning-wheel, nor even the singing of the kettle, nor the hissing of the urn, nor chilren crying, to comfort one. An old-fashioned man would have lost his senses or died of ennui before this. Not even rats in the wall, for they were starved out, or rather were never baited in,—only squirrels on the roof and under the floor, a whip-poor-will on the ridge-pole, a blue jay screaming beneath the window, a hare or woodchuck under the house, a screech owl or a cat owl behind it, a flock of wild geese or a laughing loon on the pond, and a fox to bark in the night. Not even a lark or an oriole, those mild plantation birds, ever visited my clearing. No cockerels to crow nor hens to cackle in the yard. No yard! but unfenced nature reaching up to your very sills. A young forest growing up under your windows, and wild sumachs and blackberry vines breaking through into your cellar; sturdy pitch pines rubbing and creaking against the shingles for want of room, their roots reaching quite under the house. Instead of a scuttle or a blind blown off in the gale,—a pine tree snapped off or torn up by the roots behind your house for fuel. Instead of no path to the front-yard gate in the Great Snow,—no gate—no front-yard,—and no path to the civilized world.

QUESTIONS

1. Identify the role or profession of each writer's voice. For instance, May Watts is an ecologist, and Robert Herrick is a poet. What descriptions can you give to the others?

2. Which of the writers use technical language or jargon? How does this vocabulary influence your impression of the voice?

3. One of the characteristics of a poet's voice is a habit of being conscious of the *sounds* of words. Sometimes poems rhyme or use alliteration, and most have a rhythmic pattern of some sort. Find examples of these devices in the poems here. Describe the differences among the voices of the poets.

4. Do any of the other voices seem conscious of the sounds of their words? Can you find examples of alliteration or interesting rhythms? Can a prose writer's use of sound influence the voice?

5. Imagine and describe a physical appearance for each voice. What are the clues in the language that lead you to call them male or female, old or young, dressed up or shabby?

6. Identify as closely as possible the audience that each writer hopes to reach. Do any of the writers seem to lack an idea of their audience?

7. Which of the writers are hoping to persuade an audience? What particular beliefs of the audience does the writer wish to change?

8. Does each of the writers have a thesis or central idea to communicate? If so, give a rough summary of each. What types of support are offered?

9. What was the purpose of Lewis and Clark's trip through the Louisiana Territory and beyond? Which information in the journals is relevant to the purposes of the journey? Is anything not relevant?

10. Poetry often makes comparisons. Find examples here of comparisons drawn between natural objects or events and events in human life. Do any of the prose writers do the same thing?

11. Which writers find nature cheerful, and which find it forbidding? Which writers are not concerned with the emotional impact of their descriptions?

12. Do you think any of the examples here show a poor writing job? If so, explain why.

5

Cigarettes

Do you smoke? What is it about cigarettes that makes them so attractive to some people? Is there really conclusive evidence that cigarette smoking is hazardous to health? And what role, if any, should government play in the cigarette controversy?

Classic Quotations

Pretty soon I wanted to smoke, and asked the widow to let me. But she wouldn't. She said it was a mean practice and wasn't clean, and I must try to not do it any more. That is just the way with some people. They get down on a thing when they don't know nothing about it. Here she was a bothering about Moses, which was no kin to her, and no use to anybody, being gone, you see, yet finding a power of fault with me for doing a thing that had some good in it. And she took snuff too; of course that was all right, because she done it herself.

Mark Twain, *Huckleberry Finn*

A lone man's companion, a bachelor's friend, a hungry man's food, a sad man's cordial, a wakeful man's sleep, and a chilly man's fire. . . . There's no herb like unto it under the canopy of heaven.

Charles Kingsley, *Westward Ho!*

. . . a woman is only a woman, but a good cigar is a smoke!

Rudyard Kipling, *Departmental Ditties*

A cigarette is the perfect type of a perfect pleasure. It is exquisite and it leaves one unsatisfied. What more can one want?

Oscar Wilde, *The Picture of Dorian Gray*

Overview—Health Consequences of Smoking

U.S. Public Health Service

The statement, "*Warning: The Surgeon General Has Determined That Cigarette Smoking Is Dangerous to Your Health,*" has been required by law on cigarette packaging since 1970 as a part of the Public Health Cigarette Smoking Act of 1969. This Act was a response by the U.S. Congress to the scientific information on the health consequences of cigarette smoking summarized in reports then available (the Surgeon General's Report of 1964 and the subsequent 1967, 1968, and 1969 PHS Health Consequences of Smoking). This Act was passed because a series of important questions concerning cigarette smoking and health had been answered.

The following discussion summarizes the basic questions, the methodology used to determine the anwers, and the answers themselves.

The initial question to be answered concerning the health consequences of smoking was "*Are there any harmful health effects of smoking cigarettes?*" The answer to this question was provided in two ways. First, it was demonstrated that some diseases occurred more frequently in smokers than in nonsmokers. Second, a causal relationship was established between smoking and these diseases.

Concern about the possible health effects of smoking started when scientists began looking for an explanation to account for the rapidly increasing death rate from lung cancer. The early retrospective studies showed a link between lung cancer and smoking. The first prospective studies, however, found that only one-eighth of the excess overall mortality found among smokers could be accounted for by lung cancer; the rest was largely due to coronary heart disease, chronic respiratory disease, and other forms of cancer. They also found that the effect on overall mortality was largely confined to cigarette smokers rather than the users of other forms of tobacco.

However, demonstrating an association by statistical probability is not enough to establish the causal nature of a relationship. Determining that the association between smoking and excess death rates is cause and effect was a judgment made after a number of criteria had been met, no one of which by itself is sufficient to make this judgment. These criteria as listed in the Surgeon General's Advisory Committee Report (1964) were the **consistency, strength, specificity, temporal relationship,** and **coherence** of the association.

In addition, convincing theories about the mechanisms whereby smoking contributes to the various diseases responsible for the excess mortality among cigarette smokers were developed from the evidence on the biochemical, cytologic, pathologic, and pathophysiologic effects of cigarette smoking, thereby providing the necessary support for the decision that the relationship was causal.

The most important specific health consequence of cigarette smoking in terms of the number of people affected is the development of premature coronary heart disease (CHD). Both prospective and retrospective studies clearly established that cigarette smokers have a greater risk of death due to CHD and have a higher prevalence of CHD than nonsmokers. Long-term followup of healthy populations has confirmed that a cigarette smoker is more likely to have a myocardial infarction and to die from CHD than a nonsmoker. Cigarette smoking has been shown to be one of the major independent CHD risk factors and to act in combination with other major alterable CHD risk factors (high blood pressure and elevated serum cholesterol). Autopsy studies have shown that persons who smoked cigarettes have more severe coronary atherosclerosis than persons who did not smoke. Physiologic studies and animal experiments have indicated several mechanisms whereby these effects can take place.

A second major health consequence of smoking is the development of cancer in smokers. Cigarette smoking was firmly established as the major risk factor in lung cancer. The risk of developing lung cancer was found to be 10 times greater for cigarette smokers than for nonsmokers. The risk of developing lung cancer increases with the number of cigarettes smoked per day and is greater in cigarette smokers who report inhaling, who started smoking at an early.age, or who have smoked for a greater number of years. Smokers of filter cigarettes have been shown to have a lower risk of developing lung cancer than smokers of nonfilter cigarettes, but the risk remains well above that for nonsmokers. The risk of developing cancer of the larynx, pharynx, oral cavity, esophagus, pancreas, and urinary bladder was also found to be significantly higher in cigarette smokers than in nonsmokers. Pipe and cigar smokers were found to have elevated risks for the development of cancer of the oral cavity, pharynx, larynx, and esophagus when compared to nonsmokers. Fewer pipe and cigar smokers than cigarette smokers report that they inhale. As a result lungs of pipe and cigar smokers receive much less exposure to smoke than the lungs of cigarette smokers. This is probably the primary reason for the lower incidence of cancer of the lung for pipe and cigar smokers compared to cigarette smokers.

Women have had far lower rates of lung cancer than men. This has been attributed to the fact that fewer women than men smoke and the fact that women smokers generally select filter and low tar and nicotine cigarettes. However, the percentage of women smokers in the United States has increased steadily in the last 30 years, and since 1955 the death rates from lung cancer in women have increased proportionately more rapidly than the rates for men, reflecting this increased proportion of women smokers.

The tar from cigarette smoke has been found to induce malignant changes in the skin and respiratory tract of experimental animals, and a number of specific chemical compounds contained in cigarette smoke were established as potent carcinogens or co-carcinogens. Malignant changes including carcinoma *in situ* were found in the larynx and in the sputum exfoliative cytology of experimental animals exposed to cigarette smoke.

Nonmalignant respiratory disease is a third area of smoking-induced morbidity and mortality. Cigarette smokers have been shown to have more frequent minor respiratory infections, miss more days from work due to respiratory illness, and report symptoms of cough and sputum production more frequently than nonsmokers. Retrospective and prospective studies with long-term followup have found that cigarette smoking is the primary factor in the development of chronic bronchitis and emphysema in the United States. Cigarette smokers have also been found to be more likely to have abnormalities of pulmonary function and have higher death rates from respiratory diseases than nonsmokers. Data from autopsy studies have shown that cigarette smokers were more likely to have the macroscopic changes of emphysema, and that these changes are closely related to the number of cigarettes smoked per day. Mucous cell hyperplasia has been found more often in cigarette smokers. Cigarette smoke also inhibits the ciliary motion responsible for cleansing the respiratory tract.

An additional area of health concern has been the effect of cigarette smoking during pregnancy. Mothers who smoke cigarettes during the last two trimesters of their pregnancy have been found to have babies with a lower average birth weight than nonsmoking mothers. In addition cigarette smoking mothers had a higher risk of having a stillborn child, and their infants had higher late fetal and neonatal death rates. There are some data to show that these risks due to cigarette smoking are even greater in women who have a high risk pregnancy for other reasons. These effects may occur because carbon monoxide passes freely across the placenta and is readily bound by fetal hemoglobin, thereby decreasing the oxygen carrying capacity of fetal blood.

Having established that cigarette smoking is a significant causal factor in a number of serious disease processes, two additional questions became important. They are *"Can the health consequences to the individual be averted by stopping smoking or by changing the cigarette?"* and *"What are the overall public health consequences of cessation and of the changes made in cigarettes?"*

The first question is the simpler of the two to answer. In the individual, cessation of cigarette smoking results in a rapid decline of the carbon monoxide level in the blood over the first 12 hours. Symptoms of cough, sputum production, and shortness of breath usually improve over the next few weeks. A woman who stops smoking by the fourth month of her pregnancy has no increased risk of stillbirth or perinatal death in her infant related to smoking. The deterioration in pulmonary function tests that occurs in some smokers becomes less rapid than that of continuing smokers. The death rates from ischemic heart disease, chronic bronchitis, and emphysema also become less than those of the continuing smoker. The risk of developing cancer of the lung, larynx, and oral cavity declines relative to the continuing smoker in the first few years after cessation and 10 to 15 years after stopping smoking approximates that of nonsmokers. A smoker who switches to filter cigarettes and has smoked them for 10 years or longer has a lower risk of developing lung cancer than a smoker who continues to smoke nonfilter cigarettes. The risk to a filter cigarette smoker, however, still remains well above that of a nonsmoker.

The public health benefits of cessation are more difficult to determine than the effects of cessation on the individual. Just as cause-specific death rates have reflected the effect of cigarette smoking on certain diseases, they should also reflect any substantial benefits to be gained by cessation or reduction in cigarette smoking. Several factors combined to produce a reduction in per capita dosage of tobacco exposure in the United States for the years 1966–1970. First, per capita consumption of cigarettes declined from 4,287 cigarettes per person in 1966 to 3,985 in 1970. Second, during this period there was a slow but significant decrease in the average tar and nicotine content of cigarettes as well as a decrease in the amount of tobacco contained in the average cigarette. The decline in per capita consumption during those years occurred in the face of a substantial increase in the proportion of young women becoming smokers as compared to women of previous generations and so reflected predominantly a decrease in cigarette consumption by men.

Since 1970, although the per capita consumption of cigarettes has increased, the average levels of tar and nicotine have continued to decline, making it more difficult to predict what has happened to per capita dosage.

Examination of cause-specific death rates for the period of this declining per capita consumption reveals that there was a downturn in the male death rate from ischemic heart disease beginning in 1966 which reversed the upward trend that had occurred over the previous two decades. This decline in the death rate from ischemic heart disease has not occurred in women.

The male death rate from chronic bronchitis has also been declining since 1967, and the male death rate for emphysema has declined since 1968 when it was first recorded as a separate category. Female death rates for these two diseases have not shown these trends.

Despite the impressive coincidences of the decline in death rates among males occurring at the same time that there was a decline in per capita cigarette consumption, it is impossible to be certain of the exact cause of the decline in the death rates. These diseases are influenced by a variety of factors in addition to cigarette smoking such as blood pressure and air pollution. Some of these factors have also been subject to major control efforts which may have contributed to the decline in the death rates. In addition, there have been therapeutic advances in the treatment of these problems which may also have helped lower the death rates.

A decline in male death rates from lung cancer should also follow the decline in per capita consumption. This rate would not be influenced as much by changes in other etiologic factors or changes in therapy because cigarette smoking causes from 85 to 90 percent of all lung cancer and there have been no major improvements in survival due to changes in therapy. With lung cancer, however, two additional considerations must be kept in mind. A decline in death rates from lung cancer would be expected to lag several years behind a decline in per capita consumption. In addition, the decline in consumption and switch to low tar and nicotine cigarettes occurred predominantly in the younger age groups where death rates from lung cancer are low. For these reasons, it is necessary to look at lung cancer death rates by age group rather than total lung cancer death rates. The lung cancer rates by age groups for 1971 suggest a decline in the lung cancer rates for the younger males (under 45), but the confidence limits on these trends at present remain wide enough that it is impossible to say whether this is a real decline or merely a leveling off. The national health statistics broken down by 5-year age groups are currently available only through 1971. The data by age group from a few more years will be necessary to determine whether the changes in smoking behavior which have taken place have reversed the trend of the preceding 40 years of continually increasing lung cancer rates in men. In 1971, the last year for which detailed mortality statistics are available, the accumulated exposure to cigarettes reached its peak among men born between 1915 and 1919, a group then in their early 50's. Cumulative exposure has continued to decline with each successive 5-year birth cohort born since then. The trends of the last few years offer some hope that the peak of the "lung cancer epidemic," as some have termed this phenomenon, may have been reached with this group and that future years will show a slow but consistent decline.

And the Filtered Ones Are Even Worse   William P. Moore

EDINBORO, Pa. (UPI)—Of an estimated 54 million Americans who smoke, many use filter cigarettes with the idea that doing so compensates, at least partially, for the harmful effects of which the surgeon general warns on every pack.

Gus Miller says filters don't. He says they are even more dangerous than unfiltered cigarettes.

While scientific evidence mounts on both sides of the "does smoking cause cancer?" controversy, statistical data compiled by Miller, a mathematician at Edinboro State College, support research indicating smoking shortens lifespans by about 10 years.

But Miller's work goes further. Miller, who also has degrees in chemistry and psychology, has compiled figures indicating a life expectancy for continuous nonfilter smokers of about 65 years, while it is 63 years for those who smoke filters.

Miller's study, supported in part by the Northwestern Pennsylvania branches of the Heart Association, Lung Association and Cancer Society, indicates nonsmokers have an average life expectancy of 76 to 77 years.

Through newspaper death notices, Miller traced survivors of about 7,500 residents of Erie County, Pa., who died of natural causes between 1972–74. He gathered his data through telephone interviews with relatives of the deceased.

The premature deaths reflected in Miller's study are not exclusively due to cancer or heart disease, he said. The carbon monoxide produced by cigarette smoking breaks down tissue and weakens the body's ability to deal with any disease.

Miller cites studies showing that filter cigarettes produce more carbon monoxide than nonfilters. Related studies show carbon monoxide to be a major contributing factor to cardiovascular diseases.

"It is a waste of time trying to produce a safe cigarette," Miller said. "You can't get a safe cigarette, simply because anything that burns can't be healthy. It produces carbon monoxide, tar and other unhealthy components."

Miller's theory about filters contradicts statements by the medical profession over the last 15 years that if one must smoke, it should be a filter cigarette.

The 1978 edition of "Cancer Facts & Figures," issued by the American Cancer Society, says that in addition to being responsible for 80 percent of all lung cancer deaths, cigarettes have been "implicated in other diseases, ranging from colds and gastric ulcers to chronic bronchitis, emphysema, heart disease and hazards to unborn children."

Like the wealthy Romans who contracted fatal lead poisoning from their wine glasses, Miller says, America's refusal to heed smoking warnings will lead to more premature deaths.

"Men used to live longer than women," said Miller. "Now all of a sudden women live longer. How come? Because men smoke more. The sooner people realize this and do something about it, the better off we all will be."

Miller said, however, smoking among women continues on the upswing while the reverse is true for men.

Dr. Marvin Kastenbaum, director of statistics for the Tobacco Institute, maintains Miller's study is inaccurate because persons who smoke are younger than persons who don't—and, thus, those who die at early ages would be more likely to have been smokers, without their death necessarily being related to cigarettes.

"The average age at death of people who sleep in cribs is much lower than the average age at death of people who don't sleep in cribs," Kastenbaum said.

Miller discounts Kastenbaum's criticism.

"If he had read my material, he would know I don't have average age at death, I have life expectancy after age 30. We are getting all of the people, a complete population, and it is not biased.

"They [the tobacco industry] say people who smoke are of a younger age group. That is just not true. Men have smoked for about 150 years, and some women have for about 100 years."

Miller criticized the tobacco industry for "trying to confuse the masses" by relying on data gained from studies of dubious scientific accuracy.

"Tobacco manufacturers deny the accuracy of any of the good studies, and use the poor studies that support their results," he said.

Miller claims his study is more accurate than most because it included a cross-section of the entire population, not just hospitalized persons or volunteers.

He advocates free, government-sponsored smoke-ending clinics and government-funded public information campaigns to counter the multi-million-dollar tobacco industry advertising budgets.

Miller met with HEW Secretary Joseph Califano in Washington just before Califano's department launched its recent antismoking campaign. He spends most of his time studying smoking, conducting smoke-ending clinics and spreading his views on television and radio talk shows.

Never a cigarette smoker, he does not permit smoking in his home or office.

The Unnatural History of Tobacco   Erik Eckholm

When accosting a tourist, a street waif in Cairo is as apt to beg for a cigarette as for coins. In the People's Republic of China, a country renowned for its health-care campaigns, national leaders chain-smoke as they preside over the world's largest tobacco industry. More than a decade after the United States government declared smoking to be a health hazard, four out of ten American males and three out of ten American females smoke—and the federal Department of Agriculture spends $50 million a year supporting the tobacco industry.

How is it that such a harmful product has become so firmly en-

trenched in daily life the world over? That tobacco occupies good farm-
land in India while peasants starve nearby? That the cigarette merchants
are allowed to use Madison Avenue's wiliest marketing techniques to
cajole youngsters into a lifetime of smoking? Like a dime novel, the tale of
the three-cent cigarette is one of intrigue, corporate power, and governmental hypocrisy; of human pleasure, addiction, and premature death.

"This vice will always be condemned and always clung to," wrote
the perceptive Italian physician Bernardino Ramazzini in 1713 of tobacco
use. Trying to figure out why Italian tobacco workers prized their jobs
despite the severe head and stomach ailments tobacco dust inflicted upon
them, Ramazzini, considered by many to be the father of industrial
medicine, made another observation of equal present-day weight when he
noted that "the sweet smell of gain makes the smell of tobacco less per-
ceptible and less offensive to those workers."

Although the medical case against smoking has been conclusively
established only within the last quarter century, tobacco has had powerful
opponents, as well as powerful champions, almost from the moment
sixteenth-century explorers gave Europe its first whiff. Yet from the beginning, the lure of profits, social fashions, and the association of tobacco
with relaxation have all helped propagate its use. Today, despite the
medical community's consensus and exhortations, the smoking habit continues to spread throughout most of the world. Indeed, many countries are
just now entering the era of tobacco-induced disease and death.

Native Americans were the first tobacco smokers, but their European
conquerors turned smoking and other forms of tobacco use into global
habits. Sir Walter Raleigh, the colorful favorite of Queen Elizabeth's court,
popularized smoking in England during the late sixteenth century. The
practice caught on fast and early orders for tobacco were filled in Spain's
New World colonies. Upon Elizabeth's death in 1603, however, British
rule fell to James I, who found Raleigh's smoking habit as objectionable as
he found the courtier's politics. (James eventually beheaded Raleigh for
political reasons, but one nineteenth-century writer claimed that smokers
could consider Raleigh "the first martyr in their cause.")

James declared that tobacco use was unhealthy, unholy, and altogether unbefitting a civilized society. He concluded his famous
Counter-Blaste to Tobacco, published in 1604, by characterizing smoking
as

> a custom lothsome to the eye, hatefull to the Nose, harmefull to the braine,
> dangerous to the Lungs, and in the blacke stinking fume thereof, neerest
> resembling the horrible Stigian smoke of the pit that is bottomelesse.

Even as James fumed, other people were making extravagant claims
about the salubrious powers of tobacco smoke. Some doctors prescribed
smoking as an antidote to colds and fevers; some even believed that inhaled smoke might ward off the plague. During the plague year of 1603,
all the schoolboys at Eton "were obliged to smoak in the school every

morning," reported a certain Tom Rogers, who also said that he never received a harsher whipping than the one he suffered one morning as punishment for not smoking.

Despite the antismoking campaign conducted by James and several of his English successors and the unbudging opposition of Emperor Jahangir in India, tobacco use quickly spread throughout Europe and then, through the tentacles of the colonial system, to the world. As one pipe lover exulted in 1895 over tobacco's spread, "Prince and peasant alike yielded to its mild but irresistible sway." In eighteenth-century Italy, Ramazzini reported, tobacco was smoked or inhaled by "women as well as men and even children," and its purchase was "reckoned among the daily expenses of a family."

The spreading demand and, hence, growing commercial market for tobacco in sixteenth- and seventeenth-century Europe spurred the emergence of a lucrative industry. British colonists settled in Virginia expecting to cash in on the New World's precious metals, lumber, furs, and fish; instead, they learned that only tobacco exports could keep their colony afloat. Virginia was nearly abandoned in 1614, but tobacco soon brought prosperity to the colony. It eventually became the economic backbone of the southeastern colonies despite strong opposition to reliance on this crop by the English king—and even by the founding colonial companies. The "sweet smell of gain" proved a potent force indeed, and although tobacco no longer dominates the economy of that region as totally as it once did, the tobacco industry still wields considerable force there and in other tobacco-producing areas of the world. And today, the tobacco market has a new dimension. On top of traditional public demand for tobacco, scientific image manipulation is used by the industry to try to create an ever larger market.

The popularity of one or another form of tobacco use has varied as standards of fashion have changed. Beginning in eighteenth-century England, for example, and for almost the next hundred years, the practice of sniffing snuff all but replaced the smoking habit. In this century, however, cigarettes have nearly everywhere edged out pipes, cigars, snuff, and chewing tobacco as the medium of choice. Unfortunately, cigarette smoking is probably the most dangerous of all forms of tobacco use.

Skillful marketing by the cigarette companies undoubtedly helped sell the public on cigarettes during the early twentieth century. But the power of advertising alone cannot completely account for the symbolic value with which cigarettes have been invested. Simple tubes of tobacco have come to represent modernity, *savoir-faire*, and, in the minds of children, who for decades have plunked down nickels for candy cigarettes and bubblegum cigars, adulthood. Hollywood may be one culprit. Humphrey Bogart would not be Humphrey Bogart without a cigarette drooping from his mouth, and the example of Lauren Bacall asking, "Got a match?" helped identify cigarettes as an essential social crutch. Even Bogart's death from cancer of the esophagus cannot dampen the identification of cigarettes with success and glamour that his movies and countless others continue to foster. In contemporary Soviet films, comments the satirical Moscow magazine *Krokodil*, "when an actor handsome like Apollo . . . takes a cigarette into his fingers, it isn't accidental. It means the time has come for a director to demonstrate that his character can also think."

Only recently has the compilation of an awesome medical case against cigarettes begun to tarnish the social sheen of smoking. Many thoughtful doctors had long suspected that cigarettes promoted ill health, but proof eluded researchers until the mid-twentieth century. Even in the early 1900s, cigarette advertisers could claim with impunity that their products actually promoted better health.

A startling jump in the number of lung cancer deaths in North America and Europe provided the first widely accepted proof of the hazards of smoking. In the nineteenth century lung cancer was relatively rare, but in the twentieth it rapidly emerged as the leading cause of cancer death in many countries. By 1950, studies in England and the United States showed an exceptionally close correlation between personal smoking habits and the incidence of lung cancer. By 1953, the prestigious *New England Journal of Medicine* could characterize the evidence linking cigarettes and lung cancer as "so strong as to be considered proof within the everyday meaning of the word." Then, in 1954, British and American researchers independently established that smokers have a markedly higher over-all death rate than nonsmokers. Yet the habit continued to spread, especially among adult females and teen-agers, who had lagged far behind adult males in adopting the practice, as well as among the wealthier classes in Africa, Asia, and Latin America.

In the early 1960s, two landmark public documents, which crystallized the evidence on the effects of smoking on health, caused something of a turning point in the social history of tobacco. Both a report released in 1962 by Britain's Royal College of Physicians and one published in 1964 by the Surgeon General of the United States presented the massive and growing medical case against tobacco. These and other, similar documents prompted some governments to educate people about the hazards of smoking and to place partial restrictions on cigarette advertising. As a result, the word on smoking's risks has now been fairly effectively disseminated, in the industrial countries at least. Most persons, even most heavy smokers, realize that smoking very possibly shortens their lives.

The most widely recognized health consequence of smoking is probably the heightened risk of lung cancer. The smoking–lung cancer connection is well known simply because avoidable lung cancer takes hundreds of thousands of lives around the world each year. Lung cancer deaths are much more common among males than females, but the gap is narrowing as the rise in female smoking, which began a quarter of a century ago, begins to make itself felt.

Past studies have shown that cigarette smokers are at least ten times more likely to develop lung malignancies than nonsmokers. (Those smoking newer, low-tar cigarettes may face a somewhat lower, but still dramatic, rise in lung cancer risk.) Many researchers feel that tobacco is responsible for eight or nine of every ten lung cancers. Combinations of tobacco smoke with air pollution or with toxic substances in workplaces undoubtedly add to the cancer toll; tobacco smoke and certain other pollutants operate together to drastically multiply disease risks. For example, male asbestos workers who smoke have 92 times the lung cancer risk of males who neither smoke nor come into regular contact with asbestos. But cigarettes alone almost certainly account for most lung cancer cases. Gio B. Gori, deputy director of the Division of Cancer Causes and Prevention of the U.S. National Cancer Institute, estimates that smoking two packs of cigarettes a day for a year exposes the lungs to nineteen times more benzopyrene—one of the possible carcinogens in cigarette smoke—than they would receive from breathing the polluted air of Los Angeles for a year.

Other organs and tissues, besides the lungs, become especially cancer-prone in chronic smokers. The smoking of pipes or cigars, as well as puffing on cigarettes, raises a person's odds of developing cancer of the mouth, throat, or voice box, particularly if the smoker is also a heavy drinker. Cigarette smoking also multiplies the smoker's chances of developing cancer of the esophagus, pancreas, and bladder. But, more frequent and more deadly than these other malignancies, lung cancer poses a greater threat to the smoker's life than all the other smoking-induced cancers together. After considering the entire spectrum of cancers and what is known about their causes, the president of the American Cancer Society recently stated: "Wipe out smoking and you eliminate some 15 to 20 percent of *all* cancer deaths in this and many other countries."

Despite the publicity that the cigarette-cancer connection has received, far more deaths arising from cigarette smoking involve coronary heart disease—the leading killer in most developed countries—than cancer. Smoking taxes the heart: a middle-aged American male who smokes is twice as likely as a nonsmoking male to suffer a heart attack. Female smokers experience a less marked but still significant increase in the odds of having a heart attack. Moreover, smoking combines with other major risk factors, such as high blood cholesterol and high blood pressure, to multiply manyfold the heart disease risk for both sexes.

The intense search for carcinogens in tobacco smoke has exposed tars as the principal agents provocateurs. Research on the heart and circulatory system, however, suggests that another smoke constituent—namely, carbon monoxide—influences coronary death rates. When males with heart conditions are experimentally exposed to heavy carbon monoxide concentrations, the chest pains of angina pectoris begin after less exercise than usual and persist longer than usual after exertion has stopped. Coronary patients have a limited capacity to supply their hearts with rich blood; exposure to carbon monoxide further reduces this capacity by impeding the transfer of oxygen from the blood to body tissue. Thus, carbon monoxide pollution places an added strain upon the heart and increases the likelihood that those already susceptible to heart attacks will experience them. (Nicotine inhalation seems to have the same effect.) Chronic heavy exposure to carbon monoxide may also promote the initial development of atherosclerosis, which, over time, can lead to heart attacks. Studies show that lifelong smokers tend to have more severe coronary atherosclerosis than nonsmokers do, and animals exposed to carbon monoxide develop higher blood cholesterol counts and more atherosclerosis than unexposed animals.

Not surprisingly, cigarette smokers take on tremendously increased risks of developing long-term respiratory ailments such as chronic bronchitis and emphysema. Charged with causing tens of thousands of deaths and far more disabilities each year in Europe and North America alone, these diseases have emerged as recognized public health problems only during the last century. The twin onslaught on the lungs posed by industrial air pollution and tobacco smoke undoubtedly explains why chronic respiratory diseases are growing in frequency. But cigarettes seem to be the major contributor. Cigarette smokers are five times as likely as nonsmokers to die from chronic bronchitis or emphysema.

Perhaps the most telling of all evidence against cigarettes arises from a simple comparison of annual death rates between smokers and nonsmokers. The famous 1964 U.S. Surgeon General's report noted that the death rate of males smoking ten to nineteen cigarettes daily is 70 percent higher than that of nonsmokers. For those smoking forty or more cigarettes daily, the death rate is 120 percent higher. Nearly half the excess—and presumably avoidable—deaths that occur among smokers in a given year result from coronary heart disease, while more than one-sixth are caused by lung cancer.

Since the major medical indictments of smoking appeared in the 1950s and early 1960s, further evidence that raises questions about human rights has accumulated. Voluntarily inhaling carbon monoxide and carcinogens is one thing: exhaling them into the air that others are forced to breathe is quite another. In a smoky room or car, nonsmokers inhale tars, nicotine, and carbon monoxide just as smokers do, and both groups register at least temporary changes in their bloodstreams. Breathing the exhaust of smokers can strain the heart of a coronary patient who does not smoke.

But the most potentially tragic victims of cigarettes are the infants of mothers who smoke. They are more likely than the babies of nonsmoking mothers to be born underweight and thus to encounter death or disease at birth or during the initial months of life. In an otherwise supportive environment, the infant is usually well equipped to withstand the impact of maternal smoking. But when other factors that imperil the newborn are present, for instance, poverty or poor maternal nutrition, heavy smoking by the mother nearly doubles the infant's odds of dying within a month of birth. Moreover, whether or not they are born underweight, the infants of smoking mothers suffer more chest infections, such as bronchitis and pneumonia, than other infants.

Many persons have extinguished their last cigarette after learning of the health consequences of smoking. In the United States the proportion of cigarette smokers among the adult male population has fallen from 53 percent in 1964, the year in which the Surgeon General's report appeared, to 39 percent in 1975. Among adult females, the proportion of smokers fell from a high of 34 percent in 1966 to 29 percent in 1975. In Great Britain and several other countries, smokers have also shrunk in number. As a second-best response to the perils of smoking, still other new and veteran smokers now buy cigarettes with relatively low amounts of tar and nicotine. The figures, then, show a significant, although hardly revolutionary, reversal of smoking trends in some of the more developed countries. They also show that the decline in smoking has been especially marked among those with the most education. In the United States, half of all college graduates who have ever smoked regularly have dropped the habit.

The over-all downturn in U.S. smoking rates has been marred, however, by a notable exception—one that accounts largely for the slight increase in over-all per capita cigarette consumption since it hit its lowest point in recent history in 1970. Unprecedented numbers of teen-age girls and young women now smoke. Urged on by the continuing efforts of tobacco advertisers to identify smoking with women's liberation, young women are narrowing the historic gap between male and female smoking rates. In fact, in the 15- to 16-year-old age group, a slightly higher proportion of girls (20 percent) than boys (18 percent) now smokes. Twenty-seven percent of all teen-age girls in the United States now smoke regularly and the number is climbing here and in many other countries—a trend that a World Health Organization committee has found especially troubling in light of "the clear finding that smoking during pregnancy has adverse effects on the fetus." If, as one familiar cigarette advertisement patronizingly chants, women "have come a long way," their equality with men as smokers may lead to nothing more "liberating" than premature death.

Although the percentage of its population that smokes is somewhat smaller than it was a decade ago, the United States retains its long-standing title as the world's premier cigarette-smoking country. This is partly because so many Americans smoke and also because they tend to smoke more cigarettes per day than do most other smokers. About 2,750 cigarettes were smoked in 1974 for every person in the country. Only Japan, with a 1974 per capita consumption of 2,600 cigarettes, came close to the U.S. average. Astonishingly enough, 70 percent of all Japanese males smoke, although only 9 percent of Japanese females do. Annual per capita cigarette consumption in Western European countries ranges from 1,000 to more than 2,000; average consumption in Mexico is more than 700 a year; and per capita consumption in poor African countries, such as

Nigeria and Tanzania, is still only a few hundred cigarettes per year.

These national cigarette-consumption averages provide little hint of the present smoking pandemic. While the incidence of cigarette smoking may have peaked in some of the developed Western countries, the practice has entered a dramatic growth phase in most of the less-developed countries. Cigarettes are catching on especially quickly in the cities of the poor countries. A recent Pan-American Health Organization survey in eight urban areas of Latin America revealed that 45 percent of males in those cities smoke: a higher percentage than in the United States. In contrast, only 18 percent of the females in these major Latin American cities are smokers. To capitalize on this new growth, the major cigarette companies are now as never before aiming their promotion at markets in the developing countries.

Cigarette smoking is not yet the national pastime in most of Africa and Asia that it is in Latin America, partly because average personal incomes in Africa and Asia are generally much lower than those in Latin America. Ironically, however, just when the smoking habit is being dropped by record numbers of the better-educated and better-off individuals in North America and Western Europe, the educational and economic elites of the world's poorer countries are leading their countrymen in taking up the practice. Data from India, Uganda, and elsewhere show that cigarette smoking is especially popular among university students. In hand or mouth, the cigarette in those countries bespeaks privilege and knowledge.

Perhaps the chief constraint on cigarette use in poor countries is money: only the rich can afford to enjoy more than an occasional smoke. As incomes in Africa, Asia, and Latin America rise, however, both the number of smokers and their smoking frequency climb as well. Rapid income growth usually affects smoking rates perceptibly; oil-rich Middle Eastern countries are providing cigarette merchants with a hot new market. In Nigeria, lung cancer is still rare, but a medical professor at Lagos University warns that "lung cancer will emerge with the affluence generated by our country's oil economy; there will definitely be more money for cigarettes."

Smoking in poor countries is not totally confined to urban areas. Tobacco use has long been entrenched in some rural regions. For example, shredded tobacco for hand-rolled cigarettes or pipes is a stock item in every Indonesian marketplace. In China, the amount of tobacco grown in backyard plots for personal consumption probably rivals the output of the vast state-run tobacco industry. Contemplating the dim nutritional prospects of the Gurung, a hill tribe of Nepal, an anthropologist recently wrote that, faced with a financial pinch, the tribespeople would probably let themselves become "malnourished rather than give up certain 'luxury' goods such as cigarettes."

Who profits from the tobacco business? The long list of those with a financial stake in the cigarette trade includes private and governmental tobacco farmers, huge transnational private cigarette companies and state-owned cigarette monopolies, local and national governments that depend in part upon tobacco-generated taxes and foreign exchange to survive, and the thousands of newspapers and magazines whose profits derive in part from the cigarette advertisements they carry.

The two leading tobacco-growing countries are the People's Republic of China and the United States; India, the Soviet Union, and Brazil come next but lag way behind. The world's major cigarette producers are, in order, the Chinese government monopoly, the British-American Tobacco Company, the Soviet government monopoly, the Japanese government monopoly, and Philip Morris Inc. Hence three of the top five cigarette producers are public, rather than private, enterprises.

The nearly free functioning of cigarette companies in capitalist countries is predictable. But the seemingly unchecked power of tobacco interests in the governments of controlled-market economies, such as China and the Soviet Union, is puzzling, particularly since both of those governments so strongly emphasize preventive medicine. While the Soviet government is at least trying to discourage smoking through public education, the Chinese government has done nothing to uproot the habit. When hunger and unsanitary living conditions were the overriding health challenges in China, an anticigarette campaign probably would have been a luxury. But now, following China's dramatic success in reducing undernutrition and infectious disease, cigarette-induced ailments are on the increase. Admittedly, antismoking campaigns would probably strike the Chinese as hypocritical, since many powerful national leaders—including the late Chairman Mao—are heavy smokers. But upon his recent return from a visit to China, a U.S. Senate staff member offered a second explanation: the large tax on cigarette sales "serves as a major source of investment capital for the central government—a source not easily replaced and therefore not lightly abandoned."

Many governments must view the tobacco trade with mixed emotions. As they boost cigarette and tobacco taxes and import duties—often ostensibly to discourage smoking—governments simultaneously create a major source of revenue that is far easier to justify, politically, than increases in other kinds of taxes. In many countries, the tax revenue from tobacco products exceeds the amount received by the farmers for the original tobacco crop. In 1974 in the United States, federal, state, and local governments took in about $6 billion in taxes on tobacco products, while the $4 billion in tobacco taxes received by the British government in that year constituted 70 percent of consumer expenditures on cigarettes. Even in Nigeria, where smoking's grip is less well established, tobacco taxes provided 2.2 percent of all the tax income in 1969/70.

Held hostage to the political power of the tobacco and cigarette producers or lured by self-interest in the tobacco business or both, many governments actively subsidize tobacco production. Samuel Epstein, a physician whose specialty is environmental health, calculates that the

U.S. Department of Agriculture spends about $50 million annually on price supports, tobacco research, export promotion, and other programs that support the tobacco industry. The nation's Agricultural Research Service, he notes, "assigns more space to research on tobacco than to research on food distribution. What's more, the ARS's concern is to produce a more marketable product, not a safer product."

Governmental hypocrisy in the treatment of tobacco becomes especially easy when tobacco and cigarette exports are involved. Foreign exchange is always welcomed by economic planners, and in this case, the negative health results are someone else's concern. To help keep Italy's tobacco exports competitive outside the European Economic Community, the EEC provides a subsidy of about ten cents for each pound of tobacco sold. The U.S. government ended its direct export payments in 1973, and terminated its practice of sharing equally with producers the costs of export promotion in 1975. But the federal government still finances tobacco booths at foreign trade fairs and trips of tobacco experts to and from the United States.

Perhaps the oddest and most questionable use of tobacco by the United States has been the inclusion of tobacco in the Public Law 480 "Food for Peace" program of concessional agricultural sales to needy countries. This supposedly humanitarian aid program has been manipulated to meet several goals at once: to get rid of domestic tobacco surpluses, to introduce foreigners to U.S. tobacco in the hope of nurturing a future commercial market, and to provide economic aid to politically favored governments. The amount of tobacco shipped on easy terms under P.L. 480 has ranged in value from $17 to $35 million a year over the last decade, with the bulk going to areas of "national security" concern, such as South Vietnam, Cambodia, and, most recently, Egypt.

Those who design, print, or broadcast cigarette advertisements also benefit from the tobacco business. Far from reducing promotional fever, the ban on advertising cigarettes over television and radio in the United States and several other countries merely provided a windfall for the print media. The entire $250-million advertising budget of the American cigarette companies now goes totally to magazines and newspapers. Only a few major U.S. periodicals have refused to share in this money.

The mainstays of the tobacco business are, of course, the hundreds of millions of tobacco consumers—those who pay for both the pleasures and the lethal consequences of tobacco use. Social forces encourage people to start smoking and to cling to the habit, but the $85 to $100 billion that consumers spend each year on cigarettes is what sustains global cigarette production and trade.

In the ambiguity-plagued universe of environmental health studies, only rarely does proof emerge of an unequivocal link between a particular environmental agent and a particular disease. The airtight medical case against cigarettes stands out sharply as an exception. Cigarettes, therefore, explicitly challenge the capacity of societies to use the conclusions of health research to improve daily life. The selective vision of cigarette company executives and the smokescreen of cigarette advertising notwithstanding, today's meaningful debate is not over the possibility that cigarettes might be a public hazard—the only question concerns eliminating a proven hazard.

But decreasing the hold of cigarettes is no simple task. Pollution from cigarette smoke, unlike impure water or industrial wastes in the air, results primarily from personal decisions. Smoking, overnutrition, dangerous driving, and other forms of self-destruction are all health problems rooted in personal behavior, problems that often leave health officials perplexed and frustrated. Many persons with knowledge of the risks involved still persist in unhealthy behavior. How can public health officials influence them? Draconian interventions into people's lives might reduce smoking to a minimum, but at a social price few are willing to pay.

From childhood onward, people are constantly bombarded with subtle and not-so-subtle enticements to smoke; advertisements that associate cigarettes with sexual success are reinforced by what is probably a far stronger influence—the example set by countless smoking adults. Once they become smokers, individuals grow both psychologically and physiologically dependent on cigarettes. Although teen-agers may start smoking out of a desire to appear sophisticated and mature, they may continue long after that motive has lost its relevance because they are hooked on nicotine, an addictive drug.

The full social cost of cigarette smoking has never been calculated, but the purchase price of cigarettes, the extra medical expenses incurred by smokers, and the income that smokers sacrifice to unnecessary disease and premature death constitute only a portion of the total cost. A 1975 report to the Massachusetts Public Health Association estimated that Massachusetts smokers alone cost the state's general public more than half a billion dollars a year. If no one in the state smoked, fire protection costs would fall by at least $18 million and fire damage by at least $24 million a year. State medical costs provided from public funds or health insurance to treat smoking-induced diseases are $220 million a year. Production losses in the state totaling $260 million a year result from the working time missed because of smoking-related disease.

The cost of cigarettes includes, in addition to the above factors, the many hundreds of millions of dollars in public funds spent around the world each year on research on smoking-related cancer, heart, and respiratory diseases. Moreover, nonsmokers generally pay higher life insurance rates than they would if smokers were not included in the actuarial tables. The health hazard inflicted upon innocent bystanders provides another critical justification for government intervention to deter tobacco use.

Over the last few years many local and national governments have, in fact, restricted public smoking. Moscow recently banned smoking in the city's restaurants, while smoking in public buildings and transportation has been limited or prohibited in many parts of the United States and Europe. Such laws are often laxly enforced, however. Interestingly, more than half of all current smokers polled in the United States in 1975 agreed that cigarette smoking "should be allowed in fewer places than it is now."

Governments can weed out many contradictions from their present policies by ending subsidies to the tobacco industry. But in the end, the only way to solve the smoking problem is to steer young people away from the habit and to help older smokers kick it. The vigorous, systematic use of all possible educational channels, advertising restrictions, prominent warnings on cigarette packages, tax disincentives, and so on might radically alter the smoking scene.

A different approach to the problem is to press ahead with the search for cigarettes that are lower in tars, carbon monoxide, and other toxic gases. Both the cigarette companies and the U.S. government are now involved in research toward that end. While opinions differ as to whether public funds ought to be diverted from antismoking campaigns into such research or whether all such expenses ought to be borne by the private companies, safer cigarettes can undoubtedly reduce the health costs of smoking. The two goals, a nonsmoking society and less harmful cigarettes, need not be viewed as contradictory; both can be pursued at once.

In the world's more developed countries, personal behavior has emerged as the dominant influence on health. The relevant personal choices are, in turn, influenced by the prevailing social and political environment. Societies cannot and, most would agree, should not try to dictate medically rational behavior to each individual. But neither should they encourage self-destructive behavior. As U.S. psychologist Daniel Horn, one of the pioneers in the study of smoking and health, says, today's challenge is "to identify the means whereby we can help people— whether children or adults—to develop the capability of understanding the issues in personal-choice health behavior, and the capacity to make choices both in their own self-interest and in the interest of society at large."

On Smoking   The Tobacco Institute

1   How many cigarettes are sold annually in the U.S.?

Nearly 620 billion cigarettes were purchased in 1976, about a pack-and-a-half a day by the average smoker. Sales have moved steadily upward in this decade and are continuing to increase at a rate of about 1% per year.

2   How many people smoke?

Nearly 60 million adult Americans—about 40% of the adult population.

3   Are smokers different from non-smokers?

Yes. Some doctors have concluded that smokers have behavior patterns different from non-smokers. Generally, smokers tend to be more assertive, time-conscious and energetic than non-smokers.

4   Did the Surgeon General's Report establish that smoking causes cancer and other diseases?

No. The report of the Advisory Committee to the Surgeon General in 1964 failed to establish a cause-and-effect relationship between cigarette smoking and cancer and other diseases. The report was essentially a "study of numbers"—a selective review of population studies which compared disease rates among smokers, ex-smokers and non-smokers. The report showed a statistical association between cigarette smoking and lung cancer. However, the report stated, "Statistical methods cannot establish proof of a causal relationship in an association. The causal significance of an association is a matter of judgment which goes beyond any statement of statistical probability."

5   What questions were left unanswered by the Surgeon General's Report?

Many questions were left unresolved. Why, for example, do non-smokers fall victim to heart disease, lung cancer and other diseases frequently associated with smokers? If, as some anti-smoking groups claim, cigarette smoking is the major cause of lung cancer, why is it that the vast majority of the "heavy" smokers never develop the disease? Why hasn't independent scientific research been able to identify any one or combination of the thousands of components as found in cigarette smoke as the cause of any particular disease? Why in more than forty years of research hasn't anyone been able to reproduce the type of lung cancer associated with smoking—through tobacco smoke inhalation—in laboratory animals?

6   Have scientists determined what causes cancer?

No. Scientists are continuing research to determine what causes cancer in humans. In attempts to learn the cause of lung cancer, for example, some researchers are investigating the effects of environmental agents in the air such as vapors, dust and other pollutants. Other scientists are studying the possibility that certain individuals may have a genetic predisposition to cancer. Some studies of the incidence of lung cancer by geographic area do not show correlations with levels of smoking.

7   Are cigarettes with low "tar" and nicotine "safer" for smokers?

Cigarettes have never been proven to be unsafe. Many varieties of low "tar"–nicotine cigarettes are now on the market in response to consumer preference trends. Sales of cigarettes with 15mg. of "tar" or less increased by 50% in 1976 and comprised more than 25% of the market in 1977.

8   Are "tar" and nicotine in cigarettes dangerous?

Claims that "tar" and nicotine in cigarettes harm the smoker are not supported by scientific fact. The nicotine from a cigarette is eliminated from the blood rapidly and there is little cumulative effect. By the time the cigarette is finished much of the nicotine is already metabolized. As was pointed out in the 1964 Surgeon General's Advisory Committee Report on Smoking and Health, "nicotine in quantities absorbed from smoking and other methods of tobacco use is very low and probably does not represent a significant health problem."

"Tar" is the particulate matter collected by super-cooling and condensing tobacco smoke under special laboratory conditions. This method of producing "tar" has little to do with the way we smoke cigarettes. Concern about "tar" is primarily due to early experiments which involved painting the artificially-produced substance on laboratory animals' skin. Other common substances such as tea have also been applied in much the same way, producing skin cancer on the backs of test animals. Such experiments are of little scientific value since the skin of test animals does not approximate the lining of a human lung, and because the quantities of "tar" used have been estimated to equal a man's smoking 100,000 cigarettes a day.

9   Are gases contained in cigarette smoke harmful to the smoker?

It is claimed that cigarette smoke contains harmful quantities of carbon monoxide, nitrogen dioxide and hydrogen cyanide. However, such gases occur only in low concentrations and small quantities compared to the high concentrations and large amounts necessary to produce significant effects.

Any combustion process produces carbon monoxide: cooking on a gas range, auto exhaust, garbage dump fires, etc. Dr. Helmut Wakeham said in an article published in *Preventive Medicine*, December 1977, "Cigarette smoking is an insignificant source of carbon monoxide in the overall atmosphere as compared with other natural and man-made sources."

Very little, if any, nitrogen dioxide is present in fresh cigarette smoke. As for hydrogen cyanide, the 1964 Surgeon General's Report on Smoking and Health reported that it is present in tobacco smoke only in insignificant amounts.

10   Does cigarette advertising cause young people to start smoking?

A number of independent studies have examined reasons why individuals choose to smoke. No study has demonstrated that advertising is responsible. Dr. Ernst Wynder, President of the American Health Foundation has said, "I do not believe that advertising has much influence." In a recent editorial about its cigarette advertising policy, *The Columbia Journalism Review* remarked: "What about the solid research [which indicated] that cigarette advertising rarely influences decisions to smoke or not to smoke, but [rather] that its effect and purpose is to influence the choice of brands?"

Advertising creates brand loyalties; it apparently does not create new smokers. Tobacco companies do not encourage young people to smoke. They regard smoking as an adult custom based on a mature individual's freedom of choice.

11 What organizations oppose smoking and tobacco?

Some are the voluntary health associations (American Cancer Society; American Lung Association; American Heart Association) which existed long before the 1964 Surgeon General's Report. Other organizations have sprung up since then, mostly during the last three to five years. Most are acronyms: ASH (Action on Smoking and Health); FANS (Fresh Air for Non-Smokers); GASP (Group Against Smokers Pollution) and SHAME (Society to Humiliate, Aggravate, Mortify and Embarrass Smokers).

12 What motivates the anti-smoking movement?

Despite the presence of warning notices on all cigarette packages sold in this country, there are still those who believe that it is their duty to "protect us from ourselves." Fifty years ago it was the consumption of alcoholic beverages which aroused the passion of such crusaders. Prohibition was supposed to save the nation, but, as we now know, it created more problems than it solved.

The opposition to the personal enjoyment of tobacco began soon after Sir Walter Raleigh brought the first cargo of leaf to England in the sixteenth century. As early as 1604, anti-tobacco pamphlets such as "A Counterblaste to Tobacco" authored by King James I of England were circulated. Today, with tobacco well into its fifth century of use, the controversy continues.

In the 1950s and 60s, the attack against tobacco was aimed at the product—cigarettes—and led to the package warning label, the broadcast advertising ban and higher taxes. Nevertheless, cigarette sales continued to rise. Recently, the attack has shifted to the users of the product—smokers—by attempts to make them socially unacceptable.

American Lung Association past-president Jack Hoffman has said, "Probably the only way we can win a substantial reduction of smoking is if we can somehow make it non-acceptable socially. We thought the scare of medical statistics and opinions would produce a major reduction. It didn't."

There are some who would go further, calling for an all-out prohibition of tobacco. Dr. Benjamin Byrd, a past-president of the American

Cancer Society said recently, "I think we would be better off if there were no cigarettes in the U.S. I would like to see them banned by Congress."

13 Will the anti-smoking movement succeed?

According to Dr. Peter Bourne, Special Assistant to the President for Health Issues, such proposals are not realistic. In remarks to the Ad-Hoc Committee on Tobacco and Smoking Research of the American Cancer Society on November 10, 1977, Dr. Bourne said, "Because of the political, social and economic ramifications, it is unrealistic for us to suggest a tobacco prohibition as a feasible short-term goal, and that campaign would bring into question our own credibility. It is there that we are on our weakest ground. While prohibiting use of cigarettes in public places would please non-smokers, it would not necessarily reduce overall cigarette consumption or reduce the health consequences. We have done little research on the hazards, if any, of other people's cigarettes."

14 Are non-smokers subjected to a health hazard when they breathe other people's smoke?

Public smoking in a normal environment has no known association with disease. Dr. Reuel Stallones, who was a consultant to the Surgeon General's Advisory Committee, stated, "In very direct terms, there's no medical proof that non-smokers exposed to cigarette smoke in ordinary relations with smokers suffer any damage." A study conducted by two scientists from Harvard University's School of Public Health also failed to demonstrate any health hazard to the non-smoker. The scientists took a special air sampling device into several Boston area public places (restaurants, waiting rooms, cocktail lounges) to measure the smoke concentrations. Their figures show that in order to inhale the equivalent of a single filter cigarette, the non-smoker would have to sit in a crowded cocktail lounge for more than 100 consecutive hours.

15 What about the alleged "right" to breathe smoke-free air?

Stated in terms of a "right" the issue becomes more fundamental than just the question of whether or not people should be allowed to smoke in public places. According to Federal District Judge Jack M. Gordon, the issue really involved personal freedom. That was the view expressed by Judge Gordon in his decision dismissing a lawsuit that would have prohibited smoking and the sale of cigarettes at the New Oreleans Superdome: "For the Constitution to be read to protect non-smokers from inhaling tobacco smoke would be to broaden the rights of the Constitution to limits heretofore unheard of. ... This court is of the opinion that the State's permissive attitude toward smoking in the Louisiana Superdome adequately preserves the delicate balance of individual rights without yielding to the temptation to intervene in purely private matters."

16   What is the economic impact of tobacco?

The tobacco industry has a major impact on the U.S. economy. Tobacco is grown in 22 states on some 400,000 farms and is the fifth largest cash crop behind corn, soybeans, wheat and cotton. Last year customer expenditures for tobacco products exceeded $16 billion. The U.S. is also the leading exporter of tobacco and the third largest tobacco importer. The result is a positive net contribution of more than $1 billion per year to the U.S. balance of payments.

17   What's the effect of tobacco taxes?

Federal, state and local governments realize some $6 billion annually in direct taxes on tobacco products. This revenue helps provide schools, roads, hospitals and other vital government services. Tobacco tax collections are exceeded only by those from alcoholic beverages and gasoline. Since 1863 when the Federal Government began taxing tobacco, more than $107 billion has been collected.

18   Do smokers pay their fair share of taxes?

They certainly do. Last year, for example, Virginia smokers paid over $110 million in combined federal, state and local taxes. In Fairfax County in Virginia (where a restrictive public smoking ordinance was recently enacted), smokers paid $7.8 million more than non-smokers in local, state and federal excise taxes. SMOKERS PAY THESE TAXES WITHOUT RECEIVING ADDITIONAL SERVICES. As one Virginia Congressman pointed out: "They are collecting more taxes from smokers than from non-smokers. What will happen when they succeed in forcing smokers to quit, thus losing county tax revenues? Will the Supervisors find new sources of revenue, or will they cut back local services?"

19   What is the tobacco industry doing to help resolve the smoking and health controversy?

In the last 24 years the tobacco industry has provided more than $70 million for independent research regarding questions related to smoking and health. In many of these years this commitment had exceeded that of any government department, and has been substantially more than the research expenditure reported by all the voluntary health associations who spend a major portion of their donated funds for administration and for public relations campaigns. The tobacco industry is committed to advancing scientific inquiry in this area.

20   Do the tobacco companies control the research they sponsor?

Absolutely not! The commitment of the tobacco manufacturers to resolve the smoking and health controversy has never been fully appreciated. Grants are made with no strings attached except a pledge to apply the money to legitimate scientific research. Each researcher is free to publish his study results, whatever they may be.

21   What is the tobacco subsidy program?

It is not a tobacco subsidy program—it is a tobacco price stabilization program. It is a loan program exactly like the program for wheat and other agricultural commodities to stabilize prices so farmers can get a reasonable return on their investments. The program mandates quotas limiting the acreage a farmer can use for tobacco growing and the poundage he can sell. The program also allows the tobacco farmer to borrow money, using the tobacco as collateral. Without it the tobacco supply would be larger, not smaller.

Unlike the stabilization programs for other agricultural commodities, the tobacco price stabilization program has in most years paid back more to the government than it borrowed. This is partially because tobacco stored as collateral for the loan plus interest can be held for up to ten years before being sold at a time of high demand. Since the program began in 1933, the cumulative realized loss to the federal government has been around $52 million, part of which was offset by interest income. (This compared to the loss sustained by the corn stabilization program which has cost the government $16.9 billion since 1933.) Thus, the tobacco program is one of the least expensive and most successful of the farm commodity programs.

Tobacco is one of the few crops that still utilizes family hand labor and provides a reasonable income on a small family farm. Tobacco growing is labor intensive. While it takes approximately 3.5 man-hours to grow one acre of corn, it requires over 300 man-hours to grow one acre of tobacco.

If the tobacco price stabilization program were ended, over 600,000 farm families would be affected. (Tobacco is grown on over 400,000 farms in the U.S. On many of these farms, more than one family depends on the income from tobacco sales.) Many of these farmers would be forced to seek other forms of employment, and undoubtedly many thousands would find themselves on government welfare rolls.

On October 12, 1976, then candidate, now President Jimmy Carter said about the tobacco price stabilization policy, "I personally see no need to do away with a program that costs the government next to nothing, while enabling so many hard working families to earn a living."

The Tobacco Institute recognizes that there are differences of opinion concerning smoking and health. This booklet is presented in the belief that full, free and informed discussion of the smoking and health controversy is in the public interest, and in the conviction that the controversy must be resolved by scientific research.

New Medium for the Message

Consumer Reports

On July 22, 1969, Joseph F. Cullman, then the president of Philip Morris, Inc., appeared before the Consumer Subcommittee of the Senate Commerce Committee with a startling offer. Speaking as the representative of the cigarette industry, Cullman told the subcommittee that cigarette companies would voluntarily discontinue all television advertising if Congress permitted them to take such a concerted action without fear of prosecution under the antitrust laws.

At the time, the cigarette industry was spending some $200-million a year, about two-thirds of its total advertising budget, on TV commercials, and those commercials were a major source of revenue for the broadcasting industry. The offer to leave the airwaves, therefore, was not only startling but also, in the eyes of some, a public-spirited display of corporate responsibility in the face of overwhelming evidence of the health hazards of cigarette smoking. In retrospect, however, the offer can be viewed as one of the shrewdest business decisions the industry ever made. Today, more than five years after the last cigarette commercial appeared on television, cigarette sales have never been better, and the great public concern about the effects of cigarette advertising, so evident in the late 1960's, has abated.

To understand why the voluntary departure from television worked out so well for the industry, one must look back to a critical decision made by the Federal Communications Commission (FCC) in June 1967. In response to a petition filed by attorney John F. Banzhaf (a former CU board member), the FCC ruled that, under the fairness doctrine, broadcasters were required to make available free air time for antismoking messages, since the prosmoking messages of cigarette commercials were judged a controversial matter of legitimate public importance. As a result of the FCC's ruling, thousands of messages warning of the health hazards of smoking appeared on television over the next 3½ years. Antismoking messages never matched cigarette commercials minute-for-minute—the ratio was four to five cigarette commercials to every antismoking message. Still, millions of dollars' worth of air time was turned over to the antismoking forces, and, judging by what happened to cigarette sales, their antismoking messages seemed to have at least an initial impact.

In 1964, the year the Surgeon General reported that cigarette smoking increased the risk of contracting lung cancer and exacerbated heart and respiratory diseases, domestic cigarette consumption fell sharply for a two-month period, and annual sales declined to 505 billion cigarettes from 516.5 billion the previous year. As the shock of the Surgeon General's report wore off, and as cigarette commercials continued to pound away as if nothing had happened, sales recovered, reaching a high of 540 billion cigarettes sold in 1968. But in 1969, the second full year of antismoking messages on television, cigarette sales declined more than 12 billion—a greater numerical drop in sales than immediately after the Surgeon General's report—before recovering again in 1970.

When it became clear that cigarette companies would leave TV (the last commercials were shown January 1, 1971), the FCC ruled that broadcasters need not continue running antismoking spots. As a result, the antismoking campaign on television shriveled to a relative handful of "public service" messages. In 1971, cigarette sales rose by 13 billion. Sales gained another 14.5 billion in 1972, an astounding 23 billion in 1973, and another 10 billion in 1974. Last year, cigarette sales reached a new peak, estimated at more than 600 billion.

The Shift to Print

Clearly, the departure from television hasn't hurt the cigarette industry. The industry simply shifted the bulk of its advertising budget from television to newspapers and magazines. In 1971, the first year off the air, money spent on cigarette advertising in magazines doubled, expenditures in newspapers more than quadrupled, and expenditures on billboards, posters, and transit ads (the media that largely replaced TV in reaching children and teen-agers) jumped more than five times. In 1970, the industry had spent $205-million on TV advertising out of its total advertising budget of $314.7-million. Four years later, the industry spent nothing for television, but its total ad budget remained almost as big—$306.8-million.

The big switch from television to other advertising media seems like a perfectly normal business practice, assuming one considers cigarettes a perfectly normal consumer product. But back in 1969, Senator Frank E. Moss, chairman of the Consumer Subcommittee, was one of a number of persons who wondered whether a known carcinogen and a major contributor to heart disease and other ailments should be treated like a normal consumer product. Senator Moss repeatedly questioned Joseph F. Cullman, the industry spokesman, about the industry's advertising intentions once its commercials were off the air. Cullman waffled: "I think that is too important a matter for me to answer directly, other than to say that it is a large amount of money and that we will approach it constructively . . ." he told Senator Moss.

If the cigarette industry's spokesman was evasive about the extent of future advertising plans he was quite clear about the *nature* of the advertising. Here's what Cullman, now chairman of the board of Philip Morris, told the Moss subcommittee:

> With respect to cigarette advertising in other media, it is the intention of the cigarette manufacturers to continue to avoid advertising directed to young persons . . . ; not to use testimonials from athletes or other celebrities who might have special appeal to young people; to avoid advertising which represents that cigarette smoking is essential to social prominence, success, or sexual attraction; and to refrain from depicting smokers engaged in sports or other activities requiring stamina or conditioning beyond those required in normal recreation.

Cullman further indicated that the cigarette manufacturers would abide by their voluntary Cigarette Advertising Code (now defunct), which, among many other things, stated that "Cigarette advertising may use attractive, healthy looking models . . . provided that there is no suggestion that their attractive appearance or good health is due to cigarette smoking."

Those good intentions sound a bit hollow measured against today's performance. Cigarette ads now frequently appear in magazines with high percentages of young readers—magazines such as Motor Trend, Car and Driver, Glamour, Mademoiselle, Playboy, and Penthouse. Here, a *Viceroy* ad in Motor Trend features a race car driver—certainly a profession requiring above-average stamina and conditioning. There, a *Camel* ad in Rolling Stone shows a young-looking woman casting a longing glance at a casually dressed, young-looking man smoking in a restaurant. The copy reads: "One of a kind. He does more than survive. He lives. Because he knows." The ad would appear to connect cigarettes with "social prominence, success, or sexual attractiveness," not to mention life and survival.

Women: The Special Target

The most insidious ads are those aimed at women. A Lorillard Corp. ad asks readers to "Meet *Max*," with a young-looking woman clad in bell-bottom jeans and a faded denim jacket. In a *Kent* ad, an attractive young woman holding a cigarette and a beer says, "C'mon."

Ads for *Virginia Slims*, a product of Cullman's own Philip Morris, have shamelessly exploited the women's liberation movement with the slogan, "You've come a long way, baby." Women have indeed come a long way. The widely publicized Virginia Slims Tennis Tournament has helped make women tennis stars nearly as wealthy as men tennis stars. And women have also come a long way toward equality with men in lung cancer. According to the American Cancer Society, the death rate from lung cancer among women has doubled in the past 10 years. Female death rates from lung cancer were once as low as one-sixth the death rates among males. Now they are one-fourth and "threatening to catch up," says the Cancer Society, which attributes this grim fact to the steadily increasing number of females who smoke, "partly as a result of advertising and promotion."

A study recently conducted for the Cancer Society showed that the percentage of girls 13 to 17 years old who smoke has risen from 22 per cent in 1969 to 27 per cent now, so that almost as many girls in that age-group smoke as do boys. (In that same time period the number of boys 13 to 17 years old who smoked remained a virtually constant 30 per cent.) Moreover, while only 10 per cent of those girls smoked a pack or more of cigarettes a day in 1969, now 40 per cent of them smoke at least one pack. "Smoking habits are established in the teens," the Cancer Society notes, "and in the great majority of cases, teen-age girl smokers will become adult women smokers."

Tougher Action Needed

The law requires cigarette labels and ads to carry a health warning that has proved singularly ineffective except as a legal shield for the cigarette industry. (Victims of lung cancer and their families find it difficult to win a product liability suit in the face of advertising and labeling that says: "Cigarette Smoking Is Dangerous To Your Health.")

Each year, the Federal Trade Commission dutifully reports to Congress on the advertising techniques being used by cigarette manufacturers in violation of their promise to Congress. And each year the report is filed and forgotten. As Senator Moss told CU [Consumers Union, publishers of *Consumer Reports*]: "We were able to force cigarette commercials from television because of the strong sense of public outrage at this involuntary intruder in the home, bringing the allure of jingles and animation to children not yet old enough to read. With the commercials gone, the health hazards of cigarettes have become an invisible issue. Ads in magazines and newspapers simply do not generate the same kind of outrage that TV commercials engendered."

An organization called Action on Smoking & Health (ASH), headed by the same John Banzhaf whose petition to the FCC first paved the way for anticigarette commercials, has petitioned the FTC to move against a number of obvious ills in cigarette advertising. These include the use of billboards; themes that connect cigarettes with healthy people or healthy activities; ads that fail to disclose the difficulty of quitting smoking once you've started; and ads that attempt to relieve or eliminate anxieties about the health consequences of smoking. The FTC itself has recommended to Congress that the health warning on labels and in advertising should be made much stronger and specifically cite cancer and other diseases as possible dangers associated with smoking.

CU applauds, politely, those and other measures aimed at toning down cigarette advertising. But they don't get to the heart of the matter.

In CU's view, Congress should ban all advertising of cigarettes. Period. It is uncertain whether an advertising ban would by itself, without an extensive anticigarette campaign, significantly reduce the number of new recruits to cigarette smoking. But the main argument is an ethical one: It is immoral to permit the advertising of an addictive product that causes lung cancer and contributes to heart disease, emphysema, bronchitis, and vascular disease. At the same time, the FCC should reverse its decision that the fairness doctrine no longer applied when cigarette commercials left the air. Three-and-one-half years of antismoking messages cannot compensate for two decades of cigarette commercials; anticigarette messages should be mandated at the same level at which they were aired in 1970 and should be included particularly on programs popular among school children.

Where would the money for anticigarette commercials come from? According to the Public Citizen's Health Research Group, the Department of Agriculture now spends $60-million a year to support the tobacco industry, the major portion of which goes for various export and price-support programs. Much of that subsidy to the tobacco industry should end. The money thus saved should be used to underwrite antismoking educational campaigns and to help the large number of small tobacco growers who would suffer economically from the withdrawal of Government funds.

In Search of Principle

Meanwhile, of course, it is idle to expect the cigarette industry to refrain voluntarily from advertising to the young and to women; the business of business is, after all, business. Magazines and newspapers are free to accept or reject any advertising, of course. But they, too, are businesses. A publication that turns down cigarette ads turns down substantial sums of money. Not many make the sacrifice.

A few big publications, however, have put principle ahead of profit and steadfastly refuse cigarette ads. Among them are Readers Digest, National Geographic, Good Housekeeping, The New Yorker, and The Christian Science Monitor. Principle, we might add, is probably costing them plenty. Good Housekeeping, which says cigarette ads aren't compatible with its editorial content, estimates it could book 120 pages of such advertising a year, based on comparisons with similar magazines. At a fee of $30,000 per full-color page, that would come to $3.6-million a year in additional income. Readers Digest's "lost" income is probably even greater. The magazine, which has taken strong editorial stands against smoking, charges $64,995 a page. National Geographic, which refuses cigarette ads largely because a lot of children read the magazine, receives $56,850 a page. The New Yorker, a weekly that quit taking cigarette ads following the 1964 Surgeon General's report and after an impressive antismoking article by reporter Thomas Whiteside, charges $9400 a page.

One of the many prominent publications that keep editorial principles nicely isolated from business realities is The New York Times. Not long ago, The Times commented editorially on the "distressing news" about the increase in smoking among teen-age girls. "What is still unsolved," The Times pointed out, "is how to motivate people to behave in ways that serve their long-run interests best. . . ." One can only speculate on the motivational impact of the 377 pages of cigarette advertising (about $4-million worth) carried by The New York Times last year.

In the past, The Times has recognized that its social obligations extended beyond the editorial pages. In 1969, before health warnings were required in cigarette advertising, The Times insisted that cigarette companies could advertise in its pages only if the ads carried a health warning. All the cigarette companies withdrew their ads. The Times managed to withstand the financial blow until the warnings in the ads were re-

THIS GOOD GREEN AME
THAN JUST GROW TOBACC

Millions of Americans have seen this land.

You'll find it in 22 states—green plants in neat rows, backed by a barn and h

It is Tobaccoland U.S.A.

If it were an area by itself, it would probably be a member of the United N; It is *bigger* than most U.N. member countries. And richer. It would be an extraord country, and a lovely one.

But, of course, it is not. It is *our* land, tied to the rest of our country by hist and by social custom and economic need.

Warning: The Surgeon General Has Determined
That Cigarette Smoking Is Dangerous to Your Health.

AN LAND DOES A LOT MORE

It gave us our first cash crop, over 350 years ago. It provided the economic strength and hope that sustained our first settlers and helped us win our independence.

Today it supports more than 500,000 farm families.

Last year, it paid over $6 *billion* in taxes—$2.5 billion to our national treasury, and $3.6 billion to the states, cities and counties.

It is contributing more than $1 billion to our international trade balance this year over 100 countries are buying our tobacco. It is not only the finest tobacco crop in the world, but nearly the largest—only China's is bigger.

Tobaccoland U.S.A. is a good, rich and productive land.

And it is a good land to have as part of us. **THE TOBACCO INSTITUTE**
1776 K St. N.W., Washington, D.C. 20006

quired by law and the cigarette advertisers returned to The Times.

Perhaps it's again time for the country's most influential newspaper to set an ethical example for the rest of the newspaper business.

A Counter-Blaste to Tobacco King James I

And for the vanities committed in this filthie custome, is it not both great vanitie and vncleanenesse, that at the table, a place of respect, of cleanlinesse, of modestie, men should not be ashamed, to sit tossing of *Tobacco pipes*, and puffing of the smoke of *Tobacco* one to another, making the filthie smoke and stinke thereof, to exhale athwart the dishes, and infect the aire, when very often, men that abhorre it are at their repast? Surely Smoke becomes a kitchin far better then a Dining chamber, and yet it makes a kitchen also oftentimes in the inward parts of men, soiling and infecting them, with an vnctuous and oily kinde of Soote, as hath bene found in some great *Tobacco* takers, that after their death were opened. . . .

And is it not a great vanitie, that a man cannot heartily welcome his friend now, but straight they must bee in hand with *Tobacco*? No it is become in place of a cure, in point of good fellowship, and he that will refuse to take a pipe of *Tobacco* among his fellowes, (though by his own election he would rather feele the sauour of a Sinke) is accounted peeuish and no good company, euen as they doe with tippeling in the cold Easterne Countries. Yea the Mistresse cannot in a more manerly kinde, entertaine her seruant, then by giuing him out of her faire hand a pipe of *Tobacco*. But herein is not onely a great vanitie, but a great contempt of God's good giftes, that the sweetenesse of mans breath, being a good gift of God, should be wilfully corrupted by this stinking smoke, wherein I must confesse, it hath too strong a vertue; and so that which is an ornament of nature, and can neither by any artifice be at the first acquired, nor once lost, be recouered againe, shall be filthily corrupted with an incurable stinke, which vile qualitie is as directly contrary to that wrong opinion which is holden of the wholsomnesse therof, as the venime of putrifaction is contrary to the vertue Preseruatiue.

Moreouer, which is a great iniquitie, and against all humanitie, the husband shall not bee ashamed, to reduce thereby his delicate, wholesome, and cleane complexioned wife, to that extremetie, that either shee must also corrupt her sweete breath therewith, or else resolue to liue in a perpetuall stinking torment.

Haue you not reason then to bee ashamed, and to forbeare this filthie

From James I, *A Counter-Blaste to Tobacco* (Edinburgh: E. & G. Goldsmid, 1885).

noueltie, so basely grounded, so foolishly receiued and so grossely mistaken in the right vse thereof? In your abuse thereof sinning against God, harming yourselues both in persons and goods, and taking also thereby the markes and notes of vanitie vpon you: by the custome thereof making your selves to be wondered at by all forraine ciuil Nations, and by all strangers that come among you, to be scorned and contemned. A custome lothsome to the eye, hatefull to the Nose, harmefull to the braine, dangerous to the Lungs, and in the blacke stinking fume thereof, neerest resembling the horrible Stigian smoke of the pit that is bottomelesse.

QUESTIONS

1. Compare the voices of the four short quotations at the beginning of the chapter. Do you associate cigarette smoking with certain personality types? Do these quotes sound like people who probably smoke? Which ones do you find attractive?

2. I wanted to include some cigarette ads in this chapter, but the three major cigarette companies to which I wrote refused to give me permission to publish any of their ads, so you will have to collect your own. Look at the series that shows closeups of handsome young people holding packs of Winstons, or the athletic young women who tell us why they smoke Trues. These ads are using a voice coupled with a picture to sell cigarettes. What characteristics do these supposed smokers have?

3. What is the voice in the overview of the health consequences of smoking put out by the Public Health Service? How would you describe this style of writing?

4. Which examples here are obviously persuasive? Which ones appear to be objective but have a persuasive message all the same?

5. Examine each cigarette ad in your collection for assumptions about the audience. Is the ad aimed at men or women or at a particular age group? Did the ad writer assume that the audience is interested in achieving something? Status? Sexiness? A more exciting life? Peace and quiet? Compare the assumed audience of On Smoking published by the Tobacco Institute.

6. Most people who object to smoking no longer use the sort of voice that King James I used. Why not? What sort of voice might you adopt if you wanted to persuade a friend to stop smoking? A child of yours? A parent?

7. Which of the examples contain only information that you have heard many times before, and which, if any, contain information that is new?

8. Examine carefully the disagreements among the Tobacco Institute's pamphlet On Smoking, Eckholm's article, and the U.S. Public Health Service's "Overview." Whom do you believe? Why?

9. Find an example of a cigarette ad that is set up to look like a report. Does it use language that sounds like that of the Public Health Service? What facts, if any, does it give? Why might an ad writer choose this "informative" style?

10. Define a research topic, dealing with cigarettes, on which a student in your class could expect to do a good job. In contrast, suggest some cigarette-related topics that would almost certainly result in superficial or useless papers.

6

Marriage

The subject of marriage has attracted writers in different fields from poetry to sociology to advertising. Romantics and cynics are equally fascinated. Listen to the voices especially in this chapter, and see how a writer's profession and personal attitude determine so much of his content.

Epithalamion

Edmund Spenser

Behold whiles she before the altar stands
Hearing the holy priest that to her speakes
And blesseth her with his two happy hands,
How the red roses flush vp in her cheekes,
And the pure snow with goodly vermill stayne,
Like crimsin dyde in grayne,
That euen th'Angels which continually,
About the sacred Altare doe remaine,
Forget their seruice and about her fly,
Ofte peeping in her face that seemes more fayre,
The more they on it stare.
But her sad eyes still fastened on the ground,
Are gouerned with goodly modesty,
That suffers not one looke to glaunce awry,
Which may let in a little thought vnsownd.

From Edmund Spenser, "Epithalamion," in *Spenser: Poetical Works*, edited by J. C. Smith and E. DeSelincourt (New York: Oxford University Press, 1912).

Why blush ye loue to giue to me your hand,
The pledge of all our band?
Sing ye sweet Angels, Alleluya sing,
That all the woods may answere and your eccho ring.

Nowal is done; bring home the bride againe,
Bring home the triumph of our victory,
Bring home with you the glory of her gaine,
With ioyance bring her and with iollity.
Neuer had man more ioyfull day then this,
Whom heauen would heape with blis.
Make feast therefore now all this liue long day,
This day for euer to me holy is,
Poure out the wine without restraint or stay,
Poure not by cups, but by the belly full,
Pour out to all that wull,
And sprinkle all the postes and wals with wine,
That they may sweat, and drunken be withall.
Crowne ye God Bacchus with a coronall,
And Hymen also crowne with wreathes of vine,
And let the Graces daunce vnto the rest;
For they can doo it best:
The whiles the maydens doe theyr carroll sing,
To which the woods shal answer and theyr eccho ring.

Marriage   Gregory Corso

for Mr. and Mrs. Mike Goldberg

Should I get married? Should I be good?
Astound the girl next door
with my velvet suit and faustus hood?
Don't take her to movies but to cemeteries
tell all about werewolf bathtubs and forked clarinets
then desire her and kiss her and all the preliminaries
and she going just so far and I understanding why
not getting angry saying You must feel! It's beautiful to feel!
Instead take her in my arms
lean against an old crooked tombstone
and woo her the entire night the constellations in the sky—

When she introduces me to her parents
back straightened, hair finally combed, strangled by a tie,

should I sit knees together on their 3rd-degree sofa
and not ask Where's the bathroom?
How else to feel other than I am,
a young man who often thinks Flash Gordon soap—
O how terrible it must be for a young man
seated before a family and the family thinking
We never saw him before! He wants our Mary Lou!
After tea and homemade cookies they ask What do you do?
Should I tell them? Would they like me then?
Say All right get married, we're losing a daughter
but we're gaining a son—
And should I then ask Where's the bathroom?

O God, and the wedding! All her family and her friends
and only a handful of mine all scroungy and bearded
just waiting to get at the drinks and food—
And the priest! he looking at me as if I masturbated
asking me Do you take this woman
for your lawful wedded wife?
And I, trembling what to say, say Pie Glue!
I kiss the bride all those corny men slapping me on the back:
She's all yours, boy! Ha-ha-ha!
And in their eyes you could see
some obscene honeymoon going on—
Then all that absurd rice and clanky cans and shoes
Niagara Falls! Hordes of us! Husbands! Wives! Flowers!
All streaming into cozy hotels
All going to do the same thing tonight
The indifferent clerk he knowing what was going to happen
The lobby zombies they knowing what
The whistling elevator man he knowing
The winking bellboy knowing
Everybody knows! I'd be almost inclined not to do anything!
Stay up all night! Stare that hotel clerk in the eye!
Screaming: I deny honeymoon! I deny honeymoon!
running rampant into those almost climactic suites
yelling Radio belly! Cat shovel!
O I'd live in Niagara forever! in a dark cave beneath the Falls
I'd sit there the Mad Honeymooner
devising ways to break marriages, a scourge of bigamy
a saint of divorce—

But I should get married I should be good
How nice it'd be to come home to her
and sit by the fireplace and she in the kitchen
aproned young and lovely wanting my baby

and so happy about me she burns the roast beef
and comes crying to me and I get up from my big papa chair
saying Christmas teeth! Radiant brains! Apple deaf!
God what a husband I'd make! Yes, I should get married!
So much to do! like sneaking into Mr. Jones' house late at night
and cover his golf clubs with 1920 Norwegian books
Like hanging a picture of Rimbaud on the lawnmower
Like pasting Tannu Tuva postage stamps
all over the picket fence
Like when Mrs. Kindhead comes to collect
for the Community Chest
grab her and tell her There are unfavorable omens in the sky!
And when the mayor comes to get my vote tell him
When are you going to stop people killing whales!
And when the milkman comes leave him a note in the bottle
Penguin dust, bring me penguin dust, I want penguin dust—

Yet if I should get married and it's Connecticut and snow
and she gives birth to a child and I am sleepless, worn,
up for nights, head bowed against a quiet window,
the past behind me,
finding myself in the most common of situations
a trembling man
knowledged with responsibility not twig-smear
nor Roman coin soup—
O what would that be like!
Surely I'd give it for a nipple a rubber Tacitus
For a rattle a bag of broken Bach records
Tack Della Francesca all over its crib
Sew the Greek alphabet on its bib
And build for its playpen a roofless Parthenon—

No, I doubt I'd be that kind of father
not rural not snow no quiet window
but hot smelly tight New York City
seven flights up, roaches and rats in the walls
a fat Reichian wife screeching over potatoes Get a job!
And five nose-running brats in love with Batman
And the neighbors all toothless and dry haired
like those hag masses of the 18th century
all wanting to come in and watch TV
The landlord wants his rent
Grocery store Blue Cross Gas & Electric Knights of Columbus
Impossible to lie back and dream Telephone snow,
ghost parking—
No! I should not get married I should never get married!

But—imagine if I were married to a beautiful
sophisticated woman
tall and pale wearing an elegant black dress
and long black gloves
holding a cigarette holder in one hand
and a highball in the other
and we lived high up in a penthouse with a huge window
from which we could see all of New York
and even farther on clearer days
No, can't imagine myself married to that pleasant prison dream—

O but what about love? I forget love
not that I am incapable of love
it's just that I see love as odd as wearing shoes—
I never wanted to marry a girl who was like my mother
And Ingrid Bergman was always impossible
And there's maybe a girl now but she's already married
And I don't like men and—
but there's got to be somebody!
Because what if I'm 60 years old and not married,
all alone in a furnished room with pee stains on my underwear
and everybody else is married! All the universe married but me!

Ah, yet well I know that were a woman possible
as I am possible
then marriage would be possible—
Like SHE in her lonely alien gaud waiting her Egyptian lover
so I wait—bereft of 2,000 years and the bath of life.

John Anderson

Robert Burns

John Anderson my jo, John,
When we were first acquent
Your locks were like the raven,
Your bonnie brow was brent;
But now your brow is bald, John,
Your locks are like the snow;
But blessings on your frosty pow,
John Anderson my jo.

John Anderson my jo, John,
We clamb the hill thegither,
And mony a canty day, John,

We've had wi' ane anither:
Now we maun totter down, John,
But hand in hand we'll go,
And sleep thegither at the foot,
John Anderson my jo.

Marriage

Richard A. Kalish

Marriage, for most people, represents the most important human relationship of their adult years. Only vocation can even begin to compete with the family in its impact on a person's life. The success and stability of marriage influence the emotional health of all concerned, and as a result influence the vitality of the entire country.

In the United States we believe that the goal of marriage is to make the two partners happy: it should be a worthwhile, self-actualizing, enjoyable experience for the couple. Carrying on the family name or taking care of the parents in their old age or bringing a dowry is no longer important to most Americans. These values are quite different in other areas of the world.

Who Marries Whom?

What brings two people together so that they wish to marry? The immediate answer is *proximity*: that is, they live or work or go to church or do something near each other, so that the chances are high that they will meet frequently and have the opportunity to get to know each other.

Husband and wife tend to be similar in numerous characteristics, such as race, religion, education, intelligence, social class, age, previous marital status (that is, divorced people tend to marry other divorced people), attitudes toward drinking, and number of children desired (Berelson & Steiner, 1964). Husband and wife also tend to have similar personality characteristics, although these similarities are not so consistent as those just cited. When people select the characteristics of an ideal mate, they select characteristics similar to their own (Prince & Baggaley, 1963). Thus the old idea that opposites attract is not upheld.

What Makes Marriages Successful?

Successful marriage depends on many factors, some of which are far from being understood. Nonetheless, research into this matter has been extensive, and psychologists can predict with some success which marriages will be happy and which will be unhappy. In reading the rest of this chapter, keep in mind that, although evidence may show that being happily married is *related to* some factor, this relationship does not imply that a happy marriage is *caused by* that factor. Thus happily married people are less likely to be depressed than unhappily married people (Renne, 1970), but it is not certain that depression leads to marital dissatisfaction, since the cause and effect could be exactly reversed.

Background Factors in Happy Marriages. Many childhood experiences are found to be related to later marital happiness. First, if you were brought up in a home with a happy marriage, you will have better chances of having a happy marriage; if you had a happy childhood, your chances will also be improved. Second, good relationships with parents produce later happy marriages. Third, children receiving firm discipline administered without undue harshness or frequency make better spouses. And, fourth, when parents are frank regarding sex and communicate healthy attitudes toward sex, their children seem to have happy marriages (Terman, 1938).

In addition, a happy marriage is more likely if the partners have finished high school or gone further, are happy on their jobs and with their leisure activities, and are physically healthy (Renne, 1970). Social relationships are similarly related to marital satisfaction. Happily married couples are more likely to see close friends and relatives frequently but are no more likely to join social, recreational, union, professional, or community organizations (Renne, 1970).

You have undoubtedly also heard that early marriages are less successful than later marriages. In one Midwestern city, 40% of those who had married before age 21 wished they had waited, compared with less than 10% of those married after 21 (Inselberg, 1961). Although the early life of the individual and his or her age at marriage are definite factors in marital success, they are certainly not insurmountable barriers.

Personal Factors in Happy Marriages. Marital happiness is greater when both husband and wife come from emotionally stable families and are themselves emotionally stable (Burgess & Cottrell, 1939; Lippman, 1954). Other personality characteristics have been found to be related to happy marriages: (1) consideration for others, (2) willingness to yield rather than insistence on dominating, (3) pleasantness as a companion, (4) self-confidence, and (5) ability to accept emotional dependence (Burgess & Wallin, 1953).

Husband and wife need not share everything—indeed, there is merit in being apart from each other occasionally—but enjoying many of the same things can enrich a marriage. Liking the same movies, the same sports, or the same books adds a common bond, as does having similar religious, social, political, and child-rearing values. It is interesting to note that not only do husbands and wives often share political attitudes, but each also assumes that the other agrees with him more than he actually does (Byrne & Blaylock, 1963). That is, husbands and wives overestimate the degree to which their spouses think as they do.

To some extent people re-create in their own marriage the marriage they lived with in their parents' home. They will behave much as the parent of their own sex behaved and will expect their own mate to behave much as their other parent behaved.

Marcia Sohn was the daughter of an aggressive woman who pushed her to "go with the right people" and "do the proper thing." Marcia's mother pushed her father also, until he was wealthy and terribly unhappy. As a child Marcia swore to herself that she would never push her own husband to become wealthy. Marcia eventually married a very pleasant man who enjoyed building up his business. Marcia did not push him to become wealthy, but she did push him to become better educated. He tried, but he decided he did not like college. Unlike Marcia's father, her husband refused to be bullied beyond a certain point, and he suggested a divorce. The couple decided to see a marriage counselor. Through his help, Marcia realized that she had been repeating the same pushing pattern that her mother had shown, except that she had pushed her husband to improve his education rather than to earn money.

Behavior in Marriage

When two people enter into marriage, they usually have extremely high ideals. In spite of good intentions, most newlyweds do not find adjusting to marriage easy, even when they know each other well, are well suited to each other, and come from stable homes. During the first several months of marriage, many unanticipated difficulties occur, until the couple finally work out reasonably healthy life patterns. Love, trust, the ability to communicate feelings (including anger), and the willingness to make an effort all help to produce a successful marriage and to encourage the personal growth of both individuals.

How can you contribute to making your marriage successful? A few of the many possible ways are:

—recognizing the needs of the other person and responding to them;
—learning to communicate openly, to share thoughts and feelings;
—learning to compromise;
—respecting privacy, giving the other person time and space to him/herself;
—being able to see the other person as he or she is, not as you want him or her to be;
—taking an interest in what the other person does;
—learning to listen;
—developing yourself as an individual and permitting the other person to develop him/herself as an individual.

Of Queens' Gardens

John Ruskin

We are foolish, and without excuse foolish, in speaking of the "superiority" of one sex to the other, as if they could be compared in similar things. Each has what the other has not: each completes the other, and is completed by the other: they are in nothing alike, and the happiness and perfection of both depends on each asking and receiving from the other what the other only can give.

Now their separate characters are briefly these. The man's power is active, progressive, defensive. He is eminently the doer, the creator, the discoverer, the defender. His intellect is for speculation and invention; his energy for adventure, for war, and for conquest, wherever war is just, wherever conquest necessary. But the woman's power is for rule, not for battle,—and her intellect is not for invention or creation, but for sweet ordering, arrangement and decision. She sees the qualities of things, their claims and their places. Her great function is Praise: she enters into no contest, but infallibly judges the crown of contest. By her office, and place, she is protected from all danger and temptation. The man, in his rough work in open world, must encounter all peril and trial:—to him, therefore, the failure, the offence, the inevitable error: often he must be wounded, or subdued, often misled, and *always* hardened. But he guards the woman from all this; within his house, as ruled by her, unless she herself has sought it, need enter no danger, no temptation, no cause of error or offence. This is the true nature of home—it is the place of Peace; the shelter, not only from all injury, but from all terror, doubt, and division. In so far as it is not this, it is not home: so far as the anxieties of the outer life penetrate into it, and the inconsistently-minded, unknown, unloved, or hostile society of the outer world is allowed by either husband or wife to cross the threshold, it ceases to be home; it is then only a part of that outer world which you have roofed over, and lighted fire in. But so far as it is a sacred place, a vestal temple, a temple of the hearth watched over by Household Gods, before whose faces none may come but those whom they can receive with love,—so far as it is this, and roof and fire are types only of a nobler shade and light,—shade as of the rock in a weary land, and light as of the Pharos in the stormy sea;—so far it vindicates the name, and fulfils the praise, of home.

And wherever a true wife comes, this home is always round her. The stars only may be over her head; the glow-worm in the night-cold grass may be the only fire at her foot: but home is yet wherever she is; and for a noble woman it stretches far round her, better than ceiled with cedar, or painted with vermilion, shedding its quiet light far, for those who else were homeless.

This, then, I believe to be,—will you not admit it to be,—the woman's

From John Ruskin, "Of Queens' Gardens," in *Sesame and Lilies*, from *Ruskin's Works* (Boston: Frederick Quinby Company, n.d.).

true place and power? But do not you see that to fulfil this, she must—as far as one can use such terms of a human creature—be incapable of error? So far as she rules, all must be right, or nothing is. She must be enduringly, incorruptibly good; instinctively, infallibly wise—wise, not for self-development, but for self-renunciation: wise, not that she may set herself above her husband, but that she may never fail from his side: wise, not with the narrowness of insolent and loveless pride, but with the passionate gentleness of an infinitely variable, because infinitely applicable, modesty of service—the true changefulness of woman. In that great sense—"La donna e mobile," not "Qual piùm' al vento;" no, nor yet "Variable as the shade, by the light quivering aspen made;" but variable as the *light*, manifold in fair and serene division, that it may take the color of all that it falls upon, and exalt it.

Two-Career Couples:

How They Make It Work

Mary-Ellen Banashek

Anyone with a demanding career knows how difficult it is to fit everything into a 24-hour day. Imagine the difficulties, then, of two people (or more if there are children involved) trying to juggle high-powered jobs, a home and the rest of their lives, individually and together. How do they manage, we wondered. . . . We're sorry to say there are no answers; the options available, however, are unlimited. . . .

When Marsha Petersen Kenny was growing up she wanted to be a fashion editor—"what looked like a glamorous, attractive job." After working at *Mademoiselle*, however, she changed her mind. For awhile she thought she'd work for a time, get married, have a baby and go live in the suburbs. She did get married and commuted to her job in the city while living on Long Island, but "after a year of that I changed my mind very quickly about suburban living and was ready to flee back to the city." Now at 30 she's sales promotion director for Estée Lauder International, and lives in an apartment in Brooklyn Heights. Her husband of six years, Steven Kenny, also 30, teaches economics at Suffolk County Community College on Long Island and lives in the house they bought out there last year. Steve comes into the city one or two nights during the week and Marsha spends weekends with him on the Island.

As Steve explains it, "We had a traditional marriage for three years while I was in grad school; then Marsha decided suburbia wasn't for her, so we moved to Brooklyn Heights for two years. I was the one who didn't like it there. Then a couple of things came together—we found the house

From *Mademoiselle*, September 1977.

on the Island (Marsha opted at first for a New York brownstone)—and we eventually came up with our present arrangement."

Neither of them sees anything really unique about their situation. Marsha points out that many husbands travel most of the week on business, but that's okay because it's considered unplanned or temporary. "Ours is an explicit, conscious decision—that's what throws people off. When we decided to live apart, our friends reacted frankly and adamantly—they were sure we were splitting up.

"I probably would live in the city no matter what. There are few jobs in the suburbs that interest me. And I certainly wouldn't find anything as lucrative as I have now; the money is important."

Both Marsha and Steve admit to different interests that don't conflict when they're living apart—"I can get mine out of my system without feeling guilty"—and they're freer to see their own friends. They also feel more relaxed when they are together because they've been able to unwind during the week at their own speed on their own time. Problems usually get dealt with before the weekends—"I don't discuss my job unless there's a crisis," says Marsha. "If something's really bothering me I find Steve's a good person to talk to; he's so removed from my industry that he gives me an objective point of view. But by and large our jobs are separate from us."

It would be nice to see more of each other, but both find their current setup takes a tremendous burden off the marriage. "Women who don't have any interests outside their homes and marriages make more demands on their husbands' time," says Marsha. "I don't want to make demands on Steve's time; what right have I? If he wants to do something, he's allowed." And they both talk about the fresh material and interactions from outside that they bring into the relationship. Marsha, says Steve, "is an interesting person; I look forward to being around her." What it boils down to, they agree, is "a question of freedom; it's being a grown up. We can afford to be selfish now because it's just the two of us."

They are, however, keeping their options open. If they do have a child, "it will have to be within the next few years because of my age," explains Marsha. "Unfortunately that's a major consideration; I get a little bit angry, in fact, over my age being a factor." Childcare is another major consideration. "Maybe," muses Marsha, "we'll have a baby in four years when Steve is eligible for a sabbatical and can stay home for a year. I think both parents should enjoy the children."

There are times, of course, when a traditional marriage seems easier and more appealing to them—no driving back and forth, no running for the train to Long Island on Friday night. It would be easier to stay put ". . . but easier doesn't mean better. To have a traditional marriage, we'd both have to give up a lot, one more so than the other depending on whether we ended up in the city or the suburbs. This way we have the best of both worlds." . . .

Book of Proverbs, Chapter 31

10 Who can find a virtuous woman? for her price *is* far above rubies.

11 The heart of her husband doth safely trust in her, so that he shall have no need of spoil.

12 She will do him good and not evil all the days of her life.

13 She seeketh wool, and flax, and worketh willingly with her hands.

14 She is like the merchants' ships; she bringeth her food from afar.

15 She riseth also while it is yet night, and giveth meat to her household, and a portion to her maidens.

16 She considereth a field, and buyeth it: with the fruit of her hands she planteth a vineyard.

17 She girdeth her loins with strength, and strengtheneth her arms.

18 She perceiveth that her merchandise *is* good: her candle goeth not out by night.

19 She layeth her hands to the spindle, and her hands hold the distaff.

20 She stretcheth out her hand to the poor; yea, she reacheth forth her hands to the needy.

21 She is not afraid of the snow for her household: for all her household *are* clothed with scarlet.

22 She maketh herself coverings of tapestry; her clothing *is* silk and purple.

23 Her husband is known in the gates, when he sitteth among the elders of the land.

24 She maketh fine linen, and selleth *it*; and delivereth girdles unto the merchant.

25 Strength and honour *are* her clothing; and she shall rejoice in time to come.

26 She openeth her mouth with wisdom; and in her tongue *is* the law of kindness.

27 She looketh well to the ways of her household, and eateth not the bread of idleness.

28 Her children arise up, and call her blessed; her husband *also,* and he praiseth her.

29 Many daughters have done virtuously, but thou excellest them all.

30 Favour *is* deceitful, and beauty *is* vain: *but* a woman *that* feareth the LORD, she shall be praised.

31 Give her of the fruit of her hands; and let her own works praise her in the gates.

Feminism Comes of Age: 1945–1974

Lois W. Banner

In the two decades following the Second World War, two central and divergent trends influenced women's lives. The first was their continued participation in the work force, which reflected changing economic, demographic, and medical factors. The second was a resurgent cultural emphasis on domesticity and femininity as woman's proper role.

A GENERAL CONSENSUS ON WOMAN'S ROLE

Women Under Attack

In contradistinction to the movement of women into the work force, and partly because of it, an emphasis on the importance of marriage and motherhood became widespread in the late 1940s and the 1950s. In the immediate postwar years, antifeminist rhetoric was especially virulent. During the war the nation had lauded women for their participation in the national effort, and they had emerged from the war, in the words of a contemporary, "noble, impeccable and shining." [1] But within months many opinionmakers had turned against women, criticizing them not only for having gone to work during the war, but also for having, as they saw it, destroyed the American family in the process. The attack was blatant and resembled nothing so much as the inflated antisuffrage rhetoric early in the century. The antifeminism of the 1920s and 1930s had been extensive, but subtle, and it had only rarely denied women the right to live their lives as they saw fit. But the antifeminism of the postwar 1940s held women responsible for society's ills—either because they were failures as mothers or because they had left the home for work.

As early as 1942, in his best-selling book *Generation of Vipers*, Philip Wylie accused American women of being tyrants in their homes and emasculating their husbands and sons. Taking the opposite tack in *Modern Woman: The Lost Sex* (1947), sociologist Marynia Farnham and historian Ferdinand Lundberg argued that the problems of modern society—including war and depression—could be traced to the fact that women had left the home. In their view, women had given up their essential femininity to compete in a futile battle with men, causing their children to become delinquents or neurotics, and their husbands to become alcoholics or sexually impotent. Wylie, Farnham, and Lundberg based their case, as did most antifeminists of this period, on studies that seemed to show high rates of neurosis among army draftees and career women and increasing alcoholism and impotence among American men. They concluded that the career woman was neurotic because she had rejected her natural role, while the other evils were traceable to the neurotic housewife.

Their arguments, however, grew directly out of their ideological biases. Farnham and Lundberg, for example, were Freudians. In the 1920s, Freudianism had begun to have a major influence on Americans.

But the advent of behaviorism, which offered a compelling alternative, and the onset of the depression, which made it difficult for anyone to afford psychoanalysis, had considerably diluted the Freudian impact. Also, by the late 1930s psychiatrists like Karen Horney had begun to attack Freudian views about women. But among psychiatrists in the postwar years, Freudianism prevailed. The Freudians argued that women could attain emotional stability only through domesticity and motherhood. Women who worked denied their deepest needs and risked being unable to experience love or sexual satisfaction. This, in turn, threatened the family, and, according to the most apocalyptic thinkers, the whole of Western civilization. Moreover, Freudians emphasized the importance of the early years of life on total personality development. The message to mothers was clear: they ought to stay at home to oversee their children's development.

Expert Opinion: Freud and Functionalism

The bitter antifeminism of the immediate postwar years was a transitory phenomenon, but its arguments, and particularly the Freudian ideas on which it was based, echoed throughout the 1950s, forming a body of thought that few sociological writers could avoid. As late as 1956 sociologists Alva Myrdal and Viola Klein commented that conferences of school headmasters, juvenile magistrates, probation officers, and welfare workers invariably blamed mothers, and especially working mothers, for the problems of their youthful charges.[2] Child-care experts universally recommended that mothers stay at home with their preschool children and be available when their older children returned from school. Dr. Benjamin Spock, whose book Baby and Child Care (1946) became the standard authority on the subject, recommended that the federal government pay women to raise their children so that mothers would not leave the home.[3] College educators argued for the adoption of new curricula for women that would stress courses on marriage and the family.

Within the disciplines of sociology and anthropology, some protest against these ideas was registered. But sociologists themselves were influenced by the technique of analysis known as functionalism, itself partly an outgrowth of the conservative postwar years. Functionalism stressed the value-free analysis of existing institutions and thereby left little room for criticism of them. Not all sociologists, however, were functionalists or Freudians. In her influential book Women in the Modern World: Their Education and Their Dilemmas (1953), sociologist Mirra Komarovsky criticized the Freudians and the functionalists and argued that female personality traits and women's relative lack of accomplishment in comparison to men's was due to their cultural conditioning, not to their biological inferiority. She did not deny women the right to work, and she counseled that men as well as women needed training for marriage and child-bearing. Komarovsky criticized the then-current concern about the threat to men's masculinity that competition with women posed. But she clearly implied that wives, not husbands, bore the major responsibility for the home and the family. "Everything we know and believe today about the development of the child points to the importance of mother-child relations." [4] In child-rearing, the father was a secondary figure. Like Komarovsky, Viola Klein and Alva Myrdal criticized Freud, but they approved of what they judged to be the "new and exacting standards of motherhood," and they recommended that mothers stay at home with their children—at least for the child's first three years.[5] And, while cataloguing the biological evidence that women were constitutionally superior to men and counseling that the male world of work needed woman's influence, anthropologist Ashley Montagu, in his popular *The Natural Superiority of Women* (1952), wrote that a large part of women's superiority lay in their greater gentleness and humanity, while, echoing the argument of the traditionalists, he stressed the importance of "mother love" to successful human development. Even anthropologist Margaret Mead was ambivalent. In studies like *Male and Female* (1955) she criticized the rigid sex-role definitions of American culture; at the same time she glorified woman's role as mother and homemaker.

The Evidence from Popular Culture

On a more popular level, the new emphasis on domesticity was everywhere apparent. In newspapers and magazines, on radio and billboards, Rosie the Riveter was replaced by the homemaker as the national feminine model. Advertisers in particular were quick to exploit the expanded market for domestic products that the return to a peacetime economy and the appearance of a new affluence offered. It was predictable, as before, that the model woman they would project would be either a housewife eager to buy the latest home products or a seductress whose appearance suggested special pleasure from the product she displayed. In addition, according to feminist Betty Friedan in *The Feminine Mystique* (1963), Freudian attitudes infused most articles in the mass-circulation women's magazines; the vast majority of the heroines in the short stories were housewives, and nonfiction articles were devoted almost exclusively to cooking and child care.[6]

Re-enforcing society's belief that women functioned best as sweethearts, sirens, or wives, female film stars of the 1950s were either sweet, innocent, and characterless, like Debbie Reynolds and Doris Day, or, like Marilyn Monroe, projected a complex blend of innocence and aggressive sexuality. In addition, by the mid-1950s television was beginning to beam its message into countless American homes. It also portrayed the woman either as a sex object or as a contented homebody, often flighty and irresponsible. The emphasis on domesticity was pronounced in long-running, popular shows like "I Love Lucy" and "Father Knows Best."

Women's dress styles reflected the same female images. During the war, women had worn mannish clothes: skirts were narrow; suits were popular; padded shoulders were in vogue. But in 1947 Parisian designer Christian Dior introduced the "new look," and women abandoned their masculine garb in a rush to femininity. The "new look" featured long, full skirts and emphasized a defined bosom and tiny waist, which required wearing foundation garments. By the early 1950s these fashions reached their height in the "baby doll" look. It was characterized by a cinched-in waist, a full bosom, and bouffant skirts held out by crinoline petticoats. Shoe styles emphasized ever higher heels and ever more pointed toes until, ultimately, women had difficulty walking. Not since the Victorian era had women's fashions been so confining.

The Back-to-the-Home Movement

The new arguments and styles could never have gained widespread favor had not women—and men—been willing to accept them. After the war traditionalism was in vogue, and the patriarchal past took on a romantic hue. The deprivation of the war years made a close family life attractive; women eagerly responded to the returning soldiers' desire to re-create a secure environment in the family. Rates of marriage and of remarriage after divorce and widowhood continued to remain high. The age of first marriage rapidly dropped: in 1900 the average age of first marriage for women was 22 years, while by 1940 it had lowered to 21.5 years. The Second World War occasioned the most rapid decrease over the course of the century, and by 1962 the average age of first marriage for women was 20.3 years. The size of families, which had decreased during the depression and the war, was increasing. Families with four and five children were common: the 1940s, according to one analyst, was a period of "the most rapid family formation" in the history of the United States, and the trend continued into the 1950s.[7] In keeping with these trends was the widespread influence of two movements that exalted the joys of motherhood. One, the La Leche League, was dedicated to helping mothers nurse their infants. The other movement promoted the LaMaze method of natural childbirth, which combined a humanitarian desire to free women from the pain of childbirth with a zealot's fervor to make it the most important experience of their lives.

Even most college-educated women continued to see marriage as their most important goal in life. From her vantage point at Barnard College, Mirra Komarovsky noted that, far from taking a militant feminist position, college women were defending marriage and motherhood with Freudian arguments.[8] Betty Friedan estimated that by the mid-1950s, 60 percent of female undergraduates were dropping out of college to marry.[9] One educator presciently explained this development as the result of the overwhelming influence of movies, television, and popular magazines, with their glorification of romantic love and marriage. To the young, marriage seemed both a haven and an escape from parental and social restraints.[10]

The desire to marry and to create a stable life around a romanticized version of the family (which in many ways was a middle-class luxury made possible by postwar affluence) was re-enforced by other factors. The fear that the decrease in population due to the war had weakened the nation prompted some government officials and scientists to call for a return to large families. The superficially tranquil postwar decade had its own tensions and pressures. International affairs were characterized by a series of crises and wars, including the Korean conflict, and by the perceived threat of a newly resurgent communism. Recurring cycles of inflation and depression cast an air of unease over the new affluence. As early as 1945, one analyst contended that the postwar attack against women was a classic case of scapegoating—of blaming vague fears on a definable villain.[11] Shortly thereafter, woman as virtuous wife replaced woman as villain as the central image within the cult of domesticity. But to a nation that had undergone an exhausting war and was living in a troubled peace, home as a refuge was welcome.

Also, affluent Americans increasingly clustered in suburban areas, where jobs for women were limited and domestic help was in short supply. Husbands were away from home longer because they had to commute to work, leaving wives to bear complete responsibility for the family— including the sometimes overwhelming task of transportation. With schools, stores, and the train station rarely within walking distance, the suburban housewife could spend her day behind the wheel of the station wagon, suburbia's solution to the transportation problem. The American dream of affluence in a natural, bucolic setting, away from urban squalor, often made it impossible for women to be other than housewives and mothers.

Sex and Child-Rearing. The new emphasis on Freudianism also was central to the return to the home. Americans have always respected experts, particularly when "science" is their justification and when sexuality is the issue. Marriage manuals and sex handbooks have never wanted for sales in the twentieth century. After the Second World War, as after the First, Americans were once again captivated by the notion of sexual liberation, eager to learn the style and techniques of physical gratification.[12] To this drive, Freudian theories gave the rationale: sex was an inevitable necessity of life that ruled human development. But Freudians also argued that the proper end of sexuality for women was domesticity and motherhood. Sex experts told women their mission was healthy sex; child-care experts, like Benjamin Spock, told them they must stay at home to raise their children. According to sociologist Philip Slater, this "magnification of the child-rearing role" was the most important factor in the "ultra-domestication" of the American woman in the 1950s.[13] . . .

1. Harrison Smith, "Must Women Work?" Independent Woman (December 1947), 34.
2. Alva Myrdal and Viola Klein, Women's Two Roles: Home and Work (London: Routledge and Pauls, 1956), p. 134.
3. Benjamin Spock, Baby and Child Care (1946; reprint ed., New York: Dell, 1957), p. 570.
4. Mirra Komarovsky, Women in the Modern World: Their Education and Their Dilemmas (Boston: Little, Brown, 1953), pp. 297–98.

It's easy to say we're in love.
But our diamond says we want to stay that way.

And that means being honest with each other now.
When it counts. Making special efforts to get to know each other better.
To understand how much I want a career, and why it shouldn't
end when we start a family. And knowing he can quit his job,
if he wants to try to really make it as an artist.
Yes, falling in love was pretty easy. But our diamond says
we're going to make it last.

A diamond is forever.

To give you some idea of diamond values, the half-carat ring shown here (enlarged for detail) is worth about $800. Diamond values will vary according to color, clarity, cut and weight. Ask your jeweler for the free booklet, "A Diamond Is Forever," De Beers Consolidated Mines, Ltd.

5. Myrdal and Klein, *Women's Two Roles: Home and Work*, pp. 125–30.
6. Betty Friedan, *The Feminine Mystique* (1963; reprint ed., New York: Dell, 1970), pp. 29–63.
7. John Sirjimaki, *The American Family in the Twentieth Century* (Cambridge, Mass.: Harvard University Press, 1953), p. 55.
8. Komarovsky, *Women in the Modern World: Their Education and Their Dilemmas*, p. 94.
9. Friedan, *The Feminine Mystique*, p. 115.
10. Kate Hevner Mueller, "The Cultural Pressures on Women," in Opal P. David, ed., *The Education of Women: Signs for the Future* (Washington, D.C.: American Council on Education, 1957), pp. 50–51.
11. Abraham Myerson, "Woman, the Authorities' Scapegoat," in Elizabeth Bragdon, ed., *Women Today: Their Conflicts, Their Frustrations, and Their Fulfillments* (New York: Bobbs-Merrill, 1953), p. 305.
12. To what extent Americans were successful in this quest in the 1950s—as in the 1920s— is debatable. One study of best-selling marriage manuals between 1951 and 1971 concluded that women had been granted the right to sexual pleasure but that men were always to play the dominant role. (Michael Gordon and Penelope J. Shankweiler, "Different Equals Less: Female Sexuality in Recent Marriage Manuals," *Journal of Marriage and the Family*, XXXIII [August 1971], 459–66, cited in Jessie Bernard, *The Future of Marriage* [New York: World, 1972], p. 47.)
13. Philip Slater, *The Pursuit of Loneliness: American Culture at the Breaking Point* (1970; reprint ed., Boston: Beacon, 1971), p. 66.

St. Paul's First Letter to the Corinthians, Chapter 7

Now concerning the things whereof ye wrote unto me: *It is* good for a man not to touch a woman.

2 Nevertheless, *to avoid* fornication, let every man have his own wife, and let every woman have her own husband.

3 Let the husband render unto the wife due benevolence; and likewise also the wife unto the husband.

4 The wife hath not power of her own body, but the husband: and likewise also the husband hath not power of his own body, but the wife.

5 Defraud ye not one the other, except *it be* with consent for a time, that ye may give yourselves to fasting and prayer; and come together again, that Satan tempt you not for your incontinency.

6 But I speak this by permission, *and* not of commandment.

7 For I would that all men were even as I myself. But every man hath his proper gift of God, one after this manner, and another after that.

8 I say therefore to the unmarried and widows, It is good for them if they abide even as I.

9 But if they cannot contain, let them marry: for it is better to marry than to burn.

10 And unto the married I command, *yet* not I, but the Lord, Let not the wife depart from *her* husband:

11 But and if she depart, let her remain unmarried, or be reconciled to *her* husband: and let not the husband put away *his* wife.

12 But to the rest speak I, not the Lord: If any brother hath a wife that believeth not, and she be pleased to dwell with him, let him not put her away.

13 And the woman which hath an husband that believeth not, and if he be pleased to dwell with her, let her not leave him.

14 For the unbelieving husband is sanctified by the wife, and the unbelieving wife is sanctified by the husband; else were your children unclean; but now are they holy.

15 But if the unbelieving depart, let him depart. A brother or a sister is not under bondage in such *cases:* but God hath called us to peace.

16 For what knowest thou, O wife, whether thou shalt save *thy* husband? or how knowest thou, O man, whether thou shalt save *thy* wife?

17 But as God hath distributed to every man, as the Lord hath called every one, so let him walk. And so ordain I in all churches.

18 Is any man called being circumcised? let him not become uncircumcised. Is any called in uncircumcision? let him not be circumcised.

19 Circumcision is nothing, and uncircumcision is nothing, but the keeping of the commandments of God.

20 Let every man abide in the same calling wherein he was called.

21 Art thou called *being* a servant? care not for it: but if thou mayest be made free, use *it* rather.

22 For he that is called in the Lord, *being* a servant, is the Lord's freeman: likewise also he that is called, *being* free, is Christ's servant.

23 Ye are bought with a price; be not ye the servants of men.

24 Brethren, let every man, wherein he is called, therein abide with God.

25 Now concerning virgins I have no commandment of the Lord; yet I give my judgment, as one that hath obtained mercy of the Lord to be faithful.

26 I suppose therefore that this is good for the present distress, *I say,* that *it is* good for a man so to be.

27 Art thou bound unto a wife? seek not to be loosed. Art thou loosed from a wife? seek not a wife.

28 But and if thou marry, thou hast not sinned; and if a virgin marry, she hath not sinned. Nevertheless such shall have trouble in the flesh: but I spare you.

29 But this I say, brethren, the time *is* short: it remaineth, that both they that have wives be as though they had none;

30 And they that weep, as though they wept not; and they that rejoice, as though they rejoiced not; and they that buy, as though they possessed not;

31 And they that use this world, as not abusing *it;* for the fashion of this world passeth away.

32 But I would have you without carefulness. He that is unmarried careth for the things that belong to the Lord, how he may please the Lord:

33 But he that is married careth for the things that are of the world, how he may please *his* wife.

34 There is difference *also* between a wife and a virgin. The unmarried woman careth for the things of the Lord, that she may be holy both in body and in spirit: but she that is married careth for the things of the world, how she may please *her* husband.

35 And this I speak for your own profit; not that I may cast a snare upon you, but for that which is comely, and that ye may attend upon the Lord without distraction.

36 But if any man think that he behaveth himself uncomely toward his virgin, if she pass the flower of *her* age, and need so require, let him do what he will, he sinneth not: let them marry.

37 Nevertheless he that standeth stedfast in his heart, having no necessity, but hath power over his own will, and hath so decreed in his heart that he will keep his virgin, doeth well.

38 So then he that giveth *her* in marriage doeth well; but he that giveth *her* not in marriage doeth better.

39 The wife is bound by the law as long as her husband liveth; but if her husband be dead, she is at liberty to be married to whom she will; only in the Lord.

40 But she is happier if she so abide, after my judgment: and I think also that I have the Spirit of God.

The Wife of Bath's Prologue

Geoffrey Chaucer

> Experience, though noon auctoritee
> Were in this world, is right ynough for me
> To speke of wo that is in mariage:
> For lordinges, sith I twelf yeer was of age—
> Thanked be God that is eterne on live—
> Housbondes at chirche dore I have had five
> (If I so ofte mighte han wedded be),
> And alle were worthy men in hir degree.
> But me was told, certain, nat longe agoon is,
> That sith that Crist ne wente nevere but ones   10
> To wedding in the Cane of Galilee,
> That by the same ensample taughte he me

4. **lordinges**, gentlemen. 6. **chirche dore**, the actual wedding ceremony was celebrated at the church door, not in the chancel. 11. **Cane**, Canaan. 12. **ensample**, example.

From Geoffrey Chaucer, "The Wife of Bath's Prologue," *The Canterbury Tales*, in *Chaucer's Poetry: An Anthology for the Modern Reader*, edited by E. T. Donaldson (New York: John Wiley & Sons, 1958).

That I ne sholde wedded be but ones.
Herke eek, lo, which a sharp word for the nones,
Biside a welle, Jesus, God and man,
Spak in repreve of the Samaritan:
"Thou hast yhad five housbondes," quod he,
"And that ilke man that now hath thee
Is nat thyn housbonde." Thus saide he certain.
What that he mente therby I can nat sayn,   20
But that I axe why that the fifthe man
Was noon housbonde to the Samaritan?
How manye mighte she han in mariage?
Yit herde I nevere tellen in myn age
Upon this nombre diffinicioun.
Men may divine and glosen up and down,
But wel I woot, expres, withouten lie,
God bad us for to wexe and multiplye:
That gentil text can I wel understonde.

14. **which,** what; **for the nones,** to the purpose.   16. **repreve,** reproof.   18. **ilke,** same.   **21.**
axe, ask.   **21–22.** Christ was actually referring to a sixth man who was not married to the
Samaritan woman.   25. **diffinicioun,** definition.   26. **divine,** guess; **glosen,** interpret.   27.
woot, know; **expres,** expressly.   28. **wexe,** i.e., increase.

My experience gives me sufficient right to speak of the trouble there is in
marriage, even if there were no other authority in the world; for, ladies
and gentlemen, since I was twelve years old I have had five husbands,
eternal God be thanked—if it is legal to have been married so often—and
all were fine men in their way. But not long ago I was certainly told that
since Christ attended only one wedding, in Cana of Galilee, He therefore
taught me by example to be married only once. And listen also to the
sharp words Jesus, God and man, spoke beside the well to scold the
Samaritan about this matter: "You have had five husbands," he said, "and
that man whom you now have is not your husband." Certainly He said
this; what He meant by it I can't say. But I ask why the fifth man was not
husband to the Samaritan? How many was she allowed to marry? In my
time I never yet heard of a limitation of number. Men can interpret and
gloss the text up and down, but I know surely without doubt that God
expressly told us to increase and multiply; that pleasant text I can easily
understand.

QUESTIONS

1. Describe the voice of Gregory Corso's poem. How does this character feel
   about conventions or about doing things "properly"? How do his vocabulary and sentence structure convey his attitudes toward conventions? How
   would you expect him to behave at a wedding?

2. Describe the voice of Richard Kalish's psychology textbook. Find examples of the jargon of social science. How does the voice of the historian Lois Banner differ from Kalish's voice?

3. Try to analyze the grammar of one or two of John Ruskin's sentences. Can you do it? Read the sentence aloud until your voice shows that you understand it. What message about himself does Ruskin's grammar give us?

4. Chaucer's Wife of Bath goes on to tell a long tale about her many husbands and her philosophies of marriage. What sort of character do you think she will turn out to be? Compare the voice of John Anderson's wife.

5. What guesses has Kalish made about his audience? What does he think they want to know? What audience is Lois Banner writing for? Both of these essays contain a great many facts with documentation; are the authors simply reporting, or do they seem to want to persuade their audiences with their facts?

6. At the end of his essay, Kalish suddenly changes to direct address of the audience as "you." Why may he have done this? Do you think it was a good idea?

7. Marriage has long been important to society as a way of controlling sex, children, money, and social standing. Which of these aspects of marriage are important to the writers here? Are there others that concern them as well?

8. Which of the writers are dissatisfied with the institution of marriage? What do they see wrong with it?

9. In discussing background factors in happy marriages, Kalish suggests that it is helpful if parents "communicate healthy attitudes toward sex." How do you think he would define *healthy* if he were asked to be specific?

10. Find references to sex throughout the chapter, including indirect ones. What different words are used to refer to it? Do most of these words convey particular attitudes toward sex?

11. Define a topic for a research paper on marriage. Which of the selections here, if any, would be a good source for this topic? What other sources could you use?

7

The Control of Television

This chapter deals primarily with questions relating to content. The writers here use formal voices because they wish us to concentrate on the issue under discussion: control of television.

The First Amendment to the Constitution guarantees freedom of speech and of the press. Most Americans agree that the citizens of a democracy need to be able to get information and opinions which are freely expressed. No newspaper publisher or reporter should ever fear punishment because of something he wrote. And all citizens should have an equal right to express their views.

The spread of radio and television has aroused some differences of opinion as to how the rights of the First Amendment can be secured for everyone. It has seemed to some observers that, in television, a very few people control nearly all the expressions of information and opinion. These observers suggest that somebody—probably the government—should somehow interfere to make sure that television offers a variety of viewpoints.

Other observers believe that the government has already done too much. They argue that a free press means a press that is independent of all government interference. The Federal Communications Commission issues licenses to broadcasters and enforces certain rules, like the "fairness doctrine" and the "equal time" rule. Newspapers and magazines are not regulated, and broadcasters, according to this argument, should be treated no differently.

Are there really people in this country who control the flow of information? Who are they? How can we be sure that the freedoms of speech and of the press are preserved?

The First Amendment

Congress shall make no law respecting an establishment of religion, or prohibiting the free exercise thereof; or abridging the freedom of speech, or of the press; or the right of the people peaceably to assemble, and to petition the government for a redress of grievances.

Mass Media's Conflicts of Interest

Robert Cirino

Since the primary purpose of mass media entertainment is to entertain—not inform, instruct, or manipulate—we often assume that such entertainment has little or no political bias. We sit back and allow ourselves to be entertained. Yet we are being more than entertained; we are being offered underlying messages about life and society. And these messages are getting through to us with maximum effect because our critical guard is down. Whether we are a boxer, merchant, consumer, or television viewer, when our guard is down we are liable to get zapped.

As a boxer, merchant, or consumer, we will naturally be aware after we have been hit with a punch or a bad deal, and thus try to get our guard up for the next attack. But as entertainment consumers we remain off-guard, night after night, not even recognizing we are absorbing messages that can shape our values. And the more we consume entertainment the more likely we are to absorb politically loaded words and images without question.

Many people think that most entertainment has no political bias because to them "political" refers only to politicians, political parties, laws, election, and government institutions. This is a far too limited concept of the word. Political decisions determine to a large extent what we will see on television, what we will learn in schools, what kind of goods we will produce, what wars we will fight in, and what kind of old age homes we will die in. Politicians determine to a large extent who will pay taxes, who will receive birth control devices, who will get medical care, who will get subsidies, and who will get welfare. Many other areas of life are also influenced by political decisions. In fact, it is hard to find any aspect of our life or society that is free of political significance.

Deliberately or inadvertently, entertainment is bound to include messages that say something significant about one of the above issues. In its favorable depiction of people and society, an entertainment production may support present political policy in a certain area; it may indicate that laws are needed where none now exist, or that things would be better if politicians made no laws at all.

It is impossible for a person who produces entertainment to have no ideas at all regarding life and society. Having them, it is impossible not to reflect them in his or her entertainment product. A producer may purposely try to avoid touching on politics, but this stance in itself is politically significant, for it is indirectly telling people that political matters are unimportant in life.

Some scholars, such as Marshall McLuhan, believe that the influence of mass media technology itself—not the political bias in the content—has the greatest impact on individuals and society. Indeed, it is significant that children are watching television two to six hours a day and adults are spending their evenings and weekends watching it—regardless of the political bias in the content of the entertainment. Regardless of what the President might say, it is significant that the entire nation is watching him at the same time. Viewing television for many hours a day may make children and adults more passive than they would be if they made something with their hands, played games, or talked about school or work.

Nevertheless, the importance of political bias in the content of entertainment can still be paramount. In a democratic society this bias has the potential to influence people to vote for policies that promote cooperation or competition, freedom or restriction, diversity or uniformity. Above all, the political bias will determine whether the people whose lives are being shaped by the mass media will have some measure of control over communications technology, thus giving them at least the potential to use it for their qwn benefit.

An examination of the election process provides an example. Present laws allow politicians to purchase the use of print and broadcast technology for the purpose of airing political ads designed to manipulate public opinion. If the bias in the content of the mass media persuades the people to demand that their government forbid the purchase of such time and space and require instead that stations and newspapers provide free time and space for debates and discussions, the entire election process—including the use of communications technology—would be changed drastically. The mass media, for example, would lose the hundreds of millions of dollars that they presently receive from political advertising. Talented and dedicated people who are not wealthy would have a chance of winning against politicians supported by great wealth. Third parties would be treated seriously, thus widening the spectrum of debate and adding a little life to what are usually boring exchanges between candidates with similar viewpoints. Politicians would prepare for debates and discussions instead of hire ad agencies and crown beauty queens. The politician who refused to debate would be at a great loss because the debate would still go on with the other candidates. Positions and ideology would be the major factors, not personality as communicated in political ads or staged events. And perhaps the changes could generate enough interest to get 70 to 90 percent of the people to vote, as do other democracies that restrict politicians from buying a communication advantage in the mass media.

In the end, the question is who really has the power to create bias and manage technology? For whoever has this power can control both the political bias of the content and the effects of the technology itself. The irony is that public attitudes about control of the mass media may be determined by what the mass media itself has to say about the issue.

Those who own and control the major communication technologies in the United States use them for their own purpose, which is to make a profit. But obviously, communication technologies can serve other purposes as well. They can be used to inform, enlighten, give advice, provide access for expression, and offer alternatives—and do them at the same time they entertain us. We can all think of some excellent programs that served us in some of these ways. Many private communication corporations try to fulfill as many of these laudable purposes as they can while operating primarily for profit. In some cases they find that serving these laudatory purposes increases their profits. If so, all is fine. But this is not always the case. More often than not their attempts to serve some of these good purposes—and thus serve the public interest—cause them to lose money or even go out of business.

In such cases, communication corporations may find it profitable to use their control over communications to censor, distort, or slant information and entertainment in order to increase profits, at whatever expense to the public interest. These conflicts between profits on the one hand and the public interest on the other are more numerous and important than the public is led to believe or than broadcasters or publishers will admit.

Let's look at some of these conflicts, noting in each case how the public interest conflicts with the practices and policies that increase profits for mass communication corporations.

Violence

Violence is an important aspect of life and politics; it should be dealt with, not censored. Superficial dramatic productions, such as *Starsky & Hutch* or *Baretta*, feature glorified violence for the sake of increasing excitement and actions so as to give us an emotional thrill and increase audience rating. The camera focuses on the action—the shooting, the chase, or the approval a hero gets after he kills or beats up the bad guys. In a rape scene, the emphasis is on the woman's sex appeal and the handsome man's lust. The camera quickly shows or hints at the actual sexual abuse and then narrows in on the police as they track down—and perhaps kill—the culprit.

In contrast, sincere dramatic productions, like *Roots*, don't glorify violence. They utilize violence in order to communicate serious messages about life and society. The focus is apt to be on the thinking, feeling, and motives that lead to the violence. The torn face or limb, the shock, the pain, the loss of life, the sorrow, the ruin of a life: these consequences are not glossed over quickly or ignored by such productions. In a rape scene, emphasis is apt to be on the man's psychological sickness, the woman's terror and repulsion, the humiliation, the physical damage, and the long-lasting psychological scarring.

Productions that emphasize these consequences are likely to make us hesitant about resorting to physical force or approving of its use unless there is very good cause and there seems to be no other satisfactory alternative. But these types of productions are expensive to produce and only rarely—as in the case of *Roots*—do they bring in high audience ratings. They may actually cause us to turn away from other dramatic productions that deal seriously with violence. "I've had enough," "It's too heavy," "OK, the point has been made," are common responses to productions that depict the truth about violence. These responses would be disastrous for the profit-oriented broadcasting industry. We would be switching channels, watching fewer programs, or turning the set off. We might not even turn them on again for quite a while.

To avoid this, the commercial networks continue to depict violence as glorious, painless, effective, or necessary, because it's in their interest to keep us watching all evening. But is it in the public interest to have our mass media offer so many presentations that glorify violence?

Public Affairs Programming

People in highly industrialized societies get most of their information about public affairs from television. At best, television news is a headline service, giving people a key-hole glimpse at some of the important trends, events, and issues. Even news broadcasters agree that television news by itself does not provide the public with enough information to be able to make thoughtful, reasonable choices about political matters. Realizing that this situation is not in the public interest, most democratic countries (Japan, Israel, Australia, Canada, England, and other European countries) supplement the news with prime time public affairs programs and documentaries that deal in depth with political and social issues. Such programming makes up 20 to 40 percent of prime time programming, thus providing citizens with at least the opportunity to watch serious public affairs programs every evening.

In sharp contrast, public affairs programming by the three major American networks usually amounts to less than 3 percent of regularly scheduled prime time programming and some networks frequently have no regularly scheduled public affairs programs at all. Instead, they offer the occasional special report. On most evenings then, we can choose between situation comedies, family shows, doctor dramas, or crime dramas, but there is usually no option of watching serious public affairs programs. Public television, with its cultural offerings and few cheaply produced public affairs programs, provides no real alternative.

When the matter is viewed from a purely economic standpoint, the private networks and stations can't be blamed. Their public affairs programs or documentaries attract only a small part of the audience (perhaps 5 to 10 million) compared to popular entertainment programs that reach 20 to 40 million people. Nevertheless, it is certainly in the public interest to have such programs, and important that 5 million people view them. The hard facts are that the network with the comparatively small audience of 5 million loses advertising money to the other networks and the advantage of having a large audience already tuned in on their channel when the next hour's program starts.

Children's Television

The public interest demands that the purpose of children's television should be to benefit children, not to make money by selling advertisers access to their impressionable and non-discriminating minds. Accordingly, the vast majority of democracies have banned advertising completely from children's programs. Of those that permit it, the United States places the fewest restrictions on advertisers and allows the most minutes-per-hour of ad time. The networks have made great profits from children's advertising, often as much as $20 million per year per network. But since 1968, the vocal demands of public interest groups for better children's programs and less advertising have forced the networks to be satisfied with a much smaller profit. Nevertheless, children's programs today are still saturated with ads that sell sugar-coated foods and expensive toys. Besides manipulating impressionable minds, these ads set up conflicts between parents and children. In general, it seems safe to say that what's good for children is not good for network profits.

Issue Advertising

Government regulation of industry is a controversial issue. It's in the country's interest for the mass media to present all sides of the issue fairly so that we are allowed to make up our own minds as to which regulatory policies are the best. But in 1975 even the Columbia Journalism Review, a guardian of free speech and watchdog over professional journalistic standards, began presenting numerous full-page color advertisements giving the airlines' side of the argument on the Federal regulation of airlines. Of course no advertisements with opposing views are included because people and organizations with such views usually lack the money to produce ads or buy space. The result is that we are exposed not to a debate, but to a one-sided presentation of an issue. The Review earned needed money by running these ads.

Similarly, broadcasters, daily newspapers, and mass-circulation magazines make millions of dollars by allowing oil, drug, steel, electric, automobile, aluminum, glass, and paper companies to buy time and space to present their side of a controversial issue. Opposing viewpoints, represented by consumer, environmental, public interest, or radical groups, have little money to compete. Thus large corporations are able to gain an unfair and almost insurmountable debating advantage. Media owners would lose millions of dollars if they either banned these issue ads or offered free ad time or space for counter ads.

The importance of issue advertising was shown in the 1976 election in Colorado and Massachusetts. Prior to the ad campaigns by the bottle, can, and beverage manufacturers, a large majority of people (70%) favored a mandatory deposit on beer and soft drink containers. This would cut down the production of throw-away cans and bottles. After the ad campaigns—in which the manufacturers outspent the deposit advocates by at least an 8 to 1 margin—public opinion shifted dramatically and voted against the law.

Broadcasting—The Half-Opened Media   Jerome A. Barron

The rise of broadcasting has been a direct challenge to the classic noninterventionist approach to the marketplace of ideas. The metaphor, *marketplace of ideas*, is attractive; it has helped to shape our ideas concerning the whole existing American opinion process. The modern realities of press monopoly and concentration of control have not yet penetrated popular understanding. The myth is still current that "the press" and "the marketplace of ideas" are interchangeable entities. But the mythology is increasingly under attack. The very nature of broadcasting was ultimately bound to make apparent the limits of traditional laissez-faire approach to the exchange of ideas. The dozen television channels of the VHF spectrum were and are a limited access medium. As a federal judge said of radio during broadcasting's infancy, "Obviously there is no room in the broadcast band for every business or school of thought." [1]

As a result, in approaching the electronic media, one treads on very different legal terrain than with the press. Unlike newspaper publishers, broadcasters have legal obligations to their viewers and listeners. Three of these obligations demand our attention: the fairness doctrine, the equal time rule, and the personal attack rules. The fairness doctrine requires just that—fairness in presenting controversy on radio and television. It requires broadcasters to provide reasonable opportunity for the presentation of conflicting viewpoints on controversial issues of public importance.

The fairness doctrine does not give any specific group or viewpoint a right to command air time. But it does provide a basis by which groups or individuals representing a viewpoint opposed to one that has been broadcast can sometimes secure rebuttal time. A key point is that the fairness doctrine applies only when the station has started the fray. If the station has ignored an issue, there is nothing to rebut and the fairness principle cannot be invoked.

The fairness doctrine was set forth in a 1959 amendment to section

315 of the Federal Communications Act.[2] That section also states the equal time requirement that has become part of the American language. The equal time rule requires that if a broadcaster permits a legally qualified candidate for a public office to use his station, he must also give equal opportunities to all other candidates for that office. What does "legally qualified candidate" mean? The FCC has interpreted this phrase to mean a person who has publicly announced his candidacy.[3] For example, if X is running as a legally qualified candidate for Congress for the tenth congressional district of Virginia and station WAVA–FM gives him time to broadcast, then that station must afford an equal opportunity to broadcast to all other publicly announced candidates for that office.

Fairness and equal time are the best known and perhaps the most important programming obligations of broadcasters. The fairness doctrine, however, has spun off an additional requirement; the so-called personal attack rules provide a right of reply. A personal attack is defined as an "attack on the honesty, character, integrity or like personal qualities of an identified person or group."

When a personal attack is made, the broadcaster must notify the person or group attacked of the date, time, and identity of the broadcast within a week. He must deliver a script or tape (or lacking these an accurate summary) of the attack. Finally, he must give the person or group attacked a reasonable opportunity to respond over his station.

Broadcasting is less open to debate than this account of the broadcaster's obligations might suggest. On Tuesday, April 28, 1970, President Nixon gave a nationwide television speech announcing U.S. military intervention in Cambodia. The speech nearly brought the house down and did bring down the campuses—on the heads of the administration.

Peace senators opposed to American involvement in Indochina and Vietnam sought television time to answer the President's speech. Only one network provided time and that network charged for it.

Did the senators and various peace groups opposing the war in Indochina have any legal right to time to reply to the President's speech? The disappointing answer was that there was no such right of reply.

The equal time concept did not apply because President Nixon was not running for office and there was no legally announced candidate opposing him.

The fairness doctrine was no help. The broadcasters must provide reasonable opportunity for the presentation of conflicting viewpoints, but that does not mean that every controversial subject broadcast must be specifically answered. The fairness principle requires only that there be an overall balanced presentation of conflicting viewpoints.[4] If over the three-year license period the broadcaster gives reasonable coverage to both the interventionist and the peace positions, the fairness doctrine is satisfied.

Finally, the personal attack rules did not afford the dissenting senators or anyone else a right of reply on television since President

Nixon had not attacked any person or group in his speech. It would seem that, although better than the case with the press, the legal picture in broadcasting is still inadequate.

Nevertheless, broadcasters envy the lack of obligation of their newspaper brethren. Characteristic is an editorial in *Broadcasting*, the industry house organ, lamenting the existing obligations. "The First Amendment," said *Broadcasting*, "should protect the broadcast media . . ." and called for a nationwide poll "asking the simple question whether radio and television should be accorded the protection of the First Amendment, like newspapers or magazines." [5] *Broadcasting* states the industry ideal and the newspaper reality—no public service obligations whatever. Presently, the First Amendment protects the newspapers, not their readership. In broadcasting, however, the First Amendment has been held to grant some right of participation to the audience as well. A system of broadcast regulation has made possible some entry to broadcasting by the public. These rights are not easily enforced; they are not always taken advantage of; and the agency bound to enforce them, the FCC, has not always been eager to do so.

But a panoply of public rights to broadcasting does exist and can be developed to provide still more access for the audience. Broadcasting is at least a half-opened media.

1. *KFKB Broadcasting Association v. FRC*, 47 F 2d 670 (D.C. Cir. 1931).
2. 47 U.S.C. §315 (1964).
3. *McCarthy v. FCC*, 390 F. 2d 471 (D.C. Cir. 1968).
4. See *Report on Editorializing by Broadcast Licensees*, 13 F.C.C. 1246 (1949).
5. *Broadcasting*, November 16, 1970.

Testimony by Walter Cronkite before the Senate Subcommittee on Constitutional Rights (1972)

Mr. Cronkite. Thank you. Senator. I would like to express my appreciation to this committee for going into this subject with the view to drawing up whatever corrective legislation it finds necessary to bring up to date our guarantees of free press and free speech.

I would like to make it clear that I am speaking here only for myself today, and do not represent the Columbia Broadcasting System as such, and my association with CBS news staff is that of contract talent. That is a euphemism, I am sure.

The testimony I give today is completely my own, it has not been approved by CBS. I would hope that the executives thereof agree with most of it, but am not sure they agree with all of it.

Most of us in journalism are deeply concerned over such issues as right-of-access to news sources, Government secrecy, harassment by subpoena, and the protection of news sources. These are concerns common to all communications media.

I know you are going to hear a lot about that from other media, and I would restrict my presentation, therefore, if I may, to the special problem inhibiting the freedom of broadcast journalism.

It is assumed, of course, that we do want a free press. Such is synonymous with democracy. There are a few who would argue otherwise. However, I daresay there is scarcely a public figure anywhere who has not at one time or another, perhaps more frequently than not, railed at his treatment by the press. And, of course, right here I am referring to the press as a generic term to include all media.

Senator Ervin. As I stated at the opening of these hearings, I guess I am one of the few men in political life who doesn't complain much about his treatment at the hands of the press. The press takes me to task every once in awhile, but they have always been very kind, not attributing my hypocrisy to bad motives. They have always attributed it to a lack of mental capacity.

Mr. Cronkite. I know from time to time, sir, and not always without reason, we are considered untrustworthy, disloyal, unkind, disobedient, sullen, cowardly, dirty, and irrelevant. And this is as it should be. To be trustworthy in one man's eye may not be to warrant trust in another's. While individual reporters or journalists may at one time or another place their loyalty at the feet of one man, or ideology, it is the very strength of a free press that not all reporters and journalists will do so. In this diversity, is the strength of the free press.

Down through our history, particularly at times of national stress, there have been calls for bringing the press to heel. Now, again, much is being made of that. Much is being made of the alleged prejudices and bias of newsmen, particularly those of us in this powerful new medium of television. These charges, I submit, are not unique to television.

So strident, we might be reminded, did they become that following the 1962 election that there were congressional demands then for investigation of newspaper bias. As late as the forties and fifties, there were demands for licensing of journalists. This was before television drew the attention of those who feel threatened by freedom of expression.

We newsmen are biased and we are prejudiced. We are human beings.

There is not a man who can truthfully say that he does not harbor in his breast some strong sentiments pro and con on most, if not all, of the issues of the day. Yet if there is any single hallmark of this professionalism we claim—indeed that distinguishing characteristic that makes us professionals and not mere craftsmen—is that we have learned in our journalism schools and in practice, to recognize the symptoms of personal opinions and to seek to avoid them in reporting the day's news. None of us succeeds in this difficult task in all instances, but we know the assignment and the pitfalls and, I submit, we succeed far far more often than we fail or that our critics would acknowledge.

We are far from perfect. There is a fair portion of what we do that is not done well. There are things that we are not doing, which we ought to do. There are challenges we have not fully met. We are a long way from perfection.

But that is not the point. How could we be improved by outside monitors without destroying the independence which is so essential to a free press.

Vice President Agnew was right in asserting that a handful of us determine what will be on the evening news broadcasts or, for that matter, which he didn't specify, in *The New York Times*, or *The Chicago Tribune*, or *The Christian Science Monitor*, or *The Wall Street Journal*, or anywhere else.

Indeed, it is a handful of us with this immense power, power that not one of us underestimates or takes lightly. It is a strongly editorial power.

With each item we report, we can and do seek factual honesty, fairness and balance, but we must also decide which news items out of hundreds available we are going to expose that day. And those available to us already have been culled and reculled by persons far outside our control.

The local newspaper, let us say the *Kansas City Star*, decides each day which of the events of its area will be covered. The local press service representative in Kansas City, AP or UP, decides which of those items will go onto his wire. A regional relay editor decides which of the items on the regional wire shall go on to New York, or Washington, or Los Angeles. And we decide which of these items remaining are to go on the air.

In the case of television, the decision frequently involves which items will be illustrated by film, which we freely acknowledge gives the item far greater impact than the paragraph recited by the broadcaster. And film choice, in a sense, also may be taken out of our hands by technical considerations—fogged film, unintelligible sound tracks, and a dozen things can go wrong. I don't mean to impugn my friends the cameramen, the most gallant and brave of our craft.

Many factors go into the decisions we make, so many and so complex that it would be hopeless to attempt to detail them here.

With the difficulty of proving a negative, I cannot in any way produce evidence to support the next statement. I can only give you my personal assurance—and what that is worth is only as much as you judge my veracity—but I assure you that I have never heard nor guessed nor felt that the news judgment in making any one of those decisions was based on a political or ideological consideration. Not one. I believe, I trust, that my colleagues at the other networks can say the same.

Yes, only a handful of professional journalists make the significant judgments on the news of the day, and it is a lot of power for a few men. But what would be the alternative? We would never get on the air or go to press if we attempted to submit each judgment to a committee of Congressmen, bureaucrats, sociologists, teachers, policemen, union leaders, or women liberationists, nor can we go to a plebiscite for each decision.

No one is suggesting, as far as I know, that ludicrous thought; but there are those who propose ex post facto examination of the journalist's copy's judgment, and this, on the surface, may seem innocuous enough. Far from it. It would be as effective a clamp on press freedom as direct censorship.

Any Government panel that presumes to call a news organization to account for its actions must be presumed to be hostile and scarcely would seek to investigate the reporting with which it agrees.

To place the licensed broadcast medium under the threat of such investigation, is to place it permanently under the fear of accountability to unfriendly antagonists wielding the power of legal restraint.

The effect would be more than chilling in broadcast reporting. It would put journalistic enterprise in the deep freeze with the rigidity and heart and compassion of a block of ice.

Rare, indeed, would be the station or network management willing to commit unlimited resources of its legal and executive staff to defend a documentary or daily reportage when it would be far more comfortable simply to forgo mention of the item or the subject.

Impossible would be the position of the journalist working under such understandably timid management. For each piece of potentially controversial reporting, and there is scarcely any copy, as my mail would prove, and that includes the weather, that is not controversial. He would, presumably, have to go to management for approval of every item.

Or, since this would be impractical, he would ignore the item and fill his broadcast with something less likely to involve his company and himself in lengthy review by nonprofessional and frequently politically biased critics.

It is not as if there were no monitoring on our performance in broadcast journalism. The newspapers have served this function very well. They have proved to be, and will continue to be, severe critics of the broadcast medium. There is adequate check and balance here between competing media to assure sound performance without the interference of Government.

To deny the free play of these forces by putting one of them under the surveillance of Government would be to deny the people a balance between media that can assure a free press we want.

News and dissemination cannot be accomplished without fear of failure, that is the only way that counts, and if the reporter or editor constantly must be looking over his shoulder for those who would have this product reflect their standard of right and wrong, of fairness and bias, that can't be achieved.

If broadcast journalism is brought to that state by the courts, or Congress, or anybody else exercising a right to question the judgment of its practitioners, then it ceases to be a virile seeker of the truth and becomes a pallid conduit for that propaganda which is palatable to the majority of the people, or the Congress, or the administration of the moment.

Let me go on to say, to point out, that the greatest threat to freedom of information, therefore, it seems to me, is the Government licensing of broadcasting.

Broadcast news today is not free. Because it is operated by an industry that is beholden to the Government for its right to exist, its freedom has been curtailed by fiat, by assumption, and by intimidation and harassment.

That fiat comes through the Supreme Court. It has stated that as long as we are licensed by the Government, we are not as free as the printed press and, therefore, not eligible in the same manner for its first amendment guarantees.

Astride of this constitutional protection, broadcast news stands, before those in power, now or in the future who, for whatever motive, would like to see its freedom restrained. Some do this by assumption—assuming that a Government-licensed industry is fair game for legislative inquiry. The House Interstate Commerce Committee's attempt to investigate the CBS news broadcast, Selling of the Pentagon, is the most recent case in point and a perfect one.

Whatever the gentlemen of the committee thought of the broadcast, none alleged that any crime had been committed in the reporting, editing, or broadcasting of it. What they were examining was a matter of news judgment.

In the debate over the contempt action against CBS President Stanton that ensued, several members of the House expressed the belief that there was a need for legislation to control broadcast news. We do know that there have been bills introduced in this session of Congress, to "provide for more responsible news and public affairs programs," and "prohibit the broadcasting of deceptive news and public affairs programs."

Besides the restrictions that would be imposed by this assumption of power over broadcast news by Congress, our freedoms also are curtailed or endangered by intimidation and harassment.

There are the pressures exerted by high Government officials who suggest that if we don't put our whole house in order, that is, report the news the way they would like it reported, then "perhaps it is time that the networks were made more responsive to the views of the Nation, and more responsive to the people they serve."

The speaker might, indeed, disclaim any intention of censoring broadcast journalists, but when the speaker is a high official of the administration that appoints the Commission that holds life or death power over the broadcast industry, a broadcast journalist and his employer might be excused for thinking that it sounds like a threat. A timid broadcaster might very well feel constrained to avoid offending an administration whose spokesman openly carries such a club, whether he disclaims intention to use it or not.

This sort of executive department pressure inspires ancillary pressure—the stone in the pond and ripples therefrom. Government bureaucrats, friends of the administration, Congressmen, and the general public, pick up the cue, and threaten local stations with Federal Communications Commission complaints if they do not make their news conform.

The FCC has a procedure, as you know, to handle such complaints, and it, in itself, provides a legal channel for harassment of broadcast journalism.

As you know, if the FCC thinks any complaint to it is worthy of answer, it can request an explanation from the station or network within 20, sometimes 10, days. If dissatisfied with the answer, the FCC may charge the network or station with violating the fairness doctrine and court action can ensue.

Any influential person or group can, with the most capricious complaint, fire a 20-day letter. To answer it, stations must strain their limited reserve of executive talent and time. Newsmen are diverted from their jobs to provide documentation to support the station's answer. It is only natural that station management should become timid, and newsmen should sidestep controversial subjects rather than face the annoyance of such harassment.

The ultimate intimidation is to attempt, or even threaten to attempt, through the licensing procedure, to take a station away from its owner.

Minority groups have used this practice to try to force broadcasters to pay greater attention to their aspirations. And when, shortly after Vice President Agnew's attack on *The Washington Post*, among others, that newspaper's recent acquisition of a station in Miami was challenged. *Broadcasting* magazine felt it important to note that "several persons importantly involved, in the competing application, were friends, supporters or former business associates of President Nixon."

We certainly would not want to impugn the motives of any such group, but the *Post* management might have had some cause to wonder whether this action constituted a subtle warning. In any case, one would not expect such tactics to influence the editorial position of so powerful and financially substantial a paper as *The Washington Post* and its television station manager. But can we be sure?

What about a station placed in a similar position with the resources, or, for that matter, the tradition of independence of *The Washington Post*? And, even on the *Post*, might there not be a tendency—just a tendency, ephemeral, unspoken—to "avoid offending" until this thing blows over?

Over news broadcasting then hangs perpetually this cloud of Government license.

Licensing came about because in the early days of radio, and then, again, in the first days of television, there were only a few frequencies or channels available and clearly some authority had to assign them. But even in the conception of the Federal Communications Commission Act, there was recognized a need to protect the freedom of broadcasts. The law specifically forbade censorship by the regulating agency. The law only gave the new authority the right to determine that the licensee operate it in the "public interest, convenience, and necessity."

The FCC has interpreted that right to examine a station's programing, to require a certain portion of time to be allotted to so-called public affairs programing, to provide rebuttal under the fairness and equal time doctrines.

Tribute should be paid to the wisdom of Federal Communications Commission members, past and present, that the regulatory body has not gone further. But the power to make us conform is too great to forever lie dormant. The axe lies there temptingly for the use of any enraged administration—Republican, Democrat, Wallaceite or McCarthyite. We are at the mercy of the whim of politicians and bureaucrats and whether they choose to chop us down or not, the mere existence of their power is an intimidating and constraining threat in being.

And yet the situation that caused this power to be vested in Government largely has been dissipated by technological progress. Since the law's inception the ultrahigh frequencies in television and frequency modulation (FM) band in radio have been developed and scores of additional channels have become available.

A little recognized fact is that, today, in many markets it is not the availability of channels but the capability of economic survival that limits the number of radio and television stations.

Let me repeat: In a great many cities today, including major markets, there are unused radio frequencies and television channels and the number of broadcasting stations is not limited as much by technical considerations as by a market that will support only a maximum number of stations, the same rule of the marketplace that determines the number of newspapers in a community.

Putting it more simply: The doctrine that the air belongs to the people because broadcast channels are a rare resource is today largely myth.

The myth is further exploded by the advent of cable television. The wired cities of tomorrow—not using the "people's air" at all— will have an almost unlimited number of channels available.

In passing may I note that one might be excused a certain sadness in observing the hope with which special-interest groups seek access to the airwaves. They somehow have deluded themselves into believing that access to an audience assures an audience. Nothing, obviously, could be further from the truth. If these groups were given a half hour in the middle of a network's evening prime time broadcast schedule, there is nothing to assure that a single viewer would still be with them at the end. The same is true whether they owned their own station or had unlimited access to a cable television channel. The fight to get on the air may seem like a great and heroic battle against insurmountable odds to those who so desperately seek and need a voice, but more access could prove to be a tragically hollow victory for them.

But already without the cable and without the maximum use of all the available radio frequencies and television channels, there is no monopoly in broadcasting. That myth, too, should be exposed.

Already there are more radio and television stations than there are daily newspapers in the United States. There are 1,766 daily newspapers, but there are 6,976 radio stations and 892 television stations.

It is the rare city today that is not served by more television stations and radio stations than by newspapers.

There are more television networks serving radio and television stations than there are general news agencies serving the newspapers.

The monopoly today is in publishing, not broadcasting. Broadcasting has brought this about, so splitting the advertising dollar that only one newspaper can exist in most American cities.

Unfortunately, too, broadcast news is not an adequate substitute for the newspapers it has driven out of business. I happen to believe that we do what we do rather well, but our time limitations and the transient nature of what we do will forever prevent us from taking fully the place of the printed page with its greater bulk of news and its permanent, timeless accessability. We cannot supply the wealth of detail that the informed citizen needs to judge the performance of his city, county, state or nation.

If we do our jobs thoroughly, however, we can be a superb monitor—perhaps the only one—on the monopoly newspaper to assure that it does not by plot, caprice, conspiracy, or inadvertence miss a significant story.

We can do that, gentlemen, if we are left alone to perform that essential journalistic function. The trouble is, of course, that we are not free, we are Government licensed.

So we have on the side a monopoly press that may or may not choose to present views other than those of the dominant majority. On the other side, a vigorously competitive but federally regulated broadcast industry beholden to the favor of the powerful for its existence.

This scarcely could be called a healthy situation. There is a real danger that the free flow of ideas, that the vitality of minority views, that even the dissent of recognized authorities, could be stifled in such an atmosphere.

The untrammeled, uncontrolled flow of information between our people, and our people and our Government and the essential confidence of the people that they have access to the truth could reach a parlous state in this Nation if broadcasting is not set free, as free as the printed word.

The least that must be done, and really it is only a minimal remedy, is to legislate assurances that the restrictive laws or Government decrees do not interfere with broadcast journalism's full exercise of those freedoms of press and speech guaranteed by the first amendment.

That would be a restraining influence on those who would control us, even as it has proved to be the unbreachable barrier protecting the printed press.

Even this easiest and smallest step is flawed. For even with such legal assurances, the law cannot protect a licensed broadcast station against oblique pressure from the politically powerful who may take offense at the station's news reporting. Motivation is difficult to prove, and as long as broadcasting is under Government license, harassment is possible through many means that ostensibly would have no direct relation to news operations.

The cleanest and perfect solution—clearly much harder to obtain than the first amendment guarantee would be to eliminate all Government control of broadcasting. Clearly a Federal authority would have to assign channels and monitor the station's technical performance to assure that it remained on its frequency with the proper power. But, as I have suggested here before, the time is past when there can be any legal justification for controlling broadcasting's program content. There is no monopoly today. The open competition of the market place, the laissez faire economy in which we are supposed to believe, does pertain in broadcasting. There is no reason to believe that broadcasting, set free, would not act with the same variety of motives, principles, and performance that have worked pretty well in publishing. There would be horrid stations and good, even as there are today under license. There would be some that rendered excellent journalistic service, and some that belied the trust in them— even as there are newspapers with such marks today.

As for the fairness doctrine, and equal time and the people's access to the people's air—the Nation has done rather well without imposing these artificial standards on the newspapers.

The differences between publishing and broadcasting today are mostly myth. They are perpetuated by a set of endless reflections in opposing mirrors. Broadcasting is different because it is Government licensed. Broadcasting needs to be licensed because it is different. If there is any chain of reason that binds this theory together it has rusted through time and technological development and today its weaker links have the strength of wet tissue paper. It exists because no one of authority, until perhaps now, has dared to undertake close examination of it.

This may not be the proper body to do that. But I would urge you to give the matter some consideration as you ponder means of protecting our freedoms of press and speech. It may prove an ultimate solution. Meanwhile, the most immediate need and the strongest interim measure would be to grant us broadcast journalists, imperfect as we may be but as eager and dedicated as we are, the protection of the First Amendment as surely the Founding Fathers would have intended. To fail to do so, would be to deny the people a powerful tool in their attempt to exercise their right to know and to perpetuate a system that cannot assure the freedoms fundamental to the maintenance of our democratic form of life.

Thank You, Walter Cronkite

Mobil Corporation

We listened very carefully recently when Walter Cronkite, dean of American newscasters, and, as some polls have shown, one of the most trusted figures on television, addressed a group of radio and television news directors on the state of their craft. We admired his courage and perception in expressing a weakness in TV coverage that we've been trying for some time to bring to public attention.

Basically, Mr. Cronkite complained about television's problem in covering complex news issues adequately. ". . . In the compression process forced upon us by the severe limitations of time," he said, "the job is incredibly, almost impossibly, difficult. I'm afraid that we compress so well as to almost defy the viewer and listener to understand what we say. And when that becomes the fact, we cease to be communicators."

Mr. Cronkite wasn't talking specifically about energy news. But he could have been. With nearly three-quarters of the American public getting most of its news from television, we hold TV very largely responsible for public confusion and misunderstanding over America's energy problems.

The problem, he elaborated, is "the inadvertent and perhaps inevitable distortion that results through the hyper-compression we all are forced to exert to fit one hundred pounds of news into the one-pound sack that we are given to fill each night."

"The cumulative effect is devastating, eating away at our credibility," he said. "Perhaps it will take a while for the masses to catch on—they usually are the last to know the truth. But among the informed, the opinion leaders . . . the awareness is spreading—the awareness that our abbreviated versions of the news are suspect. They or their friends and associates have been victimized by our truncated reports, and they spread the word."

As one of TV's frequent "victims" we couldn't agree more with the tube's respected dean. We often see distortions when TV reports on large oil company profits, without any mention of rate of return on investment, or other accepted yardsticks. We saw it when TV reported those 1973–74 rumors of tankers waiting offshore for higher prices, and then gave scant coverage to denials by the Coast Guard and others.

The time factor is only one shortcoming of television news programs. We'd also like to see Mr. Cronkite address the problem of television news shows being, essentially, entertainment vehicles and the fact that, in the drive for ratings, news directors—and broadcasters—will sometimes emphasize the emotional or visual aspect of a story in an effort to entertain rather than inform.

Obviously we at Mobil don't seriously expect television stations to bill their news programs as entertainment. But we do wish television

This ad appeared in *The New York Times* on January 20, 1977.

news people would emulate their print colleagues and be a little more responsive to outside views. Newspapers and magazines at least allow advertising on public issues. They also print articles by free-lance journalists, and guest columnists are regularly featured within their pages. Ideally, we'd like television to adopt similar approaches. But commercial television networks won't allow outsiders to produce news shows. We know the sort of tight control networks maintain on the free flow of information. We've tried to offer in commercials the same kind of messages we present in this space. But we've been turned down.

Mr. Cronkite does suggest longer news programs so items can get fuller development. This, he feels, would provide "enough extra time for the explanatory phrase, the 'why' and the 'how' as well as the 'who,' 'what,' 'when,' and 'where.' "

"We must redouble our efforts," he adds, "to convince all those concerned that the republic, that the people, need this hour not just so we can do a different job, but so that we can do a better, more *honest* job of carrying this tremendous responsibility that rests on our shoulders."

Well said, Walter Cronkite.

Broadcast Advertising   *Georgetown Law Journal*

With the football resting on the 35 yardline of Dallas, the Washington Redskins appeared ready to score and tie the game. For the first time that afternoon, the Redskins had gained momentum, keeping a scoring drive alive with two spectacular pass plays. As the Washington team broke their huddle, the crowd surged to its feet—and the sound of the referee's whistle signaled a time out. It was time for a "word from our sponsors."

Advertising's role in broadcast programming has transformed some elements of television into a "limited purpose" medium often concerned with marketing products, and only incidentally with entertaining viewers. While media owners originally sought advertising to finance programs and broadcasting costs,[1] they now structure their programming to sell viewing time to advertisers and advertising agencies.[2] With revenue considerations becoming a consideration in decisions on program content and quality, it may be worth evaluating the issue of whether broadcasting has betrayed its unlimited potential and its statutory obligation to serve the "public interest, convenience, and necessity." [3]

Advertiser Control

Advertising's effect on program content is not new. As early as 1943, the Supreme Court recognized that commercial sponsors in radio had a large influence on program content. In *National Broadcasting Co. v.*

United States,[4] the Court noted: "[t]o an ever-increasing extent, these [advertising] agencies actually exercise the function of program production. Thus, it is frequently neither the station nor the network, but rather the advertising agency, which determines what broadcast programs shall contain."[5]

During television's first decade, sponsors produced their own programs and retained rights to use them. Advertisers preferred that their products be identified with one show, whose quality and wholesomeness the advertiser could directly guarantee. In subsequent years, when programs were produced by television networks and independent production companies, television's largest sponsors continued policies to safeguard against publicly offensive material in programs associated with the sponsor's message. As an example, Procter and Gamble, television's largest advertiser,[6] had a policy which, though obviously not designed for everyday implementation, allowed the company to exclude any material that might offend, even by inference, "any organized minority group, lodge, or other organizations, institutions, residents of any State or section of the country, or a commercial organization of any sort."[7] Although extreme examples may be atypical, they may be useful to demonstrate at least the physical potential for a sponsor's tampering with program content, with absurd results. An electric company sponsoring a presentation of Kipling's *The Light that Failed* requested that the title be changed to avoid negative reflections upon the electric industry.[8] Automobile manufacturers, sensitive to each other's trade names, have refined "association deletion" to an art. During a football game between Southern Methodist University and Texas A & M, ABC sportcasters constantly referred to the SMU Mustangs as "horses," "colts," and "ponies" because one of the show's sponsors was the Chevrolet Camaro, a direct competitor of Ford's Mustang.[9] Equally sensitive, Ford deleted a view of the New York skyline from one of the shows it sponsored because the view included the Chrysler Building.[10] Chrysler also proved its concern by deleting President Lincoln's name from the script of *The Andersonville Trial* to avoid reference to a Ford product.[11]

Vital Role of Popularity Ratings

A drastic change occurred in the advertiser-program relation with the advent of various rating systems and improved sophistication in marketing techniques. Advertisers discovered that it was economically more efficient to discard the financial burden of producing weekly shows in favor of taking "participations"[12] in network-produced programs. By sharing participations on a variety of programs with other sponsors, the advertiser is able to expose his commercial to a larger and more diversified audience for the same dollar amount formerly spent on program production.[13] From 1957 to 1964, single sponsored shows dropped from 42.5 percent to 8.3 percent of all programs broadcast.[14]

Concomitantly, a change in sponsor influence on program content has taken place. Rather than specifically controlling a program's content, advertisers now exert an indirect influence on all programming. Although some direct sponsor influence persists,[15] the advertiser's personal power has been limited by the decision to decentralize his advertising. Now sponsors, competing among themselves for the largest audiences,[16] purchase time slots according to "cost per thousand viewers." Often the sponsor will have no choice as to which program he can sponsor, being dependent upon what "availabilities" are offered by the sponsor's advertising agency.[17] Competitive necessity has established the rating systems as "the arbiter of TV success." [18] A simple economic formula emerges—the larger the audience, the greater the price the networks can charge advertisers for a specific time slot.

Program Content and Audiences

Broadcasting corporations may have to sacrifice programming which cannot guarantee maximized audiences. The depressing, argumentative, unpopular, or controversial is excluded.[19] Judge Edward Tamm of the United States Court of Appeals for the District of Columbia Circuit has noted that "[t]o limit audience alienation, large circulation media prefer to report ideas or factual stories that are either inoffensive or on which there is relatively broad agreement or wide acceptance." [20] This observation may not be in furtherance of the Supreme Court's opinion that "a function of free speech under our system of government is to invite dispute. It may indeed best serve its high purpose when it induces a condition of unrest, creates dissatisfaction with conditions as they are, or even stirs people to anger." [21] All too often informative programs produced in good faith by networks give way to more profitable entertainment.[22] Fred Friendly, former president of CBS News, testified before the Senate Judiciary Subcommittee on Constitutional Rights that "[i]t is the dollar sign, not the government's censorship stamp, that has drastically reduced the amount of air time devoted to documentaries and public-affairs programming." [23]

As marketing analysis of audience composition has become more sophisticated, program planning has become more complex. Concern for "audience flow" [24] has encouraged networks to develop with painstaking care a program sequence which will maintain the largest continual audience possible. When the FCC limited network prime time broadcasting to three hours per night,[25] NBC sought and was granted an exception for its Sunday night broadcasts.[26] The network argued that the ruling would negate the years of hard work which had produced NBC's highly successful Sunday evening program sequence of *The Wonderful World of Disney*, *The Jimmy Stewart Show*, *Bonanza*, and *The Bold Ones*.

Programming is designed not only to attract the largest audience, but also to put the audience in the most receptive mood for the accompanying advertising message.[27] Too sad a program may result in viewers whom a particular sponsor wished to contact tuning out.[28] Dupont, a sponsor of high quality dramatic presentations, researched this phenomenon and concluded that the audience "learned" a merchandising message better during light programs, such as the comedy *Harvey*, than during productions of such "heavies" as *Hamlet* and *Ethan Frome*.[29] The avowed policy of Dupont to accept small audiences inherent in quality programming is almost unique.

Fairness Doctrine Ramifications in Broadcast Advertising

Television programmers also must consider seriously the impact of the fairness doctrine [30] before making a programming decision. In supplying rebuttal time to controversial broadcasts, broadcasters may risk losing revenue and audience flow. Although the fairness doctrine [31] has been extended to advertising, application of the doctrine was limited to cigarette commercials and anti-smoking messages which, it must be noted, involved a unique health threat.[32] The FCC has stated that "instances of extension of the ruling to other products [would be] rare, if indeed they ever occurred." [33] Advertisements for gasolines and detergents were denied controversial issue status by the FCC,[34] but this ruling was reversed on appeal.[35] Despite the reversal, the Commission's handling of the matter demonstrated its reluctance to extend application of the fairness doctrine generally to the field of product advertising. This reluctance is based upon a belief that to do so would undermine the present commercial broadcast system.[36] CBS has estimated that a general extension of the doctrine to include advertisements for cereals, gasolines, cars, oil, drugs, and detergents would inflict a $68 million loss of revenue on network broadcasters each year.[37]

Whether Advertising Regulation Would Serve First Amendment Interests

FCC reluctance to attempt to control specific program content [38] recognizes the danger to first amendment freedoms posed by government intervention in broadcasting. Protection of the public interest may be constitutionally effected, however, by regulation of advertising [39]—a matter which has occasionally been viewed as a subject of government control.[40] The law surrounding advertising's free speech status is ill-defined. Evidence exists to support the claim that the Constitutional Convention failed to consider the question of commercial advertising.[41] In *Valentine v. Christensen*,[42] the Supreme Court ruled that "purely commercial" speech is not protected under the first amendment. This ruling, however, lacked analytical substantiation or explanation. Justice Douglas, a member of the unanimous *Valentine* Court, has since called the decision "casual, almost offhand," [43] and has concluded that "[t]he extent to which such advertising could be regulated consistently with the First Amendment has therefore never been authoritatively determined." [44] Moreover, the Supreme Court has held that advertisements for religious meetings,[45] political debates,[46] and labor union activities [47] are protected speech.

Clearly, the expression of opinions and beliefs within the ambit of first amendment protection releases advertisements from the restricted category of purely commercial speech. Within the last four years, developments in both federal and state courts have elevated editorial advertising to constitutionally protected status. A ban on editorial advertising in a forum opened for commercial and public messages violates the Constitution as a discrimination between classes of ideas, which is prohibited by the first amendment.[48] Under this doctrine, the California supreme court ruled that a public transit district, which sold advertising space on municipal busses, had to make that same forum available to anti-war posters.[49] A similar ruling concerning advertising space on subway platforms was reached by the United States District Court for the Southern District of New York.[50] In the past, however, broadcasters have occasionally refused to air commercials of a nonmerchandising or nonpublic affairs nature.[51] An example of such a policy was the decision of the Westinghouse Broadcasting System ("Group W" stations) "not [to] accept paid announcements on controversial issues if [such issues] do not appear on a ballot." [52]

Case Law and the First Amendment

In August 1971, the United States Court of Appeals for the District of Columbia Circuit handed down a landmark decision in *Business Executives' Move for Vietnam Peace v. FCC*,[53] which extended the established forum doctrine to broadcasting. Wishing to purchase advertising time to advocate an end to the Vietnam War, the Business Executives' Move (BEM) ran headlong into WTOP Radio's "long established policy of refusing to sell spot announcement time to individuals or groups to set forth views on controversial issues." [54] The FCC had upheld such a policy,[55] but, in overruling the Commission's decision, the court of appeals held that a flat ban on paid public issue announcements was violative of the first amendment. The crucial factor was the discrimination between different categories of ideas. This seminal decision, however, expressly refused to hold that the right of access to an established forum is an absolute right.[56] Instead, each editorial advertisement is to be subject to a balancing test, based partially on the scarcity of broadcast time rationale cited in *National Broadcasting Co. v. United States*,[57] and partially on reasonable procedures and regulations to be established by licensees and the FCC.[58]

Evincing impatience with the FCC's hesitance to regulate television advertising effectively, the court stated: "We are convinced that the time has come for the Commission to cease abdicating responsibility over the uses of advertising time." [59] The FCC was directed to establish immediately procedures to "determine which and how many 'editorial advertisements' will be put on the air." [60]

Of paramount significance was the court's decision to retain industry and government control over advertising. Recognition of an absolute right of access would have forced broadcasters to accept all requests for time to air controversial advertisements. Such an obligation would have transformed broadcasting stations into common carriers, a result expressly contrary to the intent of the Communications Act of 1934.[61]

Social Messages Through Commercial Speech—Cultural Spillover

Today, broadcasting experts are beginning to recognize that commercial messages may transmit noncommercial ideas. Advertisements nearly always include themes of social acceptability, success, or virility and imply that acquisition and use of the advertised product is a means of attaining these goals. As a result, "[e]xternally derived solutions are thus made the prescription for life's difficulties."[62] This phenomenon is termed "cultural spillover."

Cultural spillover appears most acute in advertising during programming for children. Testifying before the FTC, Evelyn Sarson, president of Action for Children's Television (ACT), called for a ban on all but public service commercials during children's programs.[63] Mrs. Sarson cited the case of a young boy who had ingested an almost lethal dose of vitamin pills because he wanted to "grow big and strong"—as the commercials promised—faster than his peers who were taking the recommended one vitamin a day.[64]

Especially condemned has been advertising emphasis on war toys and nonnutritional foods. One study revealed that over 50 percent of the advertising during children's programs is for sweetened cereals, candy, and snacks, while no advertisements are broadcast for vegetables, milk products, meats, or fruits.[65] Critics stress that young children are incapable of making knowledgeable consumer decisions. Arguments that such cultural spillover could have little effect on the general viewer, or on young viewers in particular, ignore the fact that television advertisers spend over $1.65 billion a year [66] in the firm belief that television advertising strongly does influence viewer behavior.

There are legal precedents which may someday support regulation of cultural spillover in advertising. The fairness doctrine may apply to social values advocated by commercial advertisements. In *Friends of the Earth v. FCC*,[67] the District of Columbia Circuit applied the fairness doctrine to advertising for the second time, ruling that broadcasters had to allow a response to advertisements stressing the value of powerful automobile engines and high test gasolines.[68] Significant in this decision was the court's strong suggestion that application of the fairness doctrine was not dependent on inherent threats to the public health by the challenged advertisements. Such threats were deemed essential to the decision in *Banzhaf v. FCC*,[69] the first case in which the court had applied the fairness doctrine.

The court stated, in *Friends of the Earth*, that "[c]ommercials which continue to insinuate that the human personality finds greater fulfillment in the large car with the quick getaway do, it seems to us, ventilate a point of view which not only has become controversial but involves an issue of public importance." [70] Recent FCC rulings have enforced a similar approach to advertisements which secondarily promote a controversial national goal—the most notable example being oil company advertisements asserting the value of building the trans-Alaskan pipeline.[71]

Historically, advertising has been circumscribed substantially by common law actions for fraud and deceit, based on public policy considerations in favor of the smooth flow of commerce.[72] Considerations of public health resulted in the cigarette ruling. Public policy has also determined that it is not in our nation's interest to promote the drinking of hard liquor; this theory has resulted in the banning of liquor advertising on commercial television.[73] Clearly, if the rationale of public policy can be used to regulate commerce, protect the nation's health, and influence the country's social habits, public policy may some day be used as the justification for regulating the effects of cultural spillover in advertising.

Unsolved Fairness Doctrine Problems

The most important and most difficult problem facing commercial broadcasting today is resolution of the scope of the fairness doctrine.[74] In *Red Lion Broadcasting Co. v. FCC*, the Supreme Court recognized that the viewer's freedom of speech rights in broadcasting were paramount to those of the broadcaster.[75] Since that ruling, viewers' rights have been expanded to include access for editorial advertising [76] and fairness responses to controversial advertising.[77] The difficulties with this area of the law have led to numerous proposals. It may be interesting to examine a few of these as illustrations of proposed solutions.

Clay T. Whitehead, head of the White House Office of Telecommunications Policy, advocates changes in the fairness doctrine and the adoption of an automatic right for the public to purchase unlimited broadcast time.[78] Both suggestions, however, fail to withstand critical analysis. An absolute right of access was denied for editorial advertising by the District of Columbia Circuit, which stated: "As the *Red Lion* Court made clear, there could not be any such absolute right because advertising time, like all broadcast time, is severely limited." [79] The grant of an absolute right of access would open the floodgates of opinion to the exclusion of popular programming. The *BEM* court stressed that "[c]learly, . . . broadcasters are entitled to place an outside limit on the total amount of editorial advertising they will sell. To fail to impose some such limit would be to deny the public the other sorts of programming which it legitimately expects on radio and television." [80]

The *BEM* court delegated responsibility for developing procedures to allocate editorial advertisement time to broadcast licensees and to the Federal Communications Commission. FCC Commissioner Nicholas Johnson has advocated allotting five percent of prime time television for paid editorial advertising, the time slots to be distributed on a "first-come, first-served basis." [81] Application of such a policy, however, would raise difficult political questions concerning who would decide who is first.

Commissioner Johnson's proposal, moreover, puts a price tag on access and recognizes no correlation between currency of issues and the need for immediate access.

On January 6, 1972, the Federal Trade Commission recommended to the FCC that a "substantial" amount of time [82] be made available without cost for counter-advertising, and that a right to buy air time be established. The proposal also advocated "a substantial degree of discretion [for licensees] in deciding which commercials warrant or require access for a response." [83] General rules and guidelines promulgated by the FCC would specify which general categories of commercials would require recognition of access rights as well as the frequency and duration of replies demanded in each category. One recommendation has proposed that replies be granted to offset general cultural spillover in advertising [84] and that a flexible counter-advertisement format be permitted.[85]

1. Blalock, *Television and Advertising*, 28 FED. B.J. 341, 342–43 (1968). See Statement by Sec'y of Commerce Herbert Hoover at the First Annual Radio Conference in 1932, in 1 P & F RADIO REG. 2D 1606, 1607 (1964).
2. Barrow, *supra* note 419, at 634, 641.
3. Communications Act of 1934, 47 U.S.C. §309(a) (1970).
4. 319 U.S. 190 (1943).
5. *Id.* at 205.
6. In 1970, Procter & Gamble spent $128.5 million on network advertising. BROADCASTING, Mar. 22, 1971, at 38.
7. N. MINOW, EQUAL TIME 18 (1964). General Mills prohibited the use of "material for or against sharply drawn national or regional controversial issues." S. OPOTOWSKY, TV, THE BIG PICTURE 84 (1961). See generally C. WINICK, TASTE AND THE CENSOR IN TELEVISION 22–27 (1959).
8. Minow, *The Public Interest*, in FREEDOM AND RESPONSIBILITY IN BROADCASTING 18 (J. Coons ed. 1961).
9. TIME, Nov. 17, 1967, at 66.
10. S. OPOTOWSKY, *supra* note 7 at 83.
11. Minow, *supra* note 8, at 18.
12. A "participation" includes partial compensation to the networks for the show's production costs, plus a time slot rate dependent on the number of viewers established by one of the rating systems.
13. Blake & Blum, *Network Television Rate Practices: A Case Study in the Failure of Social Control of Price Discrimination*, 74 YALE L.J. 1339, 1346–47 (1965).
14. Cohen, *The Advertiser's Influence in TV Programming*, 8 OSGOODE HALL L.J. 91, 101 (1970).
15. NEWSWEEK, Jan. 10, 1972, at 40.
16. See N. JOHNSON, HOW TO TALK BACK TO YOUR TELEVISION SET 20–21 (1970).
17. Representing advertisers, these agencies will ask the networks for particular time slots. However, the networks retain control over time slot allocation and usually will save the best slots for their largest volume advertisers. Thus advertising agencies and advertisers are dependent on what time slots remain open—the availabilities offered by the networks.
18. Cohen, *supra* note 14, at 102; see Eck, *The Real Masters of Television*, HARPER'S, Mar. 1967, at 46–47; Washington Post, Oct. 13, 1971, §A, at 3, col. 2.
19. FCC OFFICE OF NETWORK STUDY, *supra* note 446, pt. 1, at 116; Note, *The Federal Communications Commission's Fairness Regulations: A First Step Towards Creation of a Right of Access to the Mass Media*, 54 CORNELL L. REV. 294, 296 (1969); see N. MINOW, *supra* note 7, at 74–76.

20. Hale v. FCC, 138 U.S. App. D.C. 125, 131, 425 F.2d 556, 562 (1970) (Tamm, J., concurring), *quoting* STAFF OF THE NAT'L COMM'N ON THE CAUSES AND PREVENTION OF VIOLENCE, REPORT—VIOLENCE AND THE MEDIA 81–82 (1969).

21. Terminiello v. Chicago, 337 U.S. 1, 4 (1949).

22. Successful entertainment programs will attract about 60–80 million viewers, while a documentary will average only 15 million viewers. Note, *Wasteland Revisited: A Modest Attack upon the FCC's Category System*, 17 U.C.L.A.L. REV. 868, 877 n.34 (1970). Judge Bazelon has recognized that "a broadcaster can appeal to only one audience at a time. If he devotes an hour to programs appealing to a minority taste, he forgoes the chance to compete for the greater advertising revenues consequent upon reaching a larger audience. Accordingly, it may be that even newspaper monopolies are more likely than broadcasters to serve the entire public without regulatory prodding." Banzhaf v. FCC, 132 U.S. App. D.C. 14, 32 n.76, 405 F.2d 1082, 1100 n.76 (1968); *see* N. JOHNSON, *supra* note 16, at 22–23.

23. Washington Post, Oct. 13, 1971, §A, at 3, col. 2.

24. Audience flow is the maintenance of a segment of the viewing audience between two consecutive programs. By creating a sequence of programs which appeals to the largest section of the viewing audience, broadcasters can retain a consistent audience flow. Anathema to the concept of audience flow is the interjection into a program sequence of controversial or high quality programming which will cause any part of the audience to change channels. Statement by Hugh M. Beville, Jr., NBC Vice President for Planning, *reprinted in* FCC OFFICE OF NETWORK STUDY, *supra* note 446, pt. 1, at 436; *see* Note, *A Fair Break for Controversial Speakers: Limitations of the Fairness Doctrine and the Need for Individual Access*, 39 GEO. WASH. L. REV. 532, 559 n.217 (1971). *See also* Barrow, *supra* note 419, at 636.

25. *See* N.Y. Times, Mar. 5, 1971, at 71, col. 4.

26. *Id.*

27. Cohen, *supra* note 14, at 104.

28. S. OPOTOWSKY, *supra* note 7, at 79. High quality programming often will be rejected because it tends to lower overall network ratings. Blake & Blum, *supra* note 13, at 1344 n.38.

29. Cohen, *supra* note 14, at 104.

30. *Id.*

31. *See* notes 955–972 *infra* and accompanying text.

32. Applicability of Fairness Doctrine to Cigarette Commercials, 9 F.C.C.2d 921 (1967), *aff'd sub nom.* Banzhaf v. FCC, 132 U.S. App. D.C. 14, 405 F.2d 1082 (1968).

33. Friends of the Earth, 24 F.C.C.2d 743, 745–49 (1970).

34. *Id.*

35. Friends of the Earth v. FCC, — — U.S. App. D.C. — —, 449 F.2d 1164 (1971).

36. Friends of the Earth, 24 F.C.C.2d 743, 748–49 (1970).

37. Washington Post, Oct. 22, 1971, §B, at 1, col. 6, at 4, col. 5.

38. The FCC has no authority to issue or to withhold licenses on the basis of the quality of programming. *See* FCC Network Programming Inquiry, *Report and Statement of Policy*, 25 Fed. Reg. 7291, 7293 (1960).

39. Grosjean v. American Press Co., 297 U.S. 233, 249–50 (1935). "The First Amendment embodies the fundamental idea that minority views will and must find their place in a free market of ideas and communication. When the broadcaster ignores minority tastes and serves only the majority which the advertiser seeks (and this sometimes means rejecting a program which many millions of people want to see), he is unconsciously rejecting one of the fundamental concepts upon which our society is based. . . ." Minow, *supra* note 8, at 17.

40. *See* Breard v. City of Alexandria, 341 U.S. 622 (1951).

41. Letter from the Continental Congress to the Inhabitants of Quebec, Oct. 26, 1774, *quoted in* Roth v. United States, 354 U.S. 476, 484 (1957).

42. 316 U.S. 52 (1942); *see* Breard v. City of Alexandria, 341 U.S. 622, 641–45 (1951).

43. Cammarano v. United States, 358 U.S. 498, 513 (1959) (Douglas, J., concurring).

44. *Id.* at 513. A federal district court has stated that "[i]f the advertisement is not false, defendants have a constitutional right to utilize it even though its content and blatancy may annoy both the [Federal Trade] Commission and the general public. The issue is falsity. . . ." FTC v. Sterling Drug, Inc., 215 F. Supp. 327, 332 (S.D.N.Y. 1963).
45. Martin v. City of Struthers, 319 U.S. 141 (1943).
46. Schneider v. New Jersey, 308 U.S. 147 (1939).
47. Thornhill v. Alabama, 310 U.S. 88 (1940). *Thornhill* has been significantly limited by *Giboney v. Empire Storage & Ice Co.*, which denied union picketing when in violation of valid state laws against restraint of trade, 336 U.S. 490, 497–500 (1949).
48. *See* Business Executives' Move for Vietnam Peace v. FCC, — U.S. App. D.C. —, 450 F.2d 642 (1971).
49. Wirta v. Alameda-Contra Costa Transit Distr., 68 Cal. 2d 51, 55, 434 P.2d 982, 985, 64 Cal. Rptr. 430, 433 (1967).
50. Kissinger v. New York City Transit Authority, 274 F. Supp. 438 (S.D.N.Y. 1967).
51. Station WABC(AM), the flagship station for the American Broadcasting Company, enforces a company policy not to accept commercials on controversial issues. BROADCASTING, Mar. 22, 1971, at 52. Presently, the Uniformed Fire Officers Association is appealing such a refusal to the FCC. *See id.*
52. *Id.*
53. — U.S. App. D.C. —, 450 F.2d 642 (1971).
54. *Id.* at —, 450 F.2d at 647.
55. Business Executives' Move for Vietnam Peace, 25 F.C.C.2d 242 (1970).
56. — U.S. App. D.C. at —, 450 F.2d at 659.
57. National Braodcasting Co. v. United States, 319 U.S. 190 (1943).
58. — U.S. App. D.C. at — , 450 F.2d at 663.
59. *Id.* at —, 450 F.2d at 646.
60. *Id.* at —, 450 F.2d at 646.
61. *See* 47 U.S.C. §307(e) (1970). *See also* United States v. Radio Corporation of America, 358 U.S. 334, 348–49 (1959); FCC v. Sanders Bros. Radio Station, 309 U.S. 470, 474 (1940).
62. Jones, *The Cultural and Social Impact of Advertising on American Society,* 8 OSGOODE HALL L.J. 65, 71 (1970).
63. Washington Post, Nov. 11, 1971, §C, at 1, col. 6.
64. *Id.*
65. *Id.* at 2, col. 4
66. BROADCASTING, Mar. 22, 1971, at 46.
67. — U.S. App. D.C. —, 449 F.2d 1164 (1971).
68. *Id.* at —, 449 F.2d at 1164–65.
69. 132 U.S. App. D.C. 14, 405 F.2d 1082 (1968) (cigarette commercials).
70. — U.S. App. D.C. at —, 449 F.2d at 1168.
71. Wilderness Society, 31 F.C.C.2d 729 (1971).
72. *See* Donaldson v. Read Magazine, Inc., 333 U.S. 178, 189–90 (1948); Wheeler-Lea Act §4, 15 U.S.C. §52 (1970).
73. *See generally* Lydick, *State Control of Liquor Advertising Under the United States Constitution,* 12 BAYLOR L. REV. 43 (1960).
74. Since June 1971, the FCC has been conducting an intensive review of the fairness doctrine. *See* Washington Post, Jan. 7, 1972, §A, at 1, col. 6.
75. Red Lion Broadcasting Co. v. FCC, 395 U.S. 367, 390 (1969).
76. Business Executives' Move for Vietnam Peace v. FCC, — U.S. App. D.C. —, 450 F.2d 642 (1971).
77. Banzhaf v. FCC, 132 U.S. App. D.C. 14, 405 F.2d 1082 (1968).
78. Washington Post, Oct. 7, 1971, §A, at 1, col. 6.
79. Business Executives' Move for Vietnam Peace v. FCC, — U.S. App. D.C. —, —, 450 F.2d 642, 662 (1971).
80. *Id.* at —, 450 F.2d at 663.
81. Democratic Nat'l Comm., 25 F.C.C.2d 216, 235 (1970) (Johnson, dissenting).

82. Statement of the FTC concerning The Handling of Public Issues Under the Fairness Doctrine and the Public Interest Standards of the Communications Act, FCC Docket No. 19,260, at 22 (Jan. 6, 1972).
83. *Id.* at 12.
84. *Id.* at 14–15.
85. *Id.* at 20–21.

A Modest Proposal to Pay for Excellence   Martin Mayer

Suppose you have talent ("we all have genius," an eminent music critic once shouted into a suddenly still moment at a party; "what we need is a little talent"), and you want to make a one-hour television program that is likely to appeal to five percent of the nation's households. For analytical purposes we'll ignore the likelihood that only half of that five percent will actually watch, and credit you with an audience amounting to five percent of the adult population. A best-seller with that size readership comes around maybe once every five years or so; a film with that much box office grosses $15 million to $20 million and materially contributes to the bottom line for the studio.

On commercial television, with six minutes for sale to advertisers in the hour and a good solid price of $10 per thousand homes per minute, your gross receipts are about $210,000. From that the bookkeepers quietly deduct agency commission, payments to local stations, and some share of the costs of running a network. You're lucky if there's $100,000 left; and there is no way you can make a respectably professional fifty-one-minute program for anything like $100,000.

So a television program designed for five percent of the country—an *enormous* audience by the standards of anything but television—will have to be made for public television, and it will have to be subsidized. The question promptly arises, Whence will the funding come? The foundations have almost finished their Cheshire cat act in program finance, leaving little behind but an encouraging smile. Yes, there are oil companies. But without for a moment denigrating the contribution they have made to public television, the fact is that Mobil has this thing about the BBC, and Exxon and Atlantic Richfield, for good and sufficient reason, prefer to present work by established theater repertory companies, Lincoln Center, Wolf Trap, and the like.

On their native soil, BBC programs are financed entirely through an annual license fee for the use of a television set; most semiautonomous government-sponsored broadcasting systems in the non-Communist developed nations rely on some combination of license receipts and commercials. The original Carnegie Commission that coined the phrase "public television" decided that programs for noncommercial broadcast should be paid for through an excise tax on television sets. (One commissioner—significantly, the only one with hands-on network experience—dissented. He urged a tax on commercials as the fairest system, though the one most likely to offend that great majority of viewers who watch public television rarely, if at all.) But the easiest thing to do, as the American government works, was just to get another line on the national budget. Most congressional appropriations are for things that interest only a small fraction of the public, and program money for public television has at least as much general appeal as, say, subsidies for tobacco farmers.

So there might be a source of money for your program in the annual appropriation to the Corporation for Public Broadcasting, and in the annual auction by which the individual noncommercial stations allocate government money among suggested features for the PBS network's new season. Public broadcasting, however, especially where money is concerned, is afflicted with both politics and bureaucracy. To run that gauntlet requires the patience of Job, the fortitude of Joan of Arc at the stake, and both the shell and temperament of a domesticated tortoise. If you have all of those, you don't have talent. Moreover, artistic and educational endeavors that become dependent on an annual appropriation from a legislature soon begin to smell of a peculiar fetid exhalation: the camel's nose in the tent.

But despair not. I have a good idea.

There is a potential source of significant revenue for the production of ambitious television programs, which does not require inflating the national budget or taxing the public. About one-fifth of all the advertising now carried on commercial television is not paid for. A rule that required the beneficiaries of this free advertising to pay for their time at a rate only one-tenth of what a soap-flake manufacturer would have to pay for those minutes might generate half again as much money as Congress now appropriates. And, from a public point of view, this scheme is heads we win, tails we win—even if it didn't raise the money, it would reduce the clutter on the air.

The proposal is to make broadcasters and networks pay for their "promos"—the announcements of other programs coming up tonight, tomorrow, or next week. These fall into three categories: full-fledged "commercials" for network television shows, complete with laugh track; "voice-over" announcements for coming network attractions, while the screen displays the credits at the end of a show; and "station promos," most frequently at the hour break, while the screen discloses the number of the channel you are watching.

In November 1976, shortly after Election Day, Broadcast Advertisers Reports, at the behest of the Association of National Advertisers (ANA), did a study of exactly how much of this self-promotion there was during three, twenty-hour days on each of the New York City network stations. These are the flagship stations, the most visible to the advertising agencies which contract for the time, and thus, presumably, the best behaved in the country. ANA found that on these stations, just over four percent of *all* broadcast time—almost one-fifth of the time taken up by "nonprogram material"—was devoted to program and station promos.

Apart from the football games, which are sui generis, the worst clutter is during the movies. ANA clocked an NBC "Saturday Night at the Movies" with an average of less than forty-five minutes of program time per hour (as against National Association of Broadcasters code requirements of at least fifty-one minutes in prime time). But "What's Happening!" provided only twenty-four minutes and ten seconds of program time in a half hour. Many other shows were running at a rate that would give the networks and stations more than one minute per hour over code limits to indulge in self-praise.

Costing out the value of the full-scale network promos alone ("supposedly," said Robert Liddel of Compton Advertising, who worked on the study, "we know what proper network budget sizes are"), the ANA projected the nationwide price of the network time thus occupied at $634 million in 1976–77. Station promos and voice-overs took up more time than full-scale network promos. The total price for buying time on all network stations is greater than the price of the equivalent network slots, and all prices are up this year. From the look of the ANA figures, the total market value of the time the networks and stations give themselves to promote their products approaches $2 billion a year. Let's be conservative and say $1.75 billion.

If the stations and networks were made to pay one-tenth of what they would charge advertisers for this time, the resulting fund would total $175 million a year. At an average of $250,000 an hour for program production, that would pay for almost two hours a night of programming, every night of the year, aimed at selective audiences. And there's no way the public can be a loser: If the broadcasters decide they don't want to pay for their promos, we'd have less money in the production fund—but also less infuriating noise from the carny barkers in our living rooms.

I hear only one hand clapping, and quite properly, too: I have solved only half the problem. Though income sources are extremely important in determining people's attitudes, the fact that their money was coming from a promo tax rather than from Congress probably would not depoliticize, and certainly would not speed up, CPB and PBS as presently constituted.

The fund contemplated here is a fund for producing programs; let us place its allocation in the hands of programming people. Say, a committee of seven, three from the networks, one from the National Association of Independent Stations, one from the organization of local programming directors, one from the Writers Guild, and one from the Directors Guild. Each should have one assistant of his own choice, paid from the fund. The work load for committee members should not be permitted to exceed fifty days a year, and they should serve a term of no more than two years, continuing to hold and perform their regular jobs.

Committee members should be paid by their regular employers, who should, however, have the right to reimbursement for the day a week the committee work would take, if they have the guts to put in the chit. Upper-middle-level people are what's wanted, and most such would be glad to participate, for service on this committee would clearly be one giant step on the career path.

This committee would serve no purpose other than the allocation of funds to program proposals. Completed, the programs could be offered for sale to networks or independent stations as well as made available to public television. The first charge against any sales receipts would be the reimbursement of the fund; anything over that could be split among the participants (by union contract, no doubt), with perhaps a commission for the fund. Public stations would not pay. To avoid a situation in which commercial stations and networks got first crack at everything potentially popular, perhaps PBS could procure programs at the planning stage by guaranteeing air time. Fluctuations in the fund could be avoided by setting budgets below anticipated receipts in the early years and building up a reserve; or Congress could make a one-shot appropriation to create a reserve.

Some part of the fund might be put aside to advertise the resulting programs; perhaps the networks and commercial stations might be compelled to sell a certain fraction of their promo time to the fund, at the established ten percent of commercial prices, to help draw an audience for the fund's accomplishments. In fairness, meanwhile, promos should also be restricted on public television; vulgarities like the identification of contributors, auctioneers, and successful bidders might be prohibited, and the number of claims of ineffable greatness for the current adaptation of some once popular novel might be severely rationed.

But a fatal fluency is now carrying me past the boundaries of my mandate, at the risk of obscuring the central argument. We really need a system of funding for television programs that can make it possible and attractive for a high order of talent to do what it wants to do on the air, not worrying too much about appeal to television-size audiences. We also need some sort of economic brake on the proliferation of promos, the relentless, remorseless self-advertising the networks and stations can hurl at us cost free. Now that we don't have certain public officials to kick around anymore, we know that *systemically*, not simply in reaction to unfortunate personalities or politics, we really must insulate programming decisions from government. And the sooner, the better.

QUESTIONS

1. When the Mobil advertisement uses the phrase "we at Mobil," does it refer to specific individuals? to the officers of the corporation? to the stockholders? to Mobil service station owners? What impression of the Mobil Corporation does the ad get across?

2. Suppose for a while that we could divide up everyone into two groups: TV viewers and government policymakers. Which group is Walter Cronkite talking to? What are their goals in this situation? Which group is the assumed audience of Cirino's article? Why should the control of television matter to this group? Which group is the audience of the Mobil ad? How can you tell?

3. What is the "fairness doctrine"? In what ways is it unclear or open to a variety of interpretations?

4. Explain Cirino's definition of *political*. How would this definition influence his interpretation of the fairness doctrine?

5. Which writers mention "the public interest"? Do they all mean the same thing by this phrase?

6. Walter Cronkite says that professional journalists have learned "to recognize the symptoms of personal opinions and to seek to avoid them in reporting the day's news." Watch several news programs and see whether you agree with him. Can you define *personal opinion?*

7. Explain what Barron means by "the marketplace of ideas."

8. Drawing information from each of the selections here, explain how television broadcasting is paid for. Does the process you have described seem to offer special opportunities for control by some group or groups? What group(s)?

9. Define a research topic involving television. What information would you need in order to do a good job? Is this information available? Where could you find it?

8

Writing About Literature: "Stopping by Woods on a Snowy Evening"

Most students are required to write a paper about literature sometime during their college years. This chapter is designed to make that task a little easier by showing you how other critics and students have written about one famous poem. As you read, notice the kinds of questions critics write about and the kinds of evidence they use to prove a point. You will see that what you already know about discussing voice, audience, and content can also be used when you discuss literature.

The poem under discussion is reproduced below; the commentaries follow.

Robert Frost: The Way to the Poem   John Ciardi

Stopping by Woods on a Snowy Evening   Robert Frost

Whose woods these are I think I know.
His house is in the village though;
He will not see me stopping here
To watch his woods fill up with snow.

My little horse must think it queer
To stop without a farmhouse near
Between the wood and frozen lake
The darkest evening of the year.

He gives his harness bells a shake
To ask if there is some mistake.
The only other sound's the sweep
Of easy wind and downy flake.

The woods are lovely, dark and deep.
But I have promises to keep,
And miles to go before I sleep,
And miles to go before I sleep.

The School System has much to say these days of the virtue of reading widely, and not enough about the virtues of reading less but in depth. There are any number of reading lists for poetry, but there is not enough talk about individual poems. Poetry, finally, is one poem at a time. To read any one poem carefully is the ideal preparation for reading another. Only a poem can illustrate how poetry works.

"Stopping by Woods on a Snowy Evening" is one of the master lyrics of the English language, and almost certainly the best-known poem by an American poet. What happens in it?—which is to say, not *what* does it mean, but *how* does it mean? How does it go about being a human reenactment of a human experience? The author—perhaps the thousandth reader would need to be told—is Robert Frost.

Even the TV audience can see that this poem begins as a seemingly-simple narration of a seemingly-simple incident but ends by suggesting meanings far beyond anything specifically referred to in the narrative. And even readers with only the most casual interest in poetry might be made to note the additional fact that, though the poem suggests those larger meanings, it is very careful never to abandon its pretense to being simple narration. There is duplicity at work. The poet pretends to be talking about one thing, and all the while he is talking about many others.

Many readers are forever unable to accept the poet's essential duplicity. It is almost safe to say that a poem is never about what it seems to be about. As much could be said of the proverb. The bird in the hand, the rolling stone, the stitch in time never (except by an artful double-deception) intend any sort of statement about birds, stones, or sewing. The incident of this poem, one must conclude, is at root a metaphor.

Duplicity aside, this poem's movement from the specific to the general illustrates one of the basic formulas of all poetry. Such a grand poem as Arnold's "Dover Beach" and such lesser, though unfortunately better known, poems as Longfellow's "The Village Blacksmith" and Holmes's "The Chambered Nautilus" are built on the same progression. In these three poems, however, the generalization is markedly set apart from the specific narration, and even seems additional to the telling rather than intrinsic to it. It is this sense of division one has in mind in speaking of "a tacked-on moral."

There is nothing wrong-in-itself with a tacked-on moral. Frost, in fact, makes excellent use of the device at times. In this poem, however, Frost is careful to let the whatever-the-moral-is grow out of the poem itself. When the action ends the poem ends. There is no epilogue and no explanation. Everything pretends to be about the narrated incident. And that pretense sets the basic tone of the poem's performance of itself.

The dramatic force of that performance is best observable, I believe, as a progression in three scenes.

In scene one, which coincides with stanza one, a man—a New England man—is driving his sleigh somewhere at night. It is snowing, and as the man passes a dark patch of woods he stops to watch the snow descend into the darkness. We know, moreover, that the man is familiar with these parts (he knows who owns the woods and where the owner lives), and we know that no one has seen him stop. As scene one forms itself in the theatre of the mind's-eye, therefore, it serves to establish some as yet unspecified relation between the man and the woods.

It is necessary, however, to stop here for a long parenthesis: Even so simple an opening statement raises any number of questions. It is impossible to address all the questions that rise from the poem stanza by stanza, but two that arise from stanza one illustrate the sort of thing one might well ask of the poem detail by detail.

Why, for example, does the man not say what errand he is on? What is the force of leaving the errand generalized? He might just as well have told us that he was going to the general store, or returning from it with a jug of molasses he has promised to bring Aunt Harriet and two suits of long underwear he had promised to bring the hired man. Frost, moreover, can handle homely detail to great effect. He preferred to leave his motive generalized. Why?

And why, on the other hand, does he say so much about knowing the absent owner of the woods and where he lives? Is it simply that one set of details happened-in whereas another did not? To speak of things "happening-in" is to assault the integrity of a poem. Poetry cannot be discussed meaningfully unless one can assume that everything in the poem—every last comma and variant spelling—is in it by the poet's specific act of choice. Only bad poets allow into their poems what is haphazard or cheaply chosen.

The errand, I will venture a bit brashly for lack of space, is left generalized in order the more aptly to suggest *any* errand in life and, therefore, life itself. The owner is there because he is one of the forces of the poem. Let it do to say that the force he represents is the village of mankind (that village at the edge of winter) from which the poet finds himself separated (has separated himself?) in his moment by the woods (and to which, he recalls finally, he has promises to keep). The owner is he-who-lives-in-his-village-house, thereby locked away from the poet's awareness of the-time-the-snow-tells as it engulfs and obliterates the world the village man allows himself to believe he "owns." Thus, the owner is a representative of an order of reality from which the poet has divided himself for the moment, though to a certain extent he ends by reuniting with it. Scene one, therefore, establishes not only a relation between the man and the woods, but the fact that the man's relation begins with his separation (though momentarily) from mankind.

End parenthesis one, begin parenthesis two.

Still considering the first scene as a kind of dramatic performance of forces, one must note that the poet has meticulously matched the simplicity of his language to the pretended simplicity of the narrative. Clearly, the man stopped because the beauty of the scene moved him, but he neither tells us that the scene is beautiful nor that he is moved. A bad writer, always ready to overdo, might have written: "The vastness gripped me, filling my spirit with the slow steady sinking of the snow's crystalline perfection into the glimmerless profundities of the hushed primeval woods." Frost's avoidance of such a spate illustrates two principles of good writing. The first, he has stated himself in "The Mowing": "Anything *more* than the truth would have seemed too weak" (italics mine). Understatement is one of the basic sources of power in English poetry. The second principle is to let the action speak for itself. A good novelist does not tell us that a given character is good or bad (at least not since the passing of the Dickens tradition): he shows us the character in action and then, watching him, we know. Poetry, too, has fictional obligations: even when the characters are ideas and metaphors rather than people, they must be *characterized in action*. A poem does not *talk* about ideas; it *enacts* them. The force of the poem's performance, in fact, is precisely to act out (and thereby to make us act out empathically that is, to *feel out*, that is, to *identify with*) the speaker and why he stopped. The man is the principal actor in this little "drama of why" and in scene one he is the only character, though as noted, he is somehow related to the absent owner.

End second parenthesis.

In scene two (stanzas two and three) a *foil* is introduced. In fiction and drama, a foil is a character who "plays against" a more important character. By presenting a different point of view or an opposed set of motives, the foil moves the more important character to react in ways that might not have found expression without such opposition. The more important character is thus more fully revealed—to the reader and to himself. The foil here is the horse.

The horse forces the question. Why did the man stop? Until it occurs to him that his "little horse must think it queer" he had not asked himself for reasons. He had simply stopped. But the man finds himself faced with the question he imagines the horse to be asking: what *is* there to stop for out there in the cold, away from bin and stall (house and village and mankind?) and all that any self-respecting beast could value on such a night? In sensing that other view, the man is forced to examine his own more deeply.

In stanza two the question arises only as a feeling within the man. In stanza three, however (still scene two), the horse acts. He gives his harness bells a shake. "What's wrong?" he seems to say. "What are we waiting for?"

By now, obviously, the horse—without losing its identity as horse—has also become a symbol. A symbol is something that stands for something else. Whatever that something else may be, it certainly begins as that order of life that does not understand why a man stops in the wintry middle of nowhere to watch the snow come down. (Can one fail to sense by now that the dark and the snowfall symbolize a death-wish, however momentary, *i.e.*, that hunger for final rest and surrender that a man may feel, but not a beast?)

So by the end of scene two the performance has given dramatic force to three elements that work upon the man. There is his relation to the world of the owner. There is his relation to the brute world of the horse. And there is that third presence of the unownable world, the movement of the all-engulfing snow across all the orders of life, the man's, the owner's, and the horse's—with the difference that the man knows of that second dark-within-the-dark of which the horse cannot, and the owner will not, know.

The man ends scene two with all these forces working upon him simultaneously. He feels himself moved to a decision. And he feels a last call from the darkness: "the sweep / Of easy wind and downy flake." It would be so easy and so downy to go into the woods and let himself be covered over.

But scene three (stanza four) produces a fourth force. This fourth force can be given many names. It is certainly better, in fact, to give it many names than to attempt to limit it to one. It is social obligation, or personal commitment, or duty, or just the realization that a man cannot indulge a mood forever. All of these and more. But, finally, he has a simple decision to make. He may go into the woods and let the darkness and the snow swallow him from the world of beast and man. Or he must move on. And unless he is going to stop here forever, it is time to remember that he has a long way to go and that he had best be getting there. (So there is something to be said for the horse, too.)

Then and only then, his question driven more and more deeply into himself by these cross-forces, does the man venture a comment on what attracted him, "The woods are lovely, dark and deep." His mood lingers over the thought of that lovely dark-and-deep (as do the very syllables in which he phrases the thought), but the final decision is to put off the mood and move on. He has his man's way to go and his man's obligations to tend to before he can yield. He has miles to go before his sleep. He repeats that thought and the performance ends.

But why the repetition? The first time Frost says "And miles to go before I sleep," there can be little doubt that the primary meaning is: "I have a long way to go before I get to bed tonight." The second time he says it, however, "miles to go" and "sleep" are suddenly transformed into symbols. What are those "something-elses" the symbols stand for? Hundreds of people have tried to ask Mr. Frost that question and he has always turned it away. He has turned it away *because he cannot answer it.* He could answer some part of it. But some part is not enough.

For a symbol is like a rock dropped into a pool: it sends out ripples in all directions, and the ripples are in motion. Who can say where the last ripple disappears? One may have a sense that he knows the approximate center point of the ripples, the point at which the stone struck the water. Yet even then he has trouble marking it surely. How does one make a mark on water? Oh very well—the center point of that second "miles to go" is probably approximately in the neighborhood of being close to meaning, perhaps, "the road of life"; and the second "before I sleep" is maybe that close to meaning "before I take my final rest," the rest in darkness that seemed so temptingly dark-and-deep for the moment of the mood. But the ripples continue to move and the light to change on the water, and the longer one watches the more changes he sees. Such shifting-and-being-at-the-same-instant is of the very sparkle and life of poetry. One experiences it as one experiences life, for everytime he looks at an experience he sees something new, and he sees it change as he watches it. And that sense of continuity in fluidity is one of the primary kinds of knowledge, one of man's basic ways of knowing, and one that only the arts can teach, poetry foremost among them.

Frost himself certainly did not ask what that repeated last line meant. It came to him and he received it. He "felt right" about it. And what he "felt right" about was in no sense a "meaning" that, say, an essay could apprehend, but an act of experience that could be fully presented only by the dramatic enactment of forces which is the performance of the poem.

Now look at the poem in another way. Did Frost know what he was going to do when he began? Considering the poem simply as an act of skill, as a piece of juggling, one cannot fail to respond to the magnificent turn at the end where, with one flip, seven of the simplest words in the language suddenly dazzle full of never-ending waves of thought and feeling. Or, more precisely, of felt-thought. Certainly an equivalent stunt by a juggler—could there be an equivalent—would bring the house down. Was it to cap his performance with that grand stunt that Frost wrote the poem?

Far from it. The obvious fact is that *Frost could not have known he was going to write those lines until he wrote them.* Then a second fact must be registered: *he wrote them because, for the fun of it, he had got himself into trouble.*

Frost, like every good poet, began by playing a game with himself. The most usual way of writing a four line stanza with four feet to the line is to rhyme the third line with the first, and the fourth line with the second. Even that much rhyme is so difficult in English that many poets and almost all of the anonymous ballad makers do not bother to rhyme the first and third lines at all, settling for two rhymes in four lines as good enough. For English is a rhyme-poor language. In Italian and in French, for example, so many words end with the same sounds that rhyming is relatively easy—so easy that many modern French and Italian poets do not bother to rhyme at all. English, being a more agglomerate language, has far more final sounds, hence fewer of them rhyme. When an Italian poet writes a line ending with "vita" (life) he has literally hundreds of rhyme choices available. When an English poet writes "life" at the end of a line he can summon "strife, wife, knife, fife, rife," and then he is in trouble. Now "life-strife" and "life-rife" and "life-wife" seem to offer a combination of possible ideas that can be related by more than just the rhyme. Inevitably, therefore, the poets have had to work and rework these combinations until the sparkle has gone out of them. The reader is normally tired of such rhyme-led associations. When he encounters "life-strife" he is certainly entitled to suspect that the poet did not really want to say "strife"—that had there been in English such a word as, say, "hife," meaning "infinite peace and harmony," the poet would as gladly have used that word instead of "strife." Thus, the reader feels that the writing is haphazard, that the rhyme is making the poet say things he does not really feel, and which, therefore, the reader does not feel except as boredom. One likes to see the rhymes fall into place, but he must end with the belief that it is the poet who is deciding what is said and not the rhyme scheme that is forcing the saying.

So rhyme is a kind of game, and an especially difficult one in English. As in every game, the fun of the rhyme is to set one's difficulties high and then to meet them skilfully. As Frost himself once defined freedom, it consists of "moving easy in harness."

In "Stopping by Woods on a Snowy Evening" Frost took a long chance. He decided to rhyme not two lines in each stanza, but three. Not even Frost could have sustained that much rhyme in a long poem (as Dante, for example, with the advantage of writing in Italian, sustained triple rhyme for thousands of lines in "The Divine Comedy"). Frost would have known instantly, therefore, when he took the original chance, that he was going to write a short poem. He would have had that much foretaste of it.

So the first stanza emerged rhymed a-a-b-a. And with the sure sense that this was to be a short poem, Frost decided to take an additional chance and to redouble: in English three rhymes in four lines are more than enough; there is no need to rhyme the fourth line. For the fun of it, however, Frost set himself to pick up that loose rhyme and to weave it into the pattern, thereby accepting the all but impossible burden of quadruple rhyme.

The miracle is that it worked. Despite the enormous freight of rhyme, the poem not only came out as a neat pattern, but managed to do so with no sense of strain. Every word and every rhyme falls into place as naturally and as inevitably as if there were no rhyme restricting the poet's choices.

That ease-in-difficulty is certainly inseparable from the success of the poem's performance. One watches the skill-man juggle three balls, then four, then five, and every addition makes the trick more wonderful. But unless he makes the hard trick seem as easy as an easy trick, then all is lost.

The real point, however, is not only that Frost took on a hard rhyme-trick and made it seem easy. It is rather as if the juggler, carried away, had tossed up one more ball than he could really handle, and then amazed himself by actually handling it. So with the real triumph of this poem. Frost could not have known what a stunning effect his repetition of the last line was going to produce. He could not even know he was going to repeat the line. He simply found himself up against a difficulty he almost certainly had not foreseen and he had to improvise to meet it. For in picking up the rhyme from the third line of stanza one and carrying it over into stanza two, he had created an endless chain-link form within which each stanza left a hook sticking out for the next stanza to hang on. So by stanza four, feeling the poem rounding to its end, Frost had to do something about that extra rhyme.

He might have tucked it back into a third line rhyming with the know-though-snow of stanza one. He could thus have rounded the poem out to the mathematical symmetry of using each rhyme four times. But though such a device might be defensible in theory, a rhyme repeated after eleven lines is so far from its original rhyme sound that its feeling as rhyme must certainly be lost. And what good is theory if the reader is not moved by the writing?

It must have been in some such quandary that the final repetition suggested itself—a suggestion born of the very difficulties the poet had let himself in for. So there is that point beyond mere ease in handling a hard thing, the point at which the very difficulty offers the poet the opportunity to do better than he knew he could. What, aside from having that happen to oneself, could be more self-delighting than to participate in its happening by one's reader-identification with the poem?

And by now a further point will have suggested itself: that the human-insight of the poem and the technicalities of its poetic artifice are inseparable. Each feeds the other. That interplay is the poem's meaning, a matter not of WHAT DOES IT MEAN, for no one can ever say entirely what a good poem means, but of HOW DOES IT MEAN, a process one can come much closer to discussing.

There is a necessary epilogue. Mr. Frost has often discussed this poem on the platform, or more usually in the course of a long-evening-after a talk. Time and again I have heard him say that he just wrote it off, that it just came to him, and that he set it down as it came.

Once at Bread Loaf, however, I heard him add one very essential piece to the discussion of how it "just came." One night, he said, he had sat down after supper to work at a long piece of blank verse. The piece never worked out, but Mr. Frost found himself so absorbed in it that, when next he looked up, dawn was at his window. He rose, crossed to the window, stood looking out for a few minutes, and then it was that "Stopping by Woods" suddenly "just came," so that all he had to do was cross the room and write it down.

Robert Frost is the sort of artist who hides his traces. I know of no Frost worksheets anywhere. If someone has raided his wastebasket in secret, it is possible that such worksheets exist somewhere, but Frost would not willingly allow anything but the finished product to leave him. Almost certainly, therefore, no one will ever know what was in that piece of unsuccessful blank verse he had been working at with such concentration, but I for one would stake my life that could that worksheet be uncovered, it would be found to contain the germinal stuff of "Stopping by Woods"; that what was a-simmer in him all night without finding its proper form, suddenly, when he let his still-occupied mind look away, came at him from a different direction, offered itself in a different form, and that finding that form exactly right the impulse proceeded to marry itself to the new shape in one of the most miraculous performances of English lyricism.

And that, too—whether or not one can accept so hypothetical a discussion—is part of HOW the poem means. It means that marriage to the perfect form, the poem's shapen declaration of itself, its moment's monument fixed beyond all possibility of change. And thus, finally, in every truly good poem, "How does it mean?" must always be answered "Triumphantly." Whatever the poem "is about," *how* it means is always how Genesis means: the word become a form, and the form become a thing, and—when the becoming is true—the thing become a part of the knowledge and experience of the race forever.

Letters to the Editor of the *Saturday Review*

Finding Each Other

The article "Robert Frost: The Way to the Poem," by John Ciardi (SR Apr. 12), is one of the most excellent pieces of explication I have had an opportunity to read. It is simple, thorough, and clear, and at the same time provocative of response to the deepest and most far-reaching values in poetry. The essay, just as it is, would be a boon to many students and teachers who together are seeking to find each other as they attend to a poem.

Joseph H. Jenkins.

Petersburg, Va.

Poking and Picking

Robert Frost's miracle, "Stopping by Woods on a Snowy Evening," comprises four stanzas, sixteen lines, 108 words. John Ciardi's analysis of it runs to ten full columns. This flushes an old question: Does such probing, poking, and picking really lead "The Way to the Poem"?

William L. Hassett.

Des Moines, Ia.

Critical Absurdity

I have just discovered, by way of John Ciardi's analysis of Robert Frost's poem, "Stopping by Woods on a Snowy Evening," that this charmingly simple, eloquent, lyrical little poem, long one of my favorites, is supposedly fraught with duplicity of meaning and symbolism, including a disguised death-wish, and that it is not at all about what it seems to be about.

This is really a new high in critical absurdity. If the presentation of this leading, cover-featured article were not so obviously straight-faced, I would have considered this a nice parody of much present-day "criticism." Who is Mr. Ciardi trying to kid? Or is he himself merely kidded? I am sure Mr. Frost must be highly amused or shaking his head in amazement at the awesome proportions his innocent poetic images have assumed ("By now, obviously, the horse has also become a symbol").

Mrs. Beverly Travers.

New Orleans, La.

Enhance a Rainbow

It seems to us that when a poet uses the skill Frost employs in creating a mood, sharing an experience, one should accept it as given, without further analysis. One does not enhance a rainbow by subjecting it to a spectrometric analysis.

John G. Gosselink.

Hartford City, Ind.

No Death-Wish

I was a little shocked when I read Ciardi's interpretation of the dark and snowfall in Frost's "Stopping by Woods on a Snowy Evening" as a death-wish. I suppose every person must interpret poems like this in terms of his own experience. To me, it seems to say that there is a certain deep satisfaction in stopping to lose oneself in the contemplation of beauty. The experience itself is significant in that it brings the individual into a sense of relationship to basic reality. But one cannot escape too long into these subjective experiences. There is work to do; obligations must be met; one cannot spend his whole life escaping from these practical realities.

J. Josephine Leamer.

Gardiner, Mont.

Superfluous Info

I am used to most magazines pointing out the obvious, but when SR tells me that a symbol stands for something else (John Ciardi's article on Robert Frost), I am really hurt. Chances are, if I thought a symbol was something other than something else, I wouldn't be reading *SR* or any other magazine.

Marjorie Duryee.

Everett, Wash.

Simple Narrative

Why Mr. Ciardi had to pick such, as he himself states, "a simple narrative" to expound upon I'll never know. If one thought of poetry as Mr. C does, the joy of just reading beautiful poetry would be gone completely. One would begin to spend all his time searching for symbols and such.

H. Clay Barnard.

Sausalito, Calif.

Penetrating Analysis

I have just finished reading John Ciardi's penetrating analysis of Robert Frost's familiar lyric. This is distinguished service in the cause of criticism. More articles like this and we *will* develop a poetry-reading America.

Sister Mary Denise, RSM.

Dallas, Pa.

Its Essence

Through the years I've read "Stopping by Woods on a Snowy Evening" many times and felt that with each reading I had extracted its meaning to the point where I felt certain that there was no more it could tell me. John Ciardi has exposed new and deeper meanings to me and, as an excellent teacher, has dissected and made clear its very essence.

Lloyd Rodnick.

Detroit, Mich.

Heavy Limbs

Ciardi has some very interesting ideas. But wouldn't it be better to develop them in a separate essay? It seems to me that the literary woods is too full of heavy limbs falling upon little delicate branches.

Gary Thornburg.

Losantville, Ind.

No Discords

Ciardi's calm, cleanly developed, and illuminating article on Frost's poem surely is a savory example of what his readers have clamored for all these months. In this essay one finds all of Mr. Ciardi's inspiring adherence to principles and none of those bubonic symptoms which many of his readers have denounced. Personally, I am pleased to find also fewer

coinings of discordant and sometimes hideous compounds, an in-
dulgence that often spoils the point of what Mr. Ciardi has to say.

Earl Clendenon.

Chicago, Ill.

Frost's Analyst?

The business of equating this poem with all the current philosophical
symbols that are in Ciardi's mind is, of course, Ciardi's privilege. But why
should he speak as Frost's analyst?

Harvey Parker.

Vista, Calif.

Pedantic Reparation

Ciardi very pedantically makes complete reparation for last year's
storm-provoking criticism of Anne Morrow Lindbergh's delicate and deep
poetry. Many college and high-school teachers will be able to use such an
exhaustive analysis in the classroom.

Joseph A. McNulty.

Philadelphia, Pa.

Letter to Letter-Writers
John Ciardi

I have never known a magazine with SR's knack for calling forth LETTERS
TO THE EDITOR. No one writing for SR need suffer from a sense that his
ideas have disappeared into the void: he will hear from the readers. I have
been hearing of late, and the charge this time, made by some readers, is
that I have despoiled a great poem in my analysis of Robert Frost's "Stopping by Woods on a Snowy Evening" (SR Apr. 12).

The Frost article was self-declaredly an effort at close analysis. I believe the poem to be much deeper than its surfaces, and I set out to ask
what sort of human behavior it is that presents a surface of such simplicity
while stirring such depths of multiple responses. It may be that I analyzed
badly, but the more general charge seems to be that all analysis is inimical
to poetry, and that general charge is certainly worth a closer look.

A number of readers seem to have been offended by the fact that the
analysis was longer than the poem, which, as one reader put it, "comprises four stanzas, sixteen lines, 108 words" (rather technical analysis,
that sort of word-counting), whereas my article ran to "ten full columns."

A first clear assumption in this reader's mind is the assertion that an
analysis must not be longer than what it analyzes. I can see no way of
defending that assumption. If there is to be any analysis at all, it is in the

nature of things that the analysis be longer than the poem or the passage it analyzes. One hundred and eight words will hardly do simply to describe the stanzaic form and rhyme scheme of the poem, without any consideration of the nature of the rhyme problem. Analysis and the poem are simply enough tortoise and hare. The difference from the fable is that the poetic hare does not lie down and sleep. The unfabled tortoise, however, may still hope to crawl after and, in some sense, to mark the way the hare went.

The second assumption is that analysis obscures ("does not lead the way to") a poem, and amounts in fact to mere "probing, poking, and picking." The charge as made is not specifically against my article but against all analysis. The question may, therefore, be simply located: should poetry be talked about at all?

A number of readers clearly take the position that it must not be. "One should accept it [the experience of the poem] as given, without further analysis," asserts one reader. "One does not enhance a rainbow by subjecting it to spectrometric analysis." An unwavering position and an interesting figure of speech. I am drawn to that rainbow and fascinated by this use of the word "enhance." By "spectrometric analysis" I take the gentleman to mean "investigating the physical nature of" but said, of course, with an overtone of disdain at the idea of seeing "beauty" meaningfully through any "instrument." That disdain aside, however, one may certainly ask why detailed knowledge of the physical phenomena that produce a rainbow should "unenhance" the rainbow's emotional value. Is speculation into the nature of things to be taken as a destruction of nature?

Two years ago, looking down on Rome from the Gianiculum, I saw two complete rainbows in the sky at once, not just pieces of rainbows but complete arcs with both ends of each arc visible at once in a great bridge above the city. And in what way did it hurt me as part of my instant delight to register some sense of the angle at which the sun had to hit the atmosphere in order to produce such a prodigy? I must insist on remaining among those who are willing to learn about rainbows.

Such disdain seems to be shared by many of our readers. Mr. Philip Wylie, a man described to me as an author, filed the strongest, or at least the longest, of the recent objections. My "implement," as he sees it, bounces "from the granite [of the poem] with predictable damage to the self-anointed Thor. Ciardi must be all Ph.D., and of the new academic sub-species."

Not exactly factual, since I do not own a Ph.D., but fair enough: giving lumps is a time-honored literary game and anyone with a typewriter may play. Mr. Wylie's indignation is largely against my way of dealing with Mr. Frost's poem, and that is a charge I must waive—he may be right, he may be wrong; no score. One part of his charge, however, is a more general anger at the idea that anyone should go into a detailed analysis of the rhyme scheme of a poem that "just came" to the poet. Once again the basic charge is that poetry is damaged by analysis. One should "just let it come."

Many others have joined Mr. Wylie in his defense of the untouchable-spontaneous. "Get your big clumsy feet off that miracle," says one reader I find myself especially drawn to. "What good do you think you do," writes another, "when you tear apart a thing as lovely as Mr. Frost's poem?" Another: "A dissecting kit belongs in the laboratory, not the library." And still another: "If one thought of poetry as Mr. C does, the joy of just reading beautiful poetry would be gone completely. One would begin to spend all his time dealing with symbols and such."

I must, parenthetically, reject some of the terms of that last letter. "Begin to spend *all* his time," is the writer's idea: that "all" is no part of mine. I shall pass the sneer contained in the phrase "symbols and such." But I cannot accept the responsibility for defending myself when mis-quoted. One reader, for example, accuses me of stating that a poem "is not at all about what it seems to be about." I can only reply that those are his terms, not mine, and that I have no thought of defending them.

It is that "all" in the first quotation, however, that locates the central misunderstanding. "Once one begins to analyze," the assumption runs, "he begins to spend all of his time 'merely analyzing' and the analysis not only takes the place of the poem but leads to the poem's destruction."

Were there no misconception involved, this reader's anger would certainly be justified. What is misconceived is the idea that the analysis is intended to take the place of the poem. Far from it. One takes a poem apart only in order to put it back together again with greater understanding. The poem itself is the thing. A good poem is a hanging gull on a day of perfect winds. We sit below and watch it own the air it rides: a miracle from nature. There it hangs on infallible wings. But suppose one is in-terested in the theory of flight (as the gull itself, to be sure, need not be) and suppose one notices that the gull's wings can perform miracles in the air because they have a particular curvature and a particular sort of lead-ing and trailing edge. And suppose he further notices that the gull's tail feathers have a great deal to do with that seemingly effortless mastery. Does that man cease to see the gull? Does he see nothing but diagrams of airflow and lift to the total damnation of all gulls? Or does he see the gull not only as the miracle of a perfect thing, but as the perfect thing in the enmarveling system of what encloses it?

The point involves the whole nature of perception. Do we "see" with our eyes? I must believe that it is the mind that sees, and that the eyes are only the windows we see through. We see with the patterns of what we know. Let any layman look into a tide-pool and list what he sees there. Then let him call an imaginative biologist and ask the biologist what he sees. The layman will have seen things, but the biologist will see systems, and the things in place in those systems.

He will also see many things simultaneously. A basic necessity to all poetic communication is what I have called *fluency* in an earlier article in these pages. Fluency is the ability to receive more than one meaning, impression, stimulus—call it what you please—at the same time. Analysis must always fumble and be long-winded because it must consider those multiple impressions doggedly and one by one. If such itemized dealing accurately locates true elements of the poem, the itemization will have served its purpose, and that purpose must certainly be defended as one that has summoned some of the best minds of all ages. What analysis does, though laboriously, is to establish patterns one may see with.

But there then remains the reader's work. It is up to him, guided by the analysis, to read the poem with the fluency it requires, and which analysis does not hope to achieve. Certainly, whatever is said here, poetry will be talked about and must be talked about. The one point of such talk, however, is to lead the reader more richly to the threshold of the poem. Over that threshold he must take himself. And I, for one, must suspect that if he refuses to carry anything as cumbersome as detail across that threshold, he will never furnish the house of his own mind.

The "Death-Wish" in "Stopping By Woods"

James Armstrong

Six years ago John Ciardi inadvertently unsettled a great many poetry-lovers with his analysis of Robert Frost's poem, "Stopping By Woods on a Snowy Evening" (*Saturday Review*, April 12, 1958). Mr. Ciardi's thesis was that practically all good poems are metaphorical, or symbolic, and that Frost's poem, in particular, "ends by suggesting meanings far beyond anything specifically referred to in the narrative." His attempt to elucidate some of those meanings led him to propose that "the dark and the snow-fall symbolize a death-wish, however momentary."

The response from readers was phenomenal. For weeks *SR's* letters page was filled with denunciations of Mr. Ciardi's critical ability and with general protests against "probing, poking, and picking" at poems, as one reader put it. There were letters of appreciation and congratulation as well, but the anti-analysis and anti-Ciardi responses were clearly in the majority. Mr. Ciardi defended himself and the name of Criticism with grace and good humor in a short follow-up article, and the furor, after a few more sputters, gradually subsided.

The issue was far from dead, however, as I soon began to discover. Resentment was still smoldering among Frost's admirers. What surprised me most was that where I expected to find the most sympathy for Mr. Ciardi's position—among college English teachers—I found more often displeasure. It was not the process of analysis that they objected to, as I soon learned, but the suggestion that Frost's poem expressed a "death-wish." To find such a feeling in a poem by Robert Frost, of all people, was apparently to them literary Freudianism at its worst. I began to suspect that it was really this point of interpretation, rather than criticism in general, at which most SR readers had taken offense. When I heard Mr. Frost himself at a public lecture pooh-pooh the death-wish interpretation, to the obvious and audible delight of the audience, my suspicions were confirmed.

If we feel obligated to accept Frost's disavowal as the final word, then there is no more to be said; but we need not do so. Many a poet has publicly refused to admit in his work the presence of an intention or meaning that to any discerning reader is clearly there. It may be that he justly regards his poem as his best and final statement of the matter and dislikes having it diluted or distorted by paraphrase. Or it may be that he resents having his thoughts and feelings pried at by morbid admirers who are not satisfied with the exceptional frankness about himself with which he has already complimented them in his work. For example, for Frost to admit that his poem embodies a "death-wish" would inevitably have called forth from countless well-meaning and naive admirers the question, "But for goodness' sake—why?" Few men would willingly put themselves in the position of having to answer such a question.

What is it about the idea of a "death-wish" in a Frost poem that is so disturbing? Can the impulse itself—"that hunger for final rest and surrender that a man may feel," as Mr. Ciardi described it—be so unfamiliar to us? I find it hard to think so. And even those who have never recognized it in themselves can hardly pretend that it is uncommon in literature. More than one poet has "been half in love with easeful Death." Perhaps it is hard to believe that Robert Frost ever entertained the feeling, much less gave it public expression. Yet we have only to read his poems.

I think of one, for example, called "The Onset," which begins,

> Always the same, when on a fated night
> At last the gathered snow lets down as white
> As may be in dark woods, and with a song
> It shall not make again all winter long
> Of hissing on the yet uncovered ground,
> I almost stumble looking up and round,
> As one who overtaken by the end
> Gives up his errand, and lets death descend
> Upon him where he is, with nothing done
> To evil, no important triumph won,
> More than if life had never been begun. . . .

This is not so very different a poem, in setting and mood, from "Stopping By Woods"; and the poet says, "I almost stumble . . . . / As one who . . . / Gives up his errand, and lets death descend. . . . " The inclination, the temptation, to stop and rest is clearly there.

Nor is the association of death with dark, with winter, and with snow an unnatural or a novel one. Thomas Mann, to recall a famous instance, relies heavily on this traditional symbolic significance of snow in *The Magic Mountain*, particularly in the chapter called "Snow," in which Hans Castorp becomes lost in a mountain snowstorm while skiing. Like the speakers in Frost's poems, he recognizes the temptation and resists it.

The resistance, of course, is important. The "death-wish" is not so much a wish as a temptation, a brief flirtation with the possibility. Frost's final word is always an affirmation, a turning back from death to life ("But I have promises to keep . . .") and a postponement of the rendezvous with the dark woods and the snow.

Others have recognized the compelling attraction that the woods exercised upon Frost. Mr. J. M. Cox, writing in the *Virginia Quarterly Review* (Winter 1959), says, "Confronting these desert places of his landscape, Frost needs all the restraint at his command, for the dark woods possess a magnetic attraction drawing him spellbound into them." And in "Stopping By Woods," Mr. Cox sees "the powerful fascination the woods have upon the lonely traveler . . . " who is "transfixed by the compelling invitation of the forest." Whether the whispered invitation comes from the darkness, the woods, the snow, or all three together, it is a strangely appealing one, and many men have heard it.

No one, perhaps, has heard it more clearly that the nineteenth-century English poet, Thomas Lovell Beddoes. The "death-wish"—the whispered invitation of death—is the theme of many of his poems. In "The Phantom-Wooer," there is not only a remarkable similarity of mood and theme to "Stopping By Woods," but a line occurring at a crucial point that is all but identical to a line in Frost's poem.

A "ghost" woos a lady as she sleeps. His identity is not specified, but his voice is the voice of "the little snakes of silver throat" that inhabit "mossy skulls" and whisper "die, oh! die." The poem gives us no alternative but to suppose that the voice comes from the sleeping lady's own subconscious mind. It is a persuasive voice, and a comforting one.

> Young soul put off your flesh, and come
> With me into the quiet tomb,
>   Our bed is lovely, dark, and sweet;
> The earth will swing us, as she goes,
> Beneath our coverlid of snows,
>   And the warm leaden sheet.

The "coverlid of snows" reveals a kinship at least of season with Frost's poem, but what really arrests the reader is that startling line: "Our bed is lovely, dark, and sweet. . . . " Is it unreasonable to suppose that this line was running through the head of the poet who wrote "The woods are lovely, dark and deep . . . "? Without insisting any further upon the likeness of the ideas embodied in the two poems, I will only point out that these two lines resemble each other not only in sound, but in tone and implication.

It is possible, of course, to dismiss this near-identity of line as mere coincidence, but it seems to me that to do so requires more audacity than to recognize the probability of a relationship. If we do recognize such a relationship, what does it mean? It means only that Robert Frost shared with the rest of us the common thoughts, fears, and dreams of humanity—something we knew all the time—and that he sometimes told us things about himself, and about ourselves, that we hadn't thought of before. It means, too, that a new interpretation of a familiar and favorite poem need not outrage us merely because it upsets our comfortable belief that we had it all figured out. The new idea ought to lead us instead to look at the poem again, and freshly, if we can. And if we are capable of being honest with the poem and with ourselves, we may see not only woods that are "lovely, dark and deep," but the promises that we must fulfill before we sleep.

Toward Notes for "Stopping By Woods": Some Classical Analogs

Edward H. Rosenberry

Fifteen years ago Robert Frost was quoted as saying that "Stopping by Woods on a Snowy Evening" contained all he ever knew and that he would like to print it with "forty pages of footnotes." [1] Yet as recently as 1960 John F. Lynen could write of this poem that there are "no literary parallels or signposts to guide us, much less a clear statement on the poet's part indicating the direction of his thought." [2] Even allowing for Frost's characteristic whimsy, there is a tantalizing discrepancy between the author's evident sense of the poem's opulence and the critic's sense of its stubbornly enigmatic reserve. Into this vacuum a generation of admirers has poured a relentless stream of commentary which has at once expanded the critical controversy and aggravated the author's native reticence to the point of withdrawal. "It means enough without its being pressed," he said at one time, and then added his own précis: "It's all very nice but I must be getting along, getting home." [3] The death-wish or return-to-the-womb school of readers gets even shorter shrift: "No, all that means is to get the hell out of there." [4]

A new approach (short of leaving him alone) might be to take Frost at his word, exactly as far as it goes, and to try to place the poem in a literary frame of reference which supports the author's suggesed reading in a way that structural and symbolic criticism are unable to do. This amounts to taking Lynen's observation as a challenge to show that there are literary parallels or signposts to guide us, and that the poet's remarks constitute in that light a perfectly clear statement of the direction of his thought.

The obvious reason for all the discussion of "Stopping by Woods" is that it is generally considered a major work of art, perhaps "one of the master lyrics of the English language." [5] As an important human document, for all its aesthetic singularity, it tends to occupy a crowded eminence. Great art is not less but more likely to say what has been said before, not because one work copies another but because they are equally concerned with the fundamental experience of humanity. The great ideas—a poet would say the great metaphors—persist; only the images which embody them shift with changing cultures and various imaginations. The story of Faust, for instance, notwithstanding important differences in both theme and form, is in one of its dimensions precisely the story of Odysseus, the man with a god-given destiny whose salvation depends on his ability to keep moving toward his goal, to resist the blandishments of easy satisfaction in the here and now. Culturally and aesthetically it is a greater distance from Faust to a Yankee farmer than from Odysseus to Faust, yet this is the story of Frost's homeward-bound ponderer of woods, too. The man who turns reluctantly from the transitory perfections of Helen or decides against the static immortality of Calypso's embrace is at bottom the man who says,

> The woods are lovely, dark and deep,
> But I have promises to keep,
> And miles to go before I sleep.

He hears the song, but he is bound to the mast of his own resolve. He is a universal figure, whose archetypal foil a student of mine once recognized in *Heart of Darkness:* "Kurtz came to Circe's palace," she wrote, "and stayed."

These are analogs which any student or teacher, any reader, can find for himself, as no doubt many have done. Another, less likely to be encountered by the general reader, but closer to Frost's poem in concentration of image and development of theme, is a parable occurring toward the end of the Twenty-third Discourse of the Second Book of Epictetus. The heart of the metaphor, extracted from its didactic context, runs as follows in Matheson's translation:

> What then do we see men doing? They are like a man returning to his own country who, finding a good inn on his road, stays on there because it pleases him. Man, you are forgetting your purpose! You were not travelling *to* this, but *through* it.
> "Yes, but this is a fine inn."
> And how many other fine inns are there, and how many fine meadows? But they are merely to pass through; your purpose is yonder; to return to your country, to relieve your kinsmen of their fears, to fulfill your duties as a citizen, to marry, beget children, and hold office in due course. For you have not come into the world to choose your pick of fine places, but to live and move in the place where you were born and appointed to be a citizen. . . . Some people are attracted . . . by some . . . seductive inn by the way; and there they stay on and moulder away, like those whom the Sirens entertain.[6]

Here, in yet another set of terms (but note the Homeric allusion), is the basic principle of moral life which Frost's poem dramatizes in his American setting and which he has felt impelled to explicate with such desperate clarity: "All that means is to get the hell out of there." The irony of the situation might well move a man to profanity: if the point of the parable is the importance of distinguishing between proximate and ultimate values, the author could only be exasperated by the earnest efforts of his readers to make the poem answer the merely proximate question of *what* ultimate values.

Even the context of Epictetus' parable is interesting in relation to Frost. The discourse in which it appears is entitled "On the Faculty of Expression," and it is, in effect, a sermon to poets not to confuse eloquence with substance, or the means of literature with its ends. Matthew Arnold, not surprisingly, seized on the image in this original context to underscore his case for the ethical value of Wordsworth's poetry.[7] It would hardly do to argue from such grounds that Frost, too, knew and consciously adapted Epictetus' metaphor in "Stopping by Woods"; yet the possibility of its having been as much a part of his professional equipment as Homer or Goethe is intriguingly great. Lawrance Thompson reminds us that Frost returned to college as a young man in order to "read more widely in the original texts of classical literature."

> His desultory reading in that field has continued and has been a vital stimulus to his own writing, although the effect is not at all obvious. Perhaps no American poet has ever brought to his own art such a wide acquaintance with classical literature with such a slight suggestion of it in details of direct reference or of slavish imitation.[8]

His keen interest in the classical philosophers, Thompson points out, has always been a poet's interest in their metaphors, in the analogies by which they have "sought to define spirit in terms of matter" (p. 191). The inn of Epictetus is memorable enough to have taken root in Frost's mind as it evidently did in Arnold's. A poet's knowledge, Frost has written, comes "cavalierly and as it happens in and out of books." Poets "let what will stick to them like burrs where they walk in the fields." [9]

Frost has professed himself a great believer in the role of the subconscious in poetic invention, and this could hardly have achieved freer play in his work than in the little lyric which came to him "in one stroke of the pen" at the end of an all-night session on "New Hampshire"—"the product," as he once called it, "of autointoxication coming from tiredness." [10] Somehow the ingredients of the poem boiled up and coalesced—image and theme, "stem end and blossom end"—and perhaps no one, including the poet, can ever be sure precisely what those ingredients were. All he knows, and all he needs to know, is that "he snatches a thing from some previous order in time and space into a new order with not so much as a ligature clinging to it of the old place where it was organic." [11] I think of Jean Starr Untermeyer's suggestion of an unconscious reminiscence in "Stopping by Woods" of Keats's line,

And I have many miles on foot to fare, [12]

and I find it the more plausible for the inadvertent echo of Keats that cropped up in my own preceding sentence and the unanticipated allusion to Frost in the sentence before that. ("How do I know what I think till I see what I say?") The process borders on the occult and threatens the scholar with an endemic vertigo. Just across the border lies the fact that Frost quoted Matthew Arnold three times in the last fifty lines of "New Hampshire" and called himself "a good Greek" within the last ten. I intend to let it lie.

What I wish to press for is not the establishment of an influence or a source, but the clarification of a method and a theme. In the first place, for the making of poems, doing and reading tend to produce inextricably mingled materials. The existence of analogs makes it just as likely that "Stopping by Woods" grew primarily out of Frost's reading as that it took its impulse from his having stopped by woods on a snowy evening or seen someone else do so. I believe that Lawrance Thompson should modify his opinion that this poem is prototypic of Frost's poems-from-experience, or poems in which image conceptually precedes theme.[13] Secondly, the analogs provide a thematic perspective which no work of art can have alone. The focus given to the poem's central concern with the antithesis of indolence and resolution, diversion and goal, blurs the distracting discussion over the exact limits of symbolic interpretation, and absolutely invalidates the partial view of Robert Frost as a "spiritual drifter." [14]

1. Reginald L. Cook, "Robert Frost's Asides on His Poetry," *American Literature*, 19 (Jan. 1948), 357, 355.
2. John F. Lynen, *The Pastoral Art of Robert Frost* (New Haven, 1960), p. 4.
3. Reginald L. Cook, "Frost on Frost: the Making of Poems," *American Literature*, 28 (Mar. 1956), 64.
4. Reginald L. Cook, *The Dimensions of Robert Frost* (New York, 1958), p. 33.
5. John Ciardi, "The Way to the Poem," *Saturday Review*, 60 (Apr. 12, 1958), 13.
6. *The Stoic and Epicurean Philosophers*, ed. Whitney J. Oates (New York, 1940), p. 337.
7. "Wordsworth," *Essays in Criticism*, Second Series, 1888.
8. Lawrance Thompson, *Fire and Ice* (New York, 1942), p. 151.
9. "The Figure a Poem Makes," *Complete Poems of Robert Frost* (New York, 1949), p. viii.
10. Elizabeth S. Sergeant, *Robert Frost, the Trial by Existence* (New York, 1960), p. 249; Cook, "Frost on Frost," p. 66. John Ciardi, too, reports having heard Frost say "time and again . . . that he just wrote it off, that it just came to him . . ." though he seems not to have heard what long poem Frost had been at work on through the night ("The Way to the Poem," p. 65).
11. "The Figure a Poem Makes."
12. From the sonnet "Keen, fitful gusts." Quoted by Elizabeth Sergeant, *Robert Frost*, p. 251.
13. *Fire and Ice*, p. 25.
14. Yvor Winters, "Robert Frost: or, the Spiritual Drifter as Poet," *The Function of Criticism: Problems and Exercises* (Denver, 1957), pp. 159–187.

The Ghost of Christmas Past:
"Stopping By Woods on a Snowy Evening"

Herbert R. Coursen, Jr.

Much ink has spilled on many pages in exegesis of this little poem. Actually, critical jottings have only obscured what has lain beneath critical noses all these years. To say that the poem means merely that a man stops one night to observe a snowfall, or that the poem contrasts the mundane desire for creature comfort with the sweep of aesthetic appreciation, or that it renders worldly responsibilities paramount, or that it reveals the speaker's latent death-wish is to miss the point rather badly. Lacking has been that mind simple enough to see what is *really* there.

The first line ("Whose woods these are I think I know") shows that the speaker has paused aside a woods of whose ownership he is fairly sure. So much for paraphrase. Uncertainty vanishes with the next two lines ("His house is in the village though; / He will not see me stopping here"). The speaker knows (a) where the owner's home is located, and (b) that the owner won't be out at the woods tonight. Two questions arise immediately: (a) how does the speaker know? and (b) how does the speaker know? As will be made manifest, only one answer exists to each question.

The subsequent two quatrains force more questions to pop up. On auditing the first two lines of the second quatrain ("My little horse must think it queer / To stop without a farmhouse near"), we must ask, "Why does the little 'horse' think oddly of the proceedings?" We must ask also if this *is*, as the speaker claims, the "darkest evening of the year." The calendar date of this occurrence (or lack of occurrence) by an unspecified patch of trees is essential to an apprehension of the poem's true meaning. In the third quatrain, we hear "harness bells" shook. Is the auditory image really an allusion? Then there is the question of the "horse's" identity. Is this really Equus Caballus? This question links itself to that of the *driver's* identity and reiterates the problem of the animal's untoward attitude toward this evidently unscheduled stop.

The questions have piled up unanswered as we reach the final quatrain and approach the ultimate series of poetic mysteries to be resolved. Clearly, all of the questions asked thus far (save possibly the one about the "horse's" identity) are ones which any normal reader, granted the training in close analysis provided by a survey course in English Literature during his sophomore year in college, might ask. After some extraneous imagery ("The woods are lovely, dark and deep" has either been established or is easily adduced from the dramatic situation), the final three lines hold out the key with which the poem's essence may be released. What, to ask two more questions, are the "promises" which the speaker must "keep," and why are the last two lines so redundant about the distance he must cover before he tumbles into bed? Obviously, the obligations are important, the distance great.

Now, if we swing back to one of the previous questions, the poem will begin to unravel. The "darkest evening of the year" in New England is December 21st, a date near that on which the western world celebrates Christmas. It may be that December 21st *is* the date of the poem, or (and with poets this seems more likely) that this is the closest the poet can come to Christmas without giving it all away. Who has "promises to keep" at or near this date, and who must traverse much territory to fulfill these promises? Yes, and who but St. Nick would know the location of *each* home? Only he would know who had "just settled down for a long winter's nap" (the poem's third line—"He will not see me stopping here"—is clearly a veiled allusion) and would not be out inspecting his acreage this night. The unusual phrase "fill up with snow," in the poem's fourth line, is a transfer of Santa's occupational preoccupation to the countryside; he is mulling the filling of countless stockings hung above countless fireplaces by countless careful children. "Harness bells," of course, allude to "Sleighing Song," a popular Christmas tune of the time the poem was written in which the refrain "Jingle Bells! Jingle Bells!" appears; thus again are we put on the Christmas track. The "little horse," like the date, is another attempt at poetic obfuscation. Although the "rein-reindeer" ambiguity has been eliminated from the poem's final version,* probably because too obvious, we may speculate that the animal is really a reindeer disguised as a horse by the poet's desire for obscurity, a desire which we must concede has been fulfilled up to now.

The animal is clearly concerned, like the faithful Rudolph—another possible allusion (post facto, hence unconscious)—lest his master fail to complete his mission. Seeing no farmhouse in the second quatrain, but pulling a load of presents, no wonder the little beast wonders! It takes him a full two quatrains to rouse his driver to remember all the empty stockings which hang ahead. And Santa does so reluctantly at that, poor soul, as he ponders the myriad farmhouses and villages which spread between him and his own "winter's nap." The modern St. Nick, lonely and overworked, tosses no "Happy Christmas to all and to all a good night!" into the precipitation. He merely shrugs his shoulders and resignedly plods away.

* The original draft contained the following line: "That bid me give the reins a shake" (Stageberg-Anderson, *Poetry as Experience* [New York, 1952], p. 457).

My Interpretation of "Stopping By the Woods on a Snowy Evening"

Steve Phillips

The author Robert Frost is portraying someone who is tired and needs a break from life in this poem. He finds this break one night while taking a ride through an area he always travels and this time decides to stop. This is shown by the horse when it shakes as if something is wrong or different from the usual. I think this person is tired of the life he is living and wants probably to get away from it all.

The woods offer this escape. They symbolize something beautiful and mysterious, something different that is so beautiful that it draws this person to it. The snow and frozen lake between the trees are symbolizing beauty that is so great that if the person hadn't all those promises and work ahead of him that he would just stay there forever and look at it.

The audience to this poem is everyone in general. The author wants everyone to know about his experience with the beauty of the woods and snow. Perhaps to let them know that you can get away from the life you are living and do something different, maybe something that you have always wanted to do.

The authors format is a serious one that is good for the things he wants to get across to his readers. Each line has four feet and it has a regular rhyme pattern throughout the poem except for the fourth stanza. The pattern goes like this: aaba bbcb ccdc etc. except the fourth stanza is all d. I think the author changes the pattern to emphasize his promises and duties that he has to carry out.

I think it is a good poem and I like it. The author shows everyone what it might be like to get away. He makes you think about what it would be like and wish that you could just drop everything and get away from it all.

"Stopping By Woods on a Snowy Evening"   Pat O'Donnell

Because the speaker in Robert Frost's "Stopping by Woods on a Snowy Evening" is a simple rural character riding home across the countryside in a horse-drawn sleigh, he uses everyday speech and a relaxed mood. Although he is a deeply meditative person, who contemplates the peace and mystery of the woods filling up with snow, he is also a kind, gentle man, concerned about what his "little horse" is thinking. Since he has promises to keep and obligations to fulfill, he shows responsibility by moving on, in spite of the overwhelming desire to escape from the pressure of life into restful sleep.

Frost seems to be writing to an audience who would be equally as plain and unsophisticated as the speaker, and who would readily understand his need for a moment of reverie and reflection. They, too, would be able to be deeply moved by the undisturbed serenity of the silent scene which Frost creates, and could feel the tension involved between the pull of the peace and quiet and the pull of the demands of duty.

The simplicity of speaker and audience carry over into the imagery. Watching the woods fill up with snow can be compared to a person who has emptied himself of the worries and cares of life and is allowing himself to be filled up with peace, beauty and a oneness with nature. The comparison between the inability of the little horse to understand why they're stopping and the traveler's love of revery shows a contrast between the merely natural and the human. Because the horse doesn't experience the sacredness of the moment, he disturbs the silence by shaking his harness bells. The sleep which he talks about in the last two lines seems to be more than just a well-earned reward at the end of a day's work, but the final sleep—death itself. Since it's evening, it's winter, and it's silent, the whole poem makes one think of the end of life.

The simplicity carries over into the sound, which is the musical rhythm of iambic quatrameter—"Whose woods / these are / I think / I know." He uses the simplest terms and commonest words: there is only one word, "promises," which has three syllables, seventeen words which have two syllables, and all the rest have only one syllable. The first, second and fourth lines of each stanza rhyme, and the rhyme of each succeeding stanza is that of the third and unrhymed line of the preceding verse: a a b a, b b c b, c c d c, and finally d d d d, because there is nothing to follow.

The overall effect of Frost's poem, including the speaker, audience, imagery and sound, is that of simplicity.

QUESTIONS

1. How would you describe the voice of a professional critic? How are these voices different from what you might expect in an advertisement for Robert Frost or a news report about him? Did you run into any particular jargon words that belong to criticism?

2. Compare the voices of the letters to the editor of the *Saturday Review* to the voices of the essays. Are there important differences?

3. Are the voices of the students (in the last two selections—by Phillips and O'Donnell) different from those of the professional critics? Are the two students different from one another? Do you find their voices appropriate to an English paper?

4. One of the students makes a number of mechanical errors. Can you find them? What do they add to the impression the voice makes?

5. Who reads criticism? Who reads the papers that students write about literature? Discuss how the answers to these questions might affect a critic's selection of a voice.

6. Which of these critics describe the voice or speaker of the poem? What do they say about it?

7. Which of the critics discuss the sound of the poem? Why is this an important topic? Which critic does the best job of showing a relationship between the sound and the meaning?

8. Most of the critics believe that the poem contains symbols. Do you agree? Find the two definitions of *symbol* that Ciardi gives and decide which works better for this poem.

9. Some of the critics quote things that Frost said about the poem. Did you find Frost's comments helpful? Do you think that what Frost said about the poem is more important than what others say about it?

10. What is an "analog"? Find in the library a summary of the story of Odysseus and the Sirens, or of Faust. How are these stories similar to the poem?

11. At what point did you realize that Coursen was not serious? If he *were* serious, how would you answer him?

12. The students were specifically asked to discuss the voice (or speaker), the audience, the content (or imagery), and the sound of the poem. Which areas did they cover most successfully? Where did they have trouble?

13. All of the critics say or imply that "Stopping by Woods . . ." is a great poem. What reasons do they give for these judgments? Can you suggest a general definition of good poetry?

14. Describe as specifically as you can the purpose of discussing literature (or movies, or TV programs). Is it possible to have too much discussion? Is it true that "dissecting" a work diminishes your enjoyment of it?

9

Standards for Language

We frequently hear criticism of the ways we write and speak. Sometimes it is said that the language skills of students are getting worse every year; sometimes we are told that bureaucrats are swamping the language with jargon; sometimes it is politicians who come in for a whipping.

These judgments are often made by people who have not thought carefully about how they arrived at their standards for good language. Sometimes writers or speakers are attacked for making grammatical mistakes, sometimes for using inflated or pompous language, sometimes for coining new words. Which of these things matter, and why? Can we have different standards for different situations?

As you read this chapter, think about which essays might be most helpful in making judgments about the other writings in this book.

"Grammar don't matter?" George C. Kohn

One thing seems certain: When Johnny finishes elementary school, he will know little grammar. And when he graduates from high school, he will not be much better off.

The best students undoubtedly will pick up many of the fundamentals without working hard on them. But the masses, perhaps as many as 80 percent of school kids, will not be so fortunate.

Teachers and many adults have felt that the old grammar was too rigid and irrelevant. It was unscientific. It was like Latin (and Latin is dead) and had too many rules. Many felt that no one could say what is correct. Besides, the old grammar is too hard to teach to the masses.

"Hey, man, you dig?"

"Them words don't mean nothing."

Some teachers say flatly that the grammar, the speech pattern, of any individual is all right. No one should be made to feel "inferior" because of his way of speaking and writing. Each group has a correct grammar; there is no one correct way.

What the majority says is all right with most. As the ad says, "A hundred million people can't be wrong." It is nice to promote goodwill and not criticize. And one can do both without dropping the standards of good English. One can believe in human equality without lowering the standards until there are none.

The "do-your-own-thing" method of teaching has allowed the pupils to write their own grammars. Students then can justify their mistakes as all right because they say so. Teachers can not criticize them. Teachers are only there to pour forth the rules of the past, as many as possible so the students can get an idea of what grammar is. Then they make the final conclusions. And most likely they decide that grammar is too hard to learn. It is easier to create their own.

And so a new, more relevant grammar develops, one in which rules are eliminated. The 12-year-olds develop their own particular method of study. (It doesn't matter that their "method" is different from another group's or another school's.) The important thing is that they are "creating."

Consistency and clear communication falter when those 12-year-olds try to talk with others, especially adults, and sometimes their own brothers and sisters:

"You with me, beautiful, or you a nurd?"

"You ain't got with it."

Teachers who never were able to teach the old grammar feel at home in this "do-it-yourself" atmosphere. Why do pronouns have to be categorized: personal, relative, demonstrative, indefinite, and reflexive? Just call them all pronouns; it is easier.

"His letter was sent to the Smiths and ourselves." The meaning is clear enough, but is the grammar correct? To many English teachers, this is irrelevant. English teachers who say such a thing often do not know their own tongue.

Teachers do not want the responsibility of upholding grammatical rules. Latin is not English, and our rules were founded on Latin. Latin is dead and English is alive; there must be a reason. Yes, English is always growing and changing and has survived because it has broken away from old forms and constructions. But then how can the teachers explain the use of double negatives today? They were used by Chaucer.

Teachers Have Helped

Double negatives (I don't know nothing, I never go there no more) were once acceptable, so they are acceptable today, according to many English teachers. Then ironically English has not broken away from the old form! Chaucer is right (Latin was very alive in his day). English has not grown. And modern English teachers are a lot of baloney and excuses.

As you can see, teachers of English have helped in making grammar a disaster area. Little Johnny knows no grammar because some (not all, remember) believe that Johnny will be constricted and made to adhere to "false" standards. Kids' creativity will be stifled if they have to say, "May I please have a piece of bread?" instead of "Gimme some bread." The language is changing, so why should Johnny talk like his mother or father? But, strangely, he can talk like Chaucer!

Thus nobody can tell anybody else what is grammatically correct, for he could be considered old-fashioned or uncreative or a snob. Little Johnny will continue to make up his own rules in speaking and writing as long as teachers mistake laziness for efficiency, "learning noise" for creativity, and ungrammatical constructions for individuality or even genius.

"Nobody can learn me nothing."

"All right, Johnny, we'll just be friends and play games."

"And don't give me no grammar, either, ya hear?"

"Johnny, you know we don't."

Letters to the Education Editor
of the *Christian Science Monitor*

To the education editor:

Applause for George C. Kohn, speaking out in "Grammar don't matter" (July 15). I suspect that the increasing trend to the ungrammatic will only be reversed when it becomes clear to those of the cult that it can have a limiting effect on the opportunities and accomplishments of a career.

For good grammar is as basic to understanding and respect for what is said as good, clear writing is important to the understanding and acceptance of the written word.

Gordon Jacobson
Wilmington, Del.

To the education editor:

Language is subject to an inexorable law of change. If this were not so, we would today be speaking the Anglo-Saxon of "Beowulf."

Man cannot halt the process of language change, but he can direct and channel it so that it will be gradual and orderly rather than anarchical. Some linguists advocate "leaving your language alone" and abandoning all grammatical restraint in favor of "usage," by which they mean vulgar usage.

But there is another usage which, without rejecting change altogether, restrains it and keeps it within orderly bounds, so that the language may at all times serve its basic purpose of communication and understanding, and not turn into a meaningless jargon that calls for drastic remedies.

Why not follow this sensible middle course between "leaving your language alone" and putting it into a straitjacket?

Mario Pei

Glen Ridge, N.J.

To the education editor:

No student don't need no grammar if he is to live foreever among illiterates.

Cheerful Chuck nods toward his friend. "Just between he and I, we don't believe in learning no decimals." In some circles that might be an amiable philosophy. But if I face Chuck at the cashier's window of a bank where Chuck's friend is the banker, even though I may note that he is being creative, my financial dealings would advance no further there.

The sole purpose of an education is to fit anyone for the position he will hold later: aeronautics for the flier, medicine for the doctor, and sloppy ignorance for the (expletive deleted), including teachers who don't never teach no grammer.

(Mrs.) Ruth Burton Lane

Marionville, Mo.

To the education editor:

I worked for five years at a local private college of very high academic standing and was continually horrified at the admission applications of many who graduated from high school, which means less and less each year.

I am devoutly in favor of no student being graduated from high school who is not able to meet a reasonable standard in writing, spelling, and verbalizing. Too many of our college students arrive who must take "remedial English" which they should have learned in high school.

(Mrs.) Jane McPhee

Pasadena, Calif.

To the education editor:

Grammar is a useful tool in communication. It is the attitude revealed, not the grammar, that makes the hearer feel inferior. The hearer is being "put down" when he is made to feel that it doesn't matter whether he understands or not.

"A word fitly spoken is like apples of gold in pictures of silver" (Proverbs 25:11).

(Mrs.) Miriam D. Wilson

Manitou Springs, Colo.

To the education editor:

Out of high school and no more grammar rules or lessons! Wow, that's a load off my shoulders. Now I can concentrate on something more important, creativity. Just as long as I am able to get my ideas across to other people I don't feel that I have to suppress my creativity for a capital letter or period.

Kids need a sense of freedom when they're learning how to write. A fear of grammar will only delay the great joy of creative writing. Grammar is something that is adapted through observation and experimentation in writing. Why then do we want to "teach" school kids a standard set of grammar rules? The less time teachers spend dictating these ancient rules and let kids discover rules for themselves, the faster a learning process is going to take place.

A person's writing reveals much about his-her character. Try to reduce this into a standard set of grammar rules, and what do you have left?

P.S.: To the Monitor, are you going to correct my grammar?

Julie Matey

Minneapolis

To the education editor:

As an experienced teacher, I take exception to Mr. Kohn's article. Apparently, aside from dealing in generalities about teacher and student lack of concern about grammar, Mr. Kohn fails to deal with the importance of using the child's own language as a motivational tool in teaching difficult children to read. "Experience Reading" is widely practiced and is an essential tool for learning. The use of it has not meant a compromise in grammar.

Seymour Reznitsky

New York

To the education editor:

Teachers who think grammar does not matter are certainly not equipped to teach. Let's be more careful in hiring teachers and accept only those who are well-bred and possess refinement in speech and manner.

Ethel S. Orr

Detroit

To the education editor:

It would surely be laudable to help students gain a precise command of our language. However, grammar sessions would be rather out of place in our present schools, where far too many students can barely read.

Time spent bringing a student's reading and writing skills toward some fraction of his potential should prove more profitable than time spent examining participial phrases.

Intricate knowledge of grammar is a refinement of one's education. But before we attempt the refining, we had best be certain we already have the substance.

Richard Levy

La Palma, Calif.

To the education editor:

I have reached the conclusion that there must indeed be almost total indifference to grammar in today's school teaching.

A few years ago, as an advertising copywriter, I worked on a big-city newspaper with young space salesmen, most of whom were college graduates. Their grammar was bad and their spelling atrocious.

More recently, as a mere onlooker, I have deplored the all-too-frequent mistakes in grammar and pronunciation on radio and television.

It seems to me to be an injustice to the child to allow the child to "create" his own rules or to adopt those of his parents or peers if they are incorrect.

If intelligent communication between Americans of differing age levels and backgrounds is not to become a lost art, traditional standards must be maintained in teaching English grammar, spelling, and pronunciation.

(Mrs.) Winifred Tipton

Evanston, Ill.

To the education editor:

After 20 years of college teaching, I consider it obvious that schools and colleges are almost completely incompetent in the teaching of efficient grammar. Here are some remedies:

1. Evaluate teachers and professors on how much they attend to basic literacy and how well they mark up student papers.

2. Make all the usual elements of grammar a standard part of college-entrance examinations.

3. Give up the nonsense about Chaucer's having few rules or odd ones. And stop suggesting that any patois or ghettoese lingo could possibly succeed without rule observance.

4. Keep up the discussion by having more feature articles on illiteracy.

C. D. Rollins

Storrs, Conn.

To the education editor:

I am a long-time teacher of children with a language handicap and of student teachers as well as of instructors who want refresher courses in language. I am confident that grammar does matter and that we can maintain standards without alienating our students.

Language teachers have a product to sell. If they are going to be good salespeople, they must believe in their product. Interest, continued individual growth, imagination, enthusiasm, and confidence will work wonders in developing a more effective and enjoyable program for the classroom.

Isabel S. Blish

Northampton, Mass.

To the education editor:

Nobody can understand or speak a language without knowing, at least intuitively, how it works. The parts of the system, however, may vary in importance. The grammar of English, for example, depends much more on the order of words than on their form.

To the layman, "grammar" means certain choices that are available within the system, and different and possibly unequal ways of saying the same thing. In this sense, too, grammar obviously matters, to anyone concerned with the effect of his language on listeners or readers.

Here again, though, some choices are more crucial than others. The difference between "doesn't" and "don't" involves neither clarity nor politeness. It reflects, most likely, the speaker's socio-economic or ethnic affiliation, and it exercises the listener's fair-mindedness or bigotry rather than his linguistic competence.

Donald P. Veith
Professor of English
Chico State University

Chico, Calif.

To the education editor:

This is delightful, the Monitor expressing its interest in popular revival and preservation of proper English!

In recent years it has become embarrassing to speak to an individual or group and maintain one's standards of the native tongue. Anyone within range might accuse us of affectation or pompous pedantry.

Please establish a series of articles that will be challenging to our intellect and stimulating to our sense of appreciation for the euphony of organized English.

F. Pierce Sherry

St. Petersburg, Fla.

To the education editor:

I share with Mr. Kohn the opinion that English is often badly taught. I felt, however, as I read the article that he was discussing three different topics related to the teaching of English without distinguishing between them.

One is of course incompetent teaching, which would give the impression that creativity can be taught, that writing is effortless, and that the structure of a language can be established by the majority vote of a committee. On this point I have no disagreement.

Next is the gradual displacement of what is often called "traditional English grammar." When I first started to teach, I felt dissatisfied with the traditional analysis of English sentence structure. The standard explanations seemed suitable for the Romance languages, but their logic did not always apply satisfactorily to idiomatic English construction. Extensive reading in linguistics over the years has convinced me that my problem was caused by applying the grammar of classical Latin to English.

The third point concerns the teacher's attitude toward students whose first language is either another language or a non-standard form of English.

A teacher must respect the student's heritage while at the same time showing him how to express himself in standard English and demonstrating that the standard forms are appropriate in many situations.

To understand that black English has its own grammar distinct from that of standard English does not mean that the student cannot realize the advantage of using both correctly.

Louise W. Marsh

Silver Spring, Md.

Miss Manners   Judith Martin

Q: Can you suggest a graceful way to call a friend's attention to a word that has been egregiously mispronounced? I am thinking especially of a well-educated person with a reasonably good vocabulary who makes this kind of gaffe. I recall someone saying "reticent" as if it were "re-tie-cent" with the accent on the "tie." Just recently a friend spoke of "maniac-depressive." Trying to be objective, one would like to help a friend, to help avoid a repetition of the mistake, but at the same time one would not want to seem to be putting on airs.

A: Nobody knows better than Miss Manners the joy of "helping a friend" by graciously indicating how much more one knows than he or she. For example, Miss Manners would adore pointing out that your "someone saying 'reticent' " ought to be "someone's saying 'reticent,' " but is reticent about doing so because of the unlikely chance you may then catch Miss Manners in a tiny error and the whole thing never ending, with each of us becoming increasingly bitter. At best, you may inquire of your friend, "Oh, is that the way you pronounce that? I've always heard . . . ." However, you do this at your own risk.

Why Can't Lawyers Talk Like Us?   Stuart Auerbach

Fashion designer Bonnie Cashin told her lawyer she wouldn't sign any contracts that contained legal mumbo-jumbo, especially the word "whereas."

"I tried to train my lawyer, but I just couldn't escape it," said Cashin, a designer of simple, elegant sportswear whose sense of taste is offended by wordy, incomprehensible legal language. "I spent hours with him, going over the contract point by point. But he insisted on adding some legal phrases. He said, 'It will be better understood in case there is some controversy.' "

As it turned out, the contract the lawyer insisted on—full of arcane phrases and Latin words designed to avoid confusion—now is being disputed. But a simple two-page letter Cashin wrote as a contract in another deal—"I'll do this and you do that" was all she said it contained—served well without any court challenge.

Cashin is in the vanguard of a small but growing national movement as consumers and institutions across the country are rebelling against the language of the law, which retired Yale University law professor Fred Rodell described as "almost deliberately designed to confuse and muddle the ideas it purports to convey."

The National Bank of Washington, for example, rewrote its consumer installment loan contracts in everyday English this summer. According to James F. Pilkington, assistant vice president in the consumer credit department, the bank has gotten only thanks from its consumers, and is now rewriting all its consumer contracts.

In New York, Citibank three years ago pioneered the move to write consumer loans, mortgages and bank card contracts in easily understandable, everyday English. "I haven't heard of any legal problems, although the lawyers of course died a thousand deaths when we took away some of their language," said Lamson Smith, Citibank's press spokesman.

Even President Carter is trying to reform the language of federal regulations, which contain some of the murkiest of legal verbiage. And a New York State law passed last summer ordering all consumer contracts to be written in understandable language is already under attack by the lawyers. They called the law—written by other lawyers and passed by a legislature 41 per cent of whose members are lawyers—ambiguous and said "it conflicts with existing law."

Perhaps the clearest example of the difference between legalese and readily understandable language comes from Chicago, where the Council of Lawyers drafted an easy-to-read lease form designed to protect both landlord and tenant.

The new form simply contains boxes for the date of the lease—including the exact hour it begins and ends—the amount of the rent, and the name, address and phone number of the "tenant" and "lessor." Then it begins:

"Lessor hereby leases to the tenant the apartment shown above (called the 'premises') located at the address shown above, under the terms and conditions set forth below."

This would replace the language of a typical apartment lease, which begins:

"WITNESSETH, that the said Lessor, for and in consideration of the sum of [blank] rent, and also the covenants, conditions, and agreements herein contained, and on the part of the Lessee to be paid, kept and performed, and for no other consideration except as herein expressed, does hereby let and rent to the said Lessee and the said Lessee has hereby taken as tenant of the Lessor, the following described premises:"

That paragraph is almost a perfect example of legal language, which Prof. David Mellinkoff of the University of California at Los Angeles law school called "wordy, unclear, pompous, [and] dull."

But trying to make legal language understandable appears akin to trying to bail out the Queen Mary with a teaspoon.

In 1939, Fred Rodell, the Yale law professor, wrote in a book titled, "Woe Unto You, Lawyers!": "No segment of the English language in use today is so muddy, so confusing, so hard to pin down to its supposed meaning as the language of the law. It ranges only from the ambiguous to the completely incomprehensible."

Little has changed since then. Washington attorney-writer Ronald Goldfarb called legal language "jargon elevated to pomposity."

Rodell wrote that lawyers insist on conducting their business in a jargon only other lawyers can understand because it elevates their profession into something more than it is, and gives them a reason for being.

"So long as the lawyers carefully keep to themselves the key to what the words mean," he wrote, "the only way the average man can find out what is going on is to become a lawyer, or at least to study law himself. All of which makes it very nice—and very secure—for the lawyers."

Economist John Kenneth Galbraith, who has fought against the jargon of his own profession, echoed that idea when he referred in a television discussion last week to "the desire of the lawyer, by his peculiar and obscure language, to prove that he's worth his money."

In fact, lawyers and judges often have trouble understanding the legal jargon of their peers. One Washington lawyer said a highly respected U.S. District Court judge here—the lawyer asked that both his name and the judge's not be used—issued an opinion that neither he nor the attorney on the other side could understand.

So they requested an explanation. The judge replied: "You gentlemen read and write the English language. Motion denied."

To this day, neither lawyer understands what the judge was trying to say in his opinion.

Students are indoctrinated in legalese from their first day in law school. Scott Turow, a former creative writing teacher, described the feeling in "One L," a book about his first year at Harvard Law School:

"What we were going through seemed like a kind of Berlitz assault in 'Legal,' a language I didn't speak and in which I was being forced to read and think 16 hours a day. Of course Legal bore some relation to English—it was more a dialect than a second tongue—but it was very peculiar. It was full of impossible French and Latin terms—assize, *assumpsit*, demurrer, *quare clausum fregit*, thousands more. . . .

"In reading cases," he continued, "I soon discovered that most judges and lawyers did not like to sound like ordinary people. Few said 'I.' Most did not write in simple declarative sentences. They wanted their opinions to seem the work of the law, rather than that of any individual. To make their writing less personal and more impressive, they resorted to all kinds of devices, 'whences' and 'heretofores,' roundabout phrasing, sentences of interminable length."

According to Goldfarb, who conducts seminars for judges to help them improve their opinion writing, "I have to brainwash Harvard Law School graduates to write simple, straight sentences that don't go on for pages."

Lawyers insist their language is special because it is precise. Yet lawsuits arise over the most carefully drawn, legally worded contract, and the exact shade of meaning of any law or court decision is argued and challenged by lawyers.

"Lawyers have been telling each other for so many years that the language of the law is precise that they have come to believe it, even though long preoccupation with litigation caused by their usage should have by this time made them at least skeptical," wrote Mellinkoff in his book, "The Language of the Law."

"It's not the most precise way," added Goldfarb. "It's the most imprecise way, because it isn't common usage."

In fact, much of the legal language in use today is boilerplate run up on preprinted legal forms or available in "formbooks" hidden in law libraries. Forms, said Mellinkoff in an interview, "are the only way lawyers stay in business."

And although forms are used again and again, their language can cause trouble. Mellinkoff cited a form drawn up in 1912 whose language was later rejected by the U.S. Supreme Court but still appeared in a 1955 form book. In a New York case, Goldfarb said, an attorney added to a will a boilerplate phrase directing the executor "to pay all my just debts." A court ruled that this clause, which the client had not requested, reopened a debt that was so old it was barred by a statute of limitations. What's worse, said Goldfarb, is that the phrase was unnecessary. "Dying doesn't excuse a debt. Why say the obvious?"

Where did all this come from? Mellinkoff, in his book "The Language of the Law," traces it back to Old English, larded with Latin, Old French and pure jargon. For America, legal language came from England.

"Though English is the official language [of the United States]," said Mellinkoff, "the language of the law is not officially English."

For a short period the American West declared its independence from legal mumbo-jumbo. In the 1850s, the miners beat the lawyers to the West, and those lawyers who did come "saw more promise in pick, shovel and placer pans than in lawbooks," said Mellinkoff.

As a result, the law was simple and direct. "Notis [sic]," read one sign, "to all and everybody. This is my claim, 50 feet on the gulch, Cordin to Clear Creek. Backed up by shotgun Amendments."

An 1856 rule of the Little Humbug Creek Mining District was equally direct: "Res[olved], that no persons [sic] claim shall be jumpable on the Little Humbug while he is sick or in any other way disabled from labor or while he is absent from his claim attending upon sick friends."

That didn't last long. According to Mellinkoff, "Gold meant wealth, statehood and litigation. Disputes raged over land titles. . . . California offered so many legal complications that for a time it became the paradise of lawyers."

And so the legal language of the American West returned to the legalese common today, designed, Rodell said, "to conceal the confusion and vagueness and emptiness of legal thinking."

As a result of the muddled language, people rarely bother to read insurance policies, sales contracts, mortgages or leases. The layman "will trust his lawyer—or someone else's lawyer—that it does mean something . . . and that there is a good reason for saying it in a way that prevents him from understanding it," said Rodell.

"Yet why should people not be privileged to understand completely and precisely any written laws that directly concern them, any business documents they have to sign, any code of rules and restrictions which applies to them and under which they perpetually live?"

"Why should not the ideas," Rodell continued, "be common property, freely available to anyone interested, instead of being the private and secret possession of the legal profession?"

Or, as fashion designer Bonnie Cashin put it, "I really want to understand a contract. There are a lot of people in their own businesses who can't understand lawyer language. We are successful. We can't be that dimwitted."

Tell It to Washington   League of Women Voters

Introduction

Citizens in all 50 states have an opportunity to lobby their elected officials at the local level and in the state legislatures. Unfortunately, Congress is not so readily accessible and, except for citizens living near the nation's capital, opportunities for face-to-face lobbying on national legislation are limited—but the pen is close at hand. This pamphlet is designed to help all citizens make effective use of the pen in expressing their views to their senators and representatives.

The following pages include suggested ways to write more effective letters, tips on when and how to write, and some sample approaches to letter writing. Also included are lists of congressional delegations by state and the major committee assignments.

Why Write?

"If you are wondering whether or not it is really worthwhile to communicate your views to your own senator or representative in Congress, consider this fact: Others who disagree with you are doing so constantly. . . .

"Your congressman is one person to whom your opinion definitely is important. With exceptions so rare that they are hardly worth mentioning, members of the National Congress positively do read their mail. Moreover, they are interested in its contents. The mood and tenor of the daily mail from home is a recurrent topic of conversation among members when they gather in the cloakrooms in the rear of the House and Senate Chambers or around the coffee cups in the dining rooms of the Capitol." (*You and Your Congressman* by Congressman Jim Wright.)

The mail is obviously of great importance to senators and representatives in determining thoughtful constituent opinion. During the long congressional sessions many do not get home as often as they would like and they depend on constituents' letters as a major way of "taking the pulse" back home. As a concerned citizen, you can be part of that "pulse."

You may ask, "Does my letter really make a difference?" Your voice, like your vote, does count. While one letter may not accomplish your goal, your opinion added to that of many others in your community and thousands of like-minded citizens from around the nation who are working for common goals, can make a difference.

When to Write

Whatever your writing technique, the most important thing is to take pen in hand, write and get your letter or note off to Washington. A short, simple letter or telegram stating your views can be of great value—both in stating your commitment to a goal and in adding to the voices speaking on your side of the issue.*

You must use your own personal judgment on when and how best to influence your senators and representative. There are certain times when

* You can send a 15-word telegram, called a Public Opinion Message (P.O.M.), to the President or a congressman from anywhere in the United States for only $1.25. Your name and address are not counted as part of the message unless there are additional signers. Wires sent to your governor and state legislators cost $1.00.

letters are more effective. Early in the congressional session letters are useful because they notify elected officials what issues are important to their constituents. If you write early, your letter may be the one that helps your senator or representative make up his mind.

The time to write members of a committee is when legislation is pending before the committee. Another key time comes when a bill is about to come before the full Senate or House. The letters should go to both senators or your representative, whichever is the case.

There are other times when it is appropriate to write to the President and/or a cabinet officer. Such letters are usually most effective if they are written when the executive branch is making policy decisions or drafting legislation.

A useful aid to citizens as well as Leagues is the League Action Service. Subscribers who use this service are informed when the time has come for concerted action on pending legislation. Publications provided by the service also include information on the status of legislation and background on the issue.

Writing More Effective Letters

Know the Issues

You will already know some things about a particular issue when you decide to write. But you may wish to seek additional information to back up your point of view. Whether you are supporting or opposing a piece of legislation, clear reasonable letters expressing your personal opinion will get priority treatment on the Hill, particularly if they arrive in congressional offices early in the legislative process.

There are many sources of information on issues readily available to every citizen and every member of the League. The National VOTER carries articles concerning issues and the League's position on them as well as a regular Federal Spotlight feature describing what is happening on Capitol Hill. Frequently, state Voters and local bulletins carry articles on national issues and alerts to action. In addition, members and non-members can subscribe to the League Action Service (see back cover) designed to help them keep up-to-date on both issues of concern to the League and on current congressional activity. (League positions on issues are also explained in *Study and Action: 1972–74 National Program.*)

Know Your Representative and Senators

The more you know about those you elect to represent you and about the legislative process, the easier it is to write letters and tailor them effectively. There are many sources of information about your senators and representative.

One good source is usually your local newspaper. If the paper prints voting records, clip these, along with other stories on your senators and representative.

Many senators and representatives publish newsletters to keep their constituents aware of their activities. Items in these newsletters frequently provide an excellent source of ideas for comment. Write to your senators and representative asking to be added to their mailing lists.

You should also know on what committees those you elect to Congress serve. Most national legislators specialize in legislation which comes under the jurisdiction of their committees. Is your representative, or either of your senators, the chairman of a committee or subcommittee? . . . If you don't know on what subcommittees your senators and representative serve, write and ask for this information.

Of course, the best way to get to know your elected officials is through personal or political contact during their campaigns. If your senators or representative know you, one phone call or letter from you about a piece of legislation may carry more weight than many letters from unknown citizens. If your elected representative to Washington has already made up his mind, however, even contacting him on a "first-name" basis may not be sufficient to change his opinion. But, your views, combined with similar concerns of other citizens, may make him realize that he is out of step and convince him to change his position.

The first letter can be the beginning of a long and fruitful relationship with your elected representatives. It can bring you the satisfaction of first-hand involvement in the political process. They are your elected representatives, and even if you rarely agree on issues they should know what their constituents think.

Know the Legislative Process

A piece of legislation can go through as many as 25 steps before it is enacted and funds are appropriated to carry out the legislation's intent. Citizens interested in the legislative process might find helpful the League publication, *How a Bill Becomes a Law*. Understanding the difference between the authorization process and the appropriation process is essential. Any legislation which requires federal funding must go through both processes.

If an authorization bill is passed but no funds are approved, the authorization bill is meaningless. If only limited funds are appropriated, or if executive agencies cut back on availability of funds appropriated by Congress, a program can be so restricted it really can't get off the ground.

Since major decisions on legislation are usually made in committee, an understanding of the committee system is vital to effective lobbying. There are 38 legislative standing committees—17 in the Senate and 21 in the House—and numerous select and joint committees. These committees break down into well over 200 subcommittees.

Because of space limitations, it is impossible to list the subcommittees in this pamphlet. The significance of the subcommittees should not be overlooked, however; in many cases, the basic legislation is written by the subcommittee before it is submitted to the full committee.

For example, the appropriations bill for Labor & HEW first goes to a House appropriations subcommittee. The ten members of this subcommittee handle the largest appropriations bill in Congress. Since all appropriations bills originate in the House, these ten people have substantial influence on what federal funds are appropriated for programs of primary importance to many citizens—i.e., money for education, manpower and poverty programs.

Recommended Approaches to Letter Writing

It's easy to write a good letter when your senator or representative agrees with you and you know him well enough to call him by his first name.

> Dear Harry,
>
> I was pleased to read in the Congressional Record that you gave a speech on the urgency of finding alternatives to air-polluting cars and congested highways. Does your speech mean that you are also in favor of allowing communities to use revenues from the Trust Fund to meet their transportation needs? I hope so. . . .

It is always useful to relate local needs to national legislation. If you have first-hand knowledge of what is happening in your community, include comments in your letter:

> I strongly urge you to oppose any moves in the House to prohibit busing as a tool for desegregation of schools. Some proponents of anti-busing legislation have apparently lost sight of the fact that in many communities, busing has worked. You and I both know that here in Falls City the implementation of pupil transfer using busing was the major factor responsible for the smooth integration of our school system five years ago. One hardly ever hears complaints about it now. Yet if federal funds are not available for busing, our school district will be in deep financial trouble. . . .

It is helpful to indicate your familiarity with your senator's or representative's past actions on an issue, particularly if you are trying to change his mind:

> I know that last year you opposed a bill providing the District of Columbia with an elected Mayor and City Council, but I think many of your colleagues would agree with me that this year the time has finally come for Congress to turn over local affairs in the nation's capital to those who live and work there. . . .

If you find an editorial or article in a local paper you might include it:

> Enclosed is last Wednesday's *Local Star* editorial on our local community action agency. I have been following the work of our CAA for the past two years, and this editorial confirms my observations of the effective work being done here in Katalone. . . .

If you have recently met your elected representative to Congress or heard him speak at a local meeting it is useful to relate to this experience:

It was good to see you at the King County Republican dinner. From your comments about the President's 18-month moratorium on new contracts for subsidized housing to assist low- and moderate-income people, I see that you are as distressed as I am. Because no new contracts can be signed during that time, we could have a serious gap at the end of the 18 months—a time lag during which no new subsidized housing can be built. I urge you to make it clear to the President just how serious the social and economic costs to our community will be as a result of his moratorium.

Do's and Don'ts of Letter Writing

The Fundamental Do's

DO address your senator or representative properly.

DO write legibly (handwritten letters are fine if they are readable).

DO be brief and to the point; discuss only one issue in each letter; identify a bill by number or title if possible.

DO use your own words and your own stationery.

DO be sure to include your address and sign your name legibly. If your name could be either masculine or feminine, identify your sex. If you have family, business or political connections related to the issue, explain it. It may serve as identification when your point of view is considered.

DO be courteous and reasonable.

DO feel free to write if you have a question or problem dealing with procedures of government departments. Congressional offices can often help you cut through red tape or give you advice that will save you time and wasted effort.

DO write when your spokesman in Washington does something of which you approve. Public officials hear mostly from constituents who oppose their actions. A barrage of criticism gives them a one-sided picture of their constituencies. (A note of appreciation will make your senator or representative remember you favorably the next time you write.)

DO include pertinent editorials from local papers.

DO write early in the session before a bill has been introduced if you have ideas about an issue you would like to see incorporated in legislation. If you are "lobbying" for or against a bill, and your senator or representative is a member of the committee to which it has been referred, write when the committee begins hearings. If he is not a member of the committee handling the bill, write him just before the bill comes to the floor for debate and vote.

DO write the chairman or members of a committee holding hearings on legislation in which you are interested IF you have factual information which you think should influence his or her thinking. If the chairman is not from your state or district, send a copy to your own representative or senators, since it is with them that you as a constituent have more influence.

The Fundamental Don'ts

DON'T sign and send a form or mimeograph letter.

DON'T begin on the righteous note of "as a citizen and taxpayer." Your elected representative assumes you are not an alien, and he knows we all pay taxes.

DON'T apologize for writing and taking his time. If your letter is short and expresses your opinion, he is glad to give you a hearing.

DON'T say "I hope this gets by your secretary." This only irritates the office staff.

DON'T be rude or threatening. It will get you nowhere.

DON'T be vague. Some letters received in congressional offices are couched in such general terms that it leaves the senator or representative and his staff wondering what the writer had in mind.

DON'T just because you disagree politically with your senator or representative ignore him and write to one from another district or state. Congressional courtesy calls for the recipient of such a letter to forward it to the congressman from the district or state involved.

DON'T send a carbon copy to your second senator or representative when you have addressed the letter to the first senator. Write each one individually, it's the courteous thing to do.

Correct Salutation and Closing for Letters to Officials

President
The President
The White House
Washington, D.C. 20500
Dear Mr. President:
Very respectfully yours,

Vice President
The Vice President
The White House
Washington, D.C. 20500
Dear Mr. Vice President:
Sincerely yours,

Senator
The Honorable Philip A. Hart
United States Senate
Washington, D.C. 20510
Dear Senator Hart:
Sincerely yours,

Representative
The Honorable Silvio O. Conte

House of Representatives
Washington, D.C. 20515
Dear Mr. Conte:
Sincerely yours,

Member of the Cabinet
The Honorable William P. Rogers
The Secretary of State
Washington, D.C. 20520
Dear Mr. Secretary:
Sincerely yours,

Personal Letters

Elizabeth L. Post

> If you have a mind that is entirely bromidic, if you are lacking in humor, all power of observation, and facility for expression, you had best join the ever-growing class of people who frankly confess, "I can't write letters to save my life!" and confine your literary efforts to picture post-cards with the engaging captions "X is my room," or "Beautiful weather, wish you were here."
>
> Emily Post, 1922

Letter-writing *is* becoming a lost art—in fact the practice of writing personal letters is diminishing to such an extent today that they threaten to become extinct. Since daily events are communicated by newspapers, radio, and television with great accuracy and dispatch, the circulation of general news—which formed the chief reason for letters in the stagecoach and sailing-vessel days—has no part in the hurried correspondence of the twentieth century. Yet people *do* write letters, and there are still some who possess a gift for the fresh turn of phrase that we see in old letters. It may be, though, that in the past the average writing was no better than the average of today, for naturally, the unusually gifted letters are the ones that have been preserved for us over the years.

The Letter Everyone Loves to Receive

> A perfect letter has always the effect of being a light dipping off of the top of a spring. A poor letter suggests digging into the dried ink at the bottom of an ink-well.
>
> Emily Post, 1922

The letter we all love to receive is the one that carries so much of the writer's personality that he or she seems to be sitting beside us and chatting with us. To achieve this happy feeling of *talking* through a letter, one must employ certain devices in order to detract from the stilted quality of the written word. Here are a few specific suggestions that may help to make your letters reflect your personality.

It is absolutely correct to type a personal letter, as long as the writer is a proficient enough typist so that the number of errors does not distract the reader. It does, however, destroy some of the personal touch.

Punctuation can add interest and variety to your letters, much as the change in tone of a speaker's voice adds zest and color to his story. Underlining a word or using an exclamation point after a phrase or sentence gives emphasis where you want it. A dash is effective instead of a longer, possibly more grammatical, phrase. "We went to a dance last night—what a party!" is more colorful than "We went to a dance last night, and it was a great party." Don't, however, overdo the exclamation points and dashes. A few add zest—too many become boring.

In a personal letter phrases typical of your speech should be used and not artificially replaced by more formal language. A young person who commonly uses the expression "a real doll" would sound most unnatural and self-conscious when writing, "She is a lovely girl."

Occasionally inserting the name of the person to whom you are writing gives your letter an added touch of familiarity and affection. "And, Helen, guess what we are going to do this summer!" makes Helen feel as though it will be of special interest to her.

The use of contractions is another means of making your writing natural. Since you would probably never say "I do not know" for "I don't know," or "I am so glad" for "I'm so glad," why write it that way?

Don't stop too long to think of how to say it. Decide what you want to say and then write it as quickly as possible; that way, it will seem as if you are truly talking to your friend.

And finally, brevity is infinitely more interesting than lengthy rambling. As Pascal wrote, "This letter wouldn't have been so long, but I haven't the time to make it shorter."

The Language of War   Haig Bosmajian

Resources control ... regrettable by-products ... impact area ... hardware ... hornets' nests ... protective reaction ... pacification ... strategic hamlet ... New Life Hamlet ... incursion ... Operation Ranch Hand ... Operation Independence ... Operation Sunrise ... defoliation ... advisers.

If one did not know better one would never suspect a war was going on, that human beings were being mutilated, tortured, forcibly removed from their villages, wounded, and killed. This was the language of a war in which 60,000 United States soldiers and "advisers" were killed, in which over one million Vietnamese soldiers were killed. The words and terms used by governmental officials to report what was occurring in Vietnam and Southeast Asia between 1962 and 1972 constitute an excellent case study in how language is corrupted to mask the cruelty and inhumanity of war, to attempt to justify the unjustifiable.

Linguistically legitimatizing the killing of "the enemy" during wartime has long been a preoccupation of military and civilian officials bent on waging war. Language is the tool to be used to make acceptable what civilized people would ordinarily not see as acceptable.

"War," according to Aldous Huxley, "is enormously discreditable to those who order it to be waged and even to those who merely tolerate its existence. Furthermore, to developed sensibilities the facts of war are revolting and horrifying. ... By suppressing and distorting the truth, we protect our sensibilities and preserve our self-esteem. Now, language is, among other things, a device men use for suppressing and distorting the truth. Finding the reality of war too unpleasant to contemplate, we create a verbal alternative to that reality, parallel with it, but in quality quite different from it. That which we contemplate thenceforth is not that to which we react emotionally and upon which we pass our moral judgments, is not war as it is in fact, but the fiction of war as it exists in our pleasantly falsifying verbiage." [1]

In his now famous essay "Politics and the English Language," George Orwell pointed out that "political speech and writing are largely the defense of the indefensible. . . . Defenseless villages are bombarded from the air, the inhabitants driven out into the country-side, the cattle machine-gunned, the huts set on fire with incendiary bullets: this is called *pacification*." [2]

Huxley's and Orwell's observations were especially relevant during the decade of United States military involvement in Southeast Asia. In 1972 Representative Robert F. Drinan of Massachusetts told an audience of English professors: "It is my duty to report to you that the objects of Orwell's observation are at this moment comfortably ensconced in the State and Defense Departments and, ironically or predictably, they are the very individuals who in so many other respects are bringing us closer to the Orwellian version of a sterile 1984." [3] Regarding the deceptive use of language in describing the Vietnam War Peter Farb observed: "The predominant strategy was the ornate euphemism—an effort to divert attention from the true horrors of death and destruction by labeling something the opposite of what it truly was. An aggressive attack by an armada of airplanes, which most speakers of English call simply an *air raid*, was instead spoken of as a momentary defensive strategy, a *routine limited duration protective reaction*. Defoliation of an entire forest, with the result that it may not sprout another green leaf for decades or even hundreds of years, was labeled a *resources control program*." [4]

During the war in Indochina the American military took words which carried connotations of peace, nonviolence, and conciliation and used them to hide cruelty and inhumanity inflicted on the Vietnamese people. A "pacification" program was established and month after month, year after year, government officials declared, as in some primitive incantation, that the United States was making "progress in pacification."

Writing of the situation in 1962, David Halberstam reported in his *The Making of a Quagmire*: "Some general or official would arrive in Vietnam, would spend one day in Saigon being briefed and meeting the Ngo family, and another day or two in the field inspecting selected strategic-hamlets and units. Then he would hold an airport press conference in which he would say that the war was being won, that the people were rallying to the government, that he had been impressed by the determination of President Diem, who was a great leader." All through 1963 officials in Saigon and Washington, D.C. recited the words, "We are winning in Vietnam." When in May, 1964, South Vietnamese General Khanh took the offensive and South Vietnamese casualties began to rise, the

Pentagon reported that the General was "on he right track." In August, 1965, officials in Saigon and Washington ex: ressed exuberant optimism over the course of the war. And in July 1966, Vice-President Hubert Humphrey declared: "We are gaining on all four major fronts—the economic front, the political front, the diplomatic front and the military front."

Late in the 1960's the American people were told again and again, "We now have the initiative in Vietnam." [5] During the early 1970's high civilian and military leaders announced that the end was in sight, that "the light at the end of the tunnel could be seen."

Official recitations and incantations about the war in Vietnam would have done justice to any primitive medicine-men attempting to cast a spell over members of their tribes or over tribal enemies.

The "pacification" which officials described as progressing so well turned out to be the "pacification" described by Orwell. One journalist disclosed how this "pacifying" of Vietnamese villages was carried out: "The Vietnamese woman ignored the crying baby in her arms. She stared in hatred as the American infantrymen with shotguns blasted away at chickens and ducks. Others shot a water buffalo and a pet dog. While her husband, father, and young son were led away, the torch was put to the hut that contained the family belongings. The flames consumed everything—including the shrine to the family ancestors." [6]

"Pacification" was used as a label for actions which involved entering a village with bayonets at the ready, "persuading" the people to evacuate their huts, rounding up all the males and shooting those who resisted, prodding the elderly, the women and the children into camps set up by the United States military, slaughtering the domesticated animals and burning the pitiful dwellings to the ground. A news source reported that "one village so persistently resisted pacification that finally it had to be destroyed." [7] See Webster: Pacify: to make peaceful, calm; to tranquilize.

The forcible migration of Vietnamese civilians from their villages to "strategic hamlets" was described in a variety of terms to minimize the inhumanity of it all. Paul Dickson observed in 1972 that "the forced transfer of civilians was invariably given a nice 'operation' or 'program' title like 'Operation Independence,' or 'Operation Sunrise.' Such transfers were officially termed 'compulsory relocation' and the civilians involved were either moved to 'strategic hamlets' or 'resettlement centers'—locales that were often no more than what were called 'refugee camps' in other wars. As a New York Times reporter observed . . . 'A few people were driven together, a roll of barbed wire was thrown over their heads, and the strategic hamlet was finished.' " [8]

"Pacification" in Vietnam, wrote Edward and Onora Nell in 1967, "has included at various times the construction of 'New Life Hamlets,' and of 'Prosperity Zones' containing 'strategic hamlets.' More recently a 'Rural Construction Program' came on the scene, followed by a 'Revolutionary Development Program' which in turn gave way to a 'Rural Development Program.' " [9]

What occurs when a perfectly good word like "pacification" is used as a euphemism for acts of cruelty and inhumanity is that the word loses its former meaning and cannot be uttered later without connoting some of what it attempted to hide in Vietnam. This "destruction" of words occurred in Germany under the Nazis; perfectly good words were misused and distorted with the result that after the war these same words could not be used without carrying with them the distorted meanings attributed to them by the Nazis.

Steiner has pointed out that the bestialities of Nazism infected the German language.[10] It was used "to enforce innumerable falsehoods, to persuade the Germans that the war was just and everything victorious. As defeat began closing in on the thousand-year Reich, the lies thickened to a constant snowdrift. The language was turned upside down to say 'light' where there was blackness and 'victory' where there was 'disaster.' " [11] This distorted use of language eventually has its negative effects on the language itself and as Steiner says, "there comes a breaking point. Use a language to conceive, organize, and justify Belsen; use it to make out specifications for gas ovens; use it to dehumanize man during twelve years of calculated bestiality. Something will happen to it. Make words that Hitler and Goebbels and a hundred thousand *Unterstrumführer* made: conveyors of terror and falsehood. Something will happen to the words. Something of the lies and sadism will settle in the marrow of the language." [12]

Words such as "restraint" and "protective" were debased when Richard Nixon used the former to describe United States military activities in Vietnam and when the Air Force used the latter in the term "protective reaction" to minimize large scale bombings. "Throughout the war . . . ," Nixon declared on May 8, 1972, "the United States has exercised a degree of restraint unprecedented in the annals of war." But as Ronald Kriss commented in the *Saturday Review: "Restraint?* We have grown discouragingly accustomed to the abuse, misuse, and even nonuse of words. But this was a rather blatant example, even coming from a politician. I assume the President meant that because we never supported an invasion of North Vietnam, because we never breached the Red River dikes, because we never resorted to nuclear weapons, because, in short, we never totally laid waste the country, we can congratulate ourselves for our unprecedentedly civilized behavior." [13]

"Still," Kriss added, "it requires an extraordinary insensitivity to the language to talk of 'restraint,' when we have dumped twice as many tons of explosives on South Vietnam alone as we did in all combat zones during all of World War II, when we have contributed to the killing or maiming of hundreds of thousands—if not millions—of civilians, when we have turned countless acres of once-lush forests and farmlands into hideous moonscapes, barren and brown-hued. . . . Nor does the word ring true when we consider that the Vietnam War is the longest in our history and, in terms of battle deaths, the fourth-costliest (after World War II, the Civil War, and World War I, in that order)." [14]

The extensive "protective reaction" air raids over North Vietnam were part of this "restraint." In an item titled "Terminology in Air War," the *New York Times* said on June 16, 1972: "Under 'protective reaction,' American commanders were authorized to seek out and attack enemy troops or planes or missiles that threatened them. The use of the phrase by Mr. Laird (Secretary of Defense) at the 1969 news conference marked a shift from previous American military orders in which United States ground forces were to put 'maximum pressure' on the enemy."

The *New York Times* reported that "three former members of a photo-intelligence team assigned to Pacific Air Force headquarters in Hawaii said in an interview today that at least 20 to 25 planned bombing raids later described as 'protective reaction' strikes were flown each month by Air Force planes over North Vietnam throughout 1970 and 1971. . . . All three airmen interviewed today agreed that the concept of 'protective reaction' was widely considered throughout the Pacific Air Force command as simply another way of describing bombing raids." [15] One of the airmen stated: "We were constantly hitting truck depots and storage areas and describing them as P. R. strikes." Another airman, who had seen all of the pilot reports for Seventh Air Force missions flown in Laos, Cambodia and North Vietnam, said that "invariably, after such missions . . . the pilots would enter 'protective reaction' on their reports." Finally, on April 4, 1972, "the policy of 'protective reaction' was suspended with the resumption of full-scale bombing of North Vietnam after the start of the North Vietnamese offensive." [16]

The depersonalization of the Vietnamese people reached its height in the B-52 bombers which flew from Anderson Air Force Base in Guam, six hours flying time away from their targets in Vietnam, to drop their high explosive bombs on the people and land below. To the crew aboard the B-52, it had become an "impersonal war." Joseph Treaster reports that "for the crewmen, sitting in their air-conditioned compartments more than five miles above the steamy jungle of South Vietnam, the bomb run had been merely another familiar technical exercise. The crew knew virtually nothing about their target and they showed no curiosity. Only the radar-navigator, who in earlier wars would have been called the bombardier, saw the bombs exploding, and those distant flashes gave no hint of the awesome eruption of flames and steel on the ground. No one in the plane, including this correspondent, heard the deafening blast." [17] Treaster describes the effects of the exploding bombs: "On the ground a B-52 strike—or 'arclight' as they are commonly called—is a chillingly spectacular event, sometimes electric with excitement. Tremendous clouds of smoke and dust boil up and a thunder of kettle drums splits the ears. People in the 'impact' areas are killed or sent reeling in shock." [18]

None of these devastating effects were ever perceived by the men in the B-52; nothing and nobody that had been destroyed on the ground were ever seen by the airmen. One Air Force captain declared: "Essentially I feel I'm a nonparticipant in the war. . . . I'm intelligent and I know I'm in it, but I don't feel it." A pilot "said that he often thought of himself as a long-distance truck driver. A crewman said that bombing South Vietnam from a B-52 was like 'delivering the mail.' " Another captain stated that "if we were killing anybody down there with our bombs I have to think we were bombing the enemy and not civilians. I feel quite sure about our targetting." The killing had become so impersonal that the captain could say: "As far as losing any sleep over what we're doing, how many people we kill . . . we never get to see the damage."

Here was a war in which a B-52 pilot could say as he dropped his lethal bombs: "I am a nonparticipant in the war." [19] What higher praise is there for the success of governmental officials and technology than for a military officer to make such a statement?

Keeping the killing by ground forces impersonal has always been more difficult and therefore a variety of euphemisms have been created to conceal the reality of war. During the late 1930's, according to Aldous Huxley, militarists were "clamouring for war planes numerous and powerful enough to go and 'destroy the hornets in their nests'—in other words, to go and throw thermite, high explosives and vesicants upon the inhabitants of neighboring countries before they have time to come and do the same to us." [20]

Metaphors are used to conceal the fact that human beings are killing human beings. One military officer described the parachuting of his troops into an area occupied by the Vietcong: "Our tigers jumped from the helicopters into the VC hornets' nest." For those who like their wars less picturesque and more "sanitized" there was the suggestion that a "sanitized belt" be established stretching south of the 17th parallel at the demilitarized zone. This suggestion, made during a March 1967 meeting between Presidents Johnson and Ky meant, in effect, forcibly expelling from their homes and villages all the inhabitants of the area in question, cutting down all the trees, bulldozing the land clear, and erecting "defensive positions" provided with machine guns, mortars, and mines. See Webster: To sanitize: to bring about absence of dirt and agents of infection or disease; to promote health and healthful conditions. [21]

The bombs and other means of destruction used in the Vietnam war were given names which concealed the devastation they wreaked upon the land and the people. Sydney Schanberg reported in 1972 that American briefers in Saigon who were supposed to pass on to newsmen the "facts" about the war used a language which had "no connection with everyday English" and was "designed to sanitize the war": "Planes do not drop bombs, they 'deliver ordinance.' Napalm is a forbidden word and when an American information officer is forced under direct questioning to discuss it he calls it 'soft ordnance.' In the press releases and the answers to newsmen's questions, there is never any sense, not even implicit, of people being killed, homes being destroyed, thousands of refugees fleeing." [22]

Ordnance, it turned out, meant fragmentation bombs which exploded on impact and killed or mutilated all humans and animals within range of the sharp pieces of flying metal; napalm canisters, jellied gasoline bombs which exploded and sent out showers of fiery jelly, stuck to and burned into the victim's flesh.

Even the ordnance used to destroy vegetation during defoliation operations had to be concealed behind euphemisms, " 'Operation Ranch Hand,' " Paul Dickson tells us, "was the folksy name created in 1965 for a series of concentrated airborne chemical defoliation missions during which, according to officials at that time, the chemicals being dropped were likened to 'weed killers'—even though they could kill a plant fifteen miles from the point at which they were dropped. Terms like 'Ranch Hand,' 'weed killer' ('the same as you buy in the hardware store at home,' said an American official in 1966), 'routine improvement of visibility in jungle areas,' 'non-toxic,' and 'resources control' conspired to make defoliation and crop destruction sound like a major 4-H Club project." [23]

What of the victims of all this "pacification," "sanitizing," "defoliation," and "protective reactions"? While the weapons of war had to be euphemized, the people against whom they were used had to be dehumanized. Anthony Lewis wrote in the *New York Times* on June 12, 1972, that "some of those involved in the policy of heavy bombing and shelling must, unconsciously or otherwise, regard the Vietnamese as *untermenschen*, as creatures somehow not so human as us."

In his short essay "The Nonwhite War," Herbert Mitgang recounted a government official's reference to bombed civilian installations, and presumably the people inside those buildings, as "regrettable by-products." Mitgang, after referring to the withholding of bombing raid information from the American people, wrote:

"But the greatest omission of all concerns the nonwhite people on the receiving end of the terror falling from the skies. Watching Senator Kennedy's subcommittee on refugees attempt to extract the facts from Administration spokesmen is a despairing sight. A few days ago, in the old Senate Office Building, he asked: Why is it easy for you to tell us how many bridges have been destroyed in North Vietnam and the precise number of trucks hit along the Ho Chi Minh Trail but not how many hospitals, schools, churches and other civilian installations have been hit by our bombs? The evasive response by an Assistant Secretary of State was that these were not deliberate military targets but only 'regrettable by-products' of the violence of warfare."

If the "regrettable by-product" was the death of a South Vietnamese civilian, the family of the victim was awarded thirty four dollars, officially referred to as "condolence awards." [24]

The "most shocking fact about war," Aldous Huxley reminds us, "is that its victims and its instruments are individual human beings, and that these individual human beings are condemned by the monstrous conventions of politics to murder or be murdered in quarrels not their own, to inflict upon the innocent and, innocent themselves of any crime against their enemies, to suffer cruelties of every kind. The language of strategy and politics is designed, as far as it is possible, to conceal this fact, to make it appear as though wars were not fought by individuals drilled to murder one another in cold blood and without provocation, but either by impersonal and therefore wholly nonmoral and impassible forces, or else by personified abstraction." [25]

The language and strategy of which Huxley spoke became an integral part of the Vietnam war in which politicians and military leaders distorted language to conceal and justify their inhumanity.

1. Aldous Huxley, *The Olive Tree* (New York: Harper, 1937), pp. 85–86.
2. George Orwell, "Politics and the English Language," in C. Muscatine and M. Griffith, *The Borzoi Reader*, 2nd ed. (New York: Alfred A. Knopf, 1971), p. 87.
3. Robert F. Drinan, "The Rhetoric of Peace," *College Composition and Communication*, 23 (October 1972), p. 280.
4. Peter Farb, *Word Play* (New York: Alfred A. Knopf, 1974), p. 136.
5. See my "Foreign Policy and Demons," *Frontier*, 18 (December 1966), p. 13.
6. See my "The 'Nonmorality' of Cruelty and Killing," *Christian Century*, 84 (August 23, 1967), p. 1065.
7. Cited in Edward and Onora Nell, "War Words," *College English*, 28 (May 1967), p. 605.
8. Paul Dickson, "The War of the Words," *The Progressive*, 36 (April 1972), p. 37.
9. Nell, p. 603.
10. George Steiner, *Language and Silence* (New York: Antheneum, 1970), p. 100.
11. *Ibid.*
12. *Ibid.*, p. 112.
13. Ronald Kriss, "Risk and 'Restraint' in Indochina," *Saturday Review*, 55 (May 27, 1972), p. 30.
14. *Ibid.*
15. *New York Times*, June 16, 1972, p. 3.
16. *Ibid.*
17. *New York Times*, October 13, 1972, p. 12.
18. *Ibid.*
19. *Ibid.*
20. Huxley, p. 89.
21. "The 'Nonmorality' of Cruelty and Killing," p. 1066.
22. Sydney H. Schanberg, "The Saigon Follies, or, Trying to Head Them Off at Credibility Gap," *New York Times Magazine* (November 12, 1972), p. 110.
23. Dickson, pp. 37–38.
24. Herbert Mitgang, "The Nonwhite War," *New York Times*, October 2, 1972, p. 35.
25. Huxley, pp. 86–87.

Doublespeak and Ideology in Ads:
A Kit for Teachers

Compiled by Richard Ohmann and the
Amherst Conference on Public Doublespeak, Summer 1974

> How can business defend itself? The answer is not distant. . . .
> Pick up the weapon lying idle at your side, your advertising
> budgets.
>
> Patrick Buchanan

*   *   *

Basic Principles

Ideology is the ideas of a group of people with common interests—a nation, a party, a government, a social or economic class, an occupational group, an industry, etc. The most common tactic of ideology is to show how the interests of the group are "really" the same as the interests of the whole society or of humanity in general. The famous remark of Charles Wilson some years back, "What's good for General Motors is good for the country," encapsulates the root principle of ideology. General Motors, the American Medical Association, the AFL-CIO, the National Rifle Association, garment workers, English teachers, college professors, businessmen—whatever group is organized and conscious of a common interest turns out ideology.

Ideological talk does not always amount to doublespeak, but it easily can. And for a simple reason: the interests of various groups in a society are *not* all compatible—not all the time in all respects. Poll taxes were good for white politicians but not for black tenant farmers. Higher faculty salaries at a private university with finite resources may mean *lower* salaries for secretaries or less scholarship money for students. And so on. Usually the conflict of interest is not so dramatic. Then ideology has its best opportunity—and runs its greatest risk of doublespeak. For then it can be rather abstract, hitching on to generally accepted ideas like (in this society) freedom, technological problem-solving, individualism, the family, "ecology." And if conflicts are obscure or buried, the grand concepts smooth a surface over them. Oil companies and consumers are both for a clean environment, and also for free choices in the marketplace; so (say the oil companies) let us work together to solve our problem. To paraphrase an anecdote of Lincoln's, the wolf and the sheep are both for liberty. So long as the discussion remains on this level, bystanders might be content to let the wolf and the sheep resolve their own differences, not noticing that the wolf's desired liberty is to eat the sheep, the sheep's not to be eaten. One person's solution may be the other person's problem. Not *always*, but often. And in such a situation ideology is often doublespeak.

It's an important kind of doublespeak for people to study, for these reasons: (1) If they can't decode it, they are likely to make major social choices for bad reasons, and against their interest. (2) Powerful groups in a society have ideological advantage over the poor, weak, or unorganized. Welfare mothers doubtless have an ideology, too, but lacking the resources to buy prime TV time they are less able to confuse us with doublespeak than groups that *can* buy prime time. (Remember Buchanan's advice to business.) Ideological doublespeak always tends to keep power where it is in a society. So in the Soviet Union it would be well if young people could detect Communist Party doublespeak. Here, the doublespeak of the U.S. Communist Party is less a force to contend with than that of the Pentagon. Ideology-detection is a weapon mainly of those without much wealth or power—e.g., most of us and most of our students. (3) For all that, much ideology does not *intend* to deceive. People often deeply believe their own doublespeak. And sincerity and good will make ideological doublespeak especially hard to detect.

This "kit" concentrates on advertisements. But early in a unit on this subject it is useful to have students look at some examples of more direct ideological argument, to see how it works, and how deception (conscious or unconscious) is likely to creep in. Choose one example of ideology that is unfamiliar to your students and one that is familiar. Needless to say, the choice will differ from one group of students to another, depending on their experience and stations in American society. It may be well to start with an argument quite foreign (literally) to them—say some Soviet or Chinese ideology.

How to Look for Ideology and Doublespeak in Ads:
Questions to Ask

1. Who is the advertiser?
2. What is the explicit purpose of the ad?
3. Does the advertiser have any purpose other than the explicit one?
4. What kind of person or company does the advertiser claim to represent?
5. What audience does the advertiser assume?
6. To what qualities of that audience does the advertiser appeal?
7. What self-interests does the advertiser assume the audience to have? To *think* it has?
8. How does the advertiser relate the product, company, industry, or ideas to the audience's self-interest?
9. What common interests does the advertiser claim or imply between the company or person and the audience?
10. Are there possible *conflicts* of interest between advertisers and audience?
11. Does the ad refer, directly or obliquely, to such conflicts?
12. Does the advertiser call any widely accepted values or beliefs into play in pointing to the audience's and the company or person's common interest?
13. What words does the advertiser use for such values and beliefs?

How abstract are these words? How easy are they to tie down to concrete situations and events?

14. What language does the advertiser use to suggest harmony between the company or person and the audience? Is it warranted?

Thirteen Items of Ideological Stock in Trade

Here's a highly selective list of ideological themes to look for in what American industry says:

1. Anything wrong in our society is a problem, amenable to a solution in the interest of all.
2. Corollary: all conflicts of interest are only apparent.
3. We'll all be best off if business manages the development of resources in the future.
4. It can do this only if (a) profits are high, and (b) there is a minimum of government interference.
5. Solutions to problems are generally technical; we need new technology, but not any change in the system.
6. Hence, what the experts decide is best for all. The people are often deficient in understanding.
7. On the other hand, neither business nor technocrats have much power: in the present system, *the people* are the ones who decide.
8. They decide best through individual purchases in a free market; voting is secondary, other kinds of politics a potential threat to free choice.
9. The United States can solve its problems apart from those of the rest of the world, and do so without creating problems elsewhere.
10. Freedom is good for both individuals and corporations, and pretty much the same thing for both.
11. Growth and productivity are good for all.
12. Our needs—for pleasure, love, approval, security, etc.—can best be met by consuming products.
13. Consumption should generally be done by units no larger than the nuclear family. And the nuclear family is the social ideal.

(Remember: Taken as ideas, these are of varying merit. They can be openly debated. Certainly they are not in themselves doublespeak. What earns them their places on this list is their very wide acceptance, coupled with their loose formulation: they can easily be appropriated for almost any purpose, including honest and dishonest ones. It is their abuse we should attend to.)

Short Guide to Ideological Doublespeak

Look for doublespeak in these areas of semantics and rhetoric:

1. *What you mean "we," paleface?* The homogenizing "we," and "us," and "our." Particularly, watch for shifts in the reference of "we," and for instances where "we" purports to refer to everyone in the society, but where what is said is in fact only true of some. (Recall the Lone Ranger's saying "There are Indians closing in from all sides, Tonto: we're in trouble." Tonto: "What you mean 'we,' paleface?")

2. *"America."* And "the people," "our society," etc. When you read "America needs . . ." stop and ask if all Americans need it, or only some, or some more than others. The use of "America" is often coercive, not referential.

3. *Abstraction away from people.* When someone proposes to fight "poverty," does that mean getting more money to poor people, and perhaps less to the wealthy? If not, what? Again, can we be for "ecology" without being against those who upset the ecological balance?

4. *Liberty. Or, the sheep and the wolf.* Both are for liberty, but one's liberty is the other's death. Watch for plus-words like "liberty," used as if they had the same meaning for all. In many situations they conceal conflict of interest.

5. *It's a problem.* An American habit of mind conceives any difficulty, crisis, disaster, society conflict—ANYthing BAD—as a problem. This move always implies that we're in it together, faced with the same problem, and all with the same interest in a solution. Remember that your solution *may* be my problem, or that your problem may even be *me*. Be watchful, especially, for distinterested formulation of "problems" by those who have helped create them, and whose livelihoods are at stake. Another thing: labeling something a problem obviously implies that there *is* a solution—but in some situations there may be no approved solution, or even no solution at all.

6. *The technological fix.* Fusion will solve our problem, or a new emission control device, or a new ingredient, or a new kind of glass, or just "research." The technological fix is usually aimed at symptoms, not causes. Now sometimes technical solutions are what we (all of us) need. But often they're *more* needed by those who supply the technology. And very often the technological fix is offered as remedy for social or political problems. When some technological term is the subject of an active verb, try to put people back in the picture: Technology does nothing by itself. *Who* will set the machine going? With what interest?

7. *Experts know best.* A corollary of the above, this idea always merits some skepticism. But it leads to doublespeak especially when the ideologue says (a) the people must decide, (b) the people don't/can't understand what the experts understand, (c) let the experts decide.

8. *Hard facts or iron laws.* "The hard fact is that America progresses only if business prospers." Query: What makes a fact hard? Query: What issues are excluded from debate by this hard fact? Well, the equation of progress with economic growth, for one. And the question of alternatives to free enterprise, for another. The hard fact move leads to doublespeak

when it treats a present social arrangement as iron law, and so rules out choices that might not be good for the advertiser. Watch for law-like statements in present tense (like the invented one above), which foreclose discussion of the system itself, and its assumptions. And watch for coercive uses of words and phrases like "necessary," "only possible," "required," "essential to economic health," and "inevitable unless."

9. *There's nobody here but us chickens.* Watch for formulations like "the people will decide," or "we will all be ruled by free choices in a free market." They imply that no one has more power than anyone else in determining the future—or even that big corporations have *less* power than ordinary people. Check these formulas against the facts of how decisions will be made on a particular issue. And remember to ask who paid for the ad, and whether ordinary people have any matching power.

10. *What can one man do?* To stop pollution, buy brand X gasoline. To handle the trash menace, dispose of your bottle properly. To deal with the energy shortage, turn your lights off when not using them. Some of this may be good advice (but not *all* of it), but none of the individual actions proposed will make a dent in the "problem." Watch for ads that urge independent acts of consumers, and stay silent about broader "solutions," like new laws, regulations of industry, etc.

11. *Corporations equal people.* A blend of 9 and 10. "We're all in this together—*you* conserve heat in your house, and *we'll* build more nuclear plants." Beware of hearty invitations to collaborate in making America better; ask whether the proposed "partnership" is one of equals, or one of chickens and foxes.

12. *Blurred ownership.* "The people's coal." "Your power company." "America's resources." "Our industrial system." And so on. Ask who, in cold financial and legal fact, owns the thing in question, who has power to determine its future, and why the possessive noun or pronoun is so generalized. . . .

A Consumer's Guide to Pseudoscience   James S. Trefil

I have mixed feelings about the current boom in things parascientific—movies like *Star Wars* and *Close Encounters of the Third Kind*, TV shows about weekly UFO landings, and books about spaceships that descended to earth in prehistoric times. As a physicist, I realize that today's flights of fancy may well be tomorrow's scientific orthodoxy. But it worries me that a public ill equipped to distinguish between razzle-dazzle and sound speculation is swallowing whole many pseudoscientific notions that strike me as silly at best and as a species of intellectual junk food at worst.

My concern here is not, incidentally, altogether cool and disinterested; I still brood about the time several years ago when my son, then ten, was watching a TV "documentary" about ancient civilizations that had been visited by extraterrestrials. When I ventured something mildly skeptical about the show, my son turned on me and cried, "But didn't you see? They *proved* it!"

Repeated experiences like this with my children, my students, and my contemporaries have left me convinced that the world could use a kind of do-it-yourself guide to getting one's bearings in the Alice-in-Wonderland realm of unorthodox scientific claims. Before launching into this guide, however, I'd like to make some general remarks about offbeat claims and mention some concrete examples.

As I said above, it's important to realize that unorthodox views are not alien to conventional science. When you come down to it, every accepted scientific principle started out in life as an unorthodox thought in the mind of one man. It follows, then, that in every living science there is a frontier area where new basic principles are being sought and where innovative ideas can gain a hearing. In my own field of physics there are several frontier areas, the most wide-open one being the study of elementary particles (the subatomic objects that in some way contain the key to the ultimate structure of matter). So newness in itself is not now and never has been a basis for the rejection of an idea by the scientific community.

One can visualize the situation in science in terms of concentric circles: At the *center* is that body of time-tested, universally accepted ideas that are set forth in school and college texts. The first circle out from the center is the *frontier*, which interacts constantly with the center, feeding it new ideas that the center, after lengthy testing, adopts and assimilates.

If we move beyond the frontier region of a science, however, we come to a hazy outer circle area that I like to call the *fringe*. The fringe is characterized by a scarcity of hard data and by a general fuzziness of ideas that make the average scientist very uncomfortable. It is a zone in which neither accepted scientific writ nor reasonable extrapolations of scientific knowledge seem to apply. For these reasons, it is an area that scientists generally prefer to avoid.

Yet the fringe has its uses, for it feeds ideas to the frontier, much as the frontier feeds ideas to the center: Fifty years ago, the notion that we should attempt to communicate with extraterrestrial intelligences would most emphatically have been a fringe concept. Yet today this idea has moved into the more respectable frontier circle. (Incidentally, this move illustrates an important point about the ideas contained within both the fringe and the frontier. The soundest, most useful of them keep gravitating inward, ring by ring, toward the orthodox center.)

Now there is only one thing that will make the average scientist more uneasy than talking about what lies beyond his particular frontier and that is having someone express doubts about the validity of ideas that he considers to be established at the center of his discipline and therefore no longer open to question. For example, in the time of Isaac Newton the law of gravity was a frontier subject, but now it is regarded as a principle that has been validated by centuries of experiment and use. This law has passed from the frontier of science and is firmly ensconced within the vital center. Anyone who suggests that the law ought to be abandoned or modified is not going to get a sympathetic hearing unless he presents a very convincing argument.

The progression of scientific ideas from frontier circle to "center" acceptance isn't always smooth. The germ theory of disease and the theory of continental drift are examples of ideas that were considered too "fringy" when they were first introduced. Only long, often acrimonious campaigns won them official recognition.

There have of course been thousands of fringe ideas that never made it to the frontier and thousands of frontier ideas that never gained centrist respectability. The basic problems, then, that anyone, scientist or layman, faces when confronted with a new theory are how to decide where it belongs on the concentric-circle scale and how to determine its chances of eventual acceptance.

In making such judgments, scientists have to keep two criteria in mind: A new idea may be rejected because it is too far beyond the frontier—for instance, too fringy and unprovable; or it may be rejected because it is too far behind the frontier—for instance, a clumsy, complicated way of accomplishing ends already being accomplished by simple, efficient, economical centrist theories. Thus, an overly elaborate, hard-to-prove, Rube Goldberg-like notion could be rejected because it might be at once too fringy and too inefficient in comparison with well-established centrist theories.

With this framework in mind, let's look at some current offbeat theories and the problems they pose for the citizen who is wondering whether to accept or reject their striking claims.

Velikovsky and *Worlds in Collision*

In 1950 Immanuel Velikovsky, a Russian-born psychoanalyst, published a book called *Worlds in Collision* that touched off a minor tempest among astronomers and served as a model for an entire generation of pseudoscientific writing. The premise of his work was that the recent history of our solar system has been marked by a series of catastrophic events and that these events are faithfully recorded in ancient writings. Thus, according to Velikovsky the planet we now know as Venus was ejected from Jupiter about 5,000 years ago (an event recorded in Greek mythology). Thereafter, Venus wandered about the solar system as a comet, experiencing several close encounters with our earth before settling into its present orbit. One of these encounters coincided with the parting of the Red Sea for the Israelites and another, with the stopping of the rotation of the earth for the benefit of the ancient Hebrew leader Joshua. Both of these events and other "catastrophes" too numerous to mention are recorded in the Old Testament.

To substantiate these claims, Velikovsky cited examples from other legends about massive floods and about days when the sun stood still in the sky. He also used the ancient writings to predict the properties of the planets. For example, since the manna that fell on the Israelites during their wanderings in the desert was supposed to have been material from the Venusian comet, he predicted that hydrocarbons (or many carbohydrates—the distinction between the two isn't clear in the book) would be found in the Venusian atmosphere. He also predicted that Venus would be found to be "candescent."

When these claims were made, very little was known about planetary science, so they could be classified as fringe ideas. At the same time, they required that known physical laws (such as the conservation of energy) had to have been violated at some time in the past or the events Velikovsky described would have been impossible. Thus, the scientific community rejected his thesis because his ideas were both too far ahead of and too far behind the frontier. (Velikovsky's followers also claim that a group of professors tried to suppress publication of the book. If this is true, I can only say that professors have less clout now than in the early Fifties.)

Velikovsky's claims are set forth in a book that runs to 389 pages in the paperback edition. Faced with this avalanche of fact and hypothesis, what is the reader supposed to do? Well, in Velikovsky's case we're lucky because his book caused so much furor that a number of refutations have been written. The most recent of these refutations is the published proceedings of a symposium held in 1973 by the American Association for the Advancement of Science (AAAS) (Donald Goldsmith, ed., "Scientists Confront Velikovsky," Cornell University Press, 1977). A quick look at the *Reader's Guide to Periodical Literature* or at the card catalog of a public library will turn up other books and articles contra Velikovsky. The counterarguments fall into three categories: questions of fact, questions of logical consistency, and questions of alternative explanations.

Let's take the category of factual questions. As we noted above, Velikovsky claimed flatly that hydrocarbon-based manna from Venus fell upon the Israelites during their desert wanderings. Yet National Aeronautics and Space Administration space probes have turned up no evidence of hydrocarbons in the atmosphere of Venus—although once a scientist was misquoted as saying that an early probe did find such evidence—and the temperature of the planet is about what you'd expect on the basis of the greenhouse effect. (Certainly it's not hot enough to make the surface candescent.) Such evidence helps to clear the air, but it's hardly the kind of knowledge that most of us would have at our fingertips. In keeping with my goal of providing a do-it-yourself system for analyzing theories then, I'll have to turn to the other two categories, logical consistency and alternative explanations.

About logical consistency: If you look over Velikovsky's argument, it becomes apparent that the central point is his idea that ancient writings are supposed to be taken as literal, eyewitness accounts of celestial events.

Fair enough. But when I read the Bible's account of the Israelites' wanderings, I find that the manna fell from heaven daily *except for the Sabbath*. Now I can imagine a comet whose tail contains edible material, and I can even conceive of this edible material falling only on one small area of the earth for an extended period, but I cannot for the life of me imagine a comet that keeps the Sabbath. That doesn't seem to me "logically consistent." This sort of example can be multiplied ad infinitum by anyone who looks seriously into the thousands of statements in *Worlds in Collision*.

In the same way—and here we come to the category of alternative explanations—we can ask if it's really necessary to suspend the laws of nature in order to explain the accounts of natural disasters in ancient writings. Isn't there some less complicated way of interpreting these phenomena? Surely disaster is one experience that has been shared, at one time or another, by the entire human race. And of course, the idea that ancient writers never took liberties with facts in order to achieve literary effect is a notion that doesn't stand scrutiny very well. If it did, we'd be faced with trying to explain why ancient writers were so different from their modern counterparts.

Erich von Daniken and *Chariots of the Gods?*

If there is ever a prize established for the most rhetorical questions per page, Erich von Daniken will win it hands down. Using this device, he theorizes that mythological references to flying gods actually refer to extraterrestrial visitors to earth and that many of the achievements of ancient civilizations were realized with the help of advanced technology made available by ancient space-faring astronauts. Because so many claims are made in a short space of time, the reader's rational circuits overload and he just floats along. Being unable to challenge every claim, he is reduced to the state of challenging none.

The way to cope with this blizzard of assertions and rhetorical questions (which is fairly common in pseudoscientific writing) is to resist the temptation of allowing the verbal avalanche to bury you. Instead, pick out one or two claims and look into them thoroughly. For example, here's a quote from Von Daniken about the Egyptian pyramids:

> Is it really a coincidence that the height of the pyramids multiplied by a thousand million corresponds approximately to the distance between the earth and the sun? Is it a coincidence that a meridian running through the pyramids divides continents and oceans into two exactly equal halves? Is it coincidence that the area of the base of the pyramid divided by twice its height gives the celebrated figure $\pi = 3.14159$? Is it coincidence that calculations of the weight of the earth were found, and is it also coincidence that the rocky ground on which the structure stands is carefully and accurately leveled?

Confronted with a paragraph like this, it would be an unusual reader who would not become intimidated and move on to the next paragraph, carrying with him the definite impression that the Egyptians could never have built the pyramids without outside help—even though this claim is not made explicitly. But instead, let's stop for a moment. There are five claims made in this paragraph, and checking all of them could occupy the better part of a day. Few people would want to spend that much time investigating one paragraph in a book full of such paragraphs.

So let's not. Let's pick one claim at random and check it out. For example, in Volume 18 of the *Encyclopaedia Britannica* (Plastics—Razin) I find the information that the pyramids were originally built to be 146.59 meters high and to have a square base of 230 meters to a side. A quick check shows that the claim about π can't be right (actually, any student in a freshman physics class could have told us that you can't get a dimensionless number like π when you divide an area by a height). In the interest of fairness, though, I tried a few combinations and came up with the fact that twice the length of a side of the Pyramid of Cheops divided by the structure's height is 3.138, which differs from π by only 0.1 percent. Assuming that this is what Von Daniken meant, doesn't this bit of research confirm the claim implicit in his rhetorical question?

Not necessarily. Let's take the idea one step farther. If the ancient astronauts intended to have this number be exactly π, it means they mismeasured the side of the pyramid by 0.1 percent. (For reference, 0.1 percent of 230 meters is about 9 inches.) A check through some books on surveying at the library revealed that run-of-the-mill commercial surveying is usually accurate to .01 percent (10 times more precise than the measurements done at the pyramid). A call to a man who teaches surveying yielded the information that beginning college level surveying students routinely get an accuracy of 0.05 percent; not commercial quality but still better than that at the pyramid. What I found therefore was that although an accuracy of 0.1 percent sounds very good, it is actually pretty poor by modern standards. (As an interesting aside, it turns out that all of the dimensions of the pyramid were surveyed with about this accuracy.)

So what do we have? Either the numbers quoted by Von Daniken are the result of the Egyptians' building to plan as best they could, or we have a race of ancient astronauts who could assemble and operate a spaceship but who would have flunked freshman surveying. Take your pick.

This example illustrates one important weapon in the consumer's arsenal. If you ignore an author's invitation to slide over a series of glib claims and instead take a few statements and follow them to their logical conclusion, you can get a pretty good idea of how much weight should be given to the claims that you don't verify. In the case of Von Daniken's rhetorical questions, this probably isn't much.

The pyramid-measuring example also brings up a question that is frequently asked about the pseudosciences: If they're wrong, why aren't they refuted by reputable scientists? The answer is that it would simply take too much time. It took me the better part of a morning to chase down this claim, and an exhaustive analysis of even a single chapter in this one book would take months. Very few scientists have this much time to spare for a project that will not advance their professional standing in any way and that will in all likelihood gain them nothing but a lot of crank mail. They prefer to remain silent (though disapproving) and will only do something if they are irritated beyond endurance (as they eventually were in the case of Velikovsky).

ETI and UFO Phenomena

If I had been writing this article 10 years ago, the field of extraterrestrial intelligence (ETI) and unidentified flying objects (UFOs) would have been relegated to the farthest reaches of the fringe. The whole thing reeked of little green men and bug-eyed monsters, and the Condon report had pretty well established that the great majority of UFO sightings could be assigned a perfectly natural (although sometimes complex) explanation. There seemed to be nothing more to say on the subject.

In the past few years, however, a number of developments have occurred to alter this picture. Astronomers have started to give serious thought to the idea that radio telescopes might be able to "listen in" on signals from other planetary systems. In fact, the search for evidence of ETI has already begun with existing telescopes, and proposals are in the wind to build new ones just for this purpose. In a sense, the interest in ETI constitutes a success story in which a formerly unacceptable idea has moved into the realm of serious scientific consideration.

Although the UFO phenomenon hasn't achieved this sort of status, in recent years a few reputable scientists have been willing to look into UFO sightings to see if there might be something there beyond optical illusion. The results to date are not impressive, but the fact that some scientists are willing to take the time to examine the question is itself significant. I know it may sound terribly elitist to say so, but one of the best indicators of the soundness of a new idea is the willingness of scientists to devote their time to developing it.

Most scientists aren't wealthy, so about the only things they can invest in their career are the time and effort that go into research. Like an investor looking through stock offerings, each scientist has to make a judgment as to where his energies should go to produce the maximum return. Thus, when a scientist passes up "sure thing" conventional research to devote his time to something like listening with a radio telescope for extraterrestrial signals, he's doing the equivalent of putting his money where his mouth is.

Of course, the presence of reputable scientists in a field doesn't guarantee that the ideas being investigated will turn out to be right. On the other hand, there are a lot of conventional research projects that don't prove out either. So although the ETI-UFO subject still has a very fringy flavor to it, the past few years have seen some parts of it move tentatively into the legitimate frontier area of conventional science.

Pyramid Power

This whole pyramid-power business is so far out that I wasn't-going to deal with it at all. I changed my mind when I saw the following ad in the catalog of a respected scientific-supplies company:

> CAN THE GREAT PYRAMID UNLOCK THE MYSTERIES OF ENERGY & AGING? . . . Did the ancient Egyptians build Cheops's Pyramid in such a way that the laws of nature are contradicted? Some people have been using exact scale models of the pyramids and are claiming all kinds of things . . . meat doesn't rot, razor blades stay sharp, things don't rust, and other strange phenomena. All these claims are based on energy resonating in an exact scale model of Cheops's Pyramid oriented to magnetic North.

From this ad, it's clear we're dealing with something firmly established behind the frontier. Oh well, back to Volume 18 of the *Britannica* for the pyramid dimensions. Assemble, as I did, a cardboard pyramid. Put a piece of hamburger inside and line the pyramid up with a compass. Wait a few days. Whew!

Do-It-Yourself Checklist

On the basis of the foregoing examples, I think we can now try to list general techniques that anyone can use when confronted with the next plausibly presented arguments for God-only-knows-what new idea. Here are some useful questions to ask:

Are the facts really what the author says they are? Further (and more to the point), has someone already been sufficiently irritated by the author's claims to answer this question for you?

Some of the "facts" presented in any argument just might be wrong, but it's not always convenient to check them out yourself. It's always easier if someone else does the work. For example, trying to run down all the half-truths, rumors, and inaccuracies about the Bermuda Triangle would be a prodigious task. Fortunately, you don't have to do it because it's been done and the results published by Lawrence Kusche in *The Bermuda Triangle Mystery—Solved* (Harper & Row, 1975). In a similar vein, the proceedings of the AAAS symposium mentioned previously give a pretty good overall critique of Velikovsky, so you don't have to go searching around for scattered articles.

Therefore the first thing to do is to check your local library listings on the subject you want to look into.

Is the author trying to overload your circuits?

Although Erich von Daniken is the best (or worst) example of this technique of bludgeoning the reader into quiescence, all such authors that I have read use it. The only defense against the ploy is to pick out a few statements made about a field you know something of and look into them thoroughly. The chances are that if the author hasn't gotten those right, he hasn't done too good a job on the material you don't check.

A Compact (and Highly Personal) Guide to the Frontier and the Fringe Beyond

*****Is moving into a respectable frontier position.*
***Still does not have wide acceptance, but it's moving that way.*
**Probably will never amount to anything, but you might want to keep an eye on it.*
Forget it.

*Immanuel Velikovsky and *Worlds in Collison:* The space program has pretty well taken the shine off this one.

****ESP:** Started life on the far fringe but is moving toward respectability as more hard data is collected.

***UFOs:** This old favorite is moving up in the rankings on the basis of new interest by a few scientists, but it could move down again just as fast.

*Ancient Astronauts:** If the UFOs are here now, they may have been here before, but that doesn't mean one of their crews built the pyramids.

****Extraterrestrial Intelligence:** There's a reasonable amount of effort and (more important) money going into listening for signals from space. So this subject has pretty well moved into the frontier regions of astronomy.

*Bermuda Triangle:** It turns out there are no more mysterious disappearances than you'd expect for an ocean area often hit by hurricanes and other storms.

*Lost Atlantis:** Another group that didn't build the pyramids.

Water Witching (Dowsing): Ordinarily I'd give this one star, but a student recently showed me not only that he could locate an underground water pipe but that I could too. There's probably a neurological explanation.

*Pollen Power:** Pollen collected by honeybees is supposed to be very healthful. But since the pollen is taken from the bees before they go into the hives, why not just eat the flowers and eliminate the middleman?

***Acupuncture:** It shouldn't work, but it seems to.

*Biorhythms:** People are marketing calculators that will allow you to keep separate track of your three cycles (mental, emotional, physical) according to your birth date. But statistical studies show as many successes at the low points as at the high. Another numerological fad.

*Horoscopes, Phrenology, and Palmistry:** These can be fun if you don't take them too seriously.

*Perpetual Motion Machines:** Interest in these devices, the ultimate in energy saving, has dropped considerably since the patent office began requiring a working model with each application.

*Fingertip Reading:** A few years ago the Russians caused quite a stir when they announced that they had found a woman who could read with her fingertips while blindfolded. Various professors at American universities promptly made headlines by claiming they too had located women fingertip readers. When the blindfolds were improved according to instructions from stage magicians, the powers mysteriously vanished, both here and in the U.S.S.R.

Bigfoot, the Abominable Snowman, and All That: Undoubtedly there's a measure of hoaxing here, but the discovery of something like these creatures wouldn't violate any scientific principles.

*Loch Ness Monster:** The failures of searches in a small place have pretty well ruled this one out. I draw this conclusion with regret because I was rooting for Nessie.

*Psychic Phenomena a la Uri Geller:** As far as the various keybending, spoontwisting, and remote-reading tricks are concerned, I'll believe them when they are done in front of a panel that includes at least one magician.

—JAMES S. TREFIL

Given the author's facts, is there a simpler explanation of them?

If I had to pick the single failing that characterizes pseudoscientific theories, I would choose their tendency *to propose complex solutions to simple problems.* We have already seen in the case of Velikovsky that the existence of old manuscripts describing cataclysmic events can easily be explained in terms of shared human experiences and of the known tendency of writers to exaggerate. What are we to do then when given the choice between revising almost the whole body of physics and astronomy and accepting as literal truth "facts" that may be only-too-human exaggerations? It seems to me that the most sensible path is to take the explanation that does the least amount of damage to other ideas.

I can't resist mentioning another example of how this criterion works. In the ancient-astronaut documentary mentioned earlier, there was an episode in which a subterranean vault with painted walls was shown. The announcer made a big point of claiming that there was no evidence of soot (such as a torch would have left) anywhere in the vault. The program's conclusion was that the ancient Egyptians must have had access to electric lights and hence had been visited by extraterrestrials.

Now, even assuming that it is correct that this chamber was put together without any soot being left behind by the workmen, does it necessarily follow that the Egyptians were visited by astronauts? Putting it another way, if you were an Egyptian engineer, could you think of a way to get a chamber built without leaving deposits of soot? A few minutes' reflection turns up (1) washing the soot off after the work is finished, (2) sinking a shaft to the chamber to let smoke out and light in, (3) doing it all with mirrors.

The interested citizen should always take a little time to play devil's advocate on such questions because the penchant for ignoring the very existence of a simpler explanation of the facts—an explanation that doesn't require a wildly complicated set of theories—is the besetting weakness of almost all pseudoscience.

Does the whole thing boil down to being unable to prove a negative?

It is impossible to prove that there are no unicorns. All we can prove is that we've found none so far. If the end result of a long argument (the "bottom line," if you prefer) is nothing more than the statement that a particular theory can't be disproved, you are probably safe putting it in the same class as unicorns.

Are established scientists putting time in on the phenomenon?

In the case of UFOs and ETIs, discussed above, one element in our considerations was the fact that a number of reputable scientists have been willing to bet their valuable time that the idea has something to it. While this doesn't guarantee that an idea is right, it does mean that someone has looked into it thoroughly and has come up with the conclusion that it's worth looking into a little more.

Having said this, let me hasten to add a caveat. There is no proposition on God's green earth so silly that it can't find at least one Ph.D. to support it. If you're going to use this criterion in judging a theory, find out who the scientists are. A quick check in *American Men and Women of Science* or in *Who's Who* will give you some idea of the credentials of the person involved. If you want a standard of comparison, look up Peter Sturrock, of Stanford University—he's one of the people with sound credentials who are investigating UFO sightings these days.

Finally, you have to realize that this "credentials" criterion is only one of several you should use in making a judgment. If the theory sounds fishy to you, if you feel that the conclusions are unreasonable, and if the arguments of the scientists don't convince you, then so be it. In the final analysis, you have to make up your own mind anyway.

Can you test the theory yourself?

If you have a mechanical turn of mind, you can occasionally check out a claim yourself, as I did with the pyramid-power test.

Ask such simple questions as those on the checklist when you're reading the next book that reveals the secret of the ages—they will help you decide whether you're looking at a genuine scientific breakthrough or at just another addition to the fringe. There are two areas in which such questioning will be of little help, however, and we might as well get them straight right now. If outright fraud is involved—as it is reputed to have been in the famous "demonstration" by Uri Geller at the Stanford Research Institute—going through this sort of questioning will do you little good. There is no way that fraud can be detected secondhand by the layman, and there is probably no one more ill equipped than the average scientist to deal with outright duplicity. Also, the test questions really don't apply to writings that are specifically nonrational, such as the mystical and drug-oriented books that were so common a few years ago. Such books aren't playing the same game as those by the pseudoscientists and therefore can't be judged by the same rules.

No discussion of pseudoscience would be complete without some comment on its social implications. I am well aware that many of my colleagues regard modern pseudoscience as the forerunner of an antirational swing in our society and denounce it in terms that are worthy of that doom-crying German philosopher Oswald Spengler. I feel that this is something of an overreaction. Pseudoscience has been around at least as long as (and perhaps even longer than) conventional science. Perhaps it serves some deep need of human beings to believe that there is still some mystery—something unknown—left in life. Maybe the unknown thrives because people like to see the pompous scientific establishment discomfited ("Okay, Mr. Know-it-all, explain *this* one"). Or maybe it's just that P. T. Barnum was right about a sucker being born every minute. None of these interpretations constitutes a threat to conventional science.

After all, Luigi Galvani's "animal electricity" cures in the nineteenth century didn't impair the development of the science of electricity. Mme.

Blavatsky's theosophy certainly had little effect on American science. And despite the apocalyptic terms with which it was greeted, it would be hard to show that Velikovsky's *Worlds in Collision* has had much of an effect on modern astronomy. At its worst, pseudoscience is a minor inconvenience of the cocktail party variety; and at its best, it is good entertainment. I certainly make no apology for the fact that I enjoyed reading Velikovsky and Von Daniken, even though I think they are wrong.

On balance, I'd say the best attitude to have toward pseudoscience is the one reflected in the story (probably apocryphal) about the time Groucho Marx attended a sèance. After the usual hand holding, table thumping, and light dimming, the medium announced in funereal tones that she was now in contact with the spirit world and that the participants could ask any questions they liked: Nothing, she said, was hidden from the spirits. Without hesitation, Groucho shot back, "What's the capital of North Dakota?"

Hogwash

Robert Francis

The tongue that mothered such a metaphor
Only the purest purist could despair of.

Nobody ever called swill sweet but isn't
Hogwash a daisy in a field of daisies?

What beside sports and flowers could you find
To praise better than the American language?

Bruised by American foreign policy
What shall I soothe me, what defend me with

But a handful of clean unmistakable words—
Daisies, daisies, in a field of daisies?

QUESTIONS

1. Describe the voices of the people who wrote letters to the education editor of the *Christian Science Monitor.* Are there any which make you feel put down? Which voices lead you to feel respect for them? Can you make any connections between the voices the writers choose and their attitudes toward correct grammar?

2. Describe the voice of Miss Manners. Do you like it? Which of the *Christian Science Monitor* letter writers would like it?

3. Which of these essays are addressed to people as readers or listeners, and which to people as writers or speakers? Are any addressed to both?

4. Which of these examples are clearly persuasive, trying to get us to write in certain ways or to condemn certain uses of language?

5. Which of the writers here stress the importance of the writer's awareness of an audience? Which are primarily concerned with the reliability of content? Which discuss having an appropriate voice?

6. Which writers limit themselves to a discussion of one type of writing? Does this seem to be a good idea?

7. How does "correctness" in language become established? Are there writers here who seem to have different ideas about what correctness is?

8. Do any of the writers who discuss correctness give examples which show how incorrect grammar can make language unclear? Which other writers are interested in clarity? What interferes with clear writing, according to them?

9. Pick some other chapter of this book that interested you. Which of the essays in the present chapter (on language) are most useful for evaluating the selections in that other chapter?